International African Library 14
General editors: J. D. Y. Peel and David Parkin

THE ADVANCE OF AFRICAN CAPITAL

International African Library

General Editors

J. D. Y. Peel *and* David Parkin

The *International African Library* is a major monograph series from the International African Institute and complements its quarterly periodical *Africa*, the premier journal in the field of African studies. Theoretically informed ethnographies, studies of social relations 'on the ground' which are sensitive to local cultural forms, have long been central to the Institute's publications programme. The *IAL* maintains this strength but extends it into new areas of contemporary concern, both practical and intellectual. It includes works focused on problems of development, especially on the linkages between the local and national levels of society; studies along the interface between the social and environmental sciences; and historical studies, especially those of a social, cultural or interdisciplinary character.

Titles in the series:

THE ADVANCE OF AFRICAN CAPITAL

CAPITAL

The Growth of Nigerian Private Enterprise

TOM FORREST

EDINBURGH UNIVERSITY PRESS
for the International African Institute, London

For my mother

© Tom Forrest, 1994

Transferred to Digital Print 2010

Edinburgh University Press Ltd
22 George Square, Edinburgh

Typeset in Linotronic Plantin
by Speedspools, Edinburgh

Printed and bound in Great Britain by
CPI Antony Rowe, Chippenham and Eastbourne

A CIP record for this book is available
from the British Library

ISBN 0 7486 0492 8

CONTENTS

LIST OF MAPS, TABLES AND FIGURES

FIGURES

ACKNOWLEDGEMENTS

My first debt is to my numerous informants, for without their cooperation and patience, this book could never have been written. Many took time off from busy schedules to see me at short notice. I remember my all too brief encounter with the late Faluso Longe, whose infectious enthusiasm for the subject, spurred me on and gave me some initial confidence. I am also grateful to the following, who gave me advice and logistical support in Nigeria: Professor Adebayo Adedeji, Mrs Kehinde Adekoya, Yakubu Aliyu, late Chief Samuel Asabia, Chief Joop Berkhout, Dr Sam Chukwujekwu, Chris Enenya, Chief Chuks Ikokwu, Chief Augustine Ilodibe, Chief Onwuka Kalu, Chief Arthur Mbanefo, Alhaji Aliko Mohammed, Michael Murray-Bruce, 'Bayo Olukoshi, Jean-Claude Téttégau, Chief Jerome Udoji and Chief Raymond Zard. I owe special debts to Alhaji Mohammed Koguna, whose role went far beyond that of informant, and to Freddie Scott, who helped me regain composure at a vital moment, when further work seemed impossible.

Professor Asiwaju of the History Department, University of Lagos, welcomed me and made formal arrangements for a longer visit. Nina Mba, in the same department, guided me to a literature I was ignorant of. I recall, too, the sound advice of that mercurial spirit of financial journalism, Ashikiwe Adione-Egom. I received invaluable help from two taxi drivers, Musibau Akinola and Marcus Iwu, in Lagos and Aba respectively. Their extensive knowledge of these cities, patience and good humour, allowed me to locate enterprises and kept me on time for appointments, on repeated visits to Nigeria.

In lieu of an academic office, much of this book was generated in libraries and cafés. I acknowledge the great assistance I have received from staff at the Queen Elizabeth House Library and the Rhodes House Library in Oxford. Thanks also to the proprietors of the Cafe Ariel in Berkeley, and the St Giles Cafe at Oxford, for space and forbearance. Appropriately, it was in California that I found computer sockets for use by café clientele and a congenial atmosphere in which to finish my writing.

A number of individuals made detailed comments on my work. I thank them and take full responsibility for the final product. Sara Berry read an early paper and encouraged me to extend it. Paul Kennedy criticised a draft of the book and made many positive suggestions. Later, Gareth Austin, George Deutsch, Tony Hopkins and Susan Martin read all, or part, of the manuscript. Mallam Abdulkarim Dan-Asabe shared with me his knowledge of the business class in Kano and made many suggestions. Tony Berrett, Patrick Smith and Richard Synge were a great source of encouragement throughout this project. Finally, I acknowledge the assistance of Tabitha Kanogo, with whom I conducted some early interviews in Onitsha and Nnewi. Without her understanding and support, this book would never have materialised.

LIST OF ABBREVIATIONS

AWAM	Association of West African Merchants
BCCI	Bank of Credit and Commerce International
CDC	Commonwealth Development Corporation
CDC	Constitution Drafting Committee
CFA	Communauté Financière Africaine
CFAO	Compagnie Française de l'Afrique Occidentale
CKD	completely knocked down
CMS	Church Missionary Society
DFFRI	Directorate of Food, Roads and Rural Infrastructure
ECOMOG	ECOWAS Ceasefire and Monitoring Group
ECOWAS	Economic Community of West African States
FIIRO	Federal Institute for Industrial Research, Oshodi
FMG	federal military government
GBO	G. B. Ollivant
GM	general manager
GMD	group managing director
GMT	group management team
HMV	His Master's Voice
IBRD	International Bank for Reconstruction and Development
ICAN	Institute of Chartered Accountants of Nigeria
ILO	International Labour Organisation
IMF	International Monetary Fund
ITPAN	Independent Television Producers' Association of Nigeria
ITT	International Telephone and Telegraph Corporation
IUTTC	Ijesha United Trading and Transport Company
KCTC	Kano Citizens' Trading Company
KSIC	Kano State Investment Company
LBA	licensed buying agent
LPG	liquified petroleum gas
LUTH	Lagos University Teaching Hospital

MAN	Manufacturers Association of Nigeria
MD	managing director
MUSON	Music Society of Nigeria
NAACP	National Association for the Advancement of Colored People
NAFCON	National Fertiliser Company of Nigeria
NAIPEC	Nigerian Association of Indigenous Petroleum Exploration and Production Companies
NBCI	Nigerian Bank for Commerce and Industry
NCNC	National Convention of Nigerian Citizens
NEPA	National Electric Power Authority
NEPD	Nigerian Enterprises Promotion Decree
NEPU	Northern Elements Progressive Union
NERFUND	National Economic Reconstruction Fund
NICON	National Insurance Corporation of Nigeria
NIDB	Nigerian Industrial Development Bank
Nig.	Nigeria
NLMA	Nigerian Livestock and Meat Authority
NMA	National Maritime Authority
NNDC	Northern Nigeria Development Corporation (later New Nigeria Development Company)
NNDP	Nigerian National Democratic Party
NNPC	Nigerian National Petroleum Corporation
NNSL	Nigerian National Shipping Line
NPC	Northern People's Congress
NPMC	Nigerian Produce Marketing Company
NPN	National Party of Nigeria
NRC	National Republican Convention
NTC	Nigerian Tobacco Company
OMATA	Onitsha Market Amalgamated Traders' Association
PRP	People's Redemption Party
PS	permanent secretary
PWD	public works department
SAP	Structural Adjustment Programme
SCOA	Société Commerciale de l'Ouest Africain
SDP	Social Democratic Party
SNA	Sole Native Authority
SWAN	Society of Women Accountants of Nigeria
UAC	United Africa Company
UNCTAD	United Nations Conference on Trade and Development
UTC	Union Trading Company
WAPA	West African Pilgrim Association
WPTS	Western Produce Traders' Syndicate
WRDLB	Western Regional Development Loans Board

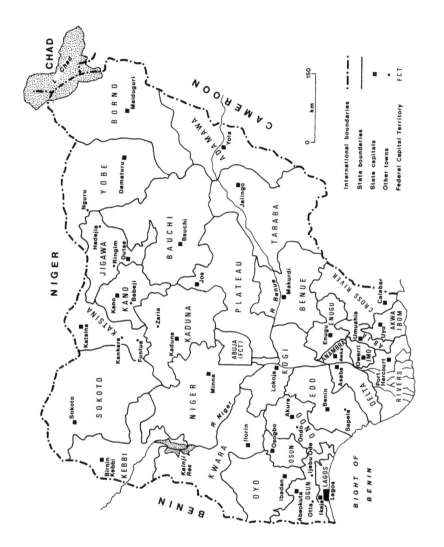

MAP 1: Nigeria: political divisions.

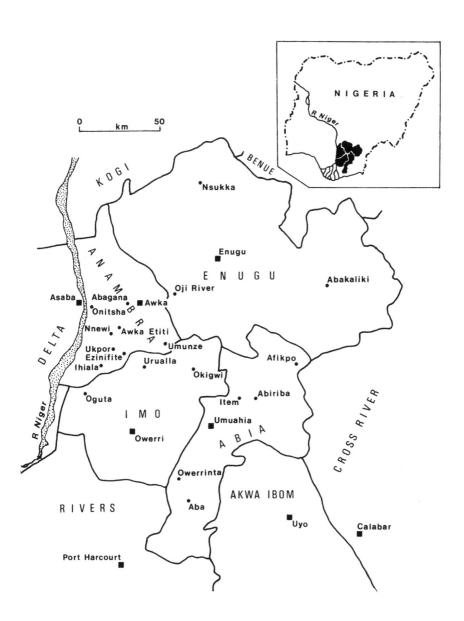

MAP 2: Anambra, Enugu, Imo and Abia States.

1

INTRODUCTION

In terms of the scale of individual enterprises, the degree of corporate organisation and the size and diversity of investment, Nigerian private capital has advanced well beyond African enterprise in Kenya, the Ivory Coast, Zimbabwe and other sub-Saharan African countries. This advance raises questions about the adequacy of existing interpretations. Certain broad generalisations and assumptions about the Nigerian case need to be questioned. The assumption that Nigerian entrepreneurs are not extensively engaged in production and long-term accumulation must now be revised.

This book aims to examine the nature of the advances that have been made by Nigerian capital since 1945. Three avenues of investigation are pursued.

First, the study aims to throw light on the growth, organisation and management of larger indigenous enterprises in Nigeria. Practically no research has been published on this important subject.[1] I will advance some reasons for this dearth of research shortly. Even in the case of Kenya, where the debate about the character, direction and strength of indigenous capital has been intense, there is surprisingly little written about the history of individual enterprises or entrepreneurs.[2] The debate was more concerned about the implications for capitalist development of relations between the state, indigenous capital and foreign capital. The debate also largely omitted the most dynamic element in Kenya's commercial and industrial sectors, East Africans of Indian origin.[3] The heat of the Kenyan debate was generated by conflicting ideological views about capitalist development within the broad Left. They could not be resolved by recourse to the evidence. Dependency and underdevelopment perspectives were pitched against those who, following the lead of Michael Cowen's historical work on capital accumulation among the Kikuyu of Central Province in the colonial period, saw a long-term path of accumulation by indigenous capital.[4]

This book is focused largely at the enterprise level and is based on studies of companies in the major business centres of Nigeria: Lagos, Sango Otta, Ibadan, Kano, Kaduna, Onitsha, Nnewi and Aba. On this basis, a more general picture of capital accumulation is built up. At the enterprise level, I am concerned with changes in organisation and management over time, with the investment and growth strategies adopted, with business culture and with questions of ownership and succession. Have long term strategies for growth and diversification been employed? How does a high-risk environment affect strategies and growth? How far have small enterprises grown into large ones? How far have groups and holding companies with significant market power emerged? How have technical, managerial, and entrepreneurial capacities changed? What strategies have enterprises adopted to acquire foreign technology and skills, and promote the development of local ones? How far has personal and family control given way to more bureaucratic forms of organisation and management as enterprises have increased in scale? What weight is given to relations with customers, employees, family and the home community? Finally, what light do business histories throw on the question of business longevity and succession across the generations? Under what conditions are enterprises likely to survive the death of the founder/owner and expand?

A second objective is to examine changes in patterns of entrepreneurship through time. Do pre-colonial patterns of trade, apprenticeship and entrepreneurship, help explain patterns of entrepreneurial activity including technical and organisational capacities, today? How have the backgrounds of business people and points of entry into business changed? What is the significance of education, experience of government or parastatals and employment with foreign companies? How have incentives to pursue careers in business and the status of business people altered?

A third objective is to examine broader patterns of accumulation and the changing political and economic conditions under which accumulation has occurred in Nigeria. What is the relative weight of various forms of accumulation – rentier, intermediary, commercial, manufacturing, service and financial? Has there been a shift from trade to manufacture and service activities? Does the specific form, character and rate of advance vary in different parts of the country? What was the impact of the shift from primary commodity exports to greatly increased exports of crude oil and the introduction of the Structural Adjustment Programme (SAP) on economic opportunities and incentives? To what extent were inflated oil revenues associated with waste and unproductive patterns of accumulation?

What role have the state and political conditions played in shaping the general conditions for accumulation? Is the great stress which some have placed on access to state resources, political connection and corruption as a means to accumulating wealth in Nigeria, warranted? Is an emphasis on political forms of accumulation and Big Men justified, and if so, what are the consequences? And how important have state policies been to the form and rate of private accumulation? Were the indigenisation and privatisation policies central to the advance of local capital? Do there exist social and economic spaces which are sufficiently independent of political and state control to allow the pursuit of private strategies of large-scale accumulation and growth? If such trajectories exist, other questions arise. Can the advance of local capital be linked to changes in the relation between business and government, and organised politics? What part has local capital played in the emergence of regional or national business organisations and have these lobbies had an impact on policy?

I am not centrally concerned in this book with values, ideas and cultural conditions and their relation to growth of enterprises. While I indicate broad shifts in values, attitudes and ideology, the influence of culture and values at the firm level really requires much more intensive local field studies of a type not undertaken here. These factors affect the motivation and aspirations of business people, the social organisation of business, corporate practice, property rights and the ways in which wealth is ultimately used and legitimated. All these dimensions have consequences for the form and extent of individual accumulation. Their relevance can be shown in many ways. For example, though a core business may well be located far from the home community of a business owner, membership of that community is likely to affect the location and management of business activities, the recruitment of extended kin, and expenditure flows. The latter flows may be aimed at enhancing the status and recognition of the individual, the legitimation of wealth and the development of the community through taking chieftaincy titles, philanthropy and contributions to community development associations, religious organisations and social clubs.

Another example comes from the work of Sara Berry. For small-scale enterprises in Yorubaland, she argues that the values of descent and seniority that underpin access to resources and shape the objectives of accumulation, lead to a considerable amount of the investible surplus being diverted into unproductive forms of social investment and political competition, with adverse consequences for the economy.[5] While Berry's arguments may be valid for small scale enterprises and the community she studied, I have reservations about their application to larger scale enterprises and the attempt to generalise them to a regional or national level.

At a higher level of aggregation, John Iliffe has argued that the presence of a widespread pragmatic hedonism has adversely affected the advance of capitalism in Africa.[6] He has found some support from Tom McCaskie who finds a powerful drive to demonstrate status as consumers among the new business class of Asante in the inter-war period.[7] Both Ali Mazrui and Jean-François Bayart have argued that African entrepreneurship has been oriented to consumption, display and munificence and has lacked the discipline associated with productive accumulation.[8] Wrigley, writing about colonial Africa, emphasises the supreme valuation of political goods – authority, recognition and power and the use of material possessions primarily as counters by which these goods could be acquired.[9]

This book has not been written from a developmental-policy perspective. Such an approach would try to determine those factors or policies which help or hinder local capital and go on to search for relevant 'lessons' and 'models'. Even on its own terms, this approach is open to the objection that causation may run in the opposite direction since indigenous capital can effect the form and content of policy in a variety of ways. More fundamentally, given the general ignorance about economic change in Nigeria, it seems quite inappropriate to begin an inquiry from a point of departure determined by considerations of policy. None the less, in the concluding chapter, a number of policy-relevant issues are addressed. Questions are raised about the growth and scale of enterprises, diversification, management practices, technology acquisition, and factors affecting longevity and succession. My view is generally longer term and less instrumental. The form, strength and trajectory of indigenous capital are the product of specific historical circumstances and slow elaboration. As Hirschman insists, the evolution of capital is embedded in a variety of national traditions, social structures and cultural values. It is subject to contradictory processes and surrounded by conflicting viewpoints and ideologies over time.[10]

Much developmental writing by economists and others suffers from a kind of policy fetishism. This is the belief that past, present and future economic performance is somehow determined by policy. This assumption is pervasive and seldom acknowledged. It finds expression in the view that certain policy conditions must be met, if capitalist development is to take place. The ambitions of social scientists, the goals of international agencies and the power of governments, converge at this point and feed off each other. With respect to entrepreneurship and enterprise growth in Africa, the most common point of departure is the notion that market deregulation and the break up of concentrations of state power will lead to a flowering of hitherto pent-up entrepreneurial capacities. This takes no account of political conditions and property rights, and the capacity of the state to provide a framework for sustained accumulation. Beyond this, research is conducted to identify the structural obstacles facing small firms and specific programmes are put forward to assist smaller enterprises with credit and technical assistance. In general, small firms are seen as the best target because in the aggregate, a larger number of small firms and the growth of small firms into larger ones, will make the greatest contribution to employment and economic growth. Another related concern of economists, with their prescriptive and predictive interests, is the efficiency, productivity and competitiveness of local enterprises. I will have little to say on this topic. Its inclusion in this work would require much more detailed quantitative information, together with a knowledge of the relevant industry and the conditions facing each company. In short, it would require a very different type of study.

Before turning to the existing literature to see how indigenous enterprise and the conditions surrounding it have been treated in the case of Nigeria, it is worth advancing some reasons for the very limited research on indigenous enterprises. More work has been done on foreign enterprises.[11] The reasons lie in the dominant perspectives on African material life, both neo-classical and Marxist. They also lie in the preoccupations of social scientists where an imperialism of short-term predictive and prescriptive interests shapes research agenda and methods and encourages broad generalisations about the continent as a whole. The emphasis on international comparison tends to support teleological conceptions of development where change is measured by the advance, or failure to advance, to some desired state. The understanding of historical change and the specific form of capitalist development in any one country is downplayed. The vision given by the developmental lens is at once wide-angled and foreshortened.

Neo-Marxist analysis in its concern with capital and class formation has often been conducted at high levels of aggregation and generalisation. As Hopkins notes, entrepreneurs tend to get subsumed under portmanteau descriptions like the bourgeoisie or capitalism and more attention is paid to the emergence of a working class than to the business class.[12] The influence of dependency and underdevelopment perspectives also directed attention away from African businessmen as active agents in the history of capitalism. In the Nigerian literature, the business class was often seen as unproductive and part of a dependent ruling class or class in formation, which gained its wealth either through privileged access to the state or through an intermediary role with foreign capital. It therefore did not merit investigation.

In the neo-classical tradition there is a long-standing presumption that market prices will call forth the appropriate response from self-interested individuals. The fittest firms will survive from a process of natural selection in the market. Corporate forms of enterprise, private-property rights and market relations are generally assumed. In other words, enterprises are not set within specific historical and cultural contexts but in a universal capitalist order.

Economists have concentrated on macro-policy, short term efficiency and project appraisal. When they have addressed enterprises, more attention appears to have been paid to the small scale informal sector than to larger-scale concerns. Since the ILO report on Kenya in 1972, which highlighted the contribution of the informal sector, the small scale sector has tended to be viewed positively as a source of enterprise and efficiency.[13] Berry has noted the populism underlying this view and has questioned the efficiency of small scale enterprises.[14]

The general image of Nigerian businessmen at home and abroad has also played a role in discouraging research. There is a perception of the business class as corrupt, unproductive and interested only in quick returns. Indigenous businessmen are thought to have a subordinate role in an economy dominated by foreign capital and public enterprises. Moreover, accumulation is often held to be heavily dependent on state patronage and political connection.

In recent books about Zaire, Janet MacGaffey has argued that much private entrepreneurial activity in Africa takes place in a second, or parallel economy, which has grown as the state has became more authoritarian and ruling classes more exploitative.[15] Despite the importance of the second economy in Nigeria, this argument is not appropriate. Most of the enterprises I consider, exist in the first economy of Nigeria, even if they originated beyond the purview of the state and the government does not effectively account for them through taxation and official statistics. Some trading enterprises in Nigeria have been engaged in the so-called second economy since the start of the colonial period and their activity is not in any immediate, causal sense, the product of an overbearing, corrupt and rapacious state.

There is now a renewal of interest in entrepreneurship in Africa. This interest stems from a concern about the weakness of African private enterprise and its role in contributing to poor economic performance. It has been heightened by Structural Adjustment Programmes that aim to deregulate economies and encourage private enterprise. It is here that views about the capacities of African entrepreneurs enter into political and economic debate. Thus it is sometimes argued that privatisation will only benefit foreign capital because local capital is too weak to take advantage of it. On the other hand, the weakness of local enterprise can also be used to support the contrary view that new foreign investment is essential to maintain adequate investment and achieve the objectives of the economic reform programmes.

I now turn to the existing literature on Nigerian enterprises. In the 1960s studies of Nigerian enterprises resulted in a picture of multiple deficiencies and low efficiency.[16] The shortcomings of management as enterprises increased in size were singled out. Among the factors held to be blocking the expansion of Nigerian enterprise were poor financial and production management (especially the latter), an inability to delegate authority on the part of the founder/owner, and a tendency to diversification and dispersion of effort. An aversion to partnership and a very strong tendency for enterprises to die with the death of their founder were also found. Peter Garlick's work on Ghanaian traders in Accra and Kumasi echoed some of these conclusions, though in his study it was the constraints on growth due to sole ownership and the diversion of funds from trade to cocoa farming and housing that were emphasised.[17] Harris thought that these problems were essentially short term and could be overcome by experience and further education.[18] Kilby doubted this and argued that the deficiencies were rooted in socio-cultural practices that would only be overcome by a long-term transformation of political institutions and ideology, in education and in technology; in short, a full blown capitalist revolution was necessary.[19] Berry has recently questioned both these interpretations with respect to small scale enterprises.[20] She argues that when proper account is taken of the conditions under which resources are acquired and access to markets is obtained, then strategies of access may well be in conflict with the demands of effective management and the exploitation of labour power.

It has been held that Nigeria exhibits the acquisition of wealth but not capitalist accumulation[21] and that much activity is heavily comprador in nature.[22] Diamond sees the bulk of the Nigerian bourgeoisie as comprador with no basis of production and accumulation outside of oil and the state.[23] Colin Leys argues that by contrast with Kenya and the Ivory Coast, domestic capital in Nigeria has been oriented to trade and has lacked a capacity to organise capitalist production.[24] Many writers place emphasis on unproductive patterns of investment and political forms of accumulation in which the state is heavily involved. Callaghy links unproductive, political forms of accumulation to the arbitrariness and unpredictability of the patrimonial state, and to statism.[25] Nigeria is compared to early modern Spain in its capacity to waste enormous earnings. Schatz, in a widely cited article, sees a transformation in Nigeria from nurture capitalism, in which the state gives assistance and support to indigenous businessmen, to a phase of pirate capitalism associated with oil boom, in which businessmen get corrupt access to state resources and manipulate the state to their advantage. He also claims, on very little evidence, that the economy was inert during the oil boom.[26] Sara Berry in a much more sophisticated argument about Yorubaland, stresses strategies of accumulation at the enterprise and regional level that are directed at securing access to, and control over, resources, rather than at increasing productivity.[27] Such strategies, which rely on kin, seniority, patronage and access to the state, rather than market relations, lead to unproductive forms of investment. Richard Joseph presents a model of prebendal politics in which individuals struggle to accumulate wealth from a swollen, fragmented state which has immense resources and a vast array of bureaucratic regulations.[28] There is no private sector, in the strict sense, in Joseph's model, only the allocation and privatisation of state resources through control of state offices and clientage.

When account is taken of other country and continent-wide studies, it can be argued that dependence of private accumulation on access to the state, and the coherence and capacities of the classes that exercise state power, have become the dominant explanations for the perceived weakness of African capital. Bayart in an ambitious attempt to identify trajectories and power and accumulation across Africa, allows a small space for private accumulation, but in his references to Nigeria, gives overwhelming priority to access to the state, to strategies of straddling between private and public domains, to income from rents and contracts.[29] Médard writing about Africa from a Kenyan perspective, views African businessmen as Big Men, who adopt multiple strategies of personal accumulation involving two-way conversions between economic and political resources. He emphasises privileged political access to a neo-patrimonial state and rental forms of accumulation.[30] These views will be taken up in the conclusion to this study.

METHOD

Five chapters in this book are based on case studies. In all, over two hundred interviews were conducted. No questionnaires were used, or research assistants employed. Ideally, the purposeful decisions of business persons should be an integral part of this type of study. Only direct, unmediated investigation can hope to achieve this. Over thirty-five years ago, Peter Bauer drew attention to the way in which an emphasis on quantification and reliance on second-hand statistics had contributed to a decline in direct observation by economists and an unwarranted narrowing of the field of study.[31] His remarks remain relevant where significant aspects of the situation cannot be meaningfully quantified. They are also apposite where statistics are unreliable or have been torn from the very context that can give them meaning. In the same vein, Amartya Sen has criticised the restrictive methods of economists, noting their extraordinarily narrow interpretation of human motivation and the low status accorded to description by the predictive and prescriptive interests that dominate the discipline.[32]

In addition to interviews, biographies, newspapers, business and financial journals and industrial directories have proved useful sources of information. Among the subjects of recently published biographies and autobiographies are Dr C. E. Abebe, Chief Francis Edo-Osagie, Alhaji Garba Nautan Hamza, Francis Arthur Nzeribe, Chief T. A. Odutola, Lawrence Omole, Chief I. A. Mbanefo, Chief Ayo Rosiji, Chief (Mrs) Bisoye Tejuoso and Madam Tinubu. These works are of variable quality and interest; yet, they all contributed to my understanding. Business histories are a much rarer commodity. The only example I found, is a history of Akintola Williams & Company.[33] In the text, case studies appear in two forms. There are brief profiles of enterprises and longer accounts of individual careers and business histories. I hope that those interested in biography will find the latter useful and relatively unencumbered by attempts to generalise or by theoretical concerns.

The criteria for selection included scale of enterprise and location within one of the major centres already mentioned. Although I did not rigidly exclude enterprises below a minimum size, most of the enterprises or groups studied employ more than 50 persons. I deliberately selected larger indigenous companies and by implication some of the most successful in terms of growth and longevity. Where I encountered enterprise failure, I have reported it. There is no readily available population of enterprises to select from. Business organisations like the Manufacturers' Association of Nigeria or local Chamber of Commerce can provide only a partial picture. Indigenous enterprises in Nigeria are not ranked by assets and turnover as they are in India, for example.

I had to make my own inquiries to identify many of the enterprises and their location. Though in principle this was only a starting point, it was a slow and arduous process that was never actually completed. It seemed at times to dominate the research. Most pieces of the jigsaw puzzle only came to light in the field. Thus when I arrived in Onitsha, I was advised to pursue my investigations in Nnewi as well.

A few non-African enterprises were included provided that they originated in Nigeria and had not diversified their activity abroad on any significant scale. From the perspective of capital accumulation, many enterprises begun in Nigeria by immigrants are indigenous, whether or not the owners have become Nigerian citizens. Their proximity to African enterprise in terms of scale and competition make them especially relevant.

I make no strong claim to national representativeness in this book. Though major centres of indigenous enterprise are covered, there remain a number of centres like Port Harcourt, Benin, Ilorin, Jos and Maiduguri with significant concentrations of indigenous capital that are outside the scope of the study. I have included, or made reference to, a few individuals and enterprises in these centres. In the case of Port Harcourt, my attention was focused almost exclusively on companies in the oil-service sector. Nor would I claim that the tables presented are comprehensive; only that a high proportion of the relevant medium- and large-scale enterprises are included. Nevertheless, I think that the scope of the studies is such that there is a basis for generalisation.

The business people I have studied are overwhelmingly male at the scale I am concerned with. The use of any other term than businessmen would be deceptive at points in the text. A few case studies of businesswomen are included. In the colonial period and after, women participated strongly in trade and distribution, dominating activity in some parts of the country. While sole trading enterprises have not, on the whole, led to large enterprises, women have made advances in areas like hotel and catering, garments, fashion design, supermarkets, insurance, laundry, maternity homes, clinics, hairdressing, and business centres.[34] Lack of access to education and the dominant perception of gender roles which saw nursing and teaching as appropriate professions in the colonial period, virtually closed off avenues to business via foreign companies and the higher echelons of the public service and public corporations. In the last two decades, a significant advance in the professions (accountancy, law, medicine, pharmacy, banking, journalism etc.) has led to entry into corporate enterprise, so that banks and multinational enterprises are headed by women like Chief (Mrs) Koforuji-Olubi, chairman of the United Bank for Africa and Mrs Adetutu Adeleke of Tate and Lyle. A few women, who have followed this path, have formed their own enterprises. They include Chief (Mrs) O. O. Olakunri, who was with the Nigerian Industrial Development Bank, before setting up Diamond Plastics and Mrs Dedun Aganga-Williams, who held positions with four banks, before launching Bullion Trust and Securities. Others, like Chief (Mrs) Bassey Etim of Port and Marine Services and Mrs Isaiah Nwafor of Nnewi worked in partnership with their husbands and have inherited and built on the business after their husbands' death, or like Mrs O. A. Alao, Executive Director of the Adegoke Group of Companies, have managed companies that were pioneered by their fathers.

Two caveats need to be entered at this point. Many Nigerian business owners have invested overseas. A few have started businesses abroad. Some of the overseas portfolios, consisting of real estate and financial assets, are substantial. Moreover, these investments are not necessarily totally 'lost' to the Nigerian economy. Income from overseas investment and business is used to fund enterprises in Nigeria and finance politics. A full account of Nigerian enterprise would need to take this international dimension into account. Yet this a difficult and sensitive area for research.

The same is true of another grey area, political corruption in the award of contracts and licences, financial corruption and other forms of illegitimate activity. I was told by friends that no Nigerian business person would talk to me because they were all very corrupt. In my experience, there is a grain of truth in this, but much depends on what you wish to discuss and what stage in their business careers informants have reached.[35] Knowledge and evidence of corruption is widespread in Nigeria and views about it are strongly held. I can only agree with readers who find some of my accounts overly sanitised. In a few cases, I found that the primary source of capital accumulation was drug trafficking. Since I name individuals and companies, I have not referred to this in the text.[36]

Another limitation of this study concerns the lack of 'hard' statistical data on enterprises. It has very rarely been possible to obtain accounts or published indicators for individual enterprises or groups of companies beyond turnover and employment figures. Thus accurate measurement of size, growth and profitability of an enterprise, or assessment of an individual's wealth is precluded. It would not be an exaggeration to say that any concerted attempt to pursue this matter during interviews was a certain way to bring discussion to an end. Where companies remain in sole ownership and are strongly identified with the founder or his family, the exposure of wealth and property to public view can be especially sensitive. Fear of liability to tax is also a potent factor preventing disclosure. This does not mean that formal accounting procedures may not be followed – the owner may well employ accountants, operate a system of financial control and monitor performance closely. Indeed, there may exist three sets of accounts – an accurate one for the entrepreneur, a second set for inquisitive banks, and a third for tax purposes.

Over time, data tends to become harder. For example, companies that have gone public on the stock exchange are obliged to reveal more information. Rankings of companies, which have begun to appear in the financial press, have large gaps in their coverage. But they do provide some information and put pressure on companies to identify themselves.

It has not been possible to give an accurate statistical summary of the size of indigenous capital by sector or industry. Industrial statistics are not comprehensive or reliable. In any case, share ownership is not a good guide to the relative strength and dynamism of indigenous capital, especially where shareholdings are in good measure the product of a recent indigenisation exercise involving the compulsory transfer of shares. Further problems of measurement exist because of the porous nature of the Nigerian economy. Unofficial flows of goods, services, currency and labour across international boundaries in West Africa are important and may alter orders of magnitude. Thus the unofficial export of manufactured goods to neighbouring countries is substantial and likely to exceed official exports by a wide margin.

Readers will notice the ubiquity of the title Chief in references to businessmen and women. I will return briefly to title taking in my conclusion, but it should be explained here that, in many cases, this does not denote tenure of a political office, or the existence of hereditary title. Generalisation about chieftaincy in Nigeria is complicated by the fact that there is very considerable variation between ethnic groups and across communities. Where wealth is often matched by social prestige and sometimes by political influence as well, a number of different elements may be bound up in chieftaincy. Runciman's distinction between the wealthy Big Man who personally constructs his power over others and chieftainships whose incumbents come to power, is useful, though often elided in practice.[37] Chieftaincy practices range from the outright purchase of new titles by the wealthy, to title taking by Big Men who climb through a hierarchy of established titles, to honorific titles bestowed by community elders, to election by interest groups and lineages to political office denoted by title, and finally to succession to high office by members of ruling families. Many titles are conferred by local community leaders to honour individuals. They are given in recognition of business achievements, philanthropy and leadership roles in the home community or wider political arena. They may, or may not, be associated with an enhanced role in the social and political affairs of a community. The recent inflation and commercialisation of chieftaincy titles in parts of Nigeria, especially in some Igbo communities, is a widely recognised phenomenon.

ORGANISATION

Chapter 2 provides a broad overview of the advance of indigenous capital in this century. It situates this development within the context of political and economic changes. The first section covers the period from the turn of the century to the outbreak of the Second War. The second section takes the story forward to the end of the Nigerian civil war in 1970. The final section covers two decades in which the economy was dominated by fluctuations in oil revenues which first brought boom conditions and then economic recession after 1982. In 1986, a Structural Adjustment Programme was introduced, the economy was deregulated and the naira underwent a steep devaluation.

Chapter 3 examines in more detail the business careers of fourteen leading business owners whose careers span seven decades (1920s to 1980s) and who were all well established in the 1950s. The group is biased towards Lagos and towards educated elements and is not representative of larger enterprises across the whole country. Large illiterate traders are not covered. It includes a number of early industrialists like Chief Odutola, and Chief Ugochukwu, traders and transporters and politician/entrepreneurs.

The next five chapters cover the growth of indigenous enterprises in the major business centres of Lagos and its environs, Onitsha, Nnewi, Aba, Kano and Kaduna.

The Lagos chapter covers business groups, more specialist enterprises and an ill-defined category of investors and middlemen. The emergence of two of the largest Lagos-based conglomerates, the Ibru Organisation and the Modandola Group, which originated in the mid-1950s, are covered separately in chapter 6. The next two chapters examine enterprises in two areas of Igboland where there has been a significant movement from trade to industry. Particular attention is given to the two specialist trading communities of Abiriba and Nnewi. The last chapter covers the old commercial centre of Kano and the much newer administrative centre of Kaduna.

My work has made me acutely aware that any of these business centres could easily be the subject of a book length study in its own right. What has been gained by a broad geographical spread has certainly entailed some losses in depth of understanding. I hope that others will go on to extend the work and that readers will draw my attention to errors of fact and interpretation.

The final chapter draws some conclusions from the study as a whole and introduces a comparative dimension.

A NOTE ON CURRENCY

Until January 1974, the unit of currency was the Nigerian £. The naira (N) was then introduced at the rate of one naira N1=$1.52. The value of the naira then fluctuated, reaching an annual average value of N1=$1.83 in 1980. Subsequently, the naira depreciated and was devalued sharply after 1986. At the end of 1992, N1=$0.05 ($1=N20).

2

THE ADVANCE OF AFRICAN CAPITAL
1900–1992: AN OVERVIEW

1900–1945

Commerce

Towards the end of the nineteenth century, there were African traders with large commercial organisations employing several thousand people. The names of Ja Ja of Opobo and Nana Olomu of Itsekiriland are outstanding. Both symbolised the wealth and influence that African middlemen had either attained or were aspiring to attain. By the 1880s, Jaja and some middlemen from Brass and New Calabar were attempting to break into the export trade, hitherto a preserve of the European firms, and in fact Jaja succeeded in arranging to ship his palm oil to a Birmingham firm.[1]

One consequence of the opening up of southern Nigeria to British trade between 1881 and 1916 was the commercial decline of the trading communities of the Oil Rivers. Both Ja Ja of Opobo and Nana Olomu were deposed, undermined by British authority and commercial interests. By their removal, the administration removed the only Delta Africans who had the resources to even attempt to establish an African export trade. The Royal Niger Company used its charter of 1886 to prohibit Lagos merchants from trading on the Niger.[2] A few of these merchants owned steamships and used them in the Niger trade.[3] As British control over the hinterland began to expand at the turn of the century, the European commercial companies shifted their operations into the interior. An influx of expatriate firms began to penetrate the hinterland, setting up buying stations for produce and retail and wholesale outlets for imported goods. The building of the railways and the extension of the road network helped to reduce transport costs, increase the supply of raw materials and expand the internal market. The trading stations of the Niger Company, the largest commercial enterprise, increased from 42 in 1900 to 54 in 1920, the year when the company was taken over by Lever Brothers.[4] These outstations reached a peak at the end of the 1920s. From its headquarters at Burutu island, the operations of the Niger Company spanned Nigeria from Ilorin to Yola and Garua in

Cameroons reaching northwards along the railway to Zaria, Kano and the Bauchi Plateau.

The coastal middlemen and their agents, on whom the firms hitherto depended for their contact with the primary producers, gradually lost their long-established monopoly to a new group of African traders in the interior. Foreign companies required inland agents to distribute goods and collect new crops like cocoa and this brought new commercial hierarchies into existence. The Aros, the inland middlemen of the pre-colonial era, lost their control over trade in Igboland. The land rights of Aro traders were challenged by their host communities.[5] The Lagos merchants were also squeezed as new expatriate companies appeared and international markets were less favourable. Many lost their independent status, becoming agents for foreign companies. Among the important traders at the close of the century were J. P. L. Davies, J. W. Cole, J. H. Doherty, Mohammed Shitta-Bey, J. J. Thomas and Z. A. Williams. The merchant prince of them all was R. B. Blaize whose financial resources in the 1890s were estimated at about £150,000.[6] Blaize left £3,000 for the foundation of the Blaize Memorial Institute at Abeokuta which opened in 1909 and provided technical training for apprentices for many years. A good indication of the importance of African traders was the prominent role they played in the Lagos Chamber of Commerce founded in 1888, and again in 1892 and 1897.[7]

The leading Lagos merchants took part in the movement inland.[8] By 1906, four African merchants, S. A. Coker, J. H. Doherty, D. A. Taylor and C. A. Oni had opened branches at Abeokuta and Ibadan. In 1914, J. H. Doherty had 10 branches including Zaria, Kano and Duala. Nevertheless, a relative loss of economic power over the first two decades of the century was signalled by the fact that African traders left the Lagos Chamber of Commerce. S. H. Pearse and P. J. C. Thomas were admitted in the early 1920s, but they were the only African members of the Chamber in the interwar years.[9]

Samuel Pearce (1866–1953) was apprenticed to MacIver and worked with Williams Brothers from 1883.[10] In 1888 he launched a business with a partner from Sierra Leone. The business closed in 1894 and he became the agent for the African and Gold Coast Trading Corporation. In 1897, he went to Calabar dealing in all imported goods and exporting palm produce, rubber and especially ivory. He returned to Lagos in 1902 with his newly acquired wealth, traded in palm produce and developed extensive property interests. He bought shares in three Gold Coast mining companies and in 1907 opened the first hotel in Lagos.[11] After World War I, the slump in the palm produce forced him to sell his hotel and dispose of his war bonds. He then entered the rubber export business until 1929, after which he shifted his activity to the import of stockfish and export of hides and skins. P. J. C. Thomas, a general merchant, began his career in Calabar before moving to

Lagos and diversifying into corn milling, tanning and a model farm. In 1920 he had twenty-five branches inland. He had eight Europeans in his employ in the early 1920s.[12]

The foreign merchant companies often combined together in the produce trade to regulate prices and to operate pooling arrangements under which the total purchase was divided among members according to previously agreed proportions. In this way they increased their profits, discouraged new entrants and forced out newcomers from the trade. When African traders attempted to control markets and prices through combinations, they could be penalised. In 1905, Kalabari canoemen and some Aboh traders combined to regulate the prices for palm oil.[13] Their alliance was backed by Calabar 'Laws'. As a result, fifty-six Kalabari traders and fourteen other African traders were tried by the Native Authority at Oguta and fined small sums.

African traders were dependent on a system of cash advances for produce buying and goods advanced on credit for resale. This system, and the superior capital resources of expatriate trading firms, together with foreign monopoly control of banking and shipping facilities, meant that it was extremely difficult for African traders to break into direct importation or direct export of produce. African traders were far more numerous than their expatriate competitors and this made collective organisation of their interests much more difficult. In shipping, the Conference Lines controlled by Sir Alfred Jones monopolised the West African export and import trades. In 1916, African shippers could secure only very limited export tonnage, 3.5 per cent of the total, or 350 tons.[14] Jones also owned the British Bank of West Africa which secured the banking business of the government of Lagos in 1894 and that of Southern Nigeria in 1903.[15]

The adverse position of African traders was compounded by the steady growth of monopoly in the import and export trade. This tendency towards a concentration of merchant capital was accelerated when poor market conditions caused many traders to go out of business and prompted amalgamations. African traders, as well as European traders, were badly hit by the deterioration in the market for palm produce and cocoa in 1921 and 1922. They had large stocks of imported goods on which they had exhausted their credits; when the price of goods crashed they could not pay their debts. African importers were generally relegated to the role of middlemen and commission brokers for the Europeans and they continued to play a secondary role between the two World Wars. The Depression of 1929–31 also affected the fortunes of many European companies disastrously. In 1929, the Niger Company Ltd and the African and Eastern Trade Company merged to form the United Africa Company (UAC). Mars calculated that of the 197 non-mining expatriate companies that existed between 1921 and 1936, only fourteen succeeded in maintaining an unbroken independent existence.[16]

Market-sharing agreements and price regulation by the expatriate trading companies provoked strong opposition and fuelled nationalist sentiment. In the 1930s, young produce traders like T. A. Odutola of Ijebu-Ode, S. O. Gbadamosi of Ikorodu and J. O. Fadahunsi of Ilesha were active members of the Nigerian Youth Movement, the leading nationalist movement in Lagos, which actively resisted the Cocoa Pool of 1937–8.

Very rarely did new companies manage to compete effectively with the established European traders and gain a significant share of the import or export market. Peter Bauer cites the experience of a group of traders in Port Harcourt who had entered the import trade in stockfish in 1937 and were undermined by price cutting.[17] When an African trader found a profitable new line, European companies would move quickly to drive them out of business. The experience of Mr C. T. Onyekwelu in Onitsha market, which is treated in chapter 3, is instructive in this regard.

On the export side, numerous attempts were made by Africans to enter the cocoa trade before the World War I and during the interwar period. Nearly all of them were shortlived and unsuccessful.[18] Schemes were initiated by Duse Mohammed Ali in the early 1920s, and in the late 1920s and early 1930s by Winifried Tete Ansa. Tete Ansa's ambitious schemes, which involved the export of produce from the Gold Coast and Nigeria, banking and the import of consumer goods from the United States, came to very little, but they caught the imagination of Nigerian produce dealers, businessmen and leaders of the National Congress. At one point, Ansa had the support of forty-five farmers' associations making up about 60 per cent of West African cocoa exports.[19] The West African Co-operative Producers Ltd, founded in 1928, closed down in 1930 due to financial irregularities, owing the Ibadan Co-operative Planters Association some £11,000.

At the end of the 1930s, there was a handful of Nigerian exporters maintaining links with mainly British brokers. In 1938–9 their total cocoa exports were only 873 tons, although this is not an adequate measure of their strength *vis-à-vis* the European trading firms.[20] The internal cocoa trade was much more stable than the export trade. Thus, T. A. Odutola of Ijebu-Ode exported 250 tons of cocoa in the 1938–9 season, yet his seasonal turnover amounted to 4,000–5,000 tons. By the late 1930s he had built his own buying organisation and largely financed his trade, although he also received advances from one of the European trading firms. The Ibadan trader, I. B. Ogun, claimed a turnover of 3,000 tons in the 1938–9 season with a staff of 35 persons and head office on Lebanon Street.[21]

Prominent because of its exceptional character was the case of Saul Raccah, by origin a Tripolitanian Jew, who was able to become one of the largest merchants in the groundnut trade in Kano. In 1938–9 Raccah's exports amounted to more than a third of the crop and exceeded the export of the UAC. His success broke the buying pool among the European merchants.

An important factor in Raccah's success was his ability to secure low cost shipping charters from Italy.[22] The largest of the Hausa groundnut traders at this time was Alhassan Dantata. He was the main groundnut buyer for the UAC and in an average year bought about 20,000 tons. He did not attempt to enter the export market.

A number of attempts were made to establish indigenous banks in the interwar period but they had little success. Two initiatives involving Winifried Tete Ansa from the Gold Coast, the Industrial and Commercial Bank Ltd (1929) and the Nigerian Mercantile Bank (1931) failed.[23] In 1933, the National Bank of Nigeria Ltd was established by Dr Akinola Maja, T. A. Doherty and H. A. Subair and attempts were made to trade directly with Europe and the United States and bypass the European trading firms. This bank was to prove more durable although its operations remained at a low level for many years. Its main function was to provide short-term finance to African importers, exporters, produce buyers and traders.

If African traders lost commercial power relative to the European trading companies during the colonial period, this did not mean that middlemen went into uninterrupted decline or that they were reduced to petty trading. The colonial economy was growing throughout the colonial period (subject to fluctuations) and thus turnover and profits could increase. There was significant commercial wealth in local terms. The European firms still relied on African agents who stood at the pinnacle of a trading hierarchy. New middlemen and women who were closely tied to the foreign companies did emerge. The arrival of Nigerian produce buyers, who had lorries, was a new competitive element; it was probably an important factor in limiting the expansion of buying stations belonging to the European trading companies.[24] Beyond trade and transport, there were some new opportunities in small-scale industries like baking and printing.[25]

In the cocoa trade, there was a hierarchy of traders with small itinerant traders at the base (pan or basket buyers). They sold to the scale men (who were traders with weighing machines). Above them were the firms' depot clerks who received a small salary and a commission on the tonnage they handled. At the top were more or less independent produce brokers. Some were really commission buyers for the firms but the wealthy and most successful ones owned their own stores and, in some cases, transport businesses. Some of them also had substantial cocoa farms. Some employed their own commission agents and maintained buying organisations very similar to those of the European firms. Produce trading could be combined with an agency from foreign firms for imported merchandise. In general, the largest trading fortunes were made on the produce-buying side.

J. D. Y. Peel has underlined the economic and political importance of the trading and transport elite in Ilesha, an important cocoa-growing area in the interwar period.[26] The enterprises, which combined trade with transport, were transient. The main objective and measure of personal success was the size of the following which an important individual could build up and the influence he could command within the community. Income was used to build up social credit in the community rather than to advance personal consumption or the enlargement of the enterprise itself.

In Kano, Hausa traders who had formerly gained wealth in the kolanut trade with the Gold Coast switched their attention to the groundnut trade, which expanded rapidly after 1912.[27] The largest traders became agents of the European trading companies with extensive networks of clients. The position of the larger Hausa traders was challenged from about 1917 by the arrival of many Lebanese and Tripolitanian Arabs. As the groundnut trade expanded, so the number of merchants increased, but of the really big middlemen, only Alhassan Dantata continued to expand his operations. It was not until the 1950s that Hausa traders began to regain their status as the most important middlemen replacing European firms as the chief buyers of crops for the Marketing Board.

The case of Omu Okwei, a prominent trader in Onitsha, illustrates that significant local wealth could be accumulated in the interstices left open by the foreign companies.[28] Omu Okwei (1872–1943) was the daughter of a prominent Ossomari family who became one of a group of wealthy women merchants based in Onitsha. In Igboland, until the 1920s, it was women who dominated the internal trade in palm produce and imported goods. Her trade in foodstuffs expanded to include retail trade in imported goods such as tobacco and cotton goods and she became an agent for the Niger Company. She then shifted her emphasis to palm and kernel oil and imported goods such as gin, lamps, matches, pots and plates. In 1910, Okwei's monthly credit with the Niger Company was valued at £400.

She employed full-time clerks and interpreters and had a network of agents in all ports of the Niger Delta. Her sons were educated and assisted her. She became a buying agent for chiefs and influential men from the hinterland and a money lender. During the 1920s she shifted from palm produce to the import of specialised and expensive items like gunpowder, ivory, and coral beads. She imported directly from Liverpool and Manchester firms using her local banking contacts. She invested part of her capital in canoes and lorries to transport her goods from the coast. At her death, she owned 24 houses in Onitsha, 6 canoes, a car and numerous plots in strategic parts of the town, which she leased.

Agriculture[29]

In the colonial period, there were locally pockets of agricultural or landed wealth, as in the large farms controlled by the Muslim aristocracy in the northern emirates[30] and the medium-scale cocoa and rubber farms in the south. Through their control of local government and patronage systems, traditional rulers in both the Northern and Western Regions exercised a great deal of power over land matters. Yet it was small farmers who dominated the rural economy and provided the vast bulk of the export produce.

Polly Hill argues that the general absence of agrarian hierarchy in pre-colonial West Africa was due to the lack of differential and transmittable rights over farmland.[31] The individual right to cultivate on a usufructuary basis derived from membership of a corporate landholding lineage or from a position as a resident member of a rural community. The fact that land was plentiful and that the great majority of households were not prevented by poverty from actively undertaking cultivation, was also important.

In Nigeria, the colonial period saw a large expansion of crops for export and food crops supported by the development of road and railway infrastructure. This was accompanied by the development of new areas of crop specialisation, population migration and the reorientation of internal trade patterns. Most production was carried out on a small scale and depended on family labour, kin or clients. Wage labour, usually temporary and seasonal, drew on labourers from other farm households and was difficult to attract and retain. Rich and powerful families were able to secure the services of various forms of unfree labour but it was always difficult to recruit and discipline.[32] In general, no clear class divisions between rich and poor farmers or between farmers and labourers emerged within rural communities in response to commercialisation and the commoditisation of land and labour. Access to resources and strategies of accumulation were very often dependent on ties of kinship, lineage and friendship and on reciprocal ties of clientage. Community identities were strong, shaping economic participation and conditioning social differentiation. A distinct peasantry, landed gentry or class of capitalist farmers did not emerge.

Capitalist agriculture did not take root during the colonial period. The colonial government generally resisted attempts to establish plantations for fear of the political consequences of widespread land alienation.[33] It had made a political alliance with the traditional authorities who controlled the land. Taxation, the mobilisation of labour for public works, and the acquisition of land for government and commercial purposes had priority and these concerns in themselves created considerable opposition. There were doubts, too, about the efficiency of plantations by comparison with smallholder agriculture in West African circumstances. Early plantations had a very poor record. This smallholder policy could draw support from ideas about colonial Trusteeship in Africa, which involved the protection of African communities and land rights from large-scale private appropriation of land.

The expansion of cocoa, a perennial crop, led to permanent transmittable rights over cocoa trees, but not land, and the development of tenancy and sharecropping. No class of capitalist farmers, cocoa gentry, or class of self-reproducing peasant households emerged. According to Berry, the possibilities of accumulation in the colonial period were limited by problems of labour supervision, by the absence of economies of scale in agriculture, by the foreign trading and banking monopolies and by colonial subordination.[34] Small prosperous farmers tended to diversify their assets rather than acquire large farms. The best opportunities for accumulation were not in agriculture but in trade, the professions and civil service.

Berry has stressed that power and wealth were sought in a political and legal context in which seniority and patronage played a large part in underpinning relations of production. The spread of cocoa and colonial rule did not undermine these relations of dependence and control, they often strengthened them. This affected access to land and labour and the organisation of production. For example, accumulators had to act as patrons to retain and recruit labour and this did not necessarily promote efficiency. It also meant that resources had to be used in establishing positions of patronage and supporting wider kin groups. In these ways, tendencies towards more capitalistic forms of accumulation, access to resources through the market, and rights in private property were checked. Peel has shown how the rise of a cocoa gentry in Ilesha was thwarted by the continued dominance of urban power and status, and by the attractions of commercial and bureaucratic careers which persuaded farmers to educate their sons and take them out of farming.[35]

Some parallels have been drawn by Martin from her work in the Ngwa region of Igboland where yam and oil-palm production were the core activities during the colonial period.[36] There was limited commercialisation of land and labour. Senior men and warrant chiefs, who did acquire wealth, did not invest in plantations or contrive to consolidate their wealth in other ways. At death, property was very often dispersed. There was a proprietary interest in controlling land and gaining power over labour which often inhibited sustained investment in agriculture. In an area where population densities were high, the costs of land acquisition were very high and there were limited technical opportunities for investment in production. Those among the younger men who had capital to invest, tended to put it into trade.

Road Transport

Road transport was an area where African enterprise was strongly represented during the interwar period. Although the largest firms were expatriate, small African transporters had a large share of the market and a competitive edge over the expatriate firms. There were no overwhelming advantages of scale. Entry was relatively easy. The seasonal nature of demand combined with the need to carry goods and passengers to inaccessible destinations required flexibility and gave advantages to small operators who could change routes and vary charges according to conditions. Africans also acquired early access to American vehicles which had a number of advantages over British vehicles.[37] They were cheaper, their lighter chassis was better suited to West African conditions, access to spare parts was better and pneumatic tyres allowed use over a variety of road surfaces.

In Lagos, the first private motor dealers, importers, and body builders, were African. The pioneer was W. A. Dawodu, the first person to import motor vehicles into Nigeria. Dawodu (1879–1930) was the son of Benjamin Fagbemi Dawodu (1830–81) a wealthy trader in salt, spirits and gun powder and court official, whose father had come to Lagos from Nupeland as a slave.[38] After secondary education and a spell at Hussey Charity Institute where he received technical training, he started bicycle repair and sales in 1905.[39] He began to import motor cars and was sole agent for Ford cars and Humber cycles. He also built up motor bodies, did conversions and built rickshaws at his Lagos works. By 1913 he was tendering for transport services near Kano and by 1920 he had become a large importer of vehicles, employing 250 persons with a branch at Oshogbo.[40] The business declined in the 1920s and did not survive the founder's death in 1930.

The first bus service in Lagos, the Anfani Bus Service, which replaced the steam tramway linking Lagos wharves to the railway terminus at Iddo, was introduced in 1914 by Mrs C. O. Obasa (b. 1873).[41] Mrs Obasa, the wealthy daughter of R. B. Blaize, spent much of her time in social work. The bus service, which was conceived more as a philanthropic than a commercial venture, ran until the late 1920s. Mrs Obasa also ran the Faji Taxi Service on the Marina and built a private toll road between Agege and the rich farmland of Ipaja.[42] In the interwar period, the Benson Transport Service, Tanimose Transport Service and Oshinowo Transport Service were all active.[43] After the war, the Union of Nigerian Transporters and Elias Transport Service entered. The largest operator was a Greek, J. N. Zarpas, who began in 1928 and provided virtually a municipal service until 1958 when the enterprise was bought by the Lagos City Council.[44] Zarpas also operated a tyre retreading plant, J.and A. Zarpas, begun in 1940.

In the West, the growth of transport services was closely linked to produce buying. Peel notes that in Ilesha after 1918 there was a rapid increase in transport owned and operated by Ijesha traders.[45] A decade later, over two dozen Ijesha owned lorries. J. D. E. Abiola, for example, a wealthy produce trader had twelve vehicles and added an agency in motor parts with the firm of Weeks. The Depression then drastically reduced the ranks of lorry owners so that by the late 1930s the field was dominated by one man. Yet during and after World War II, transport linked to produce buying remained the route to the greatest local fortunes. I. O. Ajanaku and Lawrence Omole, the two outstandingly wealthy men Ilesha produced after World War II, both moved from a base in produce to transport.

In the East, an early pioneer was Chief Elijah Henshaw who in 1923 operated a motor service between Oron, Opobo and Ikot Ekpene.[46] By the 1930s a number of motor magnates had emerged. Many of the transporters

TABLE 2.1: Size of selected immigrant groups in Nigeria.

Year	Greek	Indian	Lebanese/Syrian
1921	26	17	143
1931	67	97	419
1938	168	68	818

Source: R. Kuczynski, *Demographic Survey of the British Colonial Empire*, Table 14, pp. 613, 616.

came from Nnewi, a wealthy Igbo community that developed a number of transport specialisms. The most well known of these transport firms was to be Ojukwu Transport which began in 1937 and was based in Lagos (see chapter 3). An earlier company, based in Aba, was that of Mr J. C. Ulasi.

Ulasi originally travelled on foot from Nnewi to Aba to look for work.[47] He began to trade in cloth from Calabar in markets close to Aba. He added produce to his investments provisioning open-air stalls on several roads leading out of Aba. He recruited apprentices from Nnewi to assist him and, at one time, had as many as seventy. By the mid-1930s, he had six lorries. He secured a mail contract for Onitsha, Nnewi and Cross River, and became a warrant chief at Aba Native Court. When he died in 1944, he had ten lorries, eight property lots, and several buildings in Aba. The transport and buildings left by Ulasi were later sold to pay for the education of his children and the maintenance of his wives.

Immigrant Groups

During the colonial period, a number of new immigrant groups established themselves in Nigeria. By virtue of their small scale and type of business, they came to compete with Nigerians. Some companies were to grow to fill spaces, neglected or vacated, by European investors.

The most important of the immigrant groups in Nigeria before World War II were the Lebanese (see Table 2.1). The first arrivals came in the mid-1890s and there was a strong influx after 1918.[48] They came to Lagos and Kano first. The first Lebanese to come to commercial prominence in Lagos was a cattle dealer, Michael Elias, who by 1920 was sending 15,000 head of cattle a year to Lagos.[49] In the West, they moved to Ibadan in 1910 and then in the 1920s to smaller towns, establishing a presence in the 1930s in Benin, Ilesha and Ondo. They began as retailers and then moved into semi-wholesale with the objective of importing manufactured goods like textiles and hardware. In the late 1920s, some began to move into transport, based in Lagos and Ibadan.[50] Some became exporters of cocoa and palm kernel, like C. Zard and Co. Ltd. From the 1940s onwards, they diversified further into small-scale manufacturing, property development, catering and hotel services, cinemas and football pools.

The expansion of the Lebanese did reduce the influence of indigenous traders and in some towns they met with hostility.[51] They were not admitted to Ijebu-Ode until 1951. They tended to respond faster to economic changes in the colonial period than indigenous traders.[52] Whereas indigenous traders concentrated their attention on older patterns of demand and old market places, the Lebanese were more flexible and quick to cater for the interests of the elite and the emerging middle class. Hard working, thrifty, with family businesses and minimal overheads, they showed great tenacity with continuity of location and operations.

Indian penetration was led by Sindi textile traders, who bought Madras cloth in India for shipment to West Africa. Chellarams, which operated from Bombay, had eleven branches in Nigeria by 1939.[53] Indian companies also held agencies in electrical goods from Asian companies.

Other immigrants came from the West Indies, Sierra Leone and the Gold Coast. West Indians were prominent in the bread industry. A. S. Schackleford, who entered the bread industry in 1921, was known as the Bread King of Nigeria, and was responsible for major innovations in the baking industry.[54] Apart from his successful bakeries, which expanded to Ghana in 1934, Schackleford also operated ferry services and petrol stations. Another well-known immigrant was William Hamilton Biney, who came to Nigeria from the Gold Coast in 1907 to work as an accountant for Miller Bros. He began dock-labour contracting for Elder Dempster Lines in 1919 and built up the largest stevedoring firm in West Africa with branches in Nigeria, Ghana and Sierra Leone. His son, Kweku Biney, who trained in law, took over the business in 1955 and in 1961, W. Biney & Co. had 5,000 dockers on its register and 8 berths at Apapa.[55]

1945-1970

After World War II, political power began to shift to Africans but their economic influence was much more limited. With limited educational opportunities, many young people in the 1930s and 1940s, who were later to enter business independently, opted for correspondence courses to improve their knowledge of accounting and business practices, while holding low-level appointments in the colonial service and foreign firms. Foremost among the complaints of Nigerian nationalists was the economic power of the foreign trading companies who periodically combined in market sharing and price agreements. As a result of the wartime controls on trade, the Association of West African Merchants (AWAM) strengthened its position. In 1949, Peter Bauer estimated that six old established trading companies, which were party to a market-sharing agreement, accounted for 70 per cent of imported trade goods.[56] On the export side, where buying syndicates was common, the top six companies accounted for over 70 per cent of the value of non-mineral exports.[57] From this position of market power, the companies could control commercial credit. This was another factor working against the emergence of medium- and larger-scale African traders. The colonial banking monopolies which advanced credit to foreign enterprises and discriminated against Nigerian businessmen, also aroused hostility. There was too, a long history of concentration in shipping. The marketing boards, with their major share of demand for homeward tonnage, tended to encourage concentration in the supply of shipping services, which was dominated by three British conference lines.

In the aftermath of the war, with a shortage of consumer goods and a very profitable import trade, the activities of the trading companies became a focus of renewed agitation and nationalist opposition. There was a commission of inquiry into conditional sales by expatriate firms and, in 1947, a boycott of European firms was organised in Ibadan in protest at the distribution of consumer goods, especially textiles, which favoured the Lebanese. The operations of the Lebanese and their close ties with the expatriate companies, were resented on other grounds too. In a speech to the Legislative Council in 1950, Chief Odutola (who had pre-war experience in the Motor Transport Union) pointed out that there was hardly a single African transport operator sharing in the produce trade.[58] They had been ousted by the big Syrian transport firms. He argued that transport rates had been reduced to the extent that the Government subsidy paid on the transport of cocoa, palm kernels and other export produce from the interior to the port, went to the European licensed buying agents (LBAs) instead of being passed on to the transporters, as should have been the case. Chief Odutola commented that the Lebanese came into the country without any money and, with the help of European firms, had soon amassed a great fortune which was taken from Nigeria, and that very little was being put back into the country. He warned that the African would not stand idly by and see his resources being taken away from him by the Lebanese with the aid of British firms.

In the same speech, Chief Odutola was optimistic that a new partnership between foreign capital and Nigerian entrepreneurs was round the corner:[59]

> I have been greatly encouraged by the new sense of self confidence and responsible thinking in the country in regard to this question of outside capital. Best of all would be joint participation by Nigerian and overseas capital in the financing of industrial concerns throughout the country. It is already starting. I look forward to the time when Nigerians, by virtue of their business ability, will sit side by side with their European colleagues on the boards of directors controlling such enterprises. There is already ample evidence that a class of Nigerian businessmen is emerging which will increasingly be capable of making a genuine contribution to the industrial and commercial life of the country.

Chief Odutola's criticism of the Lebanese presence was a common refrain among nationalists and politicians in the post-war period. Toyin Falola argues that in southwestern Nigeria, the 1950s was probably a decade of contraction for the Lebanese.[60] Lebanese entry into Nigeria was certainly curtailed by changes in immigration policy that tried to exclude the poor and unskilled. There was also strong competition from Igbo traders. Osoba notes that the Igbo had pushed many Lebanese out of the Ibadan textile trade by the mid-1960s.[61] But how far there was really a contraction of Lebanese activity in the 1950s, as Falola suggests, is unclear. Under pressure from Nigerian small-scale enterprises, the Lebanese (who were basically selling imported goods like textiles and hardware) began to diversify out of the import, wholesale and retail trades. Apart from the produce trade and transport, they also invested in property companies, cinemas, hotels and catering, and light industry (soap, candles, plastics, building materials). Certainly in Kano, there was continued expansion as the Lebanese began to move into oil milling and other industrial activities.[62] Lebanese were adept at allying themselves with Nigerian politicians. They also began to apply for naturalisation as citizens of Nigeria.[63] The first application was made by an Ibadan-based trader in 1941. Yet by 1959, a total of only sixteen Lebanese had been granted naturalisation, despite the large number of applicants.

In the 1950s, Nigerian private capital was generally small scale, largely commercial in orientation, fragmented and regional in outlook. The areas where it was present on a significant scale included commerce (importing, wholesaling, retailing, and the produce trade), real estate, transport, construction, palm oil and rubber processing, saw milling and furniture, tyre retreading,[64] bakeries, printing, and shoe making and pools.[65] There was a very limited presence in banking and insurance. Small farmers, who were dependent on family labour, predominated.

Three related changes took place in the late 1940s and 1950s, each of which had an impact on the environment in which private capital operated. First, there was the gradual transfer of power to Nigerian politicians at the regional, then federal level. This brought business people closer to government and the political parties. They became prominent in the affairs of the parties which initially relied on them for financial support. It also led to a general expansion in state patronage for indigenous businessmen and an increase in the number of state agencies and enterprises. Second, from 1957 foreign capital began to invest in large-scale manufacture in order to protect its markets. The foreign trading companies also withdrew from the retail and produce trades. Various state subsidies, and later tariff escalation, also attracted a flow of new foreign investors. The third feature of significance was the breakdown of the monopolistic structure of the import trade as the overall market expanded and sources of supply widened. I will consider these points in turn.

Nigerian politicians and state officials had considerable funds at their disposal to expand the scope of state economic activity and patronage. The marketing board system, which syphoned trading surpluses away from the peasantry, provided the financial means for state expansion. The boards were statutory export monopolies that had their origins in the growing concentration in the import/export trade in the interwar period and in the wartime regulation of the produce trade. After the boards were regionalised in 1954, surplus funds were used to finance regional development programmes and party political expenditures. Helleiner estimated that a full 96 per cent of the funds for publicly owned development institutions came, directly or indirectly, from the marketing boards.[66]

The period after the war was a time of new initiatives by the government to support indigenous enterprise.[67] Between 1950 and 1965 over £4m was loaned to Nigerian entrepreneurs by government agencies.[68] The first public lending agency, the Nigerian Local Development Board, was set up in 1946. It was dissolved in 1949 and its functions were passed to the Regional Development Boards and the Colony Development Board. The latter was in operation for seven years and gave modest loans for textile, furniture, baking and saw-milling ventures. It was followed by the Federal Loans Board in 1956. This body was a modest success and generally performed better than regional agencies. Outside the mainstream activities of the regional bodies, large unsecured loans were made in each region to companies engaged in Lagos real-estate speculation.

The Regional Development Boards were followed by the Regional Development Corporations, which extended their activities from agriculture to manufacture, banking, insurance, finance, property and hotels. In 1956, the first industrial estates were opened. Investment companies were also established in the east and north in 1959 by the Commonwealth Development Corporation (CDC) as joint ventures with the Regional Development Corporations. The boards and corporations were controlled by the political class and became a source of funds for party and personal use. The boards became, in Wrigley's words, a convoluted collaboration of government, party, corporation, and private business.[69]

One result of the establishment of these boards was to impede the formation of private Nigerian capital by taxing small farmers and by funding state agencies which became the major participants in new ventures with foreign capital. The regional governments did not limit their activities to areas where indigenous business lacked the capital or technological expertise to participate. Thus in Ibadan in the early 1960s there existed seven private printing presses fully equipped with electrical cylindrical and colour printing machinery operating at less than full capacity. Yet the regional government sponsored a Government Printing Corporation, a Co-operative Press and the Caxton Press, with expatriate staff for two of these enterprises.[70] These firms were provided with semi-captive markets. Further instances of state enterprises directly undermining private enterprise could be cited in other industries, like furniture, and in other regions. Chief Odutola's vision of private Nigerian and foreign collaboration proved premature. Only very rarely did foreign companies enter into joint ventures with the largest of the indigenous entrepreneurs on anything like an equal footing.

The largest Nigerian businessmen supported an expansion of state patronage as a means of bypassing the foreign banks, getting access to credit and contracts, and bringing a state project to their home communities. State activity was not generally perceived as being in conflict with private interests. While the business class undoubtedly got new opportunities for access to capital through the activities of state agencies, it is not clear that much of it was converted into productive investment or that existing enterprises stood to gain from the new relationship between government and business. Some energies were diverted away from production towards the struggle for patronage. Another reason was that political considerations were prominent in the award of contract and licence.

The business elite, self-employed men of substance, were closely identified with the governing political parties. Most authors argue that politicians and businessmen were in close alliance and sometimes identical.[71] This is an oversimplification. There were some wealthy, independent business persons. But the need for good connections to attract business or defend an enterprise against political interference tended to lead to politicking, expediency and pragmatism. Given the attractions of politics for business people in this period, what was the impact on indigenous accumulation? There is no doubt that in some cases entrepreneurial energies were drawn off and dissipated through politics. Those independently wealthy businessmen who became closely involved in party affairs did not build up their enterprises or gain great wealth as a result of their political involvement. In a number of cases, businesses were adversely affected. A few individuals actually resigned from politics in order to concentrate on business activities.[72] There were others who gained wealth as a result of the political connections and who set up enterprises after gaining political office to exploit their connections. They tended to be involved in real estate, construction, and the direct provision of goods and services to government by contract rather than in industry.

Some leading businessmen were attracted to positions of power within government and the parties. Some took up representative positions that were opened up by constitutional changes. Others joined the boards of state companies and agencies. The close proximity of the business class with the politicians was one reason why there was an uneasy relationship between state officials and business. Businessmen were generally regarded as corrupt and seen as supplicants for favours from the state. They were not taken into confidence over state policy. They had no firm institutional presence for putting collective pressure on the government. Nationalist opposition to the dominance of foreign interests in the economy was limited and diluted by the involvement of business people in government and state bodies. It was directed mainly at small Lebanese enterprises. Periodic pressure from groups of businessmen and prominent individuals did prompt consideration of measures to restrict foreign capital but little action was taken. State policies that aimed to exclude foreign enterprise were directed first at the produce trade, transporting and the distributive sector, but in the latter case, measures were ineffective. After the public service was Nigerianised, attention was directed at expatriate employment in industry.

It was only in the late 1960s, when nationalist sentiment was strenghthened by the civil war, that Nigerian businessmen began to exercise more influence through the Small Businessmen's Committee (later the Indigenous Businessmen's Group) of the Lagos Chamber of Commerce. Although Nigerian participation in the Lagos Chamber had increased since Independence and over half the membership of the council was Nigerian by 1969, the leadership of the operational sub-groups of the Chamber (standing committees and trade groups) was firmly in the hands of the older and often more technically qualified expatriate members.[73] The Indigenous Businessmen's Group was active in pressing for a larger indigenous share of bank credit and for an indigenisation programme that would increase local shareholding in foreign companies. A breakdown of the 191 members of the Group for 1977 shows that commercial activities (50 per cent) and services (37 per cent) were dominant.[74]

A decline in business morality became evident after Independence. The tacit understandings between British rulers and British monopolies, and the market control exercised by the latter during the colonial period, did not generate much open corruption. With the transfer of power, the business environment entered a more fluid, competitive phase in which regional governments and much more diversified foreign interests including new British arrivals, vied with each other for contracts from an expanded state sector. Expatriate companies began to search for political influence. The personal insecurity of politicians and the need to fund political parties encouraged a kickback syndrome on the value of public contracts.

Table 2.2 shows the distribution of the stock of foreign direct investment by country and area of investment for 1967. In medium- and large-scale manufacture, foreign capital was dominant. In 1963, the structure of equity in large-scale manufacture comprised 10 per cent private Nigerian, 68 per cent private foreign, 3 per cent federal government, and 19 per cent regional government.[75] The presence of foreign investors created new forms of collaboration. They needed the goodwill of the new controllers of state power and politically influential businessmen. They started to appoint Nigerian directors, they hired properties from local businessmen and they appointed Nigerians as agents and representatives. Among the first Nigerians to be associated with foreign construction companies were Sir Philip Ojukwu

TABLE 2.2: Nigeria: stock of private direct investment, end 1967 ($ million).

	Canada	Denmark	France	Germany	Italy	Japan
Petroleum of which:	—	—	75.0	—	40.0	—
Production	—	—	72.0C	—	38.0	—
Refining	—	—	—	—	—	—
Marketing	—	—	3.0	—	2.0	—
Transport	—	—	—	—	—	—
Mining & smelting	—	—	—	—	—	—
Agriculture	—	—	—	—	—	—
Manufacturing	8.0	1.0	15.0	6.0	3.0	3.0
Trade	—	0.4	10.0	1.4	1.0	—
Public utilities	—	—	—	—	—	—
Transport	—	—	—	—	—	—
Banking	—	—	—	—	—	—
Tourism	—	—	—	—	—	—
Other	—	—	—	—	—	—
TOTAL	8.0	1.4	100.0	7.4	44.0	3.0

	Netherlands	Sweden	Switzerland	UK	US total	DAC
Petroleum of which:	147.0	—	—	343.0	155.0	760.0
Production	140.0	—	—	326.0	150.0	726.0
Refining	4.0	—	—	10.0	—	14.0
Marketing	3.0	—	—	7.0	5.0	20.0
Transport	—	—	—	—	—	—
Mining & smelting	—	—	—	14.9	1.0	15.9
Agriculture	—	—	—	5.0	—	5.0
Manufacturing	11.0	1.0	3.0	96.8	16.0	163.8
Trade	3.0	—	2.0	84.2	8.0	110.0
Public utilities	—	—	—	—	—	—
Transport	—	—	—	—	—	—
Banking	—	—	—	25.0	2.0	27.0
Tourism	—	—	—	—	—	—
Other	—	—	—	27.1	—	27.1
TOTAL	161.0	1.0	5.0	596.0	182.0	1,108.8

Source: *Stock of Private Direct Investments by DAC Countries in Developing Countries, end 1967.*

(Costain), Sir Mobalaji Bank Anthony (Borini Prono), Chief M. A. Aboderin (Strabag) and Chief Akin Deko (Solel Boneh).[76] Lawyers, who joined the boards of oil companies in the early 1960s, included Chief C. O. Ogunbanjo (Phillips, 1960), Chief H. O. Davies (Total, 1961) and Chief Bayo Kuku (Mobil, 1964). To get good will and integrate their companies more effectively into Nigeria, foreigners also started to sell shares to the public. Between 1959 and 1965, 9 companies sold shares worth N£600,000 to more than 6,000 shareholders.[77] Self-employed traders and businessmen, professionals and teachers were the main groups that purchased shares. Lawyers who specialised in company law were well placed to take advantage of opportunities arising from the sale of shares. Indeed lawyers, with their fee income, knowledge of land matters and political connections were in an enviable position for accumulating wealth from a variety of sources. Banks, too, liberalised the terms on which they gave loans to highly placed individuals. The Nigerianisation of middle-level management was also pursued. The United Africa Company pioneered the Africanisation of managerial staff. By 1952, 99 of the 365 positions in the middle management of the UAC operations in Nigeria were held by Nigerians.[78] This proved to be an important channel for Nigerian businessmen who left expatriate employment to set up on their own.

Some literate businessmen gradually built up shareholdings and directorships in a number of companies, creating holding companies anchored to foreign companies. From a local perspective, prominent individuals who had close associations with foreign companies, would claim to have invited them to Nigeria, just as, at an earlier date, merchants who acted as agents of the trading companies would claim to have brought the companies to their home towns.

In the 1950s, barriers to entry in the import trade were much reduced by the expansion of the Nigerian market, which permitted increased specialisation and reduced capital requirements.[79] Indian, Greek, Lebanese and Nigerian merchants all entered the import and wholesaling trade and set up companies representing foreign manufacturers. This helped to break down the concentration in the import trade and put existing companies under pressure. The older foreign trading companies gradually withdrew from general importing and retailing. They continued to invest in importing and wholesaling, concentrating on technologically more advanced lines.

New foreign entrants in this period included Bewac (British), Inlaks (Indian), and Mandilas (Greek). After a spell in general merchandise, John Mandilas secured the agency for Jaguar cars in 1951 before becoming the importer and distributor for Volkswagen in 1953 and setting up a distribution and service agency throughout the country. The company then obtained the agency for Carrier air conditioners and subsequently went into their manufacture under licence (1972). A number of other agencies and services for domestic appliances, mining equipment and fibreglass were acquired later.

Nigerian traders gradually increased their share of the import trade from 5 per cent in 1949 to about 20 per cent by 1963.[80] Among those entering the import trade during this period were Michael Ibru and Bode Akindele. They both had brief experiences of employment with the foreign merchant companies and went on to establish large conglomerates (see chapter 5). Some traders were assisted by the actions of the United Africa Company and John Holt who withdrew from general importing and provided their former Nigerian customers with clearance, warehousing and credit facilities.[81] In this way, Nigerian wholesalers were able to become importers on their own account.

Nigerian importers were able to expand into higher technical areas, obtain sole agency rights, and exploit cheaper sources of supply in the Far East and Europe. The supply of cement from Spain, Poland and Egypt by the Henry Stephens Group and the Folawiyo Group is a good example. Others obtained motor parts and consumer durables from Japan. Some traders shifted downstream into clearing and forwarding and shipping, and opened up buying offices abroad. The diversification in supply sources was reflected in a loosening of the old bilateral trading relationship between Nigeria and Britain.

On the export side, Nigerians were able to record a small increase in their share of the produce trade during the late 1950s and 1960s. Nigerians became agents for the Nigerian Produce Marketing Company (NPMC) which enabled them to ship produce and sell it abroad on behalf of the NPMC. Some traders became actively involved in the export of lesser-known commodities from the northern states, such as ginger, benniseed, sheanut, coffee, and gum arabic. They included Alhaji Nautan Hamza, Chief Henry Fajemirokun and Chief Bode Akindele. Part of the attraction of these unscheduled commodities was that they were outside the marketing-board system and therefore not subject to export tax and commission. At this time there were also no foreign exchange controls.

The export of timber was dominated by expatriate firms, but a few individuals did accumulate wealth from this source. The extraction and export of logs was more important than the export of sawn timber which was technically more demanding. Of 65 locally owned sawmills operating in the early 1960s, only 6 were engaged in the export of sawn timber though many others were exporting logs.[82] In the Mid-West, the ownership of a sawmill virtually became a requirement for the granting of additional timber concessions.[83] The international timber trade was risky, capital intensive and usually only those who had already built up capital, or had a secure base in other activities like cocoa or rubber, could consider entry. Among them were Chief Francis Edo-Osagie (b. 1914) who operated from Port Harcourt (see chapter 3), and Alfred Rewane (b. 1916), J. Asaboro and M. I. Agbontaen, who traded from Sapele.[84] Chief S. A. Oladapo of Ondo (1910–91), and Chief Ben Sutherland (B. K. Sutherland & Bros)[85] exported from Lagos.

Chief S. A. Oladapo of Ondo, after attending Ondo Boys High School (1926–30), studied at the Survey School, Oyo and worked briefly for his uncle in the produce trade, before working for expatriate companies as storekeeper, produce buyer and branch manager.[86] In the 1940s, he went independently into produce buying and the timber trade. In 1953 he bought the famous Pilot Sawmill at Aponmu, which had been set up by the Forestry Department in 1951.[87] In the early 1960s, the mill employed 156 persons. Although the business remained a sole proprietorship and slowed down in his lifetime, Chief Oladapo opened a modern saw mill in 1989, which has begun the export of semi-finished wood products. The other leg of his activities, cocoa buying with its infrastructure of warehouses, scales and long-established connections to cocoa farmers in the Ondo area, has also passed through to the next generation; a N300m. cocoa-processing plant in which Cadbury Nigeria holds 40 per cent of the equity and the Commonwealth Development Corporation provided loans, was opened in 1993.[88]

Internally, the establishment of new industries like textiles, tobacco, beer and cement opened up new opportunities for distributors and transporters. Distributorships with the Nigerian Tobacco Company (NTC) were particularly sought after and the fact that the NTC largely confined their distribution to the leading foreign merchants was an early source of opposition from Nigerian traders. Tobacco was a fast moving and lucrative line of business. Alhaji S. O. Gbadamosi was the first to secure a distributorship in the south and Alhaji G. N. A. Hamza was an early distributor in the north.[89] In 1960, the Nigerian Tobacco Company ceased distributing through the expatriate firms and began wholesaling through some sixty independent Nigerian merchants. As the principal distributor for NTC, the United Africa Company lost sales worth £6m. at one blow.[90] Jacob Tilley Gyado and Alhaji Mai Sango were both prominent distributors in the north, who went on to diversify into other areas. In textiles, Isiyaku Rabiu, who became one of the largest industrialists in Kano, was one of the first textile factors with the Kaduna textile industry. In 1963, he formed the Kano Merchants Trading Company with Nababa Badamasi and others.[91] Later, he and Nababa Badamasi both established textile industries in Kano. The distribution of cement and beer and the supply of raw materials to cement factories was another area where Nigerian entrepreneurs and transporters were active.

Transporting, which was often combined with trade, created big businessmen in every locality. Among the most well known transporters in the 1950s were F. E. Okonkwo (alias Okonkwo Kano) and Alhaji Sani Marshal of Kano, I. O. Ajanaku of Ilesha and Philip Ojukwu of Nnewi. By the mid-1960s, motor transport had displaced the railways as the major mode of north–south transport. In this field, as in the produce trade and commerce, there was sharp competition with Levantine businessmen.

Landed property and urban real estate provided enormous attractions and those larger businessmen who could get access to bank credit established residential estates. For example, in the Lagos area in the 1950s, Chief E. O. Ashamu, a pharmacist, bought land and initiated the development of the Ire-Akari Estate.[92] The St Mathew-Daniel family acquired land at Kirikiri and gave the Westminster Dredging Company a fifty year building lease. Other private estates included the Gbagada Estate, Palm Grove Estate, Okota Estate, Idimu Estate, and Dideolu Estate. Landed property was both the most secure store of wealth and a collateral with which to finance other activities like trade.

With regard to indigenous manufacture, a survey undertaken in 1965 covering some 269 of the largest enterprises over the whole country gave the following picture.[93] There was considerable occupational mobility, both with respect to previous generations and within individual careers. The immediate past employment of three-quarters of the industrialists was in the self employed category – traders, transporters, contractors and artisans. Those in government service, clerical work, teaching and the professions were represented, but people tended to move into self employment before undertaking manufacture. Former craftsmen tended to concentrate on a single line of business like printing or furniture, while those with a trading background had larger, more diversified enterprises.

Geographical mobility among manufacturers was much more limited and contrasted with the much higher mobility of traders and transporters. Apart from some movement to Lagos, inter-regional mobility was very low. Inter-provincial was also very low, only people from Ijebuland and the Igbo of Onitsha and Owerri provinces having migrated in significant proportions. In Lagos, some 75 per cent of the manufacturers were born locally or in the immediately adjacent provinces of Ijebu and Abeokuta.

The main industries in the study were saw milling, furniture, rubber processing, printing, garment making and baking. These industries were generally characterised by low barriers to entry, limited economies of scale and intense competition with excess capacity and low profitability. A large number of entrepreneurs were concentrated in these lines.

Some of the larger rubber processing units (sheet and crepe rubber and tyre retreading) provided a partial exception in terms of scale, organisation and capital requirements. The period 1954–5 saw four private Nigerian companies enter crepe processing using savings made during the high timber and rubber prices of the Korean boom.[94] A further rapid increase in capacity occurred between 1959–63. Most of these factories were located at Sapele. Some of these processors integrated backwards with rubber plantations. In 1965 there were two modern plantations with facilities for the production of high grade sheet rubber. J. A. Thomas Rubber Estates at Sapele with an investment of £110,000 had been in production since 1939 and employed over 200 persons.[95]

Other industries comprising just a few firms were beverages,[96] lime making, bone crushing,[97] paper conversion,[98] pipeline welding, gramophone records, brick making, sign making, metal working, electrical motor rewinding and rebuilding, heavy transport equipment for the oil industry, powdered drilling clays,[99] perfume blending, and tanning. In agro-processing there were also private ventures, but many were small scale and fell outside the scope of the survey. These activities comprised corn milling in the north, palm oil mills and rice mills in the south. About 20 private oil mills were operating in 1964; mostly former Eastern Nigerian Development Corporation mills purchased by major palm produce buyers.[100] They were faring slightly better than their more favourably located publicly owned competitors, largely owing to their greater efforts at fruit collection. By the early 1960s, the rice-growing area of Abakaliki in the Eastern Region had become the centre of the rice hulling and milling industry. With about 150 private diesel mills, it attracted rice from a wide area including the Northern Region. The rice was then marketed throughout the Eastern and Western Regions and to Lagos.[101]

The enterprises were commonly founded and managed by one person with very little delegation of authority. Financial controls were weak and sometimes non-existent. As might be expected, production efficiency was low in these circumstances. Mary Rowe compared the capital/labour and capital/output ratios and returns to capital of Nigerian firms to equally novice Lebanese and Greek undertakings of the same size, in the same industry and using the same equipment.[102] As a result of the far higher levels of machine utilisation, the Lebanese and Greek entrepreneurs had lower ratios and the returns to capital were two or three times those of Nigerian firms.

In his study of Lagos enterprises, Akeredolu-Ale found only very few entrepreneurs had a clear idea about succession.[103] There was a strong tendency to reserve succession to a son and so delay arrangements for their succession until they actually retired. This provided one explanation of why indigenous businesses tended to die with their original proprietors.

Finally, we need to consider the broader context of status and rewards within which larger indigenous firms were operating. In the late colonial period and 1960s, careers in the administrative arm of the government and in the professions, especially law and medicine, were ranked most highly among the educated elite and young graduates. Next in line was employment in government agencies and the foreign companies. This was usually seen as a means to financial independence and self employment. Since working conditions were poor and there was little security, jobs in corporations like the railways were often combined with other private income earning activities. In the foreign companies, Nigerians were not generally given positions of executive responsibility or policy making. They were usually found in the service positions like public relations, personnel, advertising, legal, and medical departments.[104]

At the bottom of the pecking order was employment in indigenous companies. Indigenous business had a poor image and low status associated with poor education and low technical competence. In Yorubaland, as Akeredolu-Ale points out, no word existed to describe the role of 'businessman' as distinct from 'trader'.[105] In a revealing survey of larger indigenous enterprises in Lagos in the late 1960s, Akeredolu-Ale found that among the factors limiting expansion, personnel problems were rated more highly than capital shortage or foreign competition.[106] Indigenous companies recruited personnel only after government and its agencies and foreign companies had taken their pick. Indigenous companies offered few fringe benefits and limited opportunities for training. When training was undertaken, personnel often left the company to employ their skills elsewhere.

The difficulties of securing managers and supervisory personnel was not necessarily overcome by the employment of expatriates. Employment of expatriates was seldom a success, though their performance in partnerships involving an expatriate on the technical side and a Nigerian on sales and public relations was better.[107] Experienced expatriates with requisite qualities were seldom willing to accept non-tenured contract employment in an African country under largely unknown conditions. And Nigerians often had no way of effectively assessing expatriate qualifications. Yet there may have been a reluctance on the part of Nigerian owners to employ Nigerian managers as distinct from expatriates. Rowe and Harris argue that competent Nigerian managers for saw milling were available in the 1960s, but owners were not prepared to offer them attractive salaries.[108] Salaries of expatriate managers were on average five times those of Nigerians, without even taking fringe benefits into account.[109]

Finance

Between 1945 and 1951, under conditions of high commodity prices and the high point of nationalist struggle, many indigenous banks were started. Fourteen new banks were set up in this period.[110] In 1951, only six African banks were in operation. It was estimated that they had total deposits of about £1m with advances to Africans worth £600,000.[111] The new banks were poorly capitalised and badly managed and only one, the African Continental Bank, managed to survive. For example, the Farmers and Commercial Bank was established in 1947 and grew rapidly with twenty branches and a London office by 1951.[112] It went into liquidation the following year. The banking crisis of the early 1950s and the competitive struggle for state power brought about by constitutional developments then focused attention on the colony's financial surpluses which were held in London to support sterling and give Britain control over the direction of colonial trade. These funds, which had been generated by the marketing-board system, were used by regional governments to support indigenous banks. Eventually, the indigenous banks were taken over by the regional governments. Thus, the National Bank, which had become bankers to the Cocoa Marketing Board in 1950, was formally taken over by the Western government and became a public company in 1961.[113] The National Bank was a small, but none the less significant, source of funds for indigenous entrepreneurs especially those engaged in commodity exports in the 1950s and early 1960s. In the 1970s, under the ownership of the western states, the bank stumbled from crisis to crisis having no less than twelve different boards and three periods of interregnum between 1972 and 1992.[114] 1992 proved to be the year of its final demise.

Further attempts were made to found indigenous banks in the 1950s but these made little headway and most of the new banks were foreign entrants. In 1958, Adeyemi Lawson, Chief Michael Ibru, Chief Chris Ogunbanjo, and Chief Kweku Biney went into a banking partnership with some Swiss bankers to form the Bank of Lagos. Six years later, after poor management and excessive overdrafts, the owners returned the licence and turned the bank into a finance company.

Insurance was a popular area for Nigerian businessmen providing a ready source of liquidity. Indigenous companies in the early 1950s included the African Insurance Company promoted by K. O. Mbadiwe, assisted by A. G. Leventis who brought in the Employers' Liability Assurance Corporation of the United Kingdom as technical and training partners.[115] A. Doherty and Dr A. Maja of the National Bank also promoted the Nigerian General Insurance Company in 1951 and an insurance brokerage with Glanvill Enthoven. Other significant indigenous companies included the African Alliance Insurance Company promoted by Alhaji S. L. Edu and T. A. Braithwaite with the Munich Reinsurance Company in 1960. In 1965, there were twenty-seven insurance companies with over £10,000 paid up capital in existence. Five of these were indigenous, including two companies owned by regional governments.[116] Later entrants included Law Union and Rock Insurance promoted by Sir Mobalaji Bank-Anthony in 1969, and the Marine and General Insurance in the same year, which involved Chief Henry Fajemirokun and Chief Akin-George.

Insurance brokerages were also established. Among the early firms was Dyson and Diket in 1953 (later African Insurance Brokers) founded by Sonny Odogwu, a former manager with the Norwich Union Insurance Company, who later became managing director of the African Prudential Insurance Company (1966).[117] Others involved in insurance brokerage included T. A. Braithwaite (see chapter 3) and J. Akin-George.[118] The latter, after a spell with foreign insurance companies set up J. Akin-George and Company in 1960, Sierra Leone Insurance Brokers in 1964, and Marine and General Insurance Brokers Company in Accra, Ghana in 1969.[119] In 1970, Mr Femi Johnson (1934–87) founded Femi Johnson & Co. at Ibadan. The firm had a premium income of over N50m. in 1992.[120]

1970–1990

Before considering the advance of indigenous enterprises in this period and the impact of the oil boom upon it, three other issues, which all had the potential to affect local patterns of accumulation, need to be addressed. They are the impact of Igbo withdrawal and the civil war on indigenous enterprise within the war zone and outside the war-affected areas, the effect of the indigenisation decrees; and changes in the relation between private and public sectors.

The effect of the war on private accumulation in the former Eastern Region will be taken up in chapters 6 and 7.

Little evidence is available on the impact of the war elsewhere in the federation.[121] The withdrawal of the Igbo affected the long-term pattern of business control and ownership in Lagos. The position and career prospects of non-Igbo, mainly Yoruba, in multinationals and professional firms were enhanced. Subsequently, these individuals were in a strong position to take advantage of the indigenisation exercise and secure top management positions. A further consequence of Igbo withdrawal was the transfer of wealth involved in the capital gains made by those who acquired high value Igbo properties at very low prices.

The civil war certainly opened up profitable business for contractors to the armed forces. Thus Isiyaku Ibrahim introduced an arms contractor to the Ministry of Defence for a brokerage fee of £250,000 and then became an agent of an American company selling spare parts to the Nigerian Air Force.[122] Alhaji Nautan Hamza became a large supplier of software and general goods to the army.[123] Alhaji Waziri Ibrahim was involved in arms dealing and consultancy.[124] Whether such cases were common enough to warrant recognition of a group that profited from the war is not clear. What is less open to question is that the experience of war fostered a stronger nationalism which in turn helped create the conditions for indigenisation.

As we have seen, measures to assist indignenous enterprises were taken before independence, but it was only in the early 1970s that concerted efforts were made to diminish foreign ownership in the economy. Commercial pressures to indigenise trade emerged strongly at the end of the civil war. The Indigenous Businessmen's Group in the Lagos Chamber of Commerce attacked the credit policies of the commercial banks and the record of the Nigerian Industrial Development Bank (NIDB) for favouring foreign enterprise and argued for greater Nigerian equity participation.[125] In 1971, commercial banks were instructed to give 35 per cent of loans and advances to indigenous business people, who also received more favourable access to foreign exchange from the Central Bank.[126] Such business lobbies found allies among federal civil servants and military officers, who were pressing for increased national control and Nigerian participation in the economy. It was thought that foreign capital could be pushed into higher technology areas, thereby creating opportunities for Nigerians and changing the industrial structure. Local capital accumulation would also benefit from local retention of profits.

The first indigenisation decree of 1972 was put through the Federal Executive Council in a classic exercise of bureaucratic power when civil commissioners, who opposed the decree, were not present.[127] The second decree of 1977, which was not foreseen by the promoters of the first decree, stemmed from dissatisfaction with the results of the first phase and the overthrow of the Gowon administration. Lax implementation of the first decree had led to evasion and widespread fronting. The loudest objections to the decree were reserved for the gross inequalities it encouraged and for the fact that it favoured Lagos and the western states where most of those in a position to take advantage of the decree resided. In this way, sectionalist and individual advantage combined to undermine the nationalist legitimacy of the decree and allowed nationalist and other sectional pressures to reassert themselves.

The main impact of the decrees, which enforced the outright sale or dilution of foreign shareholdings, was the transfer of shares to Nigerians on a large scale.[128] Considerable sums of local capital were absorbed by the acquisition of shares. The value of share transactions was N122m. for the first decree and N551m. for the second decree over the period 1977 to 1981.

The first decree enabled individuals to build up large blocks of equity, especially in companies that were sold privately. A few well-known Nigerians would be invited to take up 40 per cent of the equity. A company would often arrange bank loans for the share purchase, the loans to be paid off from future dividends. The monetary guidelines for 1972–3 liberalised loans for those who wanted to buy shares. Smaller companies often sold equity to a single employee who then joined the board. The sale of shares in private companies led to a high concentration of Nigerian share ownership. Ankie Hoogvelt confirmed this picture for Kano in a survey of 54 enterprises that had been affected by the decree.[129] Of the N15m. equity received by 291 individuals, 6 individuals obtained 50 per cent of the equity. This pattern of high concentration in share acquisitions was confirmed nationally. A sample of 384 private placings involving schedule-2 companies showed that 30 per cent (115 companies) had 1 shareholder and 47 per cent (185 companies) between 1 and 5 shareholders.[130]

The sale of shares marked a significant step in the level of share ownership among the bureaucratic, professional and business class and satisfied their aspirations. The outright sale of enterprises as going concerns mainly affected smaller Lebanese enterprises (textile dealers, transporters, cinemas). This reduced the potential for conflict with Nigerian competitors. Some foreign companies withdrew from retail activities.[131] Few medium- or larger-scale enterprises were sold outright to Nigerian buyers. The main exceptions were those companies purchased by the Ibru Organisation. Other instances where Nigerian entrepreneurs took shareholdings that gave them control or significantly advanced the growth of their own enterprises and their capacity for accumulation can be found, but this was not a central feature of indigenisation. A joint venture could open the way for advantageous links overseas and it could lead to eventual takeover. A longer-term influence stemming

TABLE 2.3: Former civil servants and the private sector.

Name	Birth	Rank in public sector	Retirement	Private sector board membership*
S. O. Adebo	1913	Head of service and chief secretary, Western Region (1957–62)	1972	UAC, Farmex
J. O. Udoji	1917	Head of service and chief secretary, Eastern Region (1959–66)	1966	Nigerian Tobacco Co., Wiggins Teape, Michelin, Nicherchin, Roche, Ukawoods, PGN, R. T. Briscoe, Nigerian International Bank, Power Communications Engineering, Scan Construction
S. Ade John	1924	Permanent secretary, Kaduna; Federal permanent secretary (1964–67)	1972	A. G. Leventis Group
Allison Ayida	1930	Secretary to FMG and head of federal service (1975–77)	1977	Berger Paints, Phillip Morris, Lever Bros, Ault & Wiborg, IGE, Protec-Subratel, CFAO, Coutinho Caro, Nidogas, BRGM, BEWAC, Credit Lyonnais, Fininvest Associates
Liman Ciroma	1930	Secretary to FMG and head of federal service (1977–79)	1979	UTC, Brossette, Tate & Lyle, GTE, First City Merchant Bank, City Securities Ltd, Tropical Petroleum Products
Ahmed Joda	1930	Federal permanent secretary (1967–78)	1978	SCOA, George Wimpey, Flour Mills of Nigeria, Umarco, Ingersoll-Rand, Credit Lyonnais, Food Specialities, Nigerian-French Insurance, Arc Insurance Brokers, Deutsche Babcock, New Africa Holdings, Benue Valley Meat, Tropical Petroleum Products, Centre Point Securities
I. M. Damcida	1933	Federal permanent secretary (1966–75)	1975	Enpec, Afprint, Steyr, Glaxo, Vegfru, Nigerian Technical Co., Trevi Foundations, Dynamic Industries, Kewalram, Nigerian General Motors, Nigerian-American Merchant Bank, Aeromaritime, Texaco, Capital Resources Nig, Ltd
Sule Katugum	—	Chairman, Federal Public Service Commission (1962–75)	1975	Coutinho Caro, Intra Motors, Narumal, Globe Fishing, Afprint, Caprihans, Jafco, Impex, Nigerian General Motors, Atlantic Textiles, Steel & Engineering Services, HBM General Supplies, Katugum Enterprises
P. C. Asiodu	1934	Federal permanent secretary (1965–75)	1975	Dumez, GTE, Beecham, Krupp Steel & Engineering, Nigerian Pipes, Gulf Oil, Metal Box Toyo Glass, West Africa Milk Co., SCAN Construction, Bendel Feed and Flour Mills, New African Holdings, Medife, Ecobank, Summit Furniture, Tropical Petroleum Products
Shehu Musa	1935	Secretary to the federal government (1979–83)	1983	R. T. Briscoe, Foremost Dairies, Alumaco, Juli Pharmacy, Capital Oil, Nigerian Aluminium Extrusions, Consolidated Management Services, Meridien Equity Bank

* Board membership in the private sector is not comprehensive and individuals are not necessarily associated with all companies at any one time.

Sources: Newspapers; company directories; *Who's Who in Nigeria*.

TABLE 2.4: Retired military officers and the private sector.

Name	Birth	Retirement	Private sector
General O. Obasanjo	1937	1979	Obasanjo Farms Ltd
Lt.-Gen. T. Danjuma	1937	1979	Nigeria-America Line, Comet Shipping Agencies, Ideal Flour Mills, Nigerian Eagle Flour Mills, SCOA, Michelin Motor Tyre Services, Universal Trust Bank, Tati Hotels, Sahel Publishing & Printing
Maj.-Gen. S. Yar'adua	1943	1979	Nation House Press, Africa Ocean Lines, Sambo Farms, Madara Farms, Habib Bank, Hamada Carpets, Roads Nig. Ltd
Lt.-Gen. A. Akinrinade	1939	1981	Nigerfeeds & Agriculture Operations Ltd
Maj.-Gen. G. Innih	1939	1980	Niger Valley Agro Industries, Tamasks Nig., Tecnoexportstroy Ltd, Kambag W & M Ltd, Business Publications Ltd, Bendel Feed & Flour Mill Ltd, Broad Bank

Source: *Who's Who in Nigeria.*

from the decrees was pressure to increase the number of Nigerian senior managers and directors in foreign companies. Though this was not a formal requirement for compliance, the decrees had the effect of reinforcing a trend that was already underway.

The 1970s also saw a shift in the relative status and rewards between the public and private sectors. The enhanced attractions of the private sector had consequences for the growth of indigenous private enterprises. The change was a gradual one. Public perceptions changed slowly and the movement was not confined to the decade.

A number of factors were responsible for a perceptible shift in status and rewards. First there was the arrival of the multinational oil companies in the 1960s. They offered salaries and fringe benefits that were highly competitive with the trading companies and banks which had hitherto acted as leaders in the private sector. Second, the oil boom of the 1970s created a very rapid expansion in private-sector employment with a high degree of occupational mobility. Dissatisfaction with conditions of service and with the power wielded by the administrative cadre of the civil service was widespread among technocrats in parastatal bodies and many left for the private sector. The purge of the public sector under Murtala Mohammed, which undermined security and affected morale adversely, gave further impetus to a movement from the public service. Table 2.3 lists some of the senior civil servants who retired from government service, often at a relatively young age, to join the boards of foreign companies. A few took executive positions. Some set up their own companies using connections established while in office and their name to attract bank loans. At the end of the decade, senior military officers also retired and became active in the private sector (see Table 2.4).

Indicative of the changing status accorded to private-sector employment

TABLE 2.5: Recruitment of senior personnel by indigenous companies.

Name	Background	Indigenous company	Recruitment date
Prof. Ogunseye	Extra-Mural Dept, Ibadan University	Henry Stephens	1970
J. O. Oloyode	Chief accountant, Beechams	Group financial controller, Henry Stephens	1977
B. O. W. Mafeni	Federal commissioner	Ibru Organisation	1978
A. Akinola	Deputy chief accountant, Lever Bros	MD, International Breweries	1978
Prof. Adeyemo	Accountancy, University of Lagos	Executive vice-chairman, West African Breweries	1980
M. O. Eperekun	Registrar, University of Lagos	MD, Odutola Industries	1982
S. A. Adebajo	PS, Western Region, Dunlop	Group GM, Adebowale Industries	1983
J. A. Adediran	Marketing manager, Lever Bros	Group MD, Modandola Group	1987
G. O. Adun	Coopers & Lybrand	Executive director, Majekodunmi Ventures	1990
Dr E. Omatsola	Shell Petroleum	MD, Consolidated Oil	?

and of the growth of indigenous companies was the fact that the larger ones like Henry Stephens, Lawsons Corporation and the Ibru Organisation began to recruit senior management staff from the public sector, universities and foreign companies (see Table 2.5). In the 1980s, such movements became more common. Thus, the wave of new private banks attracted banking professionals from the older banks and recruited fresh MBAs.

In the 1970s a long oil boom between 1974 and 1978 altered the incentives and opportunities for private accumulation. There was a great expansion of trading and construction. All forms of intermediary activity flourished (contracting, consultancy and commission agents) and 'arrangees' (in Nigerian parlance) had a field day. There was also an expansion of the public sector but this scarcely conflicted with strategies of private accumulation, except in a few limited areas (intercity transport, bulk importation of essential commodities, the operations of the commodity boards). In the import trade and distribution, there were further advances by Nigerian private capital, which, in some cases, led to assembly and manufacture (building materials, electronics, pharmaceuticals, educational and laboratory supplies, office equipment, vehicles and mechanical equipment, electrical and mechanical engineering). For example, Chief Adebowale began the assembly of electrical goods in Lagos in 1969. Others involved in assembly of electrical goods in the 1970s included Maiden Electronics (Chief A. S. Guobadia), Doyin Investments (Chief S. Adedoyin) and Joas (Chief J. O. Amao) in Lagos, Mike Merchandise and Ibeanu Brothers in Aba, ABG Electronics (Alhaji Bawa Garba) in Kaduna and Interworld Enterprises (Ayo Rosiji) in Kano. Many of these enterprises were forced to close down, or drastically curtail their operations, in the 1980s, when the volume of imports was much reduced

TABLE 2.6: Private indigenous investment in biscuits.

Company	Start-up	Owner
Kan Biscuits, Aba	1978	Chief Kalu Ndukwe and Chief N. O. Nwojo. N1.2m. investment. 500 employed at peak. Chiltonian Biscuits of UK, 10%
Odutola Food Industries, Ijebu Ode	1979	Chief T. A. Odutola. N5.6m. investment. Licence from Bahlsen Tet Group of West Germany
Nigerian Biscuits Manufacturing Co., Ibadan (now Diamond Biscuits)	1981	Chief Bode Akindele; 7,500 tons p.a.
Okin Biscuits, Offa	1981	Chief E. O. Adesoye. N1.3m. investment
Kaura Biscuits, Kano	1976	Alhaji Sani Marshal. 600 employed (1979)
Bagauda Biscuits, Kano	1978	Alhaji Ismaila Muhtari. 10,000 tons p.a.

Sources: Interviews; newspapers.

TABLE 2.7: Private indigenous investment in breweries.

Company	Owner	Start-up	Comment
West African Breweries, Abeokuta	Chief Adeyemi Lawson	1965–7	
North Brewery, Kano	Chief Adeyemi Lawson	1965–7	Closed
Associated Brewery, Agbara	Chief Adeyemi Lawson	1978	
International Breweries, Ilesha	Lawrence Omole	1978	Technical agreement with German brewery. 500,000 hectolitres
Continental Breweries, Ijebu-Ode	Chief T. A. Odutola	1978	French technical assistance. Joint venture with Leventis
Superbru, Agbarha-Otor	Ibru Organisation	1979	Danish technical assistance. 770,000 hectolitres
Dubic Breweries, Aba	Chief D. U. Ifeagwu	1980	German technical assistance. 600,000 hectolitres
Standard Breweries, Ibadan	Chief Bode Akindele	1981	Spanish technical assistance. 1.2m. hectolitres
Olympic Drinks Company, Abagana, Anambra State	Sir Joseph Nwankwo	1982	Belgian technical assistance. 250,000 hectolitres
Safari Breweries, Arondizuogu, Imo State	Obioha family	1983	German technical partners

Sources: Interviews; newspapers.

and the exchange rate became unfavourable. The undoubted attractions of intermediary activity and opportunities for financial gain from inflated government contracts should not be allowed to obscure the fact that there was a significant upsurge of local industrial investment towards the end of the 1970s after financial surpluses had been accumulated through trading and other services in the oil-boom period. Much of this investment was in food and beverages and in light manufacturing (see Tables 2.6 and 2.7). The size of investment and technology involved set limits to indigenous promotion and ownership. Thus, there was very minor indigenous participation in the three motorcycle assembly plants that started up in the 1970s. The major partners with Suzuki, Honda and Yamaha were Boulos, a Greek family that had been active in gold and jewellery, Leventis and John Holt. Investment in the glass industry also attracted no major indigenous private investment. On the other hand, investment in polypropylene woven sacks attracted at least three newcomers in the 1980s.[132]

The trajectory and rhythm of indigenous capital accumulation since 1970 has varied according to the location and the origin and strength of local capital. In Kano, local industrial investment appeared to gather momentum through the 1970s and continued into the 1980s. In the major commercial centres of Aba and Onitsha, where the civil war had interrupted the growth of local enterprises and set back accumulation, the increase in industrial investment at the close of the 1970s was marked. It was also apparent in the western states, the Lagos area, and Kaduna. In Nnewi, the main thrust of industrial investment did not get underway until after 1983, following the closure of the economy and the difficulty of obtaining import licences. In some newly created state capitals like Sokoto and Makurdi (1976), where local private capital was too weak to undertake investment, industrial initiatives were undertaken by state governments supported by investment agencies like Nigerian Industrial Development Bank, the Nigerian Bank for Commerce and Industry and the New Nigeria Development Company.

In Calabar, capital of Cross River State, public and private ventures were equally in evidence. A leading private investor in Calabar was Victor Akan of Oron (plastics and roofing sheets), who had trained as a quantity surveyor, developed extensive property interests and became a senator in the Second Republic.

Some enterprises started when Nigerian managers left their erstwhile expatriate employers and set up in competition with them. In the paint industry, the former production manager of Berger Paints, Mr T. T. C. Mbakwe, established Theo and Theo Paints in 1970.[133] In 1977, the former marketing manager of Chemical and Allied Products Ltd (formerly ICI), Gbenga Akinnawo, set up African Paints, the eighth company in the sector. By the end of the 1980s, African Paints was ranked fourth in terms of turnover after Berger Paints, International Paints, and Chemical and Allied Products Ltd. In 1987, Mr B. O. Abosede, a former general manager with Paterson Zochonis, set up Aboseldehyde Laboratories, a cosmetics and toiletries company which had a turnover of N151m. in 1992–3.[134] In 1990, Gbenga Daniel, an engineer and deputy chief executive at H. F. Schroeder, a multinational company in industrial electrical installation, left to set up Kresta Laurel Ltd dealing in lifts, cranes, hoists and technical systems with sole representation for Mannesmann and Sabiem lifts.[135] In 1991 the company had a turnover of over N20m and employed 65 Nigerian engineers and technicians. This company is indicative of another significant trend, the movement of Nigerian companies into the provision of technical and engineering services (supply, installation, maintenance and servicing). Other areas include computer services (Task Systems Ltd and Gicen), telecommunications (Murhi International) and oil services.

Further examples of indigenous companies spinning off from expatriate concerns can be found in the advertising industry. A wave of advertising agencies broke off from agencies that had been originally started by foreign companies like Lintas, OBM, and Grant Advertising. One of the most successful was Insight Communications Ltd, which was started by Abiodun Shobanjo after he left his post of deputy managing director at Grant Advertising in 1979.[136] In 1982, he affiliated with Ted Bates Worldwide, part of the BSB and Satchi Group. In 1989, the company was ranked number 2 in the industry, with billings of N40m. from 37 clients. Other service activities where local capital advanced include various professional services (law, accountancy, architecture, real estate), hotels,[137] casinos and restaurants,[138] the electronic media, publishing,[139] port services, aviation and shipping.

In the early 1980s, a short oil boom (1980–2), which coincided with civil rule, encouraged rentier activity and capital flight overseas. After 1982, there was severe import compression. With the introduction of the Structural Adjustment Programme in 1986, import licensing gave way to deregulation and there was a sharp devaluation of the naira. The indigenisation decrees were relaxed and a privatisation programme started. The devaluation and increased political uncertainty encouraged some divestment by foreign companies.[140]

The abolition of the commodity boards and the sharp devaluation of the naira combined to encourage the processing of agricultural produce. Thus there was fresh investment in cocoa processing (Ebun Industries, Ladgroup, Stanmark, Ile-Iluji Cocoa Products, Temple and Golders), rubber processing (Iyayi Group,[141] K. B. Omatseye, Rodco, Desam Development Group, Ferdinand Group), cotton ginning and vegetable-oil producing.

Financial deregulation, lower costs of entry, the prospect of access to foreign exchange and the opportunity to profit from currency exchange, all combined to create a mushrooming of new banks. The arrival of the new banks and increased Nigerian participation in financial services increased competition in the capital market. The opening of the Second Tier Securities Market on Lagos Stock Exchange attracted the first indigenous private companies to go public. The ideological climate also became more favourable to private enterprise as state resources dwindled and international pressures for reform intensified. Under the Babangida government, private indigenous participation was encouraged in the oil sector and the electronic media. Thus early in 1993, the first indigenous TV and radio companies received licences. The Independent Television Producers Association of Nigeria

(ITPAN) was formed with 22 members.[142] The remainder of this chapter follows the advance of local capital in the oil industry, aviation and shipping, farming and fishing, banking and insurance and overseas investment.

Oil Industry

The early development of the oil industry did not provide many direct opportunities for investment. In the 1960s, the oil industry had created opportunities for Nigerian-owned companies in furniture, printing, clearing drilling sites, welding pipelines (1964) and supplying specialised heavy transport equipment (1962).[143] The latter two companies, which were pioneered by a lawyer, an accountant and an engineer, proved very successful. There were clear indications that indigenous companies had begun to invest in the oil-service sector. This movement came to an abrupt halt with the outbreak of the civil war and was only really resumed in the 1980s. Clearly in this field, the effect of the civil war was to severely disrupt and delay the growth of indigenous capacities, the special wartime adaptations in oil refining and armaments in Biafra, not withstanding.

In the 1970s, Nigerians increased their shareholdings in oil, service and subcontracting companies, and set up petroleum transport and distribution companies as licensed independents.[144] Two oil concessions were held by Nigerian companies in 1969 (Delta Oil and Henry Stephens), but they never moved into exploration. In 1979, Nigus Petroleum owned by Alhaji Ado Ibrahim spent over $21m. to acquire two concessions, but did not find oil.[145] At this time the federal government adopted the mistaken policy of allocating crude oil to those indigenous companies which were given concessions and licensed for oil exploration. According to Jibril Aminu, federal minister for oil and natural resources, the easy earnings from crude oil, ostensibly meant to help finance development, became a disincentive to prospect for oil.[146] Some pioneer indigenous companies sold off their concessions to foreign companies. During the 1970s a number of well-connected individuals were given access to crude oil to sell. Among the early beneficiaries of 'lifting oil', as it was termed, were Alhaji Tijani Dagazau and Prince Ado Ibrahim.[147] This practice became part of political patronage at the highest levels and later involved senior military officers. Lucrative licences to bunker refined-oil products were also much sought after.

By the end of the 1980s there were indications that local companies had begun to move into capital and skill intensive areas associated with the oil industry. The movement which really got underway in the mid-1980s, gathered momentum in the early 1990s. Indigenous oil-service companies were usually launched by persons with experience of foreign oil companies (see Table 2.8). These companies were distinct from firms in which Nigerians simply went into some form of partnership with foreign companies as commission agents. For these individuals, who often formed partnerships, the risk

TABLE 2.8: Indigenous oil-service companies.

Company	Start-up	Service activity	1993 employment	Background of founders
Enosco	1972	Pipeline maintenance, construction, anti-corrosion	80	Founder worked for indigenous and foreign companies as pipeline welder
Arco Petroleum Engineering	1980	Supply and servicing of equipment	40	
Negris	1980	Supply, installation and maintenance of production equipment	150	Former Gulf Oil employee
Petrolog	1980	Mud logging	150	Former Geoservices employee
Ciscon	1985	Drilling and completion, cementing and pumping	30	Three former Schlumberger and Weatherford employees
Weltek	1986	Instrumentation	59	Two former employees of Flopetrol Schlumberger and NNPC
Zumax	1986	Wireline services	120	Two former Otis employers
Adamac Group:				
Adamac Engineering	1987	Supply of technical equipment	—	Founder traded in Aba and USA
Adadrill	1991	Well completion	60 420*	
Strasbourg	1992	Well head	30	
Benek Engineering	1987	Mechanical corrosion engineering	75	The founder worked for Shell as drilling supervisor, 16 engineers employed
Drillog Petrodynamics	1990	Directional drilling and bore-hole survey	20	Former MD, Anadrill Schlumberger (1984–90)
IMC	1992	Transportation	30	6 vessels on lease to Shell. Recruited from former NNSL staff
Kogi Oil Services	1992	Mud logging	25	Part of Dangote Group
Oil Test Services	1992	Well testing, production services, PVT laboratory, wireline logging	20–5	4 former Schlumberger employees

* Group employment.

Sources: Interviews; communications.

of initial uncertain rewards after leaving the security of foreign employment was weighed against the satisfaction and confidence of offering independent services comparable to foreign companies. With low overheads and the right to property ownership, indigenous contractors were proving competitive with foreign service companies. Located in Port Harcourt and Warri, these firms were engaged in construction of flow stations and pipeline regrinding, protection and installation, mechanical corrosion engineering, mud logging, well testing, directional drilling, wireline services, instrumentation, servicing of pumps and compressors, and specialised transport equipment.

The first private indigenous oil exploration and production company, Dubri Oil Company, started oil production in 1987. Dr U. J. Itsueli, who worked for Phillips Petroleum as Managing Director for six years, acquired part of the assets and absorbed some key personnel from Phillips when the company left Nigeria.[148] At the end of the decade, about 17 indigenous oil companies were given oil-prospecting leases by the NNPC (Nigeria National Petroleum Corporation), which started an accelerated programme for indigenous participation in all aspects of the oil industry, especially in exploration and production, and direct field services. By 1992, two companies had made discoveries of crude in commercial quantities. A Nigerian Association of Indigenous Petroleum Exploration and Production Companies (NAIPEC) was formed.

Airlines

Private Nigerian airlines operating charter flights on a regular timetable first appeared in the early 1980s (see Table 2.9). They had been preceded by the national carrier, Nigerian Airways, and a number of private airlines with foreign affiliations that met the demands of the oil industry.[149] Most of the companies emerged out of the spot charters and the aircraft spare-parts business.[150] Legislators during the Second Republic pushed for fully-fledged scheduled services but this was never achieved. The private airlines competed successfully with the state carrier, Nigeria Airways, and created a more favourable image. Their share of total passenger traffic climbed steadily through the decade despite the contraction of the domestic economy and the difficulty of generating hard currency to pay for regular maintenance overseas and major inspections. In 1989, the share of domestic traffic was around 75 per cent for private airlines, with two operators, Kabo Air and Okada Airways, carrying the bulk of the traffic.

The Kano-based Kabo Air opened in 1981. It is owned by Alhaji Dankabo, a former Nigeria Airways representative in Monrovia and Northern Sales representative. Intercontinental Airlines started as a cargo operator whose main client was the Central Bank of Nigeria. Owned by Chief Victor Vanni, the founder of Vanni Security Ltd, it was the only airline to operate an international charter with weekly flights to the United Kingdom between 1981 and

TABLE 2.9: Indigenous airline companies.*

Name	Start-up	No. of planes, 1993	Founder
Kabo Air	1981	16	Alhaji Mohammadu Dan Kabo. Former Nigeria Airways staff
Intercontinental Airlines	1981	—	Chief Victor Vanni. Ceased operations 1985
Okada Air	1983	32	Chief Gabriel Igbinedion. Management of Sierra Leone National Airline (1993)
Concord Airlines	1989	8	Bashorun M. K. O. Abiola. Started as RCN Aviation in 1977 within Radio Communications Nigeria Ltd. Not operational in 1993
Hold-Trade Air Services	1990	5	Late Aliyu Dasuki
Aviation Development Company plc (ADC)	1991	5	Started by 4 former Nigeria Airways pilots. Flew for government of Guinea for 3 years. Flies West African routes in 1993
Harco Air Services	1992	8	Alhaji Rufai Haruna
Zenith Airlines	1992	2	Ike Nwachukwu
Triax Airlines	1992	1	Prince Arthur Eze
Yvic	1992	2	Chief Yemi Akinnagbe

* Scheduled passenger airlines. Cargo and charter companies are not included. Since the advent of private airline operations, some companies have gone into liquidation. They include Barnax Airlines and Oriental Airlines. Oriental Airlines, owned by Chief Emmanuel Iwuanyanwu, was relaunched in October 1993.

Sources: Interviews; newspapers; communications.

1985. The company became indebted and its aircraft were impounded in West Germany. Okada Air began operations in 1983 after four years of spot charters. It was owned by the Esama of Benin, Chief G. O. Igbinedion, an owner of very large-scale property, who established Mid Motors Nig. Ltd in 1968 (a vehicle-distribution agency) and then moved into soft-drink bottling (Okada Bottling) and merchant banking (Crown Merchant Bank).

Shipping

The extent of Nigerian private investment in shipping is limited and has fluctuated with trading conditions (see Table 2.10). Two Nigerian traders were attracted downstream into shipping in the 1960s. The Henry Stephens Company began by chartering vessels for cement and cocoa and entered shipping in 1969. It was followed by Nigerian Green Lines owned by Alhaji Yinka Folawiyo which was involved in the cement trade from Spain. Nigerian Green Lines operated the largest indigenous fleet at the end of the 1970s with six general cargo vessels of 10,000 to 15,000 dead-weight tonnage each, plying between Nigeria and European ports.[151] The profitability of shipping over the oil-boom period attracted some other entrants, and existing owners increased their fleets. Sea Dantainer Lines, a joint venture between Alhaji Aminu Dantata and Walford Line of the United Kingdom had a short-lived existence. In the second half of the 1980s, there were three new entrants.

TABLE 2.10: Indigenous shipping companies.

Company	Start-up	Founders	Comment
Henry Stephens Shipping	1969	Late Chief Henry Faje-mirokun	Three vessels. Now charters only
Nigerian Green Lines	1973	Alhaji Yinka Folawiyo	Six vessels by 1979, totalling 87,800 tons deadweight. One vessel 1990
Equatorial Carriers	—	Sodipo Family	One vessel. Scandia Steamships of India took 40% shareholding
Sea Dantainer Lines	1978	Alhaji Aminu Dantata and Walford Lines of UK (40%)	Container shipments to Warri, ended 1979
Nigerbras	1976	Alhaji Mahmud Waziri	One vessel
Africa Ocean Lines	1985	Shehu Yar'adua and Bashorun M. K. O. Abiola	Two vessels
Bulkship (Nig.)	1985	Alhaji Hassan Adamu	One vessel and charters
Brawal Lines	1988	Part of Aeromaritime Group	One vessel
South Atlantic Seafood Company (SASCO)	1989	Olu Fashanu	Two passenger ferries and charters

Sources: Interviews; newspapers; communications.

Some foreign companies bought into indigenous companies, encouraged by the 1983 UNCTAD Code of Conduct for liner conferences which proposed that two trading countries shared cargoes 40/40, leaving the remaining 20 per cent for cross (third) parties.[152] Such pressure to increase the share of cargo for Nigerian flag vessels was taken a step further with the Shipping Policy Decree of 1987, which set up a National Maritime Authority (NMA) to monitor and promote the policy, and gave official approval to a 50/50 sharing formula for non-conference cargoes. Yet in 1988, Nigerian national carriers with 24 ships, including the state-owned Nigeria National Shipping Line, were estimated to take only 11 per cent of the cargo at Nigerian ports.[153] Apart from the financial difficulties that afflicted both private and state carriers, the main problem was that the indigenous cargo carriers lacked the facilities to attract timely cargoes allotted to them in Europe.

Large-scale Farming

Large-scale farming was not a new phenomenon of the 1970s and 1980s.[154] There had long been a class of large-scale landowners in the North, very often title holders in the emirates, who farmed on a considerable scale. Village and district heads and other large farmers often combined farming with trading and employed permanent staff and casual employees. In the Kaura Namoda area of Sokoto State in the mid-1980s, Alhaji Salabi Liman farmed 1,500 hectares and had 150 permanent staff and 600 casual staff.[155] In the same area, Alhaji Muazu Gabaki, village head of Gabaki, employed 150 permanent staff on his farm.[156] In Bauchi State, Alhaji Ibrahim Mohammed, district head of Udubo, had a farm of 1,500 hectares (Udubo Green

Farms)[157] and Alhaji Ibrahim Ganawa, former chairman of the Bauchi State Health Management Board, owned farms of 425 hectares at Azare and Ganawa.[158]

What became more apparent in the 1970s was the arrival of more capital-intensive farmers, often with a background in the civil service or army, with the connections to secure substantial bank loans. There was also large-scale acquisition of land by corporate enterprises and leading businessmen, especially in northern states. Sometimes, these acquisitions resulted from government pressures to enter farming. Access to import licences was made conditional upon evidence of farming and more emphasis was put on an import deletion programme for certain commodities that could be substituted for locally.

Several governors under the Gowon regime established large farms, for example, Governors Ogbemudia and Audu Bako. Examples of retired military officers who started farms included Lieutenant-General Akinrinade (Niger-feeds and Agricultural Operations), Major-General Shehu Yar'adua (Sambo Farms), and General Olusegun Obasanjo (Obasanjo Farms Ltd). Leading state officials included Sunday Adewusi (Nefraday Farms), Francis Ellah (Ellah Lakes PLC), Alhaji A. Howeidy (Fertile Acres), Ahmed Joda (Benue Valley Farms and Benue Valley Meat Company) and Bamanga Tukur (Gesedaddo Farms).[159] Businessmen have also invested in large-scale agriculture as part of their diversified enterprises. They include Chief Michael Ibru (Cafrad), Sanusi and Aminu Dantata (Anadariya and Asada Farms), Chief Bode Akindele (United Planters Ltd), Chief Ilodibe (Austin Farms), and Chief Abiola (Abiola Farms Ltd). Abiola Farms acquired over 17,000 hectares in five different states. A 100 hectare maize farm was developed at Dakka in Gongola State in 1989.[160] Numerous smaller examples of investment in farming, sometimes with processing facilities, could be cited. A rice-milling firm in Bendel State, Universal Grains Ltd, has established seed farms and distributes seed and gives technical advice to selected farmers.[161] The largest investments in the sector have been undertaken by foreign companies to secure raw materials for industrial use. Thus Leventis has established large maize farms, Afprint has set up cotton plantations and contract farming in Gongola State and Inlaks has invested in large-scale tomato production and processing.

Many of these large-scale farms have not proved successful. Some of them function as welfare ventures providing employment in the home community. Many of the new entrants had no prior experience of farming or were unaware of the long gestation period necessary to establish a farm. Knowledge of the skills necessary to manage a large farm was often lacking. Many adopted mechanised strategies that proved very costly when the external value of the naira depreciated.

Fishing

The Nigerian fishing industry has been largely restricted to inshore operations, inland fisheries on the Yauri and Hadejia rivers in the North and at Lake Chad, the largest source of supply.[162] The latter two fisheries gave rise to an extensive north–south trade in smoke-dried fish. Total fish imports, especially frozen fish, rose steeply in the 1970s from 67,000 tons in 1970 to 305,000 tons in 1977. Economic incentives during this period generally favoured the importation of fish and the development of a home fishing fleet made slow progress. There was some investment in shrimping for export. Among the indigenous operators were the Ibru Organisation, and the Modandola Group. Some expansion of the home fishing fleet took place in the 1980s with new entrants like the Express Fisheries, Folawiyo Group and Honeywell Group. Negotiations for fishing rights in Angola and other countries were pursued. No direct investment in middle and industrial deep sea fishing was made, though ships were chartered for this purpose in African and European waters.

Indian Enterprise

In outlining the advances made by indigenous capital, account needs to be taken of the Indian presence in the Nigerian economy. Persons of South Asian origin numbered some 14,000 in 1987.[163] Indian businessmen have come from Britain, East Africa, Indonesia and other countries in West Africa, in addition to the Indian sub-continent. Many are Sindis whose business diaspora was given further impetus by the partition of India in 1947. Total investment in Nigeria by people of Indian origin was estimated at $4bn. in 1992.[164] This presence is not widely appreciated and compared to the Lebanese, it has been neglected in the literature. One reason for this is the very low political profile of the Indian community. Another is that, for many commentators and analysts in the West, foreign investment appears to denote only investment by US, European and Japanese companies.

We noted earlier in this chapter that the origin of Indian enterprise in Nigeria lay in the arrival of firms involved in the textile trade (Chanrai, Chellaram, Kewelram, Bhojsons, Dalamal) who established a strong presence in Lagos and Port Harcourt. Subsequently, these Indian trading houses went into the production of textiles, broadened their trading activities and established supermarkets. Other traders then arrived and there was import substitution into manufacture. In the 1970s and early 1980s, a new wave of arrivals participated heavily in commodity trading and made money through currency speculation. A few of these newcomers adapted to the economic recession and redirected their activities.

In the textile sector, Indian companies established a strong position (President Industries, Afprint, Aflon, Bhojsons Industries, Churchgate Group,

Aswani Textiles, Western Textiles, Enpee, Chellco, Sunflag, Varaman, etc.). Indian firms also established a strong presence in plastics, aluminium, paints, and vegetable-oil milling. They are also present in electronics, electrical switchgear, lighting, glass, crown corks, asbestos, basic chemicals, pharmaceuticals, batteries, radiators, pipes, fish nets, fishing, agro-industry, rice production, oil-palm plantations, and banking. While some Indian companies operate in areas where the scale of capital resources and technical expertise has tended to preclude indigenous investment (glass, aluminium, basic chemicals), others are in competition with indigenous capital. In the case of vegetable-oil milling, substantial investment was undertaken by both Indian (General Agro, Nalin, Assan Industries, Premier Agro Industry, Universal Oil Mills, Grand Cereals and Oil Mills) and local entrepreneurs (Hic Oil, Ferdinand Industries, Life Vegetable Oil, Ladgroup, Sasco, Consolidated Manufacturing).

A few Indian conglomerates have emerged including Inlaks (brewing, reconstituted milk, fishing, agro-industry, packaging, computer sales, oil-services, aluminium products); Primlaks (fishing and shrimp exports, fish nets, electronics, zinc roofing, packaging, plastics, rice milling); the Tower Group, which is part of the Chandaria Group from Kenya, and has 29 companies (aluminium, basic chemicals, paints, batteries, packaging); and the Churchgate Group, which originated in the commodity trading in 1970 and then diversified into textiles, cotton ginning, fishing, shrimp processing, and dye stuffs manufacturing.[165] Birla Brothers, the Indian multinational, has invested in electrical appliances, vegetable-oil processing, motor parts, and management and consultancy services. Since 1980, as older European firms have moved out of supermarkets and tended to consolidate their activities, so Indian companies have diversified. They have been active in acquiring companies following divestment by western capital and privatisation. In addition, some established firms, both foreign and indigenous, began to employ less costly Indian managers. In turn, some of these managers acquired an interest in these firms, or started their own enterprises.

Banking

It was not until the 1970s that the pattern of indigenous participation in banking began to change.[166] In 1969, foreign banks had to incorporate locally and publish their accounts. Three major commercial banks, Barclays (later Union Bank), United Bank for Africa, and Standard (later First Bank), who controlled about 85 per cent of the deposits, voluntarily approached the stock exchange to sell between 8 per cent and 11 per cent of their equity to Nigerian interests. Nigerian participation was then increased by state involvement with further sales of equity to the public. During 1971 to 1973, the authorities attempted to put the older indigenous state banks on a stronger footing (they had been badly affected by the civil war) and supported

TABLE 2.11: The growth of financial services in Nigeria.

	1973	1989	1991
Commercial banks	17	47	66
Merchant banks	0	34	55
Mortgage institutions	1	1	23
Finance & investment companies	n.a.	28	230
Stockbrokers	10 (1980)	43	61

Sources: Central Bank of Nigeria, *Annual Reports*.

the creation of new state banks, to compete with the expatriate banks.[167] The entry of new foreign commercial banks was not encouraged. In the event, the regional banks were not able to cope and foreign banks were allowed in on the understanding that they would engage in merchant banking which, it was thought, would facilitate an inflow of long-term investment capital. In fact, they tended to finance short-term trade and contributed to the debt overhang which mushroomed after the initial oil boom.

The changes in equity structure went hand in hand with a drive to put the executive control of banking in the hands of Nigerians, thus releasing expatriate minority shareholders of the burden. By 1979, the government had increased Nigerian holding to 60 per cent and this was reflected both in the number of senior Nigerian banking executives and in board composition.

In the late 1970s, a new pattern of private Nigerian participation began to emerge when new commercial and merchant banks were established with 60 per cent private equity usually held by a few individuals (Société Générale (1977), Nigerian American Merchant Bank (1979), BCCI (Nig.) Ltd (1979),[168] and Credit Lyonnais (1983)). Under the regulations, which came into force after public concern over the inequitable outcome of the first phase of the indigenisation decree, no individual could hold more than 5 per cent of the equity.[169]

Table 2.11 shows the general expansion of financial services in Nigeria. Nigerian private participation and promotion of new banks strengthened in the 1980s with a movement from majority participation to full ownership. Of the 66 commercial banks operating at the end of 1991, over one-third were fully owned by private Nigerian interests.[170] In merchant banking, this presence was stronger with over two-thirds of the banks controlled fully by Nigerian shareholders. Well over 80 per cent of these private banks owned by Nigerians began operations between 1988 and 1991. During the 1980s a number of factors encouraged the expansion. Some banks were very profitable. Thus the Nigeria International Bank owned by a group of Nigerian individuals and Citibank (40 per cent), which opened late in 1984, declared a dividend of N34m. for 1987.[171] There had been a build-up of professional experience in the sector and the real cost of entry into banking had fallen.

There was also some relaxation of the conditions for obtaining a banking licence. For example, foreign technical partners were no longer mandatory. Instead, senior management was vetted by the Central Bank. After the Structural Adjustment Programme was introduced in 1986, there was a rush to set up new banks spurred on, in part, by the opportunity to get access to foreign exchange and take advantage of profitable opportunities for currency dealing.

A common pattern in the new banks was for a leading businessman to combine with a banking professional. Among the chief executives of the new merchant banks were former officials of the Central Bank and former staff of the older merchant banks like ICON, Nigerian Acceptances Ltd, and the International Merchant Bank. Another route to merchant banking was through stockbroking and finance companies. Stockbroking was fully indigenised during the 1970s. In 1980 only two of the ten existing companies had foreign origins. A number of these companies developed an expertise in project and corporate finance and later went into merchant banking. Examples include Centre Point Investment Ltd, Financial Trust Company, and City Securities Ltd. Among the businessmen who promoted new banks were Chief Samuel Adedoyin (Industrial Bank), Mike Adenuga (Devcom Merchant Bank), Chief S. O. Bakare (Metropolitan Merchant Bank), Alhaji Aliko Dangote (Liberty Merchant Bank), Alhaji W. I. Folawiyo (Marina International Bank), Olorogun Michael Ibru (Oceanic Bank International), Chief D. U. Ifegwu (Citizens International Bank), Chief G. O. Igbinedion (Crown Merchant Bank), Chief E. C. Iwuanyanwu (ABC Merchant Bank), Otunba M. O. Jolayemi (Victory Merchant Bank), Chief Onwuka Kalu (Fidelity Union Merchant Bank), Mr Jimi Lawal (Alpha Merchant Bank), Chief Dotun Okubanjo (Gulf Bank), Mr. G. O. Onosode (Commerce Bank), Alhaji Isiyaku Rabiu (Grindlays Merchant Bank), Alhaji Bashir Othman Tofa (Century Merchant Bank).

A leading indigenous merchant bank is First City Merchant Bank, which was set up in 1983 by Otunba M. O. Balogun. Otunba Balogun practised as a lawyer before joining the Nigerian Industrial Development Bank as legal adviser and company secretary in 1966.[172] He later became an executive director of ICON Securities (owned by the NIDB). He left in 1977 when he failed to gain the top appointment at ICON Merchant Bank. He then set up City Securities Ltd, a stockbroking and issuing house which handled a number of lucrative public share issues associated with the second phase of the indigenisation decree that required further foreign divestment. He then launched the First City Merchant Bank. No foreign technical partner was found, and 40 per cent of the stock was held in trust at Guardian Royal Exchange. The bank earned profits of N16m. before tax in 1987. In 1988, First City entered into an association with Morgan Grenfell, a leading London merchant bank.

TABLE 2.12: Structure of the insurance industry, 1988.

Ownership	No. of companies	(%)	Market share (%)
Foreign & private Nigerian	22	(20.2)	43.7
Government & private Nigerian	4	(3.7)	1.4
Government	12	(11.0)	43.1
Private Nigerian	71	(65.1)	11.8

Source: *Financial Post*, 17 August 1991.

In the insurance sector, there were some advances by indigenous capital. In 1976 the Insurance Decree cut down on the number of unregulated 'mushroom' companies. As Table 2.12 shows there were still a large number of small private indigenous companies in 1988, accounting for under 12 per cent of the insurance market. In 1988, Amicable Assurance Co. established in 1972 by Prince P. A. Adeyemo became the first insurance company to go public on the Lagos stock exchange. In 1989, Chief J. O. Irukwu, the former managing director of Unity Life and Fire Insurance (1970–82) and the Nigeria Re-Insurance Corporation (1977–89) set up the African Development Insurance Company. In 1991, the company entered a joint venture with a European insurance company, Assiwrozioni Generali Spa (25 per cent).[173] Nigerian private investors also established a number of reinsurance companies. Mr. J. O. Emanuel, an accountant, launched Universe Re-Insurance in 1985.[174] The company had a premium income of N34m. in 1991.[175] Continental Reinsurance was started in 1987 with a prominent insurance broker from Kano, Alhaji M. H. Koguna as chairman.

Overseas Investment

A further dimension to indigenous business enterprise that cannot be ignored is overseas investment. The extent of this investment by Nigerian individuals and enterprises is generally unrecorded and unknown. Yet it is generally accepted that the majority of larger businessmen have made investments overseas. This investment is seldom an integral part of the corporate strategy of an enterprise based in Nigeria. It is very often in real estate. Yet these investments are not necessarily totally 'lost' to the Nigerian economy. Income from overseas investment and business enterprises is used to fund enterprises at home and finance politics.

In addition, a few businessmen have based themselves overseas or made their initial investments abroad. Examples include the Fanz Organisation (Chief Arthur Nzeribe),[176] Chioke International[177] and Alpha Properties International (Jimi Lawal). Much more important historically for their impact on living standards and enterprises at home have been the existence of Nigerian communities trading abroad, especially within the West African sub-region. The Hausa trading diaspora is one example; the Yoruba trading community in Ghana[178] and the Igbo trading community in Cameroon are others. A more recent example, that is important for an understanding of the economic revival in Igboland after the civil war, was the establishment of Igbo trading communities in Cotonou and Lomé.

Considerable investment abroad has been financed through various forms of capital flight. With strict control over outward private capital movements and the existence of free convertibility in the parallel market for trade and capital transactions, there has been no incentive for the movement of funds through official channels. In addition, payment for various intermediary services and commissions has often been made abroad in hard currencies and has therefore been outside the scope of Nigerian controls.

Despite the paucity of information on the subject, a few isolated examples of foreign investment have been recorded in the press. In 1977, Alhaji Wahab Folawiyo participated in a consortium of Arab interests and Barclays Bank International, that acquired Edward Bates, a London bank. According to a *Financial Times* report, the Arabs were anxious to have Chief Folawiyo's participation because of Nigeria's importance as an African country and because of Arab interest in Africa.[179] Chief Adeyemi Lawson took a 14.5 per cent stake in a metallurgical plant in Dakar, Senegal in 1980.[180] Isiyaku Ibrahim, a prominent member of the National Party of Nigeria, invested in mass transportation and the fishing industry in Guinea after he went into exile in 1984.[181] The Rosiji family invested in a cashew-nut plantation in Brazil.[182] In 1988, Concord Press, owned by Bashorun M. K. O. Abiola, acquired the *Africa Economic Digest* from EMAP publishers in London. There was also some evidence at the end of the 1980s of Nigerian companies and business people making investments in West Africa. In 1985 a group of West African entrepreneurs with the active support of the West African Chambers of Commerce set up Ecobank Transnational Incorporated, a holding company based in Lomé.[183] Banking subsidiaries were established in a number of countries after 1987. By 1992, some of these subsidiaries were experiencing financial difficulties.[184] In 1990, a consortium of private Nigerian banks set up the Banque International Du Benin in Cotonou, Republic of Benin. The Nigerian banks (First Interstate, Continental Merchant Bank, First Bank of Nigeria and Union Bank) held 70 per cent of the equity with the Beninoise private sector holding the remainder.[185] The Public Finance Group founded by Chief Paul Erihri in 1982, opened a merchant bank and other financial institutions in the Gambia attracted by the highly liberalised economy.[186] In Ghana, a Nigerian who introduced Balkan Airlines to the country, has made a $4m. investment in hotels.[187] Another, who made money in second-hand clothing, invested in pineapple production for export. In Gabon, a Nigerian was reported to own the only toilet paper factory in the country.[188]

In this chapter, we have sketched in the broadest terms, the advances made by indigenous capital in this century. We have shown how the political and economic context changed and how this affected the opportunities open to indigenous entrepreneurs. In the following five chapters, we consider individual enterprises and business careers in Lagos, Ibadan, Onitsha, Nnewi, Aba, Kano and Kaduna.

3

EARLY BUSINESS PROFILES

In this chapter we present profiles of leading businessmen and one woman, whose active business careers span six decades from the 1920s to the 1980s (see Table 3.1). These individuals were all well established in the 1950s and their careers generally precede those who are treated in later chapters. They are not representative of the full range of larger-scale enterprises in this period. In particular, larger illiterate traders are not included. All, except one, had primary education and five went on to secondary schooling. They do, however, provide a range of business experience that extends and deepens the general outline presented in chapter 2. Fifteen individuals are treated (9 Yoruba, 3 Igbo, 1 Hausa, 1 Bini and 1 Itsekiri). Eight of them are Lagos based. The case of Alhaji Alhassan Dantata of Kano is treated in chapter 8.

We begin with profiles of seven industrialists, looking first at three individuals who also had extensive interests outside industry. Chief Adeola Odutola of Ijebu-Ode is perhaps the most well known of all the pioneer industrialists in the former Western Region. In 1950, he opened a tyre-retreading plant in Ibadan and launched a timber company that was one of the earliest African/European joint ventures in Nigeria. Next, we examine the career of Mathias Ugochukwu of Umunze. As a policeman, he won a fortune on the Irish Sweepstake. He invested his windfall wealth in trade, transport and property, and was a pioneer of industrial development in the former Eastern Region and chairman of John Holt. Like Odutola, Ugochukwu was an important regional figure whose significance extends beyond his business career. The third pioneer, Mr C. T. Onyekwelu, was a prominent Onitsha trader born in 1898, who, after many disappointments, eventually established a gramophone record manufacturing company in Onitsha in 1963. There follow profiles of four individuals who concentrated on a single line of industry. Otunba Ade Tuyo owned the largest bakery in Nigeria in the 1960s. Samuel Fawehinmi started a modern furniture factory in 1948 and J. K. Ladipo launched a food processing company in 1939. Chief (Mrs)

TABLE 3.1: Early business profiles.

Name	Date	Location	Business	Industry
T. A. Odutola	1902–	Ijebu-Ode, Ibadan, Kano, Onitsha	Importing, produce trade, property	Tyre retreading, plantations, tyres, biscuits, brewery
M. Ugochukwu	1926–90	Lagos, Port Harcourt, Onitsha, Kaduna, Umunze	Trading, transport, property	Tyre retreading, saw milling, foam, biscuits
C. T. Onyekwelu	1898–?	Onitsha	Trading	Gramophone records
J. Ade Tuyo	1902–?	Lagos	Bakery	Bakery
S. I. Fawehinmi	1912–	Lagos	Furniture	Furniture, saw milling
J. K. Ladipo	?–1961	Lagos	Food processing	Food processing
B. E. Tejuoso	1916–	Lagos	Trading	Plastic foam
M. Bank-Anthony	1907–91	Lagos	Importing, property, insurance, transport, investment	—
S. L. Edu	1911–	Lagos	Ship's chandler transport, insurance	—
L. P. Ojukwu	1909–66	Lagos	Transport, property, investments	—
F. Edo-Osagie	1914–93	Port Harcourt, Benin	Timber, transport, hotel proprietor	—
H. Kassim	1919–86	Kano	Trading, produce buyer, transportation, hotelier, pilgrimage agency	—
L. Omole	1915–	Ilesha	Cocoa trade, transport	Brewery
S. O. Gbadamosi	1910–93	Lagos	Importing, distribution	Singlets, ceramics
F. S. Okotie-Eboh	1912–66	Lagos, Sapele	Timber & rubber trade, property	Rubber crepe, shoes, cement

Bisoye Tejuoso after an extensive career as trader and agent to foreign companies, invested in the plastic-foam industry in 1964 and again in 1972.

Next, we turn to a group of traders and transporters. This category, whose involvement with industry was more remote, demonstrates the growth of ties with foreign companies in the 1950s. The cases of Sir Mobalaji Bank-Anthony and Alhaji S. L. Edu show some parallels. Both businessmen were involved in trading and transport (both with contracts for petrol haulage) and both founded insurance companies. Both actively sought out foreign companies that could start business in Nigeria and became board members and shareholders. In this respect, Mobalaji Bank-Anthony was a pioneer, becoming chairman of an Italian construction company in 1950. Sir Odumegwu Ojukwu of Nnewi and Lagos ran a large Lagos-based transport company. He became the first Nigerian director of Shell and was a business leader of his generation. Chief Francis Edo-Osagie, who was based in Port Harcourt, was one of the leading timber merchants of the 1950s and early 1960s. The last case is that of Lawrence Omole, one of Ilesha's richest businessmen, who started in the produce trade, moved into transport, and eventually established a brewery.

We end with two individuals who are better known as politicians than as businessmen. Alhaji S. O. Gbadamosi and Chief Festus Okotie-Eboh were the federal treasurer of the Action Group and federal minister of finance respectively. They illustrate some of the links between business, economic nationalism and politics.

INDUSTRIALISTS

Chief Adeola Odutola

Chief Odutola of Ijebu-Ode was born in 1902 and has long been known as a pioneer industrialist. As a disciplinarian of modest comportment and few words, he has been held up as an example to the youth of Yorubaland.[1] He has engaged in large-scale philanthropy and been influential in Ijebu politics. He led the educated elite against the powers of the Sole Native Authority and the Awujale of Ijebuland from the 1930s.[2] He founded a secondary school in 1945 (Ijebu-Ode Commercial College), endowed chairs at the Universities of Ibadan and Lagos, and built a church. As a member of the Legislative Council for Ijebu Province (1945–47), he had a network of contacts that allowed him to distance himself from the struggle for state patronage and party political support in which many businessmen engaged. In 1971, he became the first president of the Manufacturers Association of Nigeria.

After two years of secondary schooling at Ijebu-Ode Grammar School under the principal, Reverend I. O. Ransome-Kuti, he left for Lagos in 1921 and became a clerk in the Treasury Department.[3] Subsequently, he became a Native Authority (NA) court clerk and started trading privately in most parts of Ijebu Province between 1921 and 1933. Among the items he traded were damask, silk cloths, fishing nets and gas lamps for churches (for whom he became a major supplier). In 1933, he resigned as court clerk to enter the cocoa and palm-oil trade with his brother.[4] Stores were opened at Ife, Lagos, Ibadan and Ilesha. Two years later, lorries were purchased to take commodities direct to Lagos for export. In the same year Odutola Brothers were reported to have a turnover of £54,000 and 35 employees.[5] The size of the capital available to the firm and the firm's success as a speculator, surprised colonial officials.[6]

Chief Odutola became active in public affairs, becoming a member of the Ijebu Advisory Board and Ijebu-Ode Town Council. He was also actively involved in the Produce Buyers Union and the Nigerian Motor Transport Union. He was president of the Nigerian Youth Movement in Ijebu Division in 1938, the strongest branch outside Lagos.

Odutola Brothers was one of the largest indigenous produce companies. It was involved in direct export of cocoa overseas with Busi and Stephenson of Liverpool and was one of only 2 indigenous companies to use a wartime quota in 1941.[7] The company also participated in the short-lived cassava-starch export boom as one of 14 small shippers.[8] Later, the company became the premier buying agent for John Holt in Nigeria.[9] Chief Odutola was also involved in gold mining around Ilesha. Another wartime venture was the African Weaving Company under the management of his friend J. A. Fowokan.[10] By the end of the war the company had 25 looms and 35 employees.

In 1945 Chief Odutola became a member of the Legislative Council and immediately complained about the effect of wartime road-transport restrictions on the Ijebu who did not have the advantage of rail or river transport.[11] In the same year he became a member of the Lagos Chamber of Commerce on the recommendation of John Holt. A clear shift in Chamber policy in favour of coopting Africans only came in 1948.[12] According to Longe, Chief Odutola left the produce trade in 1948 because he foresaw the adverse impact of the marketing boards. In the same year, he also broke with his brother, Jimoh, who was to become his rival in business. In 1950, Chief Odutola started a joint venture, Omo Sawmills Ltd, with a British timber firm, Norman Ruthford. The company obtained concessions from the Forestry Department in Ijebu Province and was assisted by the Colonial Development Corporation. Some timber was exported.

The scope of Chief Odutola's interests as a legislator can be seen in a powerful speech he delivered to the Legislative Council on the Appropriation Bill in 1950.[13] He was then representing the Western House of Assembly in the Council. Many of his themes were to recur later. He attacked the rate of company profit tax as the highest in the colonies, which was adversely affecting those who wanted to start companies. He attacked restrictions on the import of American trucks which were much superior to British trucks.

He deplored the state of the Ijebu-Ode–Benin road and criticised the lethargy of the Crown Agents. In a striking passage, he contrasted the low status of engineers and their relatively poor conditions of service under colonial rule with the high esteem and rewards given to doctors and lawyers. He criticised the Department of Agriculture for excessive preoccupation with experimental work. He argued that a good clean water supply for the community should have priority over expensive hospitals. He warned that the benefits of transport subsidies were going to the Lebanese and foreign companies and not to Africans who paid the taxes. Finally, he drew a clear distinction between self-reliance which was to be applauded and self-sufficiency which he saw as the negation of progress.

In the 1940s, Chief Odutola founded two colleges – the Secondary Commercial School in 1945 and Olu Iwa College in 1948. These colleges were started in cocoa sheds in the heart of Ijebu-Ode. They amalgamated in 1963 to form Adeola Odutola Comprehensive High School (later Adeola Odutola College). Chief A. G. Leventis donated £2,000 to equip a library for the merged institutions.

Throughout the 1950s and early 1960s, Chief Odutola remained a supporter of Chief Awolowo and the Action Group. He was a shareholder in the Amalgamated Press which was controlled by the Action Group.[14] His brief detention in 1965 with Mojeed Agbaje during the western political crisis effectively ended his active political involvement.

In 1950, a tyre-retreading plant was set up in Ibadan on a three-acre site. One hundred persons, including two expatriates, were employed. This business followed a visit to England in 1948 and negotiation of a licence agreement with a British company.[15] Goodyear of the United States supplied camelback. In 1956 and 1957 other plants followed in Onitsha and Kano. Thus Chief Odutola was the first local industrialist to establish plants in all regions of the Federation. The Onitsha plant was never resuscitated after the civil war and the Anambra State government eventually acquired the waterside plot.[16] The Kano plant was the most successful of the three, experiencing little competition until recently.

His brother, Jimoh Odutola, established a rival retreading firm with superior technology in Ibadan in 1956.[17] Again there was a licensing agreement and a hired expatriate. A second plant was started at Aba in 1960. Jimoh pioneered the production of foam-rubber products in Nigeria. Technical difficulties beset this venture followed by problems in marketing the relatively expensive foam mattresses and cushions. However, lessons were learnt and put to use in the establishment of a very successful plastic-foam plant, J. A. Odutola Plastic Foam Company, whose products were cheaper and lighter.

During the 1950s, Chief Odutola established a 5,000-acre rubber and oil-palm plantation.[18] Three thousand acres were developed initially and came into production in 1965. (In the 1980s, the plantation was expanded to include cassava and soyabean cultivation.) In 1961, a rubber-compounding plant was opened in Ibadan. In 1967, a £500,000 investment was made in the production of bicycle tyres and tubes with German technical assistance. The variety of rubber products that could be compounded was also extended to include soles and heels for shoes. Michelin, a major competitor in Port Harcourt for tyre production, closed down with the advent of the civil war and this boosted production. Dunlop then became the major competitor until it ceased production. Later local competitors emerged, including Alhaji Sanusi of Lagos and GMO and Roadmaster of Onitsha. During his business career, Chief Odutola also built up a very large property portfolio concentrated in Lagos and the Apapa, Ikeja and Ijebu-Ode industrial areas.

In the 1970s, Chief Odutola entered into a series of joint ventures with the Leventis company. His friendship with Chief A. G. Leventis went back to the 1920s when Leventis, a Greek Cypriot, arrived in Abeokuta to work as an agent for A. J. Tangalakis in the produce trade. These ventures include Crown Corks (Leventis holds the Coca Cola franchise in Nigeria and is the leader in the soft-drinks market), a brewery at Ijebu-Ode, and a cannery at Otta. In 1979, a N5.6m. biscuit factory was opened as a wholly owned venture, operating under licence from the Bahlsen Tet Group of Switzerland. Leventis and Kingsway (UAC) stores were used as retail outlets, among others. A department store was also opened in Ijebu-Ode – Odutola Stores Ltd.

Apart from these, Chief Odutola also established substantial interests in a number of large enterprises operating in Nigeria. These included Kabelmetal Nig. Ltd, Western Steel Works Ltd, Bayer Pharmaceuticals Ltd, Unichem Ltd and the Continental Brewery at Aba.

The comparatively slow growth of this enterprise in later years illustrates the difficulty of effectively delegating authority for a sole proprietor. The presence of sons in the enterprise did not significantly reduce the responsibilities of the founder. Various attempts were made to appoint Nigerian managers but they found themselves without incentive where corporate procedures and responsibilities were not well established. As Longe notes, organised and continuous employment of non-relatives was a new phenomena for indigenous enterprises and for a period the severe scarcity of manpower at senior levels hampered their growth. The alternative was to employ expatriates but this was costly and far from being assured of success. It was not until 1982, when the former Registrar of the University of Lagos joined the company, that a successful appointment was made. Expatriates were employed on the technical side. Expatriate employment was reduced from eleven in 1982 to a single accountant in early 1989. This affected performance, particularly in the engineering and production areas.

Mathias Nwafor Ugochukwu

Igwe Mathias Nwafor Ugochukwu (1926–90), popularly known as Ugogbuzuo ('The white eagle that dazzles in its arrival'), was a major industrialist, investor, and property owner who pioneered large-scale industry in the former Eastern Region.[19] He was also an important Igbo leader and political figure at the regional and federal levels. While he never directly contested for electoral office, he nevertheless identified with political movements. He was, for example, one of three trustees of the NCNC (National Convention of Nigerian Citizens) in the 1950s who sided with K. O. Mbadiwe in his rift with Dr Nnamdi Azikiwe.[20] During the Second Republic, he was a member of the National Party of Nigeria and a close colleague of the vice-president, Dr Alex Ekueme. His close association with the regime led to his detention for 18 months under the Buhari regime. This adversely affected business operations. In 1980, he was awarded the title of Eze Ohazurume I of Igboland ('embodiment of the collective will of the people'). Throughout his life, he was closely associated with the church, especially St Augustine's at Umunze. The foundation stone of his Palace of the People at Umunze was laid by the Anglican Archbishop of West Africa, the most Rev C. J. Patterson.

Born at Umunze (formerly in Aguata, now Orumba Local Government Area), he was educated at St Augustine's Primary School. In 1939, he left for Jos to become houseboy to Mr Louis Offor of Enugu Ukwu.[21] He returned home in 1945 and engaged in petty trading before joining the police on a salary of £8 10s. a month.[22] The turning point in his career came in April 1951 when he won £50,000 on the Irish Sweepstake. He then left the police to pursue a career in business.

Initially, he traded in motor parts from the Gold Coast. He then built up a sizeable transport operation between Onitsha and Lagos that was second only to Ojukwu Transport. He developed trading ties with John Holt and visited Liverpool. He bought shares in John Holt and his close association with the company eventually led to his appointment as its chairman. He imported textiles and foodstuffs and became a major importer of tobacco for snuff. He also developed a strong interest in real estate, buying and selling plots and buildings all round the Federation. He had eleven properties in Port Harcourt. The most well known was 10 Aba Road, a five-storey building constructed by Eastern and General Contractors, the largest indigenous construction company in the East, owned by D. A. Nwandu and Dennis Okafor of Enugu Ukwu. The building had the first lift in Port Harcourt and was partly rented to the Bank of America (in which Chief Ugochukwu held shares).

Mathias Ugochukwu was chairman of the African Development Corporation (ADC) – an indigenous investment agency that had been founded by Mbonu Ojike, a journalist and nationalist, who became well known as the

'Boycott King' and author of *My Africa*.[23] The ADC was planned as a wide ranging development institution and it reflected the economic nationalism of the NCNC. The Corporation, which later included C. T. Onyekwelu, Sir Louis Ojukwu, and L. N. Obioha among its directors, began operations as a trading concern and acquired some assets in Lagos and the provinces.[24] The ADC bought Schackleford's bakery in Lagos after the retirement of the 'Bread King' and it became a licensed buying agent for cocoa and palm produce in the early 1950s losing its licence after a few years because it had not purchased the minimum volumes required by the boards.[25] In 1953 Ojike became a minister in the Eastern Nigeria government, and according to Michael Okpara, his duties in the Ministry of Finance made it impossible for him to manage the ADC which declined.[26]

Ugochukwu was also chairman of African Produce Dealers Ltd, a leading produce enterprise in Port Harcourt. He assisted in establishing the Nigerian Engineering and Manufacturing Company in Port Harcourt in 1957. This was Nigeria's first cement plant.[27] It imported clinker and gypsum and had an erratic history of production and closure. It suffered from competition from cheap cement imports and from the arrival in the Port Harcourt market of cement from a new plant at Nkalagu near Enugu. The company was liquidated in 1965.

In 1958, two industrial ventures were started, both of them relying on low-cost, labour-intensive operations. In Port Harcourt, a saw mill employed 300 people and in Onitsha £40,000 was invested in a tyre-retreading plant, Ugochukwu Tyres Ltd, which employed some 400 persons. Neither of these operations were reactivated after the civil war.

In 1955, Ugochukwu took the Agency of the Provincial Insurance Company of London.[28] Three years later the West African Provincial Insurance Company was launched with Provincial Insurance. Other investments during this period included a stake in the Biscuit Manufacturing Company of Nigeria and Nigerpools, one of the first Nigerian pools companies, located at Ijora Causeway, which Ugochukwu financed and organised. The company was managed by a Swiss manager and K. O. Mbadiwe, the politician, was a director. In 1962, the Central Finance Company was created to oversee real estate and shareholdings.

During the 1950s and 1960s, Chief Ugochukwu took up various appointments on federal and regional bodies. These included the Nigerian Railway Corporation, the African Continental Bank, the Nigerian Industrial Development Bank (chairman, 1964–6) the Stock Exchange, the Federal Tenders Board, and the Eastern Nigerian Marketing Board.

After the war, a major industrial investment was made at Umunze. Ugochukwu Chemical Industries produced mattresses, pillows, cushions and sheeting. The equipment suppliers, Harrison and Jones of Birmingham took a small part of the equity. Other plants were opened in Onitsha and

Kaduna. The Kaduna factory was the most successful because of a more efficient technology and higher market share. In the late 1980s, these enterprises had a turnover of around N40m and employed 800 persons.

The industry was the nucleus for a number of other developments at Umunze. Household Utilities, a furniture company, acquired from Lebanese in Lagos, was moved to Umunze. A farming enterprise that had begun before the war – Hecam Farms – was expanded to include poultry, a piggery and maize milling. Ugochukwu Tyres Ltd. was also moved to Umunze. An attempt was made to promote an oil mill – Palmke Oil Mill – with the state government and John Holt as technical partners, but the prices offered by the commodity board were unremunerative and the project closed down. (It was reactivated in 1988.) Electricity and a water supply with a mini-dam were brought to Umunze and a hotel was constructed. These developments attracted a bank and, later, a technical Federal College of Education was opened.

Unlike many Igbo businessmen, Chief Ugochukwu had the financial resources from his rental income from property to take some advantage of the indigenisation exercise. He bought 60 per cent of John Holt Insurance Brokers, which became Eagle Insurance Brokers. He increased his participation in the Biscuit Manufacturing Company by buying over the interest of John Holt and Consolidated Commercial Ltd to take over 75 per cent of the equity. He invited a few friends, like Chief Ikokwu, to take a share and join the board. In 1980, turnover was N13.5m. with 700 employed. He also bought over the interest of John Holt in Nigerian Import and Exports Services Ltd., a specialist importer of firearms. In addition, he acquired shareholdings in Yamaha Manufacturing Nig. Ltd. (motorcycles), Afprint (textiles) and Nigerian Sewing Machines. Other investments where Chief Ugochukwu was either chairman or on the board of directors included: West African Distilleries, Westminster Dredging, Nigercafé and Foods, Minnesota, Smurfit, Savannah Bank, Paktank, Scanska, and Pan African Airlines.

Chief Ugochukwu involved himself closely in his business affairs on a daily basis and worked long hours. Three sons, who were trained in the United States, came into the business before his death. The sons gradually took over responsibilities, but lack of effective delegation affected Chief Ugochukwu's health adversely.

Christopher Tagbo Onyekwelu

Christopher Tagbo Onyekwelu was born in 1898 at Nawfia, Onitsha Province.[29] He completed primary education standard 6 in 1918. He became a missionary pupil teacher and a catechist at Enugu Ukwu. He remained a devout Christian throughout his life. He was a pillar of the Anglican Church and treasurer of All Saints Cathedral, Onitsha.

In 1921, he joined the Nigerian Railway Corporation and later he enrolled in the Nigerian Police Force, although illness prevented him from taking up the appointment. He then briefly engaged in farm work. In 1924, he started to trade in palm produce in Onitsha. Only a few men from Nnobi and Nnewi were trading at this time. Trading was generally accepted as a woman's career and he was nicknamed in the market, Nwoke Mgbelafia ('a man who trades'). He sold palm kernel to the Niger Company.

In 1926, he began to import Rangoon rice, which proved to be very profitable. Rice was not grown in eastern Nigeria at that time and was only introduced into the Abakaliki area in 1942.[30] Expatriate competition forced him to leave this line of business in 1929. He then saw the need for spare parts for bicycles and sewing machines. He imported spare parts directly from a Birmingham company. Once again, foreign firms began to enter the trade and he was undersold by John Walkden. He left the trade in 1935.

Another initiative he took was to import a hand operated knitting machine and set up a small knitting factory in part of his shop (there was no electricity in Onitsha at the time). Capacity was only twelve pairs of socks a day and he eventually suspended the programme.

By 1929, he had begun to import gramophones and gramophone records. Here the expatriate companies found it difficult to compete because they could not predict which records would be popular with the public. He managed to find an overseas supplier who was willing to extend credit. He did very extensive business with Messrs Herchells and Co. Ltd of Liverpool. They became an agent of His Master's Voice (HMV) because, according to Onyekwelu, a European company would never have trusted an African businessman.

In 1939, he organised a group of singers and musicians, the Onitsha Musical Party. They were trained with the assistance of Chief L. A. Okeke of Enugu Ukwu. Sponsored by CFAO, the group went to Lagos to make recordings. The tapes were then sent to European record-pressing companies. He received two consignments of records before the war and was thus able to import and distribute records of Nigerian music, bearing his personal CTO label. During the war, he organised Onitsha traders and businesses into the Niger African Association.

After the war, production of vernacular records was stopped. German matrices used in the process were destroyed during the war. CFAO had also broken their contract with Onyekwelu to make him the sole agent in Nigeria. He therefore joined the Nigeria Association of Gramophone and Record Dealers, who were mostly of Lagos origin. They had a recording machine but no qualified technician to produce good sound.

He then decided that he must start record production in Nigeria, an objective that was not fully achieved until 1963. In 1952, he bought a portable recording machine for £2,700 but could not operate it effectively in

Onitsha. He imported a giant battery and, with the assistance of an engineer sent from England, he managed to record a few tapes in 1954, using his sitting room as a studio. These included recordings by the popular Obiligbo such as Obiageli Aku. He then bought a diesel plant for £250 but without much success.

He made two fruitless trips to Europe in 1954 and 1957 to find a foreign technical partner. Despite having substantial urban real estate, the Eastern Nigeria Development Corporation turned down a request for a loan in 1955. In 1959, he finally obtained a £30,000 loan from the Federal Loans Board, but a land-ownership dispute with Obosi people delayed construction of a factory. In the same year, he hired a German technician. He spent some £55,000 on the factory and when all funds were exhausted he was forced to turn to Phillips for working capital in 1961. A joint venture – Niger Records Ltd – was set up with the equity shared. The company, which was located in Fegge on the banks of the river Niger, employed 125 persons and 2 expatriate engineers. It competed successfully in the West African and UK markets and had an annual turnover of over £100,000. Nigerphone, his record dealership, had exclusive rights in the East, Phillips and Badejo Stores covered Lagos, while Tabansi Business Enterprises distributed in the North.

Onyekwelu was chairman of the Onitsha Chamber of Commerce and a member of the Federal Advisory Committee on Customs and Tariffs.

Joshua Ade Tuyo

Joshua Ade Tuyo was Nigeria's most prominent baker in the mid-1960s.[31] He was born in Ijebu-Ode to the Tunwase ruling house in 1902. His father mixed farming with tailoring and was an Anglican lay missionary. His mother was an indigo trader. He was sent to Lagos in 1909 and completed primary school. Joshua Tuyo entered a mission teacher-training programme at Ijebu-Ode in conformity with his parent's wishes. After three years health problems forced Tuyo to switch from teaching to a clerical career in the Railway Department. During this period (1921–4) he also took correspondence courses in shorthand and business management. In 1924, Tuyo obtained employment with the Bank of West Africa, where he stayed for a dozen years before returning to the Railway Department. With the exception of a three-year stint in the Ministry of Commerce and Industry (1948–51), Tuyo remained with the Railway Department becoming a chief clerk in 1940 and then head of personnel until his retirement in 1953.

In 1926, while stationed in Onitsha with the bank, Joshua Tuyo had met a young Ijebu girl, Alice Idowu, in the course of trading with her mother in the Onitsha market. They married the following year, and Alice, with the aid of her husband, gradually developed into a large wholesale trader specialising in textiles, sporting goods and cement. In 1950, after a major theft took her entire stock-in-trade, Mrs Tuyo determined to take up baking as a more profitable and less risky occupation. Her husband insisted on proper training and helped finance her through a two-year course at the Borough Polytechnic Institute, London. When Tuyo's first post-retirement project, trading in produce and textiles, proved disappointing, he began to take note of the high returns in bread baking. With some financial assistance from a British friend, a four-man bakery was launched in 1955. Capitalising on his wife's training and the interest of the Ministry of Commerce and Industry in promoting baking as an indigenous industry, he applied to the Federal Loans Board for a £15,000 loan. This was issued to De Facto Works Ltd in 1956 and a second loan of £6,000 was made in 1959. Tuyo became president of the Lagos Chamber of Commerce and a member of the Lagos Executive Development Board.

By the mid-1960s the De Facto bakery was one of the country's largest bakeries, with more than 200 employees engaged in the production and distribution of bread. Annual turnover was £170,000 in 1964 and the bakery had a delivery range of 90 miles. By 1969, the enterprise was employing 310 persons and arrangements had been made to expand the business to Benin under the management of one of his sons. The manufacturing process was by far the most modern and capital intensive of Nigeria's several hundred mechanised bakeries. In addition to operating with water-tempering and measuring devices, flour sifters, oil-fired reel and drawing-plate ovens (in contrast to wood-fired peel ovens) and embossed English bread pans, the bakery made bread that included such atypical ingredients as full cream dried milk and malt extract.

The principal markets for De Facto's high-quality, high-cost bread were the hotels and food stores servicing the large Lagos European community. Even allowing for a higher sales price, heavy overhead costs in the form of a large administrative staff (nearly a quarter of all employees), and the services of an English accounting firm gave De Facto a considerably lower profit margin on sales than that of its competitors who catered to the mass market. The biggest problem was the arrival in 1962 of Nigerian Flour Mills, owned by the federal government.[32] Soon after its establishment, the government placed a heavy duty on imported flour supplies. This raised flour prices and was one reason why De Facto decided to go into catering. Nevertheless, its earnings and its ability to borrow were sufficient to finance a De Facto restaurant and five retail bake-shops, as well as to take a small interest in a Swedish-sponsored reconstituted-milk factory, of which Ade Tuyo was chairman.

Samuel Ibitayo Fawehinmi

Fawehinmi Furniture Factory Ltd was one of the first indigenous companies in West Africa to employ the latest techniques and machinery in furniture production. Other companies followed largely in the 1970s when there was considerable investment in furniture production.

Samuel Ibitayo Fawehinmi was born in 1912.[33] His father was a trader at Ondo. He attended the Boys' High School, Ondo and Government College, Ibadan. He then studied at Higher College, Yaba for three years. It had been his intention to study medicine but in 1934 he found himself having to wait one year for a pre-medical course. Because he appeared to have an aptitude for wood- and metalwork, he was advised to train in those subjects. As there was no specialised syllabus, he took a civil engineering course. In 1936 he was awarded a technical instructor's diploma and in 1937 was appointed to the staff of Government College, Umuahia. In 1939 he transferred to King's College, Lagos where he remained until 1946.

He then decided to go into the manufacture of furniture and persuaded his father to finance his training in England. He studied at Shoreditch Technical College where the vice-principal was, fortunately, a member of a family of furniture manufacturers – A. G. Clark and Co. He trained at the Clark factory and at Harrod's factory for upholstery.

He returned to Nigeria and with funds from his father and a loan of £350 from Irving and Bonnar, he was able to build a house in Surulere in 1948. From here he launched his business. In 1950, he obtained a loan of £1,500 from the Colony Development Board. With an annual turnover of £3,000 to £4,000 he was able to repay the loan of £5,000 from Barclays Bank to purchase modern equipment. The loan was repaid in two-and-a-half years.

In 1953, a four-acre site was purchased in Yaba. All building was done by direct labour under his direction. The company has remained and expanded at this location ever since. There was a continuous increase in turnover until the 1980s. Showrooms were built in Yaba, Surulere and Broad Street, Lagos. The firm has remained a family business, employing between 150 and 300 persons. The two eldest sons were both trained in the United Kingdom for management and technical positions within the company and a sister studied accountancy.

This case study shows single-minded determination to concentrate on one line of activity and achieve excellence in it. The company kept abreast of new methods and techniques. The only other investments made outside the business were in saw mills at Otta and Ondo. Expatriate competition was welcomed and one expatriate company assisted with the training of employees in some processes. All available funds were ploughed back into the enterprise. Mr Fawehinmi rode a bicycle long after he was able to afford a motor car. He followed a policy of cash payments so the company had no creditors. Attempts to bring him into politics failed and family rivalries that have disadvantaged other companies were absent.

Josephus Kayode Lapido

J. K. Lapido was a pioneer of food processing and packaging in Nigeria.[34] He was educated at Abeokuta Grammar School between 1921 and 1925 and then trained in agriculture at Moor Plantation, Ibadan. He joined the Ministry of Agriculture and was a research chemist at Samaru, Zaria for many years before returning to Moor Plantation. He resigned from government service in 1936.

Lisabi Mills was set up on Lagos Island in 1938. The market for packaged Nigerian foods was a limited one and the main outlets were department stores, hotels, hospitals and the armed forces. Cocoa and coffee were processed for drinking and frozen chicken sold. Also processed were cut and dried okra, ewedu and agborom, rice, bean flour, milled melon seed and fried plantain. Two more retail outlets were established in Ikorodu and Yaba.

After the war, the business was moved to Commercial Avenue, Yaba. In the 1950s, there was an expansion to a site at Maryland where there was an orchard and a maintenance department. Among the products were lard in tins, jollof rice, egusi soup, cereal food, wheat flakes, canned and bottled palm oil, tapioca flakes, groundnut oil, ground shrimp, and pepper. Yam and cassava flour were developed after J. K. Lapido died. The enterprise remained a family one and the owner stayed with one activity, reinvesting the profits. J. K. Ladipo was widely respected for his hard work, integrity, and honesty of purpose.[35] He was a zealous campaigner against corruption and placed 'No Bribe' advertisements in newspapers.

The business experienced a downward trend with the civil war and the oil boom. During the oil boom, the affluent imported food and there was a scarcity of raw materials. Vegetable oil was imported and packaged. The number of lines was reduced. In 1974, a son who had trained abroad and taken a doctorate in food science, returned and became managing director.

The company was in the process of investing in new machinery for vegetable-oil processing and production of baby foods and breakfast cereals when the Structural Adjustment Programme raised the cost of credit and the cost of imported items, such as corn starch. The company has recently concentrated on enriched custard powder and short-term contract and batch work (e.g. corn grits for breweries). Employment has fluctuated between 50 and 100 persons.

Chief (Mrs) Bisoye Tejuoso[36]

Born in 1916 at Abeokuta, Mrs Tejuoso, attended primary and secondary schools in her home town. Her father, Chief J. A. Karunmi, was a farmer. At the age of eighteen, she married Mr J. S. Tejuoso who worked for the railways in Lagos. In 1940, her husband was transferred to Zaria where she spent seventeen years. While in Zaria, she used the railways to trade in foodstuffs (onion, tomato, maize and groundnut) with the South. The trade became lucrative and the family was able to build houses of their own in Zaria. In the early 1950s, she became an agent of the UAC selling provisions and textile materials to traders from Funtua and Gusau.

She left Zaria in 1957 for Lagos and continued her connection with UAC, specialising in hardware and enamelware. When Vono Products was established in 1960, she became a very successful agent, selling beds, mattresses and cushions from her showroom on Broad Street. One particular design of bed, Bisi Bed, was named after her.

In 1964 she collaborated with a Norwegian and Mr E. E. Eribo,[37] a Benin-based businessman in a plastic foam venture, Nigerian Urethane Company. The factory was located in Benin and she acted as sales director, selling products in Lagos. A carpet industry was also established in Benin, the Nigerian Carpet Manufacturing Company. At the end of the 1960s, she became dissatisfied with the way the business was run and withdrew her partnership.

She obtained a loan from the NIDB and land from the Lagos State Development and Property Corporation to start a foam venture, Teju Industries, at Ilupeju in 1972. An expatriate production manager stayed with the company from 1972 to 1987. Her son, Dapo, a medical doctor, became managing director in 1971. The industry expanded to over 2,000 employees with 18 depots outside Lagos. A devastating fire outbreak in 1984 halted production and the industry now functions at a much reduced level. Other business ventures undertaken include a poultry farm, a hotel, a property company, petroleum distribution and a furniture venture in partnership with an Italian.

Both Chief Tejuoso and her son have taken chieftaincy titles that have progressively involved them in chieftaincy affairs in Egbaland. In 1982 Mrs Tejuosho became Iyalode Egba, leader of all Egba women. She was the third person to hold the title following Madam Tinubu and Madam Miniya Jojola. In 1989 her son became Osile of Oke-Ona, Egba.

TRADERS AND TRANSPORTERS
Sir Mobalaji Bank-Anthony

Mobalaji Bank-Anthony was born in Boma, Belgian Congo, where his mother had gone to trade.[38] His father, Pa Alfred, was a successful businessman in Lagos who founded a firm of undertakers, A. Bank-Anthony and Sons.[39] His secondary education was at Methodist Boys High School, Lagos, Ijebu-Ode Grammar School, CMS (Church Missionary Society) Grammar School and Baptist Academy. He then worked with the Post and Telegraph Department for six years between 1924 and 1931.

He entered private business as a general merchant (M. de Bank Brothers) in 1929 and built up a business trading in palm oil. He travelled to Germany in 1932, looking for machinery to speed up palm oil pressing, but the boom in whale oil killed his scheme. He brought some patent-medicine samples home and set up in the patent-medicine business. A store was opened in 1933. He broadened his range of commodities to include German watches and clocks until the war stopped his source of supply. He eventually managed to import fountain pens, becoming the third largest dealer after UAC and UTC. Soldiers in transit in Lagos during the World War II were among his best customers for pens.[40] Another profitable line was the import of marble angels for tombstones from Italy. Later he tried to set up a marble business with an Italian partner, but there was a disagreement and the business collapsed. The failure to develop a Nigerian marble industry was his most frustrating business experience.[41]

He briefly participated in politics helping to found the Lagos Youth Movement in the early 1930s along with Dr J. C. Vaughan, and Samuel Akinsanya.[42] An early issue was the content of the medical curriculum of the Yaba Higher College. He left the Nigerian Youth Movement in 1938 to concentrate on business and never again developed direct affiliations with political parties. He did however participate as an individual in the work of the Lagos Trade and Industrial Advisory Council, a body established in 1950 by the colonial administration to discuss commercial issues with African and European business interests.[43] He was also a leading figure in the Ad Hoc Committee of All Nigeria Businessmen of 1956 which complained about the minor participation of African businessmen in the economy.

1950 marks the beginning of a strong association, as board member and occasional shareholder, with a number of foreign companies which started operations in Nigeria. Mobalaji Bank-Anthony, a man with ideas and projects and numerous foreign connections, was a pioneer in this regard. An indefatigable correspondent and constant traveller, he was a very frequent visitor to Europe.[44] His links with Italian, German and American companies reflect the broadening of Nigeria's international economic ties away from Britain during the decade. Not all his efforts to get foreign companies involved in Nigeria were successful. For example, he tried to convince the German electronics company, Telefunken, to establish a manufacturing plant, to no avail.[45]

In 1950 he sold property for a speculative business trip to Europe and was assisted by the financial secretary, Eric Harmsworth. He introduced the Italian construction firm, Borini Prono, to Nigeria and became chairman of their Nigerian subsidiary. Amongst other projects, the company was involved in swamp clearance in central Lagos, a stadium project at Surulere, the Ijora Causeway and the Benin–Asaba road. Further foreign trips brought more companies to Nigeria and more directorships. In 1951, he became chief agent of Law Union and Rock Insurance Company, a London firm. He was the first Nigerian to secure such an agency. An insurance agency, Bank and Braithwaite, founded with Mr T. A. Braithwaite, his cousin, also flourished for a while. He became managing director of the biggest cinema circuit in the country. Bank-Anthony was awarded the OBE in 1956. His transport company, Bank's Transport Ltd., obtained a haulage contract from Mobil Oil. In 1957, he joined the board of Mobil Exploration Nigeria Ltd and was instrumental in securing an exploration licence for the company. In 1958, he became chairman of Holman Brothers, a company selling road-making and mining machinery. In the same year he became chairman of Motor Parts Industries Ltd, a joint venture with Italian partners. The following year he became chairman of Weide and Company, dealers in electronic and electrical equipment. Another company he was associated with was Foremost Dairies which was originally incorporated in Nigeria as the Swedish African Milk Company (SAMCO) in 1959. In addition, he was on the board of Embechem, a pharmaceutical company and British Insulated Callender Cables. Finally for fourteen years he was the owner of Aerocontractors, a private air-charter company, which he later sold to Michael Ibru of the Ibru Organisation.

Mobalaji Bank-Anthony was the founding father of the Nigerian-American Chamber of Commerce, creating the Nigerian-American Friendship Club in 1960.[46] He was chairman of the Lagos Stock Exchange for two terms and was chairman of the Federal Rehabilitation Appeal Board set up to assist Nigerians in the war-affected areas after the civil war. He was associated with the YMCA, the Boy Scouts of Nigeria and St John's Ambulance and was patron of many sporting organisations. He was a large scale philanthropist and built a N500,000 accident ward at the National Orthopaedic Hospital, Igbobi and funded a similar facility in honour of his mother at Lagos State General Hospital, Ikeja. He also endowed a fellowship in nephrology at the University of Ibadan and was awarded an honorary doctorate by the university.

Chief Shafi Lawal Edu

Chief Edu was the tenth child of Bale Edu of Epe, a devout Muslim.[47] His mother was a wealthy trader who had organised Epe's fishing industry. He was educated at Government Moslem School and Epe Government School.

In 1929, he joined the Unilever subsidiary, African Oil and Nuts. He then moved to Holland West Afrika Lines and remained between 1931 and 1946, becoming head manager. He was the sole agent in Epe, and then moved to Apapa, opening branches for the Line in Badagry, Warri and Sapele.

Shipping flourished but he noticed gaps in services available to shipping lines. He became a ship's chandler, supplying provisions to shipping lines. He was also a food contractor to the Nigerian army in Lagos.

Drawing on his experience of the shipping business, S. L. Edu and Sons became more broadly based. It entered the export trade and allied services sector. Chandling was expanded to include stevedoring and later, transport.

S. L. E. Transport Ltd became sole haulage contractor for British Petroleum in the Western Region. By 1950, the business included buying and exporting of timber, and a stake was taken in the Wata Timber Company, established in 1954. In 1960, he established the African Alliance Insurance Company (a life-insurance concern) in partnership with a German company, Munich Reinsurance, which offered him better terms than any British company.

He was the director of some ten companies, including Aluminium Manufacturing Company, Niger Petroleum Company, British Petroleum, Blackwood Hodge, Glaxo, Whessoe Engineering, Hademac, Brown Boveri, Nigeria Oil Refining Company and Palm Lines.

In 1949, Edu represented the colony in the review of Richards constitution. In 1951, he entered politics as a member of the Western House of Assembly, Epe Division (1951–6), he was a member of the House of Representatives (1952–4).

Sir Odumegwu Ojukwu

Odumegwu Ojukwu, one of the business leaders of his generation was the most outstanding of a group of transport magnates from Nnewi. Born in 1909, the son of a farmer, Odumegwu Ojukwu attended primary school in Asaba and secondary school at Hope Waddel College, Calabar.[48] He joined the Agricultural Department briefly as a produce inspector before going to Lagos to join John Holt as a junior sales clerk, dealing in tyres. It was during his time at Holts that his interest in transport was really aroused. He had established his own textiles-trading business at Onitsha and discovered how textile traders from the East were handicapped by lack of transport.

He left Holts to establish his own transport company in Lagos and purchased his first second-hand lorry in 1937. In the 1940s, he rapidly built up a large fleet of vehicles, with lorries, Buick station wagons, town limousines and buses that worked for the West African Airways Corporation. This was a time of economic expansion with great demand for transport. Ojukwu was able to supply transport for the Produce Control Board. In the early 1950s, he had over 200 vehicles and employed 600 persons, including 3 expatriate technicians. Meticulous attention to detail was one ingredient in his success. In his own words, he got up before the drivers to check the vehicles, look at their oil dipsticks and look under the vehicle himself. A passionate believer in the virtues of transport, he once organised a shop on wheels, believing that this was the way the African could defeat the overseas trader in Nigeria.

As a business leader of his generation, Ojukwu became vice-president of the Lagos Chamber of Commerce. He was also director of the Shell D'Arcy Petroleum Development Company, Costain (West Africa), Thomas Wyatt and Son (West Africa), the African Development Corporation, Lion of Africa Insurance Co., African Continental Bank, and others. His eldest sons trained in medicine, engineering and in the army and became directors of the transport company, Ojukwu Transport Ltd. His attempts to persuade his son, Odumegwu Ojukwu, who was to became military governor of the Eastern Region and leader of secessionist Biafra, to join his business failed. At one point he tried to induce him with the offer of an annual income in excess of £40,000, being the value of the allowances accruing from his company directorships.[49] At home, he was a trustee of the Nnewi and District Schools Association, patron and founder member of the Nnewi Patriotic Association, and patron of the Nnewi Community Hospital.[50] He financed the construction of the first post office in Nnewi in 1953.

In the mid-1950s the transport industry became increasingly competitive and Ojukwu started to shift his investments into property and industrial companies.[51] He also became heavily involved with government companies. He was on the board of the Nigerian Coal Corporation, the Nigerian National Shipping Line, the Eastern Region Marketing Board, the Motor Licensing Board, the Lagos Liquor Licensing Board, the Lagos and Ikoyi Prisons Visitors, the Public Relations Advisory Committee and the Nkalagu Cement Company. He did not diversify into other industries of his own. A plan to introduce steam ferries on the Niger river did not materialise.

Though never really an active politician, he studied politics closely, mediating between factions within the NCNC. Later he briefly gained a parliamentary seat having felt deprived as a businessman of the public acclaim and recognition that politicians enjoyed in this period.[52] With branches of his business in all parts of Nigeria, he believed strongly in strengthening Nigerian unity through the development of trade and commerce.

Sir Louis Ojukwu died in 1966 shortly before the Nigerian civil war. His estate, which included large properties and shareholdings, has been the subject of controversy.[53] His will was abandoned at Government House, Enugu, when the city fell to Federal troops. It was moved to Lagos and was subsequently lost. In a reconstituted will (1990), a memorial hospital is to be built at Nnewi and a memorial Education and Scholarship Trust Fund established.

Chief Francis Edo-Osagie[54]

Chief Edo-Osagie is descended from the Edogiawerie Osagie-Oloke family in Benin. His great-grandfather, Ogbomo, was the Okavbiogbe of Benin, and was in charge of land matters during the reign of Oba Osemwede (1816–47). His father joined the Forestry Department in 1902 and was known as 'Olakparaba', meaning 'rubber police'. He later became a farmer and died in 1921. Edo-Osagie entered the Baptist Primary School, Benin in 1925 when he was about eleven years old. He attended schools at Ifon and Sapele, and Baptist High School, Ibadan, where he enrolled for courses in book keeping and accountancy with a British correspondence college.

He returned to Benin in 1932 and took a variety of jobs, including transport clerk with Armels Transport Company at Benin, beach master with the produce merchants, Messrs S. Thomopolus at Ondo, newspaper sales agent with Duse Mohammed Ali, proprietor of the *Comet* (1940–2),[55] auditor with the Army Command Pay Office in Lagos (1942–6) and book keeper and assistant accountant with J. Allen and Co. at Aba where he opened their office in 1947.

While in the East, he saw the potential of the timber business in the Oguta, Owerri and Rivers area. He formed a partnership with M. I. Agbontaen and John Edokpolo[56] to export mahogony, Opepe, Iroko and Abura wood but the company folded when timber prices fell in 1952. On the advice of an expatriate bank manager, who allowed him credit, he stayed in the timber trade and registered his own company, F. E. Osagie and Sons. With the assistance of a visiting English timber broker, he discovered that large quantities of unsold mohogany at Abonnema, Ahoada, Owerri and Port Harcourt, which had been badly affected by toredo worms, could be dressed and the core saved. The export of this wood to the United Kingdom proved a very lucrative business and in conjunction with his agent, Austen Taylor & Co, the market was extended into Europe and the United States. The West Africa Conference Line declared a 5 per cent commission for shippers of timber which increased profits. At this time Edo-Osagie also ran a transport enterprise with a fleet of lorries which carried the name 'By the Grace of God'. In 1961 Osagie was elected vice-president of the Nigerian Timber Association. In this capacity, he successfully convinced the federal government that the export of Abura logs, which required less capital to exploit, should be reserved exclusively for Nigerians.

Port Harcourt, then known as the Garden City, experienced rapid growth in the early 1960s spurred on by the arrival of the Shell-BP Petroleum Development Company headquarters in 1961. As a successful timber merchant, Chief Edo-Osagie, or 'Franco', as he was popularly known, was at the centre of elite social life in the city. His home, 'Nigertimba House', became a meeting point for the business elite. His hallmark was his Cadillac, cigars and liberal use of champagne. Osagie was a leading member of the Recreation Club, the Rotary Club and the Port Harcourt Dining Club and he founded with Chief H. K. Offonry, his biographer, the Port Harcourt Friendship Society which drew together the different nationalities then flooding into Port Harcourt. Though a non-Easterner, he was invited by the Eastern Premier, Dr Michael Okpara, to be a member of the Leaders of Thought in the Eastern Region.

Chief Osagie's popularity and his refusal to become involved in partisan politics, attracted the attention of foreign companies and in 1962 he became an adviser to Shell-BP. The following year he and Alhaji Sanusi Dantata were appointed directors. He was already a director of Palm Line Agency, a division of UAC. He played a large role in overcoming various tensions that arose within Shell between Nigerian and expatriate staff, in breaking down strong suspicions about company operations and easing relations with host communities, regional and federal governments. Among the important issues were salary differentials and conditions of service, Nigerianisation and recruitment. There was, too, a serious mismatch in perceptions about job titles and actual responsibilities between a corporate entity like Shell and views prevalent in the civil service and in Nigerian society, which was highly status and title conscious. Titles and words would often speak louder than the responsibilities and decisions entailed in a position. Chief Osagie was instrumental in getting Nigerians redesignated from 'assistant' and 'supervisor' to managerial status, so that they did not lose respect in their dealings with civil servants and others in the wider society. When the outbreak of war shifted the centre of oil operations to Warri, Chief Osagie moved to Benin and again played a vital diplomatic role, communicating between the company, the Mid-Western State government and local communities. Shell's debt to, and affection for, Chief Osagie were vividly demonstrated when he left the board in 1984. A farewell party organised in his honour in London was attended by seven of the managing directors, who had chaired the board in his presence.

In Benin, Chief Osagie built the first modern hotel, the Motel Benin Plaza, a forty-bedroom chalet complex and established a large private art collection. A state-owned hotel quickly followed and he was given a ten-year contract to run it. The contract was terminated after two years, following a change in government. While in Port Harcourt, he had joined the board of the Nigerian Ports Authority and his involvement with parastatal bodies now increased. He became chairman of the Mid-Western Nigeria Development Corporation, but relinquished his position after two years because board policies and decisions were never complied with by members of the management. Other state agencies with which he was involved included the Bendel State Specialist Hospital Management Committee, the New Nigeria Bank, and the Bendel State Land Use amd Allocation Committee.

Alhaji Haruna Kassim

Alhaji Haruna Kassim was born in 1919 at Ringim, the birthplace of many successful Kano merchants.[57] His family were originally from Bornu. With the construction of the railway from Kano to Nguru, which was completed in 1939, Ringim became a collection centre for groundnuts and later tobacco and its prosperity was assured.

Young Haruna came to Kano in 1930 as a Koranic student (*almajiri*) and sought to support himself through work and begging. His aptitude was such that he gave up studies and became a shop boy with G. B. Ollivant. By 1939, he had become a messenger and was soon an agent distributing imported goods. Though not literate in western script, he was very shrewd and quickly accumulated commissions. By 1944, when only 25 years of age, he was of sufficient means and prominence to undertake the Hajj to Mecca by land through Chad and the Sudan. He was classified as wealthy by the tax authorities in 1948.

In 1948 he became an agent for the pilgrimage, joining Ibrahim Gashash and Mahmud Dantata to found the first well-organised pilgrimage agency – the West African Pilgrim Agency, better known as WAPA. In 1959 he broke away to establish his own agency, Hajj Air, with a controversial loan from the Northern Regional Development Corporation on which payments were delayed.[58] Haruna Kassim never specialised in traditional items of trade being an agent of foreign companies. He became a licensed buying agent and a transporter and was a founding member of the Kano Transport Syndicate. In the early 1970s he built the Kandara Palace Hotel, the first modern hotel in Kano to be owned by a local businessman.

Like many other wealthy merchants in Kano, he affiliated with the Tijaniyya brotherhood of Ibrahim Niass after the Senegalese scholar made his second visit to Kano in 1951. He built a Tijaniyya mosque near his shop in Fagge and sponsored the pilgrimage of many *mallams*, including the famous musician Mamman Shata. By the mid-1950s he had become involved in politics and in 1961 won a seat in the Northern House of Assembly for the Northern People's Congress (NPC). He allied himself closely with Ahmadu Bello, the Sardauna of Sokoto, supporting him in the crisis that led to the deposition of the Emir of Kano in 1963 and providing a bridge between the Sardauna and *mallams* in Kano.[59] In his case, participation in politics gave him access to licence and bank loans and appears to have been advantageous to business. Ill health and disenchantment with politics led him to withdraw from public view during the Second Republic.

Lawrence Omole

Lawrence Omole was born in Ilesha in 1915.[60] His father after a varied career, worked with the Railways and became a native Foreman Plate-Layer. Though he was a promising student, his primary education was not completed. His father could not afford the fees after retirement from the railways because his gratuity was wasted in an unsuccessful cattle trading venture. The family was forced into farming and from 1928 to 1935 he worked on his father's farm. He wanted to become an *osomaalo* trader but the family lacked the connections that would allow them to raise the initial capital.

Osomaalo, which means, 'I will sit until I have collected my money', was a term applied to aggressive Ilesha textile traders, who travelled outside Ilesha with their children and apprentices and sold textiles on an instalment basis, typically giving customers about three months to pay.[61] The trade was at its height in the 1920s and 1930s and involved a high proportion of male migrants. The aim was to get married, build a house, educate children and then come home to farm. The trade was strongest outside the cocoa belt in the northern savanna areas that were relatively poor and politically peripheral. As fixed retail outlets spread and trade became more diversified, so the opportunities for the *osomaalo* trade diminished. As a youth, Omole was impressed by the flamboyance of these traders, who would come home at Christmas and introduce new styles of dressing and house construction and decoration into the community.

After a short spell as a clerk with Nigerian and Lebanese shop owners, he became a produce clerk for Pa Aluko (1938–9) and then J. J. Ibironke (1939–44). While working with Ibironke, he made contact with N. K. Zard, an Ibadan-based, Lebanese cocoa trader who encouraged him to buy low-grade cocoa. This he successfully did out of hours, engaging a clerk of his own and selling cocoa to Zard. In 1944, he was transferred to become the produce manager of the Ijesha United Trading and Transport Company (IUTTC) which had been set up by some leading Ilesha business men. This attempt to pool resources was a failure. The enterprise was undercapitalised from the outset and suffered from the divided loyalties of the proprietors, each of whom was an agent of foreign companies to whom they were financially committed. According to Peel, joint enterprises like the IUTTC tended to be short lived.[62] They were plagued with managerial disagreements and divided responsibilities and the most capable and energetic of the individual partners gave their best efforts to their own projects.

In 1945, Omole left to become a produce depot buyer with the UAC. He successfully stockpiled cocoa against price rises, made large profits and purchased his first lorry in 1947. Attempts to purchase more lorries were frustrated by UAC, which did not want him to expand beyond certain predetermined limits. He therefore resigned his appointment and became a member of the Western Produce Traders Syndicate (WPTS) with five other partners between 1950 and 1953. In 1951 along with two other Ijesa produce traders, he was able to negotiate a loan for the development of a transport company from the Western Regional Development Loans Board (WRDLB) which had been established the previous year.[63] He started his own transport business, Omole Transport Service, on the Ilesha–Omuo–Ekiti and Ilesha–Ibadan routes in 1951. The company expanded to link Ilesha with the major towns of Ondo State and Oyo, Lagos and Onitsha. The WPTS met the same problems as the IUTTC, so he left in 1954, to start his own produce-buying company and was appointed a licensed buying agent. Later, the transport and produce ventures were merged to form Lawrence Omole and Sons Ltd. Omole joined local government in 1947, and stood unsuccessfully for election for the Action Group in 1956 and 1959. Politics was not viewed as a means of amassing wealth. It proved a drain on his resources and affected business adversely. He was able to expand business through bank loans (life insurance policy for £10,000 accepted as collateral) extending operations to Ife, Ekiti and Ondo. Only N. K. Zard in Ibadan could rival him in the cocoa markets. His success was partly due to payment of bonuses and cash advances, which attracted agents because it allowed them to speculate. He was younger and more flexible than most of his rivals. And his annual trade forecasts, which he provided without payment for Gill and Duffus, the London commodity brokers, proved more accurate than those of others. In 1957, he began to invest seriously in property, eventually establishing estates at Ilesha, Ile-Ife, Ibadan and Lagos.

He held a vision of an industrialised Ijeshaland and was concerned that the *osomaalo* tradition had not brought about permanent development at home. His first strategy, which was to get the Action Group government to bring industry to Ilesha, was frustrated by lack of political support for the party in the area. His second idea – planning and financing industry through an Ijesa Planning Council – was thwarted by the lack of enthusiasm of educated elements. His last solution, which was eventually successful, was to bring together a small group of wealthy individuals including I. O. Ajanaku, another Ijesa produce trader and transporter, and T. A. Oni, an Ibadan-based civil engineer.[64] It came to fruition in 1978 in the form of International Breweries Limited.

The brewery currently employs over 1,000 persons directly and has a network of over 1,000 distributors. *Osomaalo* traders came back home to invest their capital in beer distribution. There has been no retrenchment. There is a technical agreement with a German brewery. The high cost of imported capital equipment has constrained capacity to 500,000 hectolitres.

A farm was established for the production of maize and sorghum and a grains-processing plant set up. A plastics venture was established in 1983. In the same year, financial investments were consolidated in Cardinal Investments Ltd. They included shares in SCOA, Leventis Motors, Daily Times, Triplex and three banks. Trade in cocoa has continued and in 1987 the company was ranked sixth in terms of non-oil export earnings. The produce and transport company employed approximately 500 people.

The Dr Lawrence Omole Foundation was launched in 1985 by children and cousins. It has funded scholarships and the building of a library complex and health centre at the Oyo State College of Education. Omole gave financial assistance to both Christian and Muslim associations. Lawrence Omole did not seek chieftaincy titles, but was awarded an honorary doctorate by the University of Ife. He successfully supported his elder brother for the second-highest title in Ilesha, that of Obanla.

Of his many children, only three sons are actively involved in the family business. Omole attributes their reluctance to polygamy, with which he has become disenchanted. The urge to pursue business independently is even stronger with his wives than with the children. The root cause of this lack of involvement, he attributes to the fact that the business belongs, 'to everybody and therefore to nobody'.

POLITICIANS/BUSINESSMEN

Alhaji S. O. Gbadamosi[65]

Alhaji Gbadamosi was born in 1910. He was sent to school at the age of eight. His education was interrupted when his father withdrew him for fear of him becoming a Christian. He studied to standard 6 and then went out to work, taking responsibility for his brother's school fees. He secured employment with Karl Stark, a German importing company in 1934. In 1935, he started the Ikorudu Trading Company in partnership with his cousin, Alhaji R. A. Allison.[66] The first line of business was importing picture postcards from Germany, but Japanese goods had started to enter Nigeria at this time and he imported handkerchiefs, canvas shoes, electric bulbs, bicycles and wall clocks.

He became a major importer of underwear. Competition from the UAC, the largest importer, proved very strong, so he approached the company for distribution rights, but this was declined. He then decided to go into the manufacture of singlets. He imported sewing machines and established a small factory at Balogun Street in 1937 with 35 employees. Subsequently he moved to Apapa Road, Ebutte Metta, where he employed 200 persons. Employees were sent to Manchester for training. Three expatriate managers were employed. Knitting and weaving were added later.

A second industrial venture was the Ikorudu Ceramics Industries, a partnership with Alhaji Allison and Dr Akinola Maja. It started in 1948 with a loan of £20,000 from the Nigerian Local Development Board. This company was not successful. It was taken over by the Production Development Board in 1953 and closed down in 1960 after sustaining large losses. Alhaji Gbadamosi became the first Nigerian distributor for the Nigerian Tobacco Company after political pressure had been exerted on the company to appoint Nigerian distributors. Gbadamosi also rented a store in Balogun Street to the Guinness brewery. He subsequently became a member of the Guinness board, and then chairman. He was also a distributor for Nigerian Breweries and the Portland Cement Company. He was on the board of the Nigerian Railway Corporation and the Western Nigerian Development Corporation.

Gbadamosi's business career demonstrates a strong linkage between organised politics, economic nationalism and state patronage. Before World War II, he played an important role in the National Bank, and was a member of the Nigerian Youth Movement. During the war, he was a founder member of the Nigerian Association of African Importers and Exporters, which struggled to get a larger share of the wartime trade for Africans. In 1948, he was a member of the Commission of Enquiry into Conditional Sales which was the result of agitation against the trading practices of the

European merchant firms. He became a prominent member of the Action Group and acted as federal treasurer. From the regional house of assembly he was elected to the Federal House of Representatives. He was a partner in the National Investment and Properties Company, which was the main channel for Action Group funds between 1959 and 1961, along with Dr Akinola Maja, Chief S. O. Sonibare, and Alfred Rewane.

Chief Festus Sam Okotie-Eboh

At the time of Nigerian independence, Chief Okotie-Eboh was not only Nigeria's most colourful minister, he was also one of its wealthiest business-men.[67] He was born in 1912, son of a minor Itsekiri chief. After completing standard 6, his first position was that of assessment clerk for the Sapele township, followed by four years as a teacher in a Baptist primary school. In 1937, he joined the Warri branch of the Bata Shoe Company. He advanced in this company to become deputy manager of the regional office in Sapele by 1943. In this same year he launched the first of a string of five schools. He was appointed to the Sapele Township Advisory Board and the Warri Ports Advisory Committee.[68] In 1947, Bata sent their able young manager to Czechoslovakia for further training. The following year he returned with diplomas in business administration and chiropody. Soon afterwards, Okotie-Eboh struck out on his own in the timber and rubber trade. In 1951, he was elected to the Western Region House of Representatives and in 1954 to the Federal Parliament in Lagos. He was made Minister of Labour in 1955 and then minister of finance in 1957, a position he still held at the time of his assassination in January 1966. He was credited with attracting the Federal Government College to Warri and was instrumental in establishing the Koko port complex.[69]

Chief Okotie-Eboh's first wholly owned industrial venture was a rubber-creping factory opened in 1958. This, like the Omimi rubber and canvas shoe factory (opened in 1963), was run by a succession of hired expatriate managers. Despite the Ministry of Finance's much publicised excise of tax of 1964, which discriminated against competing leather and plastic footwear, Omimi never achieved profitability. There were quality-control problems and a succession of poor expatriate managers. Chief Okotie-Eboh could not devote much time to the plant and this was a recipe for disaster. In other ventures, the Mid-West Cement Company and Unameji Cabinet Works, management was provided by the co-investors, Cutinho Caro and Dissengoff, respectively. These co-investors were machinery-merchant firms who delivered turnkey projects financed by short-term supplier credits. The drawbacks of this type of investment, which became increasingly common in Nigeria after 1961, are well known. Problems with equipment and management, inflated costs and the creation of a substantial foreign debt were commonplace.[70] In 1967, not a single turnkey project was earning a profit.

Mrs Okotie-Eboh, the former manageress of her husband's schools, was also active in the business world, holding directorships in a number of overseas companies doing business in Nigeria.

CONCLUSION

With the exception of three individuals, all the business people we have considered had experience in trade early in their business careers. The three exceptions all concentrated on a single line of business (food processing, furniture and baking), after pursuing careers with government departments. The same pattern was true of the Ibadan-based civil engineer, T. A. Oni, who was with the Public Works Department for fifteen years before setting up his own construction company in 1945.[71] This confirms the proposition that a trading background tended to be associated with larger, more diversified enterprises. Although only one individual was primarily a transporter, five others also had transport interests, confirming the importance of transport as an area of indigenous accumulation. Among the larger businessmen, we see the beginnings of property and investment portfolios (Odutola, Ugochukwu, Ojukwu and Okotie-Eboh) that extended beyond area of origin to different parts of the Federation and in two cases (Odutola and Ojukwu), enterprises which were national in the scope of their operations. Share ownership and board membership in foreign companies started from around 1950.

We noted earlier that all individuals had primary education and five went on to secondary education. After schooling none went directly into business on their own account. Before 1960, the presence of persons with secondary schooling in private business was rare since government service was the preferred career. Pursuit of a career with a government department or as a teacher was the norm and this meant that the entry point for private business could be late. Exceptionally, Mr Ade Tuyo did not begin his business career until he was more than 50 years old.

Five persons had experience with one or more foreign companies (Unilever, Holland West Afrika Lines, John Holt, Patterson Zochonis, Karl Stark, Bata). Overall, this experience does not appear to have been crucial to subsequent success. Only two had prolonged experience with foreign companies that shaped their subsequent career (Edu and Okotie-Eboh). No fewer than nine concerns employed expatriates, while employment of senior Nigerian management from outside the family was extremely rare.

How far did the new opportunities brought about by the gradual shift in political power and economic nationalism – distributorships, licensed buying agencies, government loans, board membership of foreign companies and parastatals – effect patterns of accumulation? If distribution rights and agencies contributed to local commercial advances, the impact of other measures and responses was much less clear. Although four of the five persons we covered who took government loans used them successfully (Onyekwelu,

Fawehimni, Ade Tuyo, Omole), this is not an accurate overall picture. Others have shown that political considerations were paramount and that this led to waste and unproductive use of resources.

Board membership and shareholding in foreign companies and government agencies was an important attraction to business persons and professionals as the opportunities expanded in the 1950s and 1960s. How far such associations and the energies they absorbed, impeded the growth of indigenous companies is a question which is difficult to answer with any precision. The existence of these opportunities at a time when Nigerians were starting to set up corporate enterprises may have diverted energies away from the growth of their own enterprises and encouraged the growth of rentier activity.

While individual business fortunes may have become more dependent on political and state patronage in the 1950s, it would be an exaggeration to say that this became the only route to wealth or that all those who entered politics were primarily concerned to accumulate wealth. A few like Edo-Osagie avoided partisan politics altogether. Other businessmen who entered politics were independently wealthy before their entry. Entry into politics by businessmen did not necessarily lead to the greater accumulation of wealth. In no case, did it lead to the development of strong corporate enterprise. In the case of Okotie-Eboh, his enterprises flourished before his energies were absorbed by full-time politics. After entry into politics, his businesses were managed by expatriates and were altogether less successful. Alfred Rewane, the Action Group politician was later to adopt the strategy of promoting companies and leaving the management to foreign partners who had substantial shareholdings (see chapter 2). The success of Ayo Rosiji in business came after he had formally left the political arena (see chapter 4). Richard Sklar's assessment of Dr Nnamdi Azikiwe, the Eastern Region premier, seems appropriate to other businessmen who were independently wealthy before they entered politics. He argues that Azikiwe's political activities were not intended in any important or meaningful sense to increase his private wealth. On the contrary, he could have become much wealthier if the accumulation of wealth had been his major object.[72]

When individual careers or company histories are carried forward to the present day, a very mixed picture emerges. In the case of Ojukwu Transport and the late Chief Festus Okotie-Eboh, the original enterprises have gone and family disagreements over sharing the estates have arisen. In the case of S. L. Edu, S. O. Gbadamosi and the late C. T. Onyekwelu, highly trained sons (law, economics, accountancy) have pursued their own business careers in other directions. The specialist enterprises have either died or shown very modest growth. The larger groups founded by T. A. Odutola, M. Ugochukwu and L. Omole have survived, though it is too early to assess their long-term prospects.

4

LAGOS ENTERPRISES

In this chapter we examine the growth of enterprises and patterns of accumulation in Lagos. Some attention is also given to enterprises located in other centres in the western states like Sango Otta (Ogun State), Ibadan (Oyo State) and Ijebu-Ode (Ogun State). We start with a brief historical account of the economic development of Lagos in this century. The next section looks at the growth of a number of the larger business groups. There follows an account of more specialist enterprises. Finally, an ill-defined, though important, category of property investors, shareholders, financiers, consultants and intermediaries is considered. Two of the largest Lagos-based conglomerates, the Ibru Organisation and the Modandola Group, are examined separately at greater length in the following chapter.

THE GROWTH OF LAGOS

In this century, Lagos has experienced rapid population growth and commercial and industrial development. It was the capital of the Colony and then the nation. In 1967, it became capital of the newly created Lagos State. The total population of the metropolitan area grew from 267,407 in 1952 to 665,246 in 1963.[1] By 1988 the population stood at 6 million. In 1963, 73 per cent of the population were immigrants. A large majority of the population has always been Yoruba. The 1950 census found that 37 per cent of the population were locally born Yoruba, 37 per cent were Yoruba immigrants and only 26 per cent non-Yoruba immigrants.[2] All Yoruba sub-groups have been represented in this migration to Lagos. Historically the first to come were freed slaves. They were followed by Egba migrants, then by Ijebu and people from Oyo. By 1968 only 16 per cent of the population of the metropolitan area were non-Yoruba.[3]

Lagos Island, which in early colonial days served as the seat of government, and as the residential and commercial centre, has remained the main centre for large-scale commerce and finance. The Yaba district on the mainland, which was planned as a residential area for colonial servants, attracted a number of African enterprises in the late 1940s and early 1950s. Among them were the West African Pilot, John Okwesa Printers, Lisabi Mills, Pacific Printers, Ojukwu Transport, Fawehinmi Furniture and Biney Zoo. Hotels (Ambassador and Niger Palace) and nightclubs were run by Lebanese. Around the time of independence, the more affluent residents of Yaba started moving beyond Lagos Island to Ikoyi. Ikoyi, and later Victoria Island, developed as residential areas for the government and business elite. Recently, the banking boom has led to banks and other financial institutions spilling on to Victoria Island.

The greater Lagos area in 1964 accounted for over 37 per cent of value added and 35 per cent of employment in large-scale industry.[4] It was the policy of the former Western Region government to attract industry to the Ikeja industrial estate near Lagos. By 1975 these figures had risen to 69 per cent and 43 per cent respectively, implying that productivity was growing faster in Lagos than elsewhere. In the last two decades, industry has expanded beyond the older industrial areas of Apapa port and Ikeja into new industrial estates encouraged by the new expressways to Badagry and Isolo. Industry has also been attracted to Sango Otta in Ogun State where land has been relatively cheap.

Among the reasons for the attraction of Lagos were economic incentives which favoured industries using imported raw materials and the port location. Three-quarters of the total import and export trade, excluding petroleum, went through the Lagos ports. There was, too, the large size of the local market and the fact that Port Harcourt, the other comparable location, suffered severe war damage and was slow to attract new industry after the civil war. The close proximity of Lagos has tended to draw large scale private investment away from other centres in Yorubaland. The passing of Ibadan as a regional capital has also increased the attractions of Lagos as a business centre for Ibadan and Oyo people. Apart from the early investment by the Odutola brothers and private investment in saw milling, it was state agencies that undertook most of the major investment outside Lagos in the late colonial and early independence periods. It was not until the latter half of the 1970s that many new private industries were established.[5] There was then a pause until a number of agro-industrial investments were initiated in the early 1990s.

Four African groups were active in the commercial development of Lagos at the turn of the nineteenth century.[6] First, there were Afro-Brazilian emigrants who had purchased their freedom from slavery. Second, there were liberated slaves from Sierra Leone and their descendants, known as Saros, from whom most of the prosperous indigenous merchants came including members of the Chamber of Commerce. The third group of merchants were the indigenes among whom were the white cap chiefs, the traditional landowners of Lagos. Under the *baba isale* system of clientship, some of the chiefs acted as the trading customer, commercial representative or broker for hinterland communities. The last group were the immigrant traders and merchants from Egba, Ijebu, Ibadan/Oyo, Ilesha and Ondo.

Kristin Mann gives a detailed picture of the rise of a Lagos merchant, Taiwo Olowo, who came from lowly origins in the hinterland to build up great power and wealth during the second half of the nineteenth century.[7] Taiwo was an archetypal Big Man with a large following of dependents, great fame, and influence with the British. He was a trader in palm oil, palm-oil plantation owner, urban property owner, money lender and occasional supplier of guns. He also acted as an intermediary in the supply of goods for hinterland towns. After the annexation of Lagos by the British, he took advantage of land grants from the Crown, and new legal provisions which underpinned the development of individual land ownership and a market in real estate. Under a dual system of land tenure, individual ownership came to coexist with communal ownership in the hands of indigenous descent groups. As a result, rights in land were not always well defined and claims to property were often disputed. Taiwo had the resources to employ the best lawyers to protect his interests in the courts.

Taiwo was able to build up a large urban property holding. Land was crucial to his accumulation strategy in many ways. His own land was mortgaged as security for advances of cash and goods from European companies which he used to buy palm oil. Taiwo also registered over eighty properties mortgaged to him to guarantee the loans he made. Mortgages and debt gave him power over people and increased his large following. Property was used for stores and warehouses and to house his dependents and slaves. He also rented land and buildings to European firms thus joining the ranks of the Lagos rentier class towards the end of the nineteenth century. The fourth generation of his family still derives considerable income from this property today.

Other merchants, sometimes of slave or external origin, who were able to build up individual property holdings, created family property at their death by means of wills which entailed the estate to all their descendants.[8] The most affluent might attempt to create a corporate land-holding entity and establish individual rights in land through bequests to children and friends. Apart from underpinning credit relations between merchants, property also provided more economic continuity and psychological security than did trading; sudden reversals of fortune among the Lagos merchant class were common.

As we saw in chapter 2, independent merchants came under pressure towards the end of the nineteenth century from expatriate competition. Some merchants were able to acquire land for the production of cocoa in the 1890s at Agege on the outskirts of Lagos. The Agege Planters Union, formed in 1909, was dominated by about a dozen large farmers headed by J. K. Coker who had 1,500 acres.[9] Farming, the management of family property and professional careers were combined. Under economic pressure, the attractions of formal education and careers in the professions and the colonial administration increased. Lagosians were the first to become involved in white-collar occupations in the colonial administration.

Among the wealthier families, income from urban properties could be used to fund higher education and lengthy professional training, often overseas. Law was especially popular as a means to manage property and to protect and secure land rights, which were often under threat of litigation. Land litigation was an important source of fee income and lawyers sometimes acquired land from their clients in lieu of monetary payment. The land issue led lawyers into the political arena and formed the legal profession into an economic interest group.[10] The attractions of the professions (law, medicine, accountancy, insurance, banking, real estate, architecture and real estate) have persisted and it is from a base in professional practice that some have built up wealth since the 1950s by creating substantial investment portfolios in shares and property and by extending their interests in corporate business.

Throughout this century, the attractions of land-owning and property development in Lagos have scarcely diminished, though with new opportunities to earn income and reduce risk, the economic linkage between trading and property holding is less central than it was to the merchant class at the turn of the century. Community and family interest in land remains strong and a sentimental attachment to land underscores a tendency to maintain holdings and to lease property rather than sell. Otherwise impecunious families have tried to develop their plots in Lagos with financial assistance from outside parties. Wealthier families have been able to consolidate their plots and develop them or create private estates. In economic terms, land is a relatively secure investment acting as an inflationary hedge. The annual income obtained from rental property could be seen as a 'retirement plan'. The return on real estate in Lagos in the early 1960s was estimated at 10–35 per cent, considerably higher than in other urban centres.[11] It could be greater than this when up to five years rental payments were paid cash in advance in the select Ikoyi area of Lagos.[12] Property could be used as a base from which to diversify into areas of higher risk and as a collateral for bank and trade credit. The benefits of land ownership and property development are not only economic. Sandra Barnes in her study of Mushin shows how land ownership has given high status and provided the initial base for political advancement.[13]

The process of land reclamation and allocation of plots by government to the rich and powerful has been a systematic feature of Lagos property development since the late colonial period. Land reclamation has continued with the infamous bulldozing of Maroko (now known as Victoria Island extension), the displacement of slum dwellers and the opening-up of the Lekki peninsula beyond Victoria Island. Profits from banking and insurance have been used to invest in private estate development at Lekki.

In the 1970s the oil boom and more recently the banking boom acted to fuel property prices at the top end of the market. In the early 1980s professionals (architects, quantity surveyors, town planners and real-estate agents) began to move into private property development as the number of state contracts dwindled. Thus real-estate surveyors, who acted as letting agents, set up property development companies, and approached banks and insurance companies for finance. These individuals were often members of Lagos land-holding families.

The attractions of land ownership and property in Lagos and the access it gave to credit for trading, weakened the incentives for Lagosians and Yoruba immigrants to move into other economic activities. In respect of property ownership, a survey of residential areas in Lagos in 1960 showed that Lagosians were strongly represented, followed by the Egba and the Ijebu.[14] Although Igbo immigrants in Lagos were numerically larger than each of the latter groups, the Igbo had surprisingly little property in Lagos, contrary to popular beliefs. It was in other urban centres – Port Harcourt, Calabar, Jos and Kano – that most of the Igbo investment in property was located.

Outside Lagos, it was Ijebu people who were commercially dominant in Yorubaland during the colonial period. Akeredolu-Ale has advanced historical and geographical reasons for this dominance.[15] Strategically located on the boundary with Colony Province, they were able to take advantage of the blockade of the produce trade which Ibadan/Oyo farmer entrepreneurs were carrying on with Lagos. Through military force, they succeeded in reserving to themselves the role of middlemen in the trade between coast and hinterland. Three entrepôts – Epe, Ejinrin and Ikorudu – were located in Ijebuland. Thus they had stronger economic incentives to pursue commercial ventures than did other Yoruba groups. The Ijebu were not prominently involved in cash crop farming and clerical occupations were deprecated for a longer period than in other parts of Yorubaland. They preferred to trade as middlemen and use their transport to evacuate produce over a wide area of Yorubaland. They traded directly with Iseyin cloth producers and settled in large numbers in Ibadan acquiring substantial properties and becoming in some cases, landlords to indigenes.

Ijebu commercial dominance was not later translated into a dominant position in larger-scale enterprises in Lagos in the 1960s. Akeredolu-Ale from his work on larger wholly owned indigenous enterprises in Lagos in the late 1960s, argued that Ijebu dominance was already eroded by other sub-groups.[16] According to him, the Ijebu displayed less ambition and aggression and less organisational ability than businessmen from other Yoruba sub-groups and were slow to take up new opportunities in manufacture. They also exhibited extreme reluctance to delegate authority to others and showed a tendency to reserve leadership and direction of enterprises to blood relations, especially sons. Ayandele takes a contrary view, arguing for Ijebu economic ascendancy.[17] Although my own work did not systematically address the issue, it suggests that Ijebu are well represented in larger Lagos enterprises, though in no sense dominant. In Akeredolu-Ale's work, Lagosians were only slightly represented in the entrepreneurial group, a picture confirmed in my own work (see Table 4.1). People from the ethnically heterogeneous state of Bendel, on the other hand, were relatively well represented among the business groups in Lagos.[18] A survey of 164 of the largest manufacturing enterprises undertaken in 1965, before the departure of the Igbo, found Yoruba ownership of 128 enterprises (78 per cent), with Igbo 23 (14 per cent) and Bini 8 (5 per cent).[19]

BUSINESS GROUPS

We now turn to look at the origins and growth of some of the larger Lagos business groups (see Table 4.1). The profiles are presented by age of birth of the founder. The inclusion of enterprises in this table is not meant to indicate equivalence in terms of size or wealth; a few enterprises, which have virtually disappeared with the death of the founder, are included for the historical record. Some business trajectories are like shooting stars that burn brightly on ascent, only to fade quickly with age, a turn to religious activities and family demands on the estate. Lawsons Corporation, was created by a former chairman of Lagos City Council, who established a brewery. Chief Henry Fajemirokun, the founder of the Henry Stephens Group, had a very high profile as a business leader before his death in 1978. The Folawiyo Group has specialised in cement importation and shipping. The next case, the Okada Group, has extensive property interests and owns the largest private airline in Nigeria. The Doyin Group under Prince Adedoyin has emerged from a start in petty trade to become a significant industrial investor and property owner.

The section ends with profiles of four younger groups, which have emerged since 1970. Chief M. K. O. Abiola, chief executive of the Concord Group, is probably the most high-profile businessman in Nigeria. His image has coloured popular perceptions of the Nigerian business tycoon. His case shows how an individual can bargain effectively with a multinational company. The Honeywell Group developed a strong trade in baker's yeast during the oil boom and subsequently diversified into a mini-conglomerate. Devcom Group originated from trade and construction during the late 1970s and has developed a strong presence in banking, property and oil exploration. The South Atlantic Seafood Company (SASCO) has grown rapidly since 1985 with interests in shipping, vegetable-oil processing and light engineering.

TABLE 4.1: Lagos-based groups.

Name	Owner	Birth	Origin	Start	Initial business	Major activities
Lawsons Corporation	Adeyemi Lawson	1924	Yoruba (Egba)	1964	Beer brewing	Brewing, real estate, insurance
Ugochukwu Group	M. N. Ugochukwu	1926	Igbo (Umunze)	1951	Import/transport	Foam, biscuits, trading, insurance
Henry Stephens	Henry Fajemirokun	1927	Yoruba (Ondo)	1958	Import/export	Import/export, agencies
Folawiyo Group	Yinka Folawiyo	1928	Yoruba (Lagos)	1957	Import/export	Cement import, shipping, poultry, fishing
Ashamu Group	E. O. Ashamu	1929	Yoruba (Oyo)	1954	Pharmacy	Real estate, agro-industry
Ibru Organisation	Michael Ibru	1932	Urhobo	1956	Import frozen fish	Conglomerate
Modandola Group	Bode Akindele	1932	Yoruba (Ibadan)	1956	Import/export	Conglomerate
Odogwu Group	Sonny Odogwu	1932	Igbo (Asaba)	1953	Insurance broker	Property, packaging, insurance
Gicen Group	G. I. C. Eneli	1932	Igbo (Obosi)	1970	Investment services, insurance brokerage	Computer agencies, food & beverage engineering, chemicals trade
Hamza Holdings	G. N. Hamza	1934	Hausa (Kano)	1948	Retail trade	Import/export
Okada Group	G. Igbinedion	1934	Bini	1968	Motor distribution	Real estate, airline, shipping
Doyin Group	S. O. Adedoyin	1935	Yoruba (Kwara)	1950	Retail trade	Property, banking, detergents, agro-industry, pharmaceuticals
Alexander Ajanaku Holdings	Dr A. Ajanaku	1936	Yoruba (Ilesha)	1975	Medical practice	Medical practice, fast food, plastics/fibre glass, real estate, publishing
Concord Group	M. K. O. Abiola	1937	Yoruba (Egba)	1971	Telecommunications	Telecommunications, farming, publishing, oil exploration
Desam Group	Dr E. J. Amana	1938	Oron	1972	Consulting engineer	Engineering services, rubber production and processing, property
Eleganza Group	R. A. Okoya	1940	Yoruba (Kwara)	?	Retail trade	Plastics, ceramics, property
Imesco Enterprises	Dr Ime Umanah	1943	Annang	1963	Retail trade	Import/export, BMW agency, farming, banking, publishing
Honeywell Group	Oba Otudeko	1944	Yoruba (Ijebu)	1975	Import foodstuffs	Trading, flour milling, construction, plastics, fishing, security services
Devcom Group	Mike Adenuga	1953	Yoruba (Ijebu)	1978	Importing	Banking, property, agro-industry, oil exploration
Onwuka Interbiz	Onwuka Kalu	1955	Igbo (Abiriba)	1972	Importing	Trading, engineering, banking
Dangote Group	Aliko Dangote	1957	Hausa (Kano)	1976	Importing	Commodity trade, property, fishing, banking, cotton ginning and textiles
SASCO	I. K. Olu Fashanu	1958	Yoruba (Okpe)	1985	Wholesaling & shipping	Shipping, agro-industry, engineering

Sources: Interviews; company directories; newspapers.

Older Groups
Lawsons Corporation (Nig.) Ltd

Chief Adeyemi Lawson (1924–93) was educated at Baptist Academy, Lagos (1931–5) and CMS Grammar School, Lagos (1936–41).[20] He studied law in London (1945–8) and then engaged in private legal practice (1948–64). He was chairman of Lagos Town Council (1954–60) and the Lagos State Development Board and became president of the Lagos Chamber of Commerce and Industry (1975–9).

His first step into corporate business was as a pioneer shareholder of the Bank of Lagos (1958–64) which ended in failure with poor management. He founded West African Breweries Ltd, Abeokuta, in 1964, taking 30 per cent of the equity alongside the Western Region Development Corporation (30 per cent), Dizengoff (20 per cent), German technical partners (10 per cent) and A. G. Leventis (10 per cent) to assist with distribution. After a difficult start, the operation proved successful after some capital reconstruction. North Brewery was established in Kano as a venture with the federal government. Associated Breweries was established in Lagos and on the Agbara Industrial Estate in 1977. Both the Lagos and Kano breweries have closed. Investment in advertising and distribution may not have been sufficient to sustain a competitive position.

The Agbara estate covering 450 hectares with 27 factories and a residential area was originally promoted by Chief Lawson in the mid-1970s as part of larger landholding. When Ogun State was created in 1976, there was controversy and the state government took over the whole area, including the estate. After 15 months of negotiation, the state government decided to grant Chief Lawson half of the property for a lease of 99 years.

Other interests include insurance (Grand Union Insurance 1979), advertising (Grant Advertising), and investments in Metal Box Toyo Glass, Pharma-Deko (formerly Park Davis), Ecobank, and in SOFAM (Dakar,Senegal)

Chief Lawson introduced the Grail Movement to Nigeria. In later years, a considerable amount of his time and money was invested in this religious movement. From 1970, a large estate called Grailland was developed at Iju suburb, Agege.

Henry Stephens Group of Companies

Chief Henry Fajemirokun (1927–78) was born in Ile-Oluji, Ondo State and educated at Ondo Boys High School and CMS Grammar School, Lagos. He left college at the age of 18 to join the West African Frontier Force and served in India.[21] He then joined the Post and Telegraph Department in Lagos where he studied privately for the Cambridge School Certificate. He became a leading figure in the trade-union movement, becoming president-general of the Nigerian Civil Service in 1957, a post he held until 1968. He represented labour on the board of the Electricity Corporation of Nigeria

(1957–60) and served as a member of the Salaries Review Commission for Western Nigeria (1959).

After he had developed his import/export business in the 1960s, Chief Fajemirokun became prominent in the Lagos Chamber of Commerce of which he was president from 1971 to 1975. During the Gowon regime he was a leading exponent of the Economic Community of West Africa (ECOWAS) and was President of the Federation of West African Chambers of Commerce (1972–8). He achieved a very high profile during this period both in Nigeria and in London. When, for example, foreign investors expressed disquiet over the second phase of the indigenisation exercise, it was Chief Fajemirokun who went to London to reassure western interests. Together with Sir Adam Thompson, chairman of British Caledonian, he was instrumental in founding the Nigeria-British Chamber of Commerce in 1977.[22]

In 1958 Chief Fajemirokun started an import/export company, exporting cow bones, shea nuts, hides and skins, rubber and coffee. In 1960 the company was the first to import cement on a large scale from cheap sources of supply like Egypt and Poland. Importation was arranged through London using 90-day credit facilities. The company was to remain a large-scale importer of cement for many years. The importation of construction machinery and mechanical equipment was started. The assembly of cement mixers began in 1970.

On the export side, the company became an exporter of cocoa for the Nigerian Produce Marketing Company. Rubber and palm kernels were also shipped. In 1969 a commodity brokerage was opened in London and a seat obtained on the London Commodity Exchange.

In 1962 Nigerian Maritime Services (NMS) was formed with an expatriate partner who had assisted him with the export of commodities. This company pioneered the household packaging and removals business in Lagos and got custom from embassies. The company also developed clearing and forwarding and took shipping agencies. In 1968 two companies were hived off from NMS – Nigmarship Agencies which chartered vessels for the cement and cocoa trade and the Nigerian Shipping Company which bought its first ship in 1970. The latter company went into partnership with the East Asiatic Company (49 per cent) which finally withdrew in 1979. The Nigerian South American line was opened during the 1970s to take advantage of the increase in trade between Nigeria and Brazil.

A number of other ventures took off in the late 1960s. In 1967 Afro-Electro Konsult was set up to represent an American telecommunications company, with his cousin, an engineer, in charge. A trading company, the Adriatic Company, was acquired and became a small property company. Gilco, an Apapa-based company with a number of important agencies was acquired from an Englishman who was retiring. The company specialised in electrical equipment and radar repair for the navy and held agencies for GEC, Marconi and Hawker Siddeley. Chief Fajemirokun was also active in setting up Marine and General Assurance with Chief Akin George, Michael Ibru, Adeyemi Lawson and Chris Ogunbanjo. Finally an attempt was made to go into oil exploration with an American partner. Investment was undertaken but oil was not found in commercial quantities.

In the 1970s, shares were acquired in a number of companies. An attempt was made to buy out the foreign stake (46 per cent) in the Daily Times of Nigeria.[23] The stake was held by IPC of United Kingdom and had to be divested as part of the indigenisation exercise. The deal was successfully opposed by Babatunde Jose, chairman and managing director of Daily Times, who gained the support of Allison Ayida and General Gowon. He argued that it would be undesirable for such a large stake to be held by a single individual. Both the Daily Times and Henry Stephens were in negotiation with Rank Xerox, the American multinational which wanted to invest in Nigeria. The two local companies could not agree on terms for holding the 40 per cent local stake. Eventually the Daily Times withdrew leaving Henry Fajemirokun with a 40 per cent share. Other large shareholdings were taken in Johnsons Wax, Fan Milk and two construction companies.

When Chief Fajemirokun died in 1978 a number of ventures were in the pipeline. They included a truck-assembly plant, a brewery, fishing, hotels and a bank. The truck assembly and brewery were both planned for a 84-hectare site at Oke-Igbo, Ondo State. No licence was approved for the assembly venture with Daf of Holland and an agency for Steyr vehicles which planned to build trailer bodies was overtaken by Steyr's decision to build their own plant in Bauchi. With the exception of the Nigerian American Merchant Bank, none of these ventures materialised following the death of Chief Fajemirokun. This demonstrated how far the success of the initiatives was dependent on the founder and his ability to deal with government.

After Fajemirokun's death, Professor Ayo Ogunsheye became managing director of the Group. He had joined the company in 1970 from the Department of Extra-Mural Studies at the University of Ibadan. His recruitment was one of the first examples of a senior Nigerian professional joining an indigenous company. Other senior Nigerian recruits included the chief executive of the Nigerian National Shipping Line who joined in 1971 and the Chief Accountant at Beechams who became chief financial controller in 1977.[24] Expatriates were also recruited and numbered about 10 at the peak of their employment.

The Group was very closely associated and identified with the founder and it suffered a sharp setback with his sudden death. His son, 'Dele Fajemirokun who had gained some business experience with Bank of America and Bhojsons was appointed Group executive director. He has developed his own business interests independently of the Group which is owned by twelve children who share the estate. The corporate structure and divisions of the Group have not altered since 1978.

The Yinka Folawiyo Group of Companies

This group of companies owned by Alhaji Chief W. I. Folawiyo, the Baba Adini of Nigeria, is involved in international trade and shipping and has assets in excess of N400m.

Yinka Folawiyo was born in 1928, the son of Lagos merchant. He was educated at Olowogbowo Methodist School, Lagos and Ilesha Grammar School before becoming a management trainee with the United Africa Company (1947–9).[25] He joined Socony Vacom Oil (now Mobil Oil) setting up his own import and export company in 1957. In 1958 Alhaji Folawiyo visited Eastern Europe and was the first Nigerian to develop strong trading ties with the Eastern Bloc.[26] Sugar and cement were imported from the former USSR. Trade links were extended to Bulgaria and Romania and commodities imported included bagged cement, fertilisers and food items. A company was formed in 1967 to charter ships and it became a carrier of cocoa, palm kernels and groundnuts for the Nigerian Produce Marketing Company.

In 1972 a shipping company was founded (Nigerian Green Lines) and in 1975 a regular liner service between Europe and Nigeria was inaugurated. The size of the fleet has fluctuated between six general cargo vessels with a total of 87,800 tons dead-weight (1979) to a single vessel in 1990. The company was accorded the status of a national carrier by the federal government and became a member of two conference lines. An agency based in London was opened in 1975 for purchasing, chartering and ship management and Alhaji Folawiyo became a member of the Baltic Exchange.

Investment was undertaken in lighterage facilities (Marine and International Lighterage Ltd) and a transport fleet. N40m. was invested in a deepwater berth for the Nigerian Spanish Cement Company (1976). This company is a joint venture with Hispacement Co. of Spain and forecasts a turnover of N180m. in 1991. Overseas investment includes the West Afrika Holland Trading Company of Antwerp founded in 1973, which has 800 metres of warehouse facilities. A stake was also taken in the Allied Arab Bank in London in 1977.[27]

During the 1970s the group diversified into property (1971) and construction (1977). Further attempts were made to diversify away from international trading and shipping in the 1980s. A rice-farming venture with the Rivers State government and the federal government, which acquired 6,000 hectares of land, failed. An integrated poultry complex costing N50m. has been established at Ilora, Oyo State and another unit is scheduled for the Lekki peninsula.[28] A fishing company with four trawlers started operations in 1990 and a merchant bank, Marina International Bank, was launched in the same year. Other investments were made in two banks, in a construction company (G. Cappa), in plastics, aluminium, and insurance.

The Group remains a family business closely controlled by the founder who has brought in some members of the family. Alhaji Folawiyo made large contributions in excess of N20m. towards the construction of Lagos Central Mosque and is chairman of its executive council.

The Okada Group

This Group has assets conservatively estimated at N500m. and includes the largest private airline in Nigeria.

Chief Igbinedion, the Esama of Benin, was born in 1934.[29] His father was a road builder in the Public Works Department and his mother traded in smoked fish. He completed primary education in Benin in 1944 and then spent three years buying rubber and timber near Benin. He also assisted an uncle in block moulding.

In 1955 he returned to Benin and was employed as a messenger in the Adult Education Department. He then joined the police force (1958–64). It was during this period that he met an English lady, a school principal, whom he married. His parents-in-law in the United Kingdom were to assist his business ventures through introductions in England and his wife negotiated on his behalf.

From 1964 to 1968 he worked for Leventis Motors becoming a Sales Manager. In 1968 he established Mid-Motors (Nig.) Ltd. His wife negotiated bank loans for the enterprise. The company assembled Hino trucks during the oil-boom period but by the end of the decade it had contracted drastically. A soft-drinks venture, Okada Bottling Company was begun in 1977 with technical assistance from Canada Dry. Okada Airlines began operations in 1983 after four years of spot charters and by 1993 operated 32 aircraft. Chief Igbinedion also promoted Crown Merchant Bank which began operations in Lagos in 1988.[30]

The real-estate portfolio of the Group is very large with four estates in Benin where the properties of deceased Bini chiefs have also been acquired. There are properties in Lagos, Ibadan, Jos, London and New York. A vast estate, Okada Wonderland, has been built near Benin and was absorbing a quarter of the group earnings while under construction. Over 1,500 houses were planned together with a church, golf course, swimming pool and tennis courts. The Igbinedion Hospital and Medical Research Centre is located on the estate.

Chief Igbinedion's limited education has had political consequences. While his ambitions extended beyond the governorship of Bendel State, his lack of education precluded running for the Presidency. He has therefore supported his sons' political careers. His eldest son failed in his bid for the Bendel governorship in 1992. A patron of the National Party of Nigeria during the

Second Republic, Chief Igbinedion's political motto is 'Any government in power'.

Doyin Group of Companies

Prince Dr Samuel Adedoyin was born in 1935 at Agbamu, Kwara State.[31] He was educated to standard 4 and at the age of 14 he started petty trading in Lagos with £48. He later moved into importation, concentrating on handbags and umbrellas.

In 1968 Doyin Investments Nig. Ltd was established. This was a labour-intensive industry making travel goods (suitcases, wallets and purses). During the 1970s it employed up to 500 persons. In 1969 he established Doyin Motors representing Volvo. Later Starco was founded to distribute Peugeot motors. A third investment in the 1970s was in the assembly of electronic goods. The factory employed 200 persons and closed in 1985. A fishing venture with Polish partners failed.

In the 1980s the Group attempted to invest in areas with more stable demand that were less vulnerable to changes in industrial policy. There are no joint ventures and expatriates are not employed. Industries were chosen in areas where Nigerians could readily be trained. Industries include mat manufacture (1984), grits for beer making (1985), soap and detergents (1984), pharmaceuticals (injectibles) (1989) and cosmetics (toothpaste, vaseline, body cream in 1990). Global Soap and Detergent Industries located at Ilorin with an investment of N200m., employs over 700 persons. It is the only sizeable indigenous competitor for foreign firms like Lever Brothers and Patterson Zochonis.

The Group has a large property portfolio. This is a major area of investment and provides a secure base. From its beginnings with a trading premises in Idumota and the first house in Mushin, the property portfolio has been steadily upgraded through areas like Ikeja and Surulere until it covers the prime residential areas of Victoria Island and Ikoyi.

Other investments have been made in 7Up, Metoxide, and include a controlling interest in a merchant bank. An office for investment in London was established and an expatriate employed.

Philanthropy for the Agbamu community includes provision of a 50-bed hospital, electricity and water supply, and a post office. Educational endowment funds have been given to the Univeristy of Ilorin, Kwara State Polytechnic and Kwara State College of Education.

Younger Groups (Post-1970)

The Concord Group

Bashorun M. K. O. Abiola is probably the most high-profile businessman in Nigeria. His image has coloured popular perceptions of the Nigerian business tycoon as an individual engaged in a constant round of contract making and philanthropy with access to the highest levels of the state. He has combined business with large-scale philanthropy and holds over 140 titles across the country including Aare Ona Kakanfo ('Generalissimo') of Yorubaland. In the manner of an archetypal 'Big Man', wealth is converted into political capital; the legendary flow of philanthropy constantly replenishes his following, advances his reputation, and keeps his name in the public eye. His business operations and style are not intelligible without an appreciation of his political ambitions. As a leading member of the National Party of Nigeria during the Second Republic, he failed to secure the party's nomination as presidential candidate for the 1983 elections. In 1993 he won the presidential elections for the Social Democratic Party, securing an overall majority in 19 states and Abuja, only to have victory denied him by a military government that annulled the elections. His successful campaign was populist and was fought on the theme of a promise to do away with poverty. Abroad, his publishing interests, philanthropy, Pan African position and political activity have ensured considerable publicity. He gave assistance to President Museveni before he came power in Uganda[32] and mounted a campaign for reparations from the West for the costs inflicted on Africa by the slave trade.

The twenty-third child of his father's three wives, he grew up to become the first surviving child.[33] His mother, a kolanut trader, provided support for his early education. At the age of 9 he was trading in firewood at Abeokuta to support the family. After one year he had saved enough money to hire *tanioroko*, an old military Austin lorry sold by tender after World War II. Business expansion was cut short by resistance from villagers where the firewood was collected.

At 14 he entered the Baptist Boys High School, Abeokuta (1951–6). Here he encountered pressure on him to convert to Christianity.[34] He countered that his father had sent him to come and read books and not to change his religion. His fees were not paid, but he was kept at school because of his strong academic performance. During this period he established an *agidigbo* orchestra, Kashy Mambo Orchestra, to entertain at social functions in Abeokuta. His one-third share of total income gave him savings of over £700. Through school he gained connections and a thorough knowledge of the Christian educated elite of Yorubaland. General Obasanjo, who was to become head of state, followed a year behind him at the Baptist Boys High School.

After school he had a spell as a bank clerk before obtaining a Western Region scholarship to study abroad.[35] He studied accountancy at the University of Glasgow (1961–3) and completed his professional qualifications in three years with distinction in all papers. He returned home in 1966 with the intention of joining Guinness, the multinational brewer. He encountered discrimination against Nigerian senior staff and opted instead for the post of accountant with Lagos University Teaching Hospital. He then joined Pfizer Products Ltd, the American pharmaceutical multinational and was given considerable managerial authority. He was involved in building a feed-mill plant in Kumasi, Ghana. But the bar on holding shares in the company rankled him and he resented the 'perpetual status of a bridesmaid'. He therefore left to set up independently as a chartered accountant. However, he soon responded to an advertisment asking for a first class chartered accountant in Africa and found out at the third and final interview in New York that he was being recruited by the International Telephone and Tele-graph Corporation (ITT). He joined ITT as comptroller in 1969.[36] This proved to be the turning point in his career.

The federal government had owed ITT £3.5m. for telecommunications equipment for three and a half years. Abiola's first assignment was to collect this debt. Early one morning he confronted Lt.-Col. Murtala Mohammed, Inspector of Signals, who had just returned from the war front. The Chief of Staff, Army, Brigadier Usman Katsina found them arguing and Alhaji Yusuf Gobir, Permanent Secretary, Ministry of Defence was called in. Even-tually payment was made. Armed with the cheque, Abiola flew to London and was able to oust the expatriate managing director of ITT Nigeria. He also requested a 50 per cent shareholding in ITT Nigeria wishing, as he put it, 'to be a landlord rather than a tenant to the company'. When ITT refused, he promptly formed his own telecommunications company, Radio Communications (Nig.) Ltd (1971) and secured a small, £3m. contract from the army. News somehow leaked to ITT that Radio Communications had secured a £30m. contract, whereupon they offered him 49 per cent of ITT (Nig.) which he accepted while retaining 100 per cent control of Radio Communications in which ITT had wanted a shareholding.

Chief Abiola was to become vice-president for Africa and the Middle East thereby joining the inner circle of ITT. The post helped to launch him internationally and further his political ambitions. In 1975 ITT (Nig.) secured a very large contract for telephone exchanges in all parts of the country. Radio Communications also received substantial military contracts providing communications for the Signals division and setting up training programmes in the United States and United Kingdom.

After the success of ITT (Nig.) and Radio Communications, Chief Abiola set up a number of other ventures and also entered politics. He was chair-man of the National Party of Nigeria (NPN) in Ogun State (1978–82). He left the party after his ambitions for the Presidential nomination were dashed at the party convention. When the NPN took power in 1979, Abiola supported the party through two newspapers, the *National Concord* and *Sunday Concord*, which he launched simultaneously. The Concord Press engaged some talented journalists like Ray Ekpu and Dele Giwa. The papers achieved a good distribution throughout the country. When he left the NPN and stopped opposing Chief Awolowo of the Unity Party of Nigeria, circulation increased in Yorubaland. *Business Concord* and a weekly, *African*

Concord followed, together with vernacular newspapers. His wives have been important in his business affairs. His first wife, Simbiat Abiola (1938–92), was vice-chairman of the Concord Group of newspapers and played a large role in setting up the newspapers and other ventures like the Wonder bakery.[37] She was the founder and financier of the Kakanfo Queens, a female football team. His fourth wife, Dr Doyin Abiola, a journalist, became editor of the *National Concord* before her marriage and in 1985 became managing director and editor-in-chief of the Concord Press. In 1988 *African Economic Digest* was purchased from the EMAP Group in London for £300,000. His publishing interests were instrumental in gaining favour with the black caucus in the United States and promoting his Pan African vision. Chief Abiola became Patron of the Congressional Black Caucus in the United States and won the Black Heritage Award of the NAACP (National Association for the Advancement of Colored People) in 1987 and 1988.

Another venture was a N2.5m. investment in a modern automated bakery in Lagos.[38] The Wonder Baking Company opened in 1980 and employed 140 persons in 1981. It operated on the specific Wonder bread recipe used in a large chain of continental bakeries in the United States and Britain under the brand name of Mother's Pride. A second plant planned for Abeokuta did not materialise. The bakery was under the management of Chief (Mrs) Simbiat Abiola and later her son, Deji. A soft-drinks plant was established in Abeokuta where the Alake of Abeokuta gave him land and a title in appreciation of his national success. Prominent Egbas have generally conducted their business in Lagos and have not invested at home.

In the mid-1980s Chief Abiola began to make investments in agriculture. About 50,000 hectares were purchased in five states (Ogun, Kwara, Gongola, Akwa Ibom and Lagos).[39] Small scale cultivation of maize in Gongola started in 1988 (100 hectares) and a further 1,500 hectares were cleared in 1989. N10m. was invested in a 10,000-ton drying silo complex in 1987. It is planned to produce maize oil and animal feed.

Other ventures include Concord Airlines, African Ocean Lines (1985), Abiola Bookshops (1986), Summit Oil and an interest in Decca (WA) Ltd. In the case of African Ocean Lines, the largest shareholders were Chief Abiola and retired Major-General Shehu Yar'adua (27.5 per cent each).[40] Two ships were purchased from East Germany in 1986, at a time when shipping policy was changing to assist local operators with the establishment of the National Maritime Authority. However the company had problems attracting cargo and in 1988 the ships were sold. Chief Abiola and Major-General Yar'adua are also the largest Nigerian shareholders in the Habib Nigeria Bank Ltd, Kaduna, which is 40 per cent owned by Habib Bank of Pakistan and started operations in 1983.[41] Summit Oil was the recipient of a discretionary allocation by the Federal government of two exploratory blocs in the Niger Delta and discovered oil in commercial quantities in 1992.[42] It

TABLE 4.2: The Honeywell Group.

Company	Start-up
Honeywell Enterprises	1976
Honeywell Technical Enterprises	1978
Nigerian Eagle Flour Mills	1979
Polyventures, Ibadan	1984
Acepolymers, Ibadan	1984
Quality Printing and Paper	1984
Coral Products	1984
Pivot Engineering	1987
Honeywell Construction	1988
Honeywell Fisheries	1988
Pavilion Technology	1990

Source: Interview.

employs Nigerian chemical and petroleum engineers and is managed by Kola Abiola, the first son of the founder who studied business administration and also manages Abiola Farms and Concord Airlines.[43] In general, it has been policy to bring in sons to manage businesses in the Group at a young age.

Large scale philanthropy has included support for two football teams, the establishment of a comprehensive high school in Abeokuta in 1979, donations to many state development funds and support for Colleges of Arabic and Islamic Studies in Sokoto and Abeokuta. According to the Sultan of Sokoto, Chief Abiola has financially and morally assisted the propagation of Islam probably more than any other Nigerian in contemporary history.[44] Chief Abiola has been involved in fund raising for 63 secondary schools, 41 libraries and 21 water projects in 17 different states.[45] In 1990 he donated N1m. to each state university and other monies for student welfare, for publications and polytechnics. Over two decades, he has awarded over 1,000 scholarships.

The Honeywell Group

This Group employs over 3,000 persons and has grown rapidly since its inception in 1976 (see Table 4.2).[46]

Mr Oba Otudeko was a bank clerk at the age of 17. Through private tuition he became an Associate of the Institute of Bankers at the age of 20. He was then sponsored by his bank to study accountancy in Leeds, England. He was the best final-year student in 1967 and gained third place in his accountancy examinations.

He returned to Nigeria in 1969 and pursued an accelerated career in the Cooperative Bank, Ibadan, becoming acting general manager. Thus he had early exposure to management and became part of the elite of the financial system in the early 1970s.

His father came originally from Ijebuland and settled in Ibadan in 1909.

He worked with Nigerian Railways before going into produce dealing in cocoa and palm kernels. This was combined with gold mining at Ilesha. This led to an investment in EO Waters, a mineral water and soft drink bottling plant in Ibadan in the 1940s. Other prominent traders in Ibadan at that time were the Asuni family, and Animashaun of Idi-Ikan. They were produce merchants as well as UAC factors.

His mother was a very energetic trader and great traveller. She settled in Sokoto where she pioneered the introduction of grinding machines in the early 1950s. Her trading network in foodstuffs extended to Minna, Zaria and Kaduna and she traded abroad to Niger, Ghana and Abidjan.

Honeywell Enterprises gradually evolved out of the translation and redirection of his mother's business in foodstuffs in terms of modern management. Capital from that source was used to develop the importation of sugar and milk. Honeywell Trading developed links with a Dutch company and became a major importer of baking yeast. The group introduced the manufacturer's brand names of Engendura Active Dry Yeast and Fermipan Instant Yeast into the Nigerian market. These two brands were promoted to first-place position in the baking industry in Nigeria. The group was active in most Lagos markets but principally at Oke-Arin. In 1978 Honeywell Technical Enterprises was established for the supply, installation and servicing of power equipment.[47]

Knowledge of the baking industry informed the decision to set up a flour mill in Ibadan with British Lebanese who had the technical know-how. Ideal Flour Mills had a turnover of N34.0m. in 1986 and employed 295 persons.[48] After the wheat ban, part of the mill's production line was retooled for corn milling. A substantial part is out of production owing to inadequate local wheat supply. A second flour-milling venture with the Ogun State government was overtaken by the wheat ban. Machinery was purchased but never used. Ideal Flour Mills was followed by Polyventures, a packaging venture which provided sacks for the mill. The venture had a turnover of N4.9m. in 1986 and employed 300 persons.[49] In addition a polythene plant for plastic bags was established. Further investment was undertaken in 1984 in a paper conversion and printing factory and a plastic household-ware unit, both sited at Odogbolu in Ogun State, the owner's home town.

In order to take advantage of government expenditures and contracts and get a better balance in the group's activities, the Group then expanded away from manufacture. An electrical contracting firm, Pivot Engineering was set up in 1987 and this was followed by a construction company (1988) and a company specialising in security systems (1990). The Group also diversified into fishing. The Group has invested in the Sheraton Hotel and the Universal Trust Bank. A merchant bank is in the pipeline. The Group has also invested in property and real estate.

The diversified nature of the Honeywell Group is partly a reaction to instability in industrial policy and partly due to expectations of political change that will enhance the importance of state contracts as a source of profit. The Group is moving towards the development of group-level management with a four-man team to cover merchandising and marketing, public relations, corporate management and engineering. It includes the owner, a brother, one Indian expatriate, and a former university professor.

Devcom Group

Mike Adenuga was a student in the United States in the early 1970s and majored in business administration. He entered construction and commodity and general merchanting in the late 1970s and established a reputation for new products and price cutting.[50] Some of the profits from trade were invested in international real estate and caught the European property boom in the 1980s.

Devcom Merchant Bank started operations in 1989. In the first fifteen months of operation it lead managed a syndicated loan of N82.5m. to Lagos State government and handled a N54m. public-equity issue for Tate Industries Ltd. It was also financial adviser to Bendel State privatisation programme. In 1990 a commercial bank, Equatorial Trust Bank was opened.

Consolidated Oil, which began as an oil-marketing company, was given exploratory rights in the South Western Delta Region in 1990. A number of Nigerian oil specialists were recruited and exploratory work conducted without foreign partners. Oil was found in December 1991 after hiring an oil rig for $5m.[51]

Consolidated Manufacturing was originally set up to manufacture decorated aluminium panels, but it has diversified into food processing and has made a N200m. investment in cocoa and vegetable-oil processing. The Group also has a N300m. property portfolio through Sancomex.

The South Atlantic Seafood Company (SASCO)

This group has exhibited rapid growth and diversification since its inception in 1985 and employed 550 persons in 1992.[52] Idieli Koitu Olu Fashanu was born in 1959 and educated at Government College, Ughelli.[53] He studied commerce at the University of Madras, India and then took an MA degree in International Trade and Marketing at Strathclyde University, Glasgow. His father-in-law, a Singaporean businessman gave him moral support and encouraged him to take risk. He began trading in Lagos, buying commodities like salt and cement from a group of northern traders in Apapa. The traders had import licences but were first-time importers with no storage facilities nor the will to take the risk of wholesaling and distributing commodities. Money was raised for trading from an indigenous merchant bank and direct importation begun.

To complement trading, he entered shipping encouraged by a brother who had trained as a marine engineer. His father-in-law also gave guarantees to help finance the purchase of ships. In 1987 he bought an oil tanker for $8m. with assistance of First City Merchant Bank and provided a charter service for oil firms including the Nigerian National Petroleum Corporation. A 22,000-ton dead-weight vessel was bought and used to import cargo from Brazil. Later it was put on charter in Europe.

Other areas of investment include cinemas, light engineering, agro-industry and farming. The decision to invest in vegetable-oil processing followed a visit to Malaysia. After a long gestation period at a time when the naira was being constantly devalued, an automated vegetable-oil mill and refinery was established in 1991. Okhebo Farms Industries Ltd was located at the site of an old cocoa plantation initiated by his grandfather. Chalets, a dining room, recreational facilities and a housing estate were constructed. The financing of the $7.5m. investment caused a contraction in trading activity and on completion the project had to be refinanced. Five engineers were sent to Malaysia and Thailand for training and two to Belgium to study equipment fabrication. A major concern has been to encourage with various incentives a culture of substantial oil sales among market women who are accustomed to trading in small quantities.

Udofe Metal Industries (1988) with an investment of N40m. was set up in Bendel State with the assistance of the African Development Bank. It manufactures wheelbarrows, sinks and cutlasses and had a turnover of about N35m. at the end of 1990. Machinery including a 400-ton press was acquired from a Singapore company that was under pressure from the Singapore government to shift into higher-technology, less land-extensive operations. In 1992 a licence agreement was signed with Peugeot to manufacture body components (fenders, boots, door panels) and spare parts for the assembly plant in Kaduna.

Entry into cinemas in 1986 followed a privatisation exercise by Bendel State and was originally part of a strategy to secure participation in a Bendel bank. Five cinemas were leased from the Bendel government for seven years at the cost of N600,000. N2m. was spent on renovation. Cinema audiences proved very discriminating and the enterprise was not profitable.

An attempt to set up a coastal ferry and cargo business between West African countries ended in frustration after a promising start and was probably before its time. A passenger service between Lagos and Tema was launched in 1989 and a second service between Port Harcourt and Abidjan in 1990.[54] There had been an increase in demand as west–east coastal passenger movement increased due to the high cost of movement to Europe. Yet the enterprise foundered on excessive bureaucratic and security interference as power brokers in each domain prevented coordination and efficient operation. The vessel was put on charter with the ECOMOG forces in Liberia.

The Group is managed by Olu Fashanu and his twin brothers, a marine engineer and a banker. Technical, financial and manpower/political functions are divided. Each company is run independently with general managers reporting to the brothers. Three expatriate managers from France, India and England are employed.

SPECIALIST ENTERPRISES

This section begins with profiles of a number of more specialist companies that started before 1970. First we examine the business career of William Murray-Bruce who founded a chain of retail stores in 1964. We then trace the business career of Chief Ayo Rosiji, former Action Group secretary and federal minister, who pioneered the first indigenous distillery in Nigeria. We then turn to two professional firms in accountancy and insurance broker-age, Akintola Williams and T. A. Braithwaite. Next, we cover a supplier of electrical appliances, a leading stationary and paper-recycling company, and a steel stockist.

Younger concerns that have been established since 1970 include two higher-technology enterprises in the manufacture of air conditioners and electrical cables, Gacol and MicCom; a small foundry, Easitech Projects; a plastics firm, Diamond Plastics; two enterprises in commodity trading and agro-industry, Ladgroup and Majekodunmi Ventures; two engineering ser-vice companies, Desam Group and Negris; a pharmaceutical concern, Contin-ental Pharmaceuticals; Liz Olofin, a small company that went public in 1990; and one of the largest, most successful, private hospitals in Nigeria, Eko Hospitals. Finally we look at two concerns that are located primarily in Ibadan and Ijebu-Ode: the Joas Group, which has diversified out of electronics assembly, and Bisrod Furniture.

Domino Stores

William Murray-Bruce was born in 1914.[55] His father was a Scot who worked for the Royal Niger Company and married a lady from Akassa. He was educated in Onitsha and worked for the United Africa Company in many different locations for thirty-six years before his retirement in 1964. Towards the end of his career, he worked as credit controller with Kingsway Stores and was assistant manager at the general bulk store in Apapa. In 1959 he underwent training with John Lewis department stores in England.

In 1959 UAC started a series of small retail stores with an optimum size of 2,000 sq. ft. The intention was to complement the larger Kingsway Stores. These stores would, it was thought, be less intimidating for Nigerian consumers and penetrate the lower income market. The stores could also act as a training ground for Kingsway Stores. Several of these stores were established by 1964, but the strategy did not prove very profitable. William Murray-Bruce who was then supervisory manager of the stores requested that UAC sell him the store outlets. They agreed to sell him two stores in Lagos. He financed the purchase by forgoing his retirement benefits and taking goods in stock on credit. Only a few staff stayed with him. Later he bought the Domino trade name for £4,000 from UAC.

His strategy was to bring the stores closer to the people. He extended working hours from 8 a.m. to 8 p.m. (2 shifts) and introduced Sunday trading; locations near churches were considered positively advantageous. Junior staff and management trainees were recruited from middle-ranking secondary-school leavers who turned over relatively quickly (average five years). Staff were encouraged to undertake further education part time. Graduates, who would expect superior working conditions, were not recruited.

A wholesale operation was begun in 1965 and by 1968 the company had become the largest distributor for Lever Brothers. By 1980, there were 210 sub-distributors and the directors of Lever Brothers had become alarmed at the rapid expansion and market share of the wholesale operation. Without consultation, they began to supply sub-distributors directly and encourage them to undercut Domino. This nearly caused the collapse of Domino Stores.

In 1979, prior to these events, a son of the proprietor, Michael Murray-Bruce, who trained as a mechanical engineer and had work experience with multinational companies in the United Kingdom and United States, took over as managing director from his father who became non-executive chairman. Subsequently, the company placed more emphasis on the retail trade and the number of stores expanded to seventeen before adverse economic conditions reduced outlets to thirteen. Lagos and Port Harcourt have been the main locations and the company has not expanded to the northern states. Wholesale distribution was undertaken for International Distillers and a small shareholding taken up. Integral to the growth of a successful retail operation was the development of a property company, Manilla Properties. The appreciation of company properties has been substantial, the stores acting as a catalyst for property revaluation in their vicinity. A residential property development has been opened in Lagos.

Murray-Bruce was chairman of Food Specialities (Nestlé) and a major shareholder. Apart from landed property, Domino Stores has diversified its investment through Manilla Properties in other directions: entertainment and media activities, a frozen-foods company, the production of baby foods, the export of cashew nuts and sesame seeds and an oil-services company.

The company holds a controlling interest in Silverbird Productions, which originated when Ben, another son, returned from university education in the United States to initiate musical promotions in Lagos. Later, local and international beauty contests were promoted and the company acquired the franchise for pageants previously held by Times Leisure Services, the organisers of Miss Nigeria contests. Later the rights from Warner Brothers to supply TV programmes were acquired and the company applied for licence to establish private TV and radio stations. Former staff of the NBTV were recruited and a TV village constructed at Lekki.

In 1974 as a result of the indigenisation exercise, Domino Stores took a 40 per cent interest in Nigeria Food Supply and Cold Storage Company, a company importing frozen meat. This company had been started in 1956 by an expatriate who sold out to Union International, a member of the Weddel Group owned by the Vestey family. In the early 1980s, Union International divested. Domino Stores acquired its interest and took management control.

A controlling interest is held in a baby-food plant (Buckingham Ltd) which opened in Apapa in 1992 employing 50 persons. Rights in the production of Soy Ogi were purchased from FIIRO (Federal Institute for Industrial Research, Oshodi). The company sources soybeans and maize locally and fabricated equipment locally. Equity was taken up by 13 private shareholders through private placement and a NERFUND (National Economic Reconstruction Fund) loan was obtained.[56]

In 1992 an investment was made in IMC Ltd, an oil-service company specialising in transportation. The company operates six vessels on lease to Shell at Warri and there is the prospect of further expansion in the Port Harcourt area. Many of the crew recruited were former staff of the Nigerian National Shipping Line.

Chief Ayo Rosiji

Ayo Rosiji was born in 1917 at Abeokuta.[57] He was educated at Ibadan Grammar School, Government College, Ibadan, and Yaba Higher College where he studied engineering. In 1942 he worked with Shell. From 1944–8 he studied law in England returning to Nigeria to set up a legal practice in Ibadan. During the 1950s he acquired some plots in Ibadan from clients.[58] He became active in politics and became federal general secretary and legal adviser to the Action Group from 1953. He became a federal minister in 1957–9 in the Balewa government. Rosiji kept his business interests separate from the Action Group and did not join the inner group of businessmen who controlled party finances. He sided with Chief Akintola in his split with Chief Awolowo and led the NNDP in the house.

In 1957 he acquired three plots in Apapa from the Lagos Executive Development Board for the immediate deposit of £500.[59] To develop the plots, he took a loan of £3,000 from the National Bank and then borrowed £7,000 from the Lagos Building Society. The plots were developed using contractor finance, and the property rented to British Petroleum who paid him £6,400 in advance for 4 years. He incorporated a property-development company, Onikan Ltd. When the Rosiji family moved to Apapa in 1960, there were only three other Nigerian families there, including those of two other lawyers who developed business interests, Adeyemi Lawson and Chris Ogunbanjo. Law practice and property investments would provide the initial capital for business.

To promote business, Rosiji turned to US investors. He recruited an African-American economist to conduct feasibility studies into various industries. One project which was seriously investigated was a sugar complex and two companies were incorporated in 1961, the Nigerian Chemical Company in the United States and Nigerian Distilleries Ltd., to convert molasses from the newly established government sugar company at Bacita to alcohol. This plan was obstructed by his political opponents who set up Nigerian Fermentation Industries (later West African Distilleries) to import and bottle foreign brand names.

Trials of sugar were conducted along the Ogun River (in his constituency) with the assistance of Dr T. S. B. Aribisala, chief agricultural officer and PS Western Region, and B. O. Amon, head of research at Moor Plantation Agricultural Research Station, Ibadan. 20,000 acres of land was surveyed. This project was promoted by Midaf, an offshoot of an international business consultancy, which Rosiji introduced to Nigeria. The project was overtaken by the 1966 military coup.

In 1962 he formed Nigerian Electronics with himself as chairman and majority shareholder together with an American investor and Westinghouse, the US multinational. This was the first plant for the assembly of TV and radio sets. A Nigerian electronics engineer, Anofi Guobadia, was assistant manager.[60] A plan to diversify to air conditioners was thwarted by Nigerian distrust of locally made goods. Guobadia became general manager in 1964, but the company did not survive Rosiji's absence in Britain after the military coup of 1966.

Other interests developed before 1966 included a small share in Sanitas, a toilet-tissue company with a close friend Stanley Powell and Bowater, the UK multinational. This investment was later liquidated after Sanitas sold out under the indigenisation decree and new interests became involved. A stake was also acquired in Gulf Fisheries with Italian and Kuwaiti interests. The company operated eight trawlers, a mother ship, and exported shrimps and imported fish.

Three further projects associated with Midaf were undertaken. Midaf leased the loss-making Pepsi Cola plant at Mushin from the Western Region government and turned it round. However, the company was compulsorily reacquired by the Western government after the coup. A second business interest developed by Midaf before the civil war was Masco, a wholesale distribution outlet for locally made goods at Ijora opened in 1964 and the Masco supermarket at Ikeja which was sold to foreign interests in 1992. Midaf and Rosiji also joined forces with a Hungarian company to establish Paper Sack Nigeria Ltd to sell sacks to a cement company. Rosiji retained his 20 per cent shareholding when the civil war erupted, while his partners sold their shares to Chief Olu Aboderin.

While in Engand, Rosiji kept contact with Stanley Powell, a former neighbour in Apapa, who was the owner of Brian Munro, an agency for consumer goods with an import, wholesale and distribution arm. Powell invited Rosiji to become a director and shareholder in Pioneer Ltd, a company which made Birds custard powder in Lagos. When Rosiji returned to Nigeria he became an executive director of Brian Munro in 1973 and later became a substantial shareholder through the indigenisation exercise. He also started a clearing and forwarding agency which took over clearing and forwarding functions for Brian Monro. He became joint managing director and later executive chairman of Brian Munro until 1982.

Ayo Rosiji resuscitated Nigerian Distilleries to become the first indigenous distillery and the largest in Nigeria. Know-how was acquired from a Dutch-man and an expatriate was employed up to 1983. The company started at Ikeja, in the warehouse of Brian Munro with the bottling of brands like Dubonnet owned by Paul Ricard of France to whom samples of finished drinks were sent for monitoring. The company moved to Otta in 1981 and developed a strong set of own brands like Seaman's schnapps, Regal gin, Black Knight whisky and Bacchus tonic wine. A nationwide distribution network was also established. A son of the founder, Ola Rosiji, who graduated at Ibadan and studied accountancy, worked his way up the company, to became managing director in 1984. Another venture at Otta is the Anita Shoe Co. Begun in 1980 as a partnership with a Dutchman, the company is now wholly owned by Ayo Rosiji.

Another son, Abimbolu, who studied in United States and took a doctorate in Brazil, set up a cosmetics and toiletries company with his father. The economic recession undermined the viability of the venture and the plant was closed down.

Ola Rosiji has also ventured into cashew-nut farming in Kwara State and Brazil. Ayo Rosiji, who visited Abimbolu when he studied in Brazil, became aware of the investment potential and encouraged Ola to transfer his cashew-nut venture to Brazil. With the assistance of Abimbolu, an existing plantation of 7,000 acres was purchased and a processing plant built, so nuts could be exported to the United States. This business is managed by a sister, Olande, who trained as a lawyer.

Since retirement, Ayo Rosiji has directed his energies to education and the arts. He has been active in the Ogun State University Foundation and was chairman and then patron of the Music Society of Nigeria (MUSON).

Akintola Williams and Co.[61]

Akintola Williams was born in 1919. His father, Ekundayo Williams, was a clerk in the colonial service, who after legal training in London, set up a legal practice in Lagos. He also had interests in farming and real estate. The real estate was inherited from his grandfather, Z. A. Williams, a merchant prince from Abeokuta.

He was educated at Baptist Academy and CMS Grammar School, Lagos, before taking a higher diploma in Commerce at Yaba Higher College. He then proceeded to England where he qualified as the first Nigerian chartered accountant. On his return to Nigeria, he was briefly an assessment officer in the Inland Revenue, before setting up his own firm in 1952.

At this time, five big foreign firms monopolised the accounting business in Lagos and many firms in Nigeria had their accounts audited by overseas firms. There were small local accountancy firms like S. O. Ogundiya and Co., but they were certified, not chartered accountants.

Akintola Williams secured early patronage from a number of indigenous companies like Fawehinmi Furniture, Ojukwu Transport, the African Insurance Company owned by K. O. Mbadiwe and the *West African Pilot* owned by Nnamdi Azikiwe. The arrival of new statutory corporations also constituted an early business opportunity and among the clients were the Electricity Corporation of Nigeria, the Western Nigeria Development Corporation, the Eastern Nigeria Development Corporation, the Nigerian Railway Corporation and the Nigerian Ports Authority. The first foreign client was Czechoslovak-Nigerian Import and Export Company.

In 1957 the first partner, Charles S. Sankey, was appointed and he was followed by Mr Njoh Litumbe, a Cameroonian who opened offices for the firm in Port Harcourt and Enugu and later played a leading role in the overseas expansion of the firm. The firm was run as a collective responsibility based on mutual consultation with the very clear understanding that no partner was indispensable.

Akintola Williams played a leading role in the establishment of the Association of Accountants in Nigerian in 1960 which became the Institute of Chartered Accountants of Nigeria in 1965. The local training of accountants was one of his highest priorities.[62]

A branch was established in 1964 in the Cameroons. This was followed by branches in the Ivory Coast and Swaziland. Affiliates were established in Ghana, Egypt and Kenya. The overseas expansion was a deliberate hedge against the possibility of economic and political risk at home. At 31 March 1992, there were 19 partners with 535 staff.

The Companies Act of 1968, which made it mandatory for all companies operating in Nigeria to incorporate locally and make annual audited accounts, boosted the demand for the firm's services, as did the indigenisation exercise of the early 1970s.

From the core activity of accounting and auditing, a Group emerged. A management consultancy unit, AW Consultants Ltd, was hived off in 1973, headed by Chief Arthur Mbanefo. A company secretarial service and an acquisition in a computer-services company, followed. In 1977, an international link was established with Touche Ross International. This company was chosen because it allowed local firms independence. Akintola Williams and Co. could keep its work and name and undertake work referred to it by Touche Ross on the basis of a profit-sharing agreement. Akintola Williams secured a seat on the governing body of Touche Ross. In 1991, the firm became the sole representative in Nigeria of DRT International, a firm that resulted from a merger of Touche with Deloitte of the United States and Tohmatsu of Japan.

Apart from the development of his own firm, from which he retired in 1983, Akintola Williams was a board member and leading shareholder in John Holt Investments Co., Bentworth Finance Nigeria, Boulos and BEWAC. Since retirement, he has been deeply involved in the establishment of a music centre and concert hall for the Music Society of Nigeria (MUSON).

T. A. Braithwaite

T. A. Braithwaite was born in 1928.[63] His father was a teacher and a keen churchman. He attended CMS Grammar School, Lagos and in 1946 passed examinations giving him exemption from London matriculation. The family inherited some property from his maternal grandmother, so there was sufficient income to pay for his further education. Whereas most of his contemporaries went into law and medicine, he wanted a training in business, but opportunities were very limited in Lagos at that time. He worked for Kingsway Stores as a salesman and then joined the Railway Training School at Iddo, followed by a spell with Royal Exchange. In 1949, he left for London to join Royal Exchange Assurance and passed his associate exams in two years.

On return to Lagos, he became chief agent of London and Lancashire operating in the name of his cousin, Mobalaji Bank-Anthony. Other chief agencies at that time were UAC and Patterson Zochonis. In 1958, he opened his own insurance-broking office.

In the early 1960s, he was able to secure important business for the London insurance market, including the Lagos Executive Development Board, the Nigerian Ports Authority and commercial banks. The Nigerian government suggested that a number of leading Nigerian brokers should go into partnership with a leading British firm, but T. A. Braithwaite preferred to be independent. In 1970, Braithwaite Steel Brokers was established as Lloyd's brokers under the management of Cayzer Steel Bowater.

In 1960 he founded with S. L. Edu, the African Alliance Insurance Co. in which the Munich Reinsurance had a 40 per cent stake. He was chief executive for 15 years. In 1974, he founded a property company with properties on Lagos Island and Ikeja. In 1976 he formed Metalum Ltd, an aluminium construction company with some expatriates who had formerly worked for

Alumaco. This firm has recently created a subsidiary with a German company
at Abuja. He also acquired a stake of 30 per cent in Elder Dempster
Agencies (Nig.) Ltd, a shipping agency.

Adebowale Group of Companies

Chief A. B. Adebowale was born in 1929. His father was a farmer and his
mother a petty trader. After primary and secondary education and teacher
training, he taught for some years at Epe (1951–9). He then joined SCOA as
a shop master for 10 months. In 1959 he opened Adebowale Stores on
Lagos Island, a retail outlet for electronic goods and home appliances.

In 1969, Adebowale Electrical Industries were established to assemble
electrical goods (domestic appliances and audio-visual equipment). Television
assembly began in 1972. The main source of components for assembly was
the Nichimen company of Japan. The company also imported from Britain.
In 1986 the company had a turnover of N35m. and employed 800 persons.[64]
Adebowale Engineering Services was set up to provide technical services.

In 1975 Debo Industries was opened along the Oshodi expressway for the
manufacture of refrigerators, freezers, air conditioners, cabinets and kitchen
units. Technical assistance was provided by Zanussi of Italy. The manufacture
of gas cookers was added later. In 1986 turnover was N26m. and employment
stood at 530 persons.[65]

The Group was hit by the smuggling of electrical goods in the late 1970s
and then by the decline in oil revenues and the closure of the economy.
Group employment fell from about 2,000 persons at the end of the 1970s to
under 550 in 1990. The company was forced to close down retail branches
in Kano, Ilorin, Zaria, Enugu and Ibadan.

In 1983 a former permanent secretary in the Western Region government
was recruited from Dunlop as group managing director. In 1987 a foreign
company was bought and Adebowale Foundry and Metal Fabrication Ltd
established at Sango Otta. A retail store was also opened on Lagos Island.

Onward Stationary

This indigenous firm is number 2 in the field of paper products after
Thomas Wyatt, the British multinational and pioneer and leader in Nigeria.[66]
The company is notable for the way in which it has specialised, diversifying
only in related fields of activity.

Chief Obagun was born in 1932. He did not complete secondary education
and started trading. He specialised in stationary, buying from G. B. Ollivant
and Thomas Wyatt and selling to printers. He set up a shop on Lagos
Island selling school materials. In 1960 he began direct importation from
Scandinavia. He acquired a guillotine and larger premises so that he could
service a larger market. He bought from Thomas Wyatt in large quantities
and concentrated on exercise books. A paper-conversion plant was established

at Matori, Lagos in 1973 with the support of Scandinavian suppliers. Over 100 lines were produced with employment fluctuating between 100 to 700 persons. In 1975, a printing press, Nigerprint, was set up. This was followed by Scanink, a manufacturer of printing ink in Ibadan in 1984 with employment of 80 persons. A facility for the production of computer paper was also established in 1986.

A major investment of N100m. in a recycling plant to manufacture jumbo rolls from waste paper was completed in 1991. This is the fourth plant in the country after Star Paper and Dubic Industries in Aba and Boulos in Lagos. Nigerians were sent to Italy for training by the Italian equipment supplier. There is no management or technical agreement.

Sanusi Group of Companies

This group has a turnover of between N70m. and N80m. and employs about 2,000 persons. It is owned by Alhaji A. R. O. Sanusi, pioneer member and president of the Islamic League of Nigeria and Babalaje of Egba Muslims.[67]

Alhaji Sanusi was born in 1932 and began his education at Arabic School in Abeokuta. He attended primary school in Lagos and at the age of 11 started business with his brothers who were building-materials merchants. He worked for them for 13 years. After differences with his brothers over the pace of expansion, he set up on his own and registered R. O. Sanusi and Brothers in 1956. He became an agent for an expatriate company, Thomas Aplinx, then at Kakawa street.

In 1960 he attempted to buy the West African Steel and Wire Company in the belief that the company could be revived. Despite the fact that the Nigerian Industrial Development Bank was prepared to help finance the deal, the company was sold to expatriates. This strengthened his resolve to found his own factories. At this time he concentrated on the import of building materials, hardware and agricultural equipment.

In 1971 the Pioneer Chemical Manufacturing Company (later known as Sanusi Rubber Works Ltd) was set up to manufacture bicycle tyres and tubes. This was followed by a factory to manufacture wire nails, wire netting, iron rods and twisted bars in Ibadan (1975). A company was also established to take advantage of the trade in imported foodstuffs. It expanded rapidly and employed about 1,000 persons at the peak. Finally a galvanized roofing-sheet factory was opened in Ikeja in 1981.

In the 1980s, the company became a major distributor for the National Steel Mills, the main source of wire rods for galvanizing. This link has been central to the success of the company in recent years. A son of the founder who completed business studies in the United Kingdom became vice-chairman of the group.

Younger Specialist Enterprises
Gacol

Dr M. Akinrele was educated at King's College, Lagos and studied engineering at Cambridge University.[68] His father was a schoolmaster at Ondo and trained at Fourah Bay College. On return to Nigeria in 1961, he spent two years with the Western Region Development Corporation at a sheet galvanising plant which was a joint venture with a Japanese company. He visited Japan for six months.

In 1965, he joined British Petroleum and stayed five years. He also became a lecturer and consultant with the Nigerian Institute of Management. Dissatisfied as an employee, he wanted to run his own business and make good the deficiency in production which he observed. He tried small-scale industry with paper clips and school chalk in a garage (1973–75). He then saw an opportunity in refrigeration and air conditioning and was assisted with finance by the Odua Investment Corporation, a Western State parastatal. This was an area with considerable domestic competition from Patterson Zochonis, Mandilas, Phillips, and Birla brothers.

An Italian production design was used and two expatriates employed for short periods. He could not invest in a large-scale modern plant. He therefore innovated with a condenser and evaporating unit which reduced the volume and weight of the heat exchangers. A patent was taken out for a 'balanced evaporation and condenser design of reduced heat transfer surface and enhanced refrigeration effect'. Since 1991, condensers have been supplied to the Peugeot assembly plant in Kaduna. The company received a merit award from the Ministry of Science and Technology. In addition to the manufacture of refrigeration and air-conditioning units, the assembly of cookers was started. At the low scale of production, an enamelling furnace could not be justified, so a thermal spraying process is under investigation.

Mass production has been adversely affected by problems of labour discipline and motivation. Anticipation of likely problems in production has also been lacking. With the shrinkage of disposable income under the Structural Adjustment Programme, consumers have switched to used units and this has effected demand adversely. Numbers employed have fallen from 200 in 1986 to 100 in 1991.

MicCom Engineering Works Ltd

This enterprise managed by Mr Tunde Ponnle and Mrs Olu Ponnle manufactures electrical cables.[69] In 1991 it had a turnover of N25m.

Tunde Ponnle was born in 1939. After graduating from teacher-training college in 1960, he entered technical college in Ibadan in 1962 and studied electrical engineering. He also trained at the Post and Telegraph School, Oshodi. After working for Nigerian External Communications, he joined the University of Ife, at Ibadan, as a technical officer. During this period, he opened a repair shop at Mokola market employing apprentices. He then left to start a technical section at the Government Trade Centre, Oshogbo.

From 1970–2 he studied electrical engineering at the Polytechnic of North London. Soon after his return to Nigeria, he started a business doing repair work, electrical installation, and house wiring. He secured contracts at the Murtala International airport, at the army barracks, Shaki, and the naval base, Ojo. This experience gave an insight into the demand for cables and problems of acquisition from existing cable companies.

Mrs Olu Ponnle was born in 1944 at Ibadan. Like her husband, she trained as a teacher and studied at the Polytechnic of North London where she qualified in electrical engineering. On return to Nigeria, she worked with Western Nigeria Television, Adebowale Electrical Industries, and Maiden Electronics. She then took an appointment as a training officer with the Industrial Training Fund before resigning to work with her husband in 1977.

An initial approach to a British company failed because the capital intensive investment was too costly. Mr Ponnle then went to India and saw cable manufacture that was within his means. Machinery was imported from India (1981) and Indian expatriates were employed until Nigerians replaced them. Initial competition from established manufacturers, and poor market reception due to low quality were eventually overcome. The enterprise was sustained in this period by income from earlier property investment. By the end of the decade, the patronage of government agencies like NEPA (Nigerian Electric Power Authority) and DFFRI (Directorate of Foods, Roads and Rural Infrastructure) was assured and in 1991 turnover was N25m. The factory has been relocated and expanded at cost of N60m., again with Indian technology.

Sons and daughters are being brought into the company and given responsibility for subsidiary activities like copperwire production. Over 200 persons are supported with scholarships by a foundation for educational development.

Easitech Projects

This small foundry at Ikeja started operations in 1977 and had a turnover in excess of N5m. in 1991 with 60 workers employed. including 4 engineers, artisans and apprentices.[70] No expatriates are employed. The company fabricates industrial machinery like blockmoulding machines, oil expellers, pulleys and shafts, and cosmetic and paint mixers, at far lower cost than imported models. Spare parts are manufactured for corporate clients like Guinness, Dunlop and Portland Cement. Sales have been made to customers from other countries in West Africa. Raw materials are sourced locally from scrap-metal markets at Owode-Onirin, Orile and Idiroko. The growth of this small company contrasts favourably with efforts by Lagos and Ondo

State governments to establish foundries, both of which have failed to take off.

Diamond Plastics

Chief (Mrs) O. O. Olakunri was born in 1937.[71] Both parents were well educated. Her maternal grandfather was Chief J. H. Doherty and her paternal grandmother owned the Tika Tore Press in Lagos. She attended CMS Girls School in Lagos and was then educated in England.

She decided early that she wanted to be a chartered accountant and served articles in Dorset and the City of London. Her university education at Birmingham was interrupted by her marriage in 1957 and the birth of two children in quick succession. With part-time employment in broadcasting and advertising, she continued her articles and qualified as the first African female chartered accountant in 1963.

She worked for a while with Peat Cassleton Elliot in London and Lagos and joined the Nigerian Industrial Development Bank (NIDB) in 1966. She became an assistant general manager and an executive director of ICON Stockbrokers. She was a founder member of the Institute of Chartered Accountants of Nigeria (ICAN) and became the first President of the Society of Women Accountants of Nigeria (SWAN).

She resigned from NIDB in 1972 to have more time for the family and bought a plastics factory in Apapa, which had been started in 1968 by an Italian engineer. She was interested in buying CTB Stockbrokers and though this did not materialise, she took a management contract with the company and was its managing director (1974-8). In 1973, she joined the board of Bata Nigeria and later became its chairwoman. In 1977, she was nominated to the Constituent Assembly. She also became a founding director in two state banks, Eko Bank International and Gateway Bank. During the oil boom, she began to import pre-fabricated housing units but found that they had little appeal as permanent residences in Nigeria.

At the outset, Diamond Plastics had been established for the production of toys. Mrs Olakunri shifted production entirely to industrial containers made to customer specifications. An expatriate general manager was appointed. Employment rose to 300 and 2 expatriates were employed. A plant was opened in 1982 at Koko Port for Total Oil and customers in Bendel and the northern states. The Koko plant was not very successful; customers preferred to purchase containers direct from Lagos. The plant was closed in 1985 and sold to Total Oil. At this time, the increased cost of imported resin and problems obtaining import licences cut production and 100 workers were retrenched.

Ladgroup

This company with a turnover of N200m. and employment of 150 persons in 1990 is the leading indigenous cocoa exporter.

Mr B. A. Onafowokan was educated at King's College, Lagos and the University of Ibadan where he graduated in mathematics.[72] He joined Shell (WA) in 1956 eventually rising to the position of retail sales manager before he left in 1972. Encouraged by Shell, he initially wanted to enter the plastics industry to manufacture plastic products for the oil industry. This motivated him to go into business, but adverse conditions for importing deterred him from the plastics industry. Noting that the large trading conglomerates had often started in the produce trade, he decided to go into the export of commodities.

His initial capital was £34,000 made up of pension and gratuity from Shell (£11,000), a bank loan of £5,000 and £18,000 from the sale of his house in southwest Ikoyi. He first tried to export coffee but found difficulties dealing with existing brokerage companies. He then turned to ginger from the Kafanchan area, chillies and shea nuts. Initially he was caught with stocks of ginger for an export contract in a falling market because of strikes in the United Kingdom and a friend lent him some money. Within 2 years however he was obtaining annual credit of N6m. from Nigerian Acceptances Ltd (a merchant bank) to finance commodity exports. The company became a major exporter of cocoa after 1986 when the Cocoa Board was abolished, establishing a network of dealers in four states. In 1989 it was the fourth largest exporter of cocoa after two Ibadan-based Lebanese companies and Afro-Continental, a Geneva-based commodity trader.

The import side was developed from the beginning. The company was the first to import Thai rice on a large scale. Other items included canned fish (Japan), frozen fish, stockfish, and sugar. In the late 1980s the company was the largest importer of frozen fish. Attempts to import textiles were discontinued because of difficulties over credit advances to textiles traders.

The company is undertaking a $15.2m. investment in machinery for cocoa processing and shea-nut crushing. This is expected to be the first shea-nut crushing facility in the country. These investments were undertaken after assurances from overseas customers that they would purchase the processed products. The investment in cocoa butter has gone ahead despite the lifting of the ban on cocoa exports.

Majekodunmi Ventures

This company had a turnover of about N180m. in 1991 and employed 438 persons.

The founder, Mr A. O. Majekodunmi was born in 1955.[73] He left the University of Lagos before completing his degree, to begin petty trading in

Oke Arin market, Lagos. He became a distributor of soaps, detergents, milk, and sugar before starting direct importation. The export of palm oil to the United States was a very profitable venture.

The company acquired a 20 per cent shareholding in Cocoa Products Ltd of Ile Iluji after the Nigerian Cocoa Board monopoly was abolished. Cocoa Products had been set up to process cocoa for the Nigeria Cocoa Board, but could not buy cocoa because of an inadequate capital base. A further 15 per cent of the equity was bought from foreign technical partners. A refurbishment of the presses was undertaken with a loan from the African Development Bank.

The company continued in the oil-palm trade and in 1982 acquired ownership of an abandoned palm-oil estate. In 1991 it bought an additional 2,500 hectares in Edo state. A soap factory was also purchased. Trading has expanded with the development of a superstore and warehousing complex with a daily turnover of N300,000 (1991). The company has an active research and development division and has systematically tried to develop an adaptable corporate culture with occupational flexibility and weekend staff retreats.

The Desam Group

Chief Edet Amana was born in 1938 and educated at Methodist College, Uzuakoli and King's College, Lagos.[74] He attended Imperial College, London (1961–6) before working with a British firm of consulting engineers. On return to Nigeria he was employed as a service engineer with Shell-BP (1968–72).

In 1972 he set up Amana Consulting Engineers. Over a 15-year period this firm was responsible for the design and implementation of projects valued at about $2bn.[75] The engineering-service division held agencies for A. W. Chesterton of Boston, Mass., and Hewlett Packard (1982). In 1981 a joint venture was set up with Earth Technology Corporation of California for geotechnical and geophysical surveying and mapping. Another venture involving Israeli interests covered architectural planning. At its peak the company employed 30 engineers, including 10 expatriates.

The company had undergone some diversification and overall Group employment was 550 persons in 1993. From 1980, the Group began to develop rubber farms and has recently established a rubber-processing venture. The Group is also involved in insurance brokerage and trading in supplies for the oil industry. Investments have been made in banking, publishing and property. The property portfolio in Lagos, Uyo, Calabar and Abuja yields an annual income of about N5m.

Negris Group

Mr Abidoye Ayoola, the owner of this oil-service company, which employs 150 persons, trained in mechanical engineering at the University of Lagos.[76] He left in 1970 to join Gulf Oil as a petroleum engineer. He then went to the United States, studied for a Masters degree, and worked for Gulf Oil and a solar turbine company in California.

In 1978 he returned to Nigeria to represent an American company. Two years later he launched his own oil-service company, then known as Capital Equipment Company. Encouraged by the NNPC, he secured contracts for the installation and maintenance of production equipment. Projects were also undertaken for the Central Bank and NEPA. The main difficulty was to get a stable pool of dedicated Nigerians and expatriates in an environment where there was great job mobility and many people aspired to go independent. This was achived so that the company could move beyond representation of foreign companies to undertake installation and servicing work of its own.

As a long-term insurance policy, the company has diversified into property. In the early 1980s, it also established a 2,000 hectare maize farm at Ogbomosho, the owner's home town. The original plan for farm mechanisation had to be shelved after the Second Republic when imported machinery and spares became very expensive. Maize production has been halted and the farm now concentrates on pigs and livestock. A finance company has also been set up.

Continental Pharmaceuticals

This company began in 1975 as an importer and distributor of cosmetics, toiletries and baby products and has become one of the largest integrated indigenous pharmaceutical companies in the country with wholesale distribution depots nationwide.[77] It is owned by two brothers one of whom trained as a pharmacist in the United States. In 1989 it had a turnover of N25m. with 425 persons employed.

In 1976 the company acquired the total assets, plant and machinery, formulations and manufacturing processes of Barclay Pharmaceuticals, a British company in Lagos. It subsequently also acquired the premises and manufacturing facilities of Colgate Palmolive (Nig.) Ltd in Lagos where a first class manufacturing facility was established. Integrated manufacturing facilities were completed in 1980. The company inherited a franchise for Revlon Afro products. Gradually it developed its own products (Afro Cocoa Butter Cream and Lotion) with the assistance of a two-and-a-half-year research project with the Federal Institute of Industrial Research, Oshodi, and the franchise became redundant. Three expatriates are employed (1989) for liquid tablets and plastics technology. The company embosses tablets and produces its own plastic containers. The quality-assurance department is staffed by 5 graduates.

The company produces a wide range of over-the-counter drugs and ethical medicines, toothpaste, cosmetics, disinfectants, toiletries and baby products. It supplies bulk essential drugs for the federal and state governments. Foreign companies which dominate the pharmaceutical industry have done little drug formulation with the exception of Pfizer. In 1990 the company joined the newly created Nigerian Indigenous Pharmaceutical Manufacturer's Association, in the belief that the interests of indigenous manufacturers were not given due attention by the Pharmaceutical Group of the Manufacturers Association of Nigeria which is dominated by multinationals.

Liz-Olofin and Co. PLC

This small group had a turnover of N10.5m. in 1991 and went public the previous year.[78] Mr O. K. Atewologun attended secondary school at Ido-Ekiti in Ondo State (1956–60) and trained as a banker in London (1963–6), before starting a career in banking.

He started importation of foods and drinks for supermarkets and restaurants in 1973. A bread-production unit (1979) was converted to biscuit production in 1983. With the ban on the importation of wheat, the company developed the production of cereal from maize and went into candle production in 1985. It has 20 per cent of the national market for candles and has made one acquisition. In terms of production, it is one of the top 3 among the 65 producers registered with the Candle Producers Association of Nigeria. Two maize and cassava farms totalling 200 hectares are in operation and the company produces curled maize puffs. In 1991 a crude vegetable-oil factory was opened. A share was also purchased in Araromi Aiyesan Oil Palm Estate, Ondo State.

The Group owns a medium-sized hotel and has acquired land at the Lekki Peninsula Tourism Zone for hotel development with a view to attracting a technical partner for equity and management participation.

Eko Hospitals PLC

In 1976 three consultants at the Lagos University Teaching Hospital (LUTH), Alexander Eneli, Sunny Kuku and Francis Isanghedigbi were engaged in solo private practice in Surulere sharing overheads.[79] The doctors planned to establish a group practice but Isanghedigbi left Lagos for Calabar. Amechi Obiora then joined the practice. In 1978 the doctors resigned their appointments at LUTH to set up the Mercy Specialist Clinic. Their departure was triggered by a decree that banned private practice by professionals in government service. Eko Hospitals was incorporated by the three partners in 1980 and a bank loan of N80,000 raised. In 1985, five full specialities were in operation: surgery, obstetrics, gynaecology, paediatrics and psychiatry; and the hospital was recognised for training of house officers. In 1991 the hospital had over 550 employees and a turnover of N39m. and preparations were underway for expansion using funds from a public-share issue.[80] There were 45 doctors, 16 full-time consultants and 16 senior administrative staff. The company held over 200 corporate retainerships.

Joas Group of Companies

Chief Amao after primary and secondary education in Ibadan, trained as a motor mechanic with GL Gaiser in Lagos.[81] With limited prospects of becoming an auto engineer, he moved to Kano after his uncle died in 1957. Here he successfully entered the electronics trade in 1963, forming Joas Trading and Technical Company. With the civil war, he returned to Lagos and in 1973 Joas Electrical Industries became sole distributor for Sony. Capital was accumulated through the oil boom with the assembly of TV and radio. Employment was about 450 persons at the peak. At the end of the 1970s, Chief Amao diversified into carpets (Atlantic Carpets) and foam mattress production in Ibadan (Bodefoam Industries). Four expatriate engineers were employed initially, but left by 1984. Combined employment in the two factories was 190 persons in 1993. The old electronic assembly lines in Lagos were converted to furniture manufacture and gas-cooker assembly. Chief Amao is a major investor in a mortgage bank. He has also invested in a merchant bank and in an indigenous starch factory. The latter company, Farbest Industries (1991), located near Ibadan, owns a 1,200 hectare cassava farm and was promoted by Dr Jide Koleoso, former director of the Federal Institute of Industrial Research.

Bisrod Furniture

Bisrod is owned by Giwa Bisi Rodipe and manufactures office and institutional furniture at Ijebu-Ode.[82] The plant is fully equipped with facilities for square-section tubular-steel frames, laminated panels and powder coating. Employment has fluctuated from about 350 persons at the peak in 1982, to 100 in 1993.

Chief Rodipe, whose father was a farmer, attended Yaba Trade Centre from 1958 to 1961. After a brief period with Cooperative Woodworks, he joined the Western Region Television and Broadcasting Service, staying for 14 years (1961–74). From 1971, he engaged simultaneously in roadside carpentry. This straddling between occupations continued until he had sufficient capital to become fully established as a furniture manufacturer in Ibadan. His finances were boosted at this point by earnings from the design of a stage for the Nigerian tour of the American musician James Brown.

With the creation of new states in 1976, demand increased and orders were received from all over the country. The national scope of the market was crucial to the decision to relocate production to a large factory (60,000 sq. ft.) at Ijebu-Ode (Ogun State). Currently over 90 per cent of demand is from outside Ogun State and includes 12 polytechnics and 18 universities.

Chief Rodipe developed a middle range of office and classroom furniture avoiding sophisticated products and capital intensive equipment. A very successful range of school furniture (classmate range) was introduced and it eventually became the specification accepted by the federal Ministry of Education. Only one bank loan for N400,000 was taken in 1978. This, together with the fact that demand has proved steadier than in the oversaturated market for domestic furniture, has allowed the company to maintain satisfactory levels of production in depressed economic conditions. Thorough investigation of the export market found very demanding specifications (e.g. all white wood removed from teak chairs) that could only be met with high additional costs.

Collaboration with a UK firm of furniture manufacturers involved the supply of equipment and recruitment of two expatriates (1980–83) but no equity participation or technical agreement. Eight Nigerians were sent for overseas training; of these, two remained in 1993. Four executive directors to cover production, marketing and projects were appointed from within the company and a profit-sharing scheme introduced.

INVESTORS, INTERMEDIARIES AND ENTREPRENEURS

Our concentration on corporate groups and specialist enterprises misses a range of private enterprise which is harder to classify and more difficult to measure. It is none the less relatively important in Nigeria, especially in the Lagos area. Its size reflects the weight of the opportunities available in the public sector and foreign companies from the 1950s when Nigerians were only beginning to establish corporate concerns of their own. At one extreme, it shades into the other categories with the active promotion of enterprises in commerce, industry, banking, finance and property. At the other, it involves essentially rentier or intermediary roles as investor, commission agent, consultant, facilitator and occasional trader. In many cases, these functions overlap and it would be erroneous to describe the business activities of these persons as simply comprador, rentier or arrangee. The degree to which these activities are formally organised and managed through investment and holding companies or other agencies varies. Generally, individuals have not built up corporate organisations, taken partners, or actively managed those companies in which they have participated.

Often the full-time pursuit of private business has come relatively late in their careers. After secondary education and in many cases higher education or professional training, individuals have pursued careers with the civil service, parastatals, foreign companies or professions. The security, financial rewards and high status of these occupations was sufficient to overcome, at least temporarily, aspirations towards self-employment and independence.

Premature or forcible retirement from executive positions in the public sector has been common in the last two decades. The high turnover has contributed to the flow of individuals starting new enterprises. A gradual shift in favour of private-sector employment in terms of rewards and status, which we noted in chapter 2, also contributed.

Career paths vary and may exhibit, at some stage, the holding of multiple positions on the boards of parastatals and foreign companies while private business is promoted. The experience, connections and reputation gathered in the course of a career can be used in a number of ways; to secure access to bank loans and property; as a springboard to shareholding and board membership in major foreign companies; as a means of securing privileged access to information about state policies; and as a means of securing benefits from state discretionary policies and patronage. In this regard, institutions like the Western Nigeria Development Corporation, the Nigerian Industrial Development Bank and the New Nigerian Development Company have all been prominent foci for training, the building of networks, and state patronage.

By virtue of their headstart in education and the professions, their proximity to Lagos, and the early expansion of state institutions in the former Western Region, Yorubas are well represented in this category. Igbo people for obvious reasons are not so prominent. However, conscious strategies to broaden ethnic recruitment by companies and the operation of the principle of federal character at the national level have tended to widen ethnic representation.

We now examine briefly some individual business careers. There are many different strategies and paths of accumulation. The following instances are intended to be illustrative and by no means exhaust the possibilities.

Former Private and Public Sector Employees

In the following case, employment with the United Africa Company and parastatals provided the springboard to a substantial presence in foreign companies and the simultaneous development of own companies.

Otunba Adekunle Ojora was born into the royal family of Lagos in 1932.[83] He received his primary and secondary education in Lagos and studied journalism in London at Regent Street Polytechnic. After a spell in broadcasting, he worked in public relations in the Office of the Premier, Western Region. In 1962 he joined the UAC as a public relations manager. He became an executive director of the company.

He was a nominated member of Lagos City Council (1966–73) When he left the UAC in 1967, he was appointed managing director of a parastatal property company, Wemabod Estates (1967–73) and chairman of the Nigerian National Shipping Line (1967–73).

From this springboard, he started his own companies at the turn of the decade and became a major shareholder and board member in a number of leading foreign companies. He actively sought foreign companies to invest in, and where he was invited to join the board he took shareholdings as a matter of policy. Companies include AGIP (a multinational oil company), Union Trading Company (UTC), Sun Assurance, National Cash Register, Inchape Oil (oil-inspection services), Dresser Manufacturing Co (oil-service materials), Schlumberger (oil-services), Avon Cosmetics, Associated Pharmaceutical Products (joint venture with Merck) and Phoenix Assurance. Other significant holdings were acquired in 7Up and Ecobank Nigeria. Recently majority shareholdings were taken in the UK firm of Evans Brothers, the publishers, and an affiliated company in Nigeria and Chief Ojora became vice-chairman of the London company.

His own companies include a holding company, Lagos Investments Ltd (1970), a property company with a nationwide portfolio, and a fishing company. He acquired the stockbroking interests of the Bowring Group (Capital Trust Brokers) and took a stake in their insurance brokerage. He also acquired the plastic-container division of Pfizer in 1975 (Ivory Products Ltd) and set up a company (Nigerlink) to represent English and German companies including Deutz-MWM (sales and service of auto generating sets). A construction company, Unital Builders, was opened up in 1975 and employs 8 expatriates. A motor franchise for Volkswagen was also started. A rice mill set up in Ibadan proved unprofitable in the face of smuggling and was closed.

For some individuals, the route to substantial private shareholding was a close connection with foreign companies without experience of the public sector. Three examples are given.

Chief N. O. Idowu was born in 1935 and after education in Ibadan and Zaria, became a teacher.[84] He joined Bhojsons Group, a large Indian company, as personnel manager in 1964 and rose to be deputy group chairman and managing director (1979–85). He assisted Indian companies wanting to set up in Nigeria and subsequently took shareholdings and created a holding company. Indian companies in which he became a board member include Rolled Steel Products, Karamu Plastics, Cash and Carry, General Agro Industries, Lucky Fibres, Reliance Textiles, and Premier Industries. Others investments were made in Horizon Fibres, Communications Associates (a joint venture with Decca and Racal of United Kingdom), Ferodo, and a South Korean electronic-assembly plant. Chief Idowu promoted Nigbel Merchant Bank and has interests in three other banks. He also promoted a factory for maize grits near Ibadan.

Prince Ado Ibrahim was born in 1929, the son of Alhaji Ibrahim, the late Atta of Ebiraland.[85] After secondary schooling at Okene Middle School, Ondo Boys' High School, and Oduduwa College, Ife, he joined the UAC as an entrant for an accelerated management-training course designed for selected school leavers of northern Nigerian origin. After experience with Kingsway Stores in Kaduna, he moved to Amalgamated Tin Mines of Nigeria in Jos as personnel manager in 1953 and became an area manager. He took an external London degree in statistics (1954) and later earned a Harvard MBA (1959).

In the early 1960s he started his own companies. He floated a mining company, an investment and property company and an insurance company. In the 1970s, Nigus Petroleum won oil concessions and the right to lift crude oil. He acquired over three-million shares in Food Specialities Ltd, the largest baby-food and beverage manufacturer in Nigeria (Nestlé) and became chairman of Atlas (Nig.) Ltd

In 1976 he established the Ado Ibrahim Foundation for the award of university scholarships. The foundation endowed three university chairs, and a Centre for Law and Diplomacy at the University of Jos. The foundation made a donation of £1m. to the Association of Commonwealth Universities in 1987.

Dr M. O. Omolayole was chairman and chief executive of Lever Brothers for ten years (1974–84). In 1984, he established a consultancy firm, Omolayole Associates, whose clients include multinational corporations, the International Institute for Tropical Agriculture, Ibadan, the International Labour Organisation and the Federation of Kenyan Employers.[86] He is chairman of Chemical and Allied Products where he held 54 per cent of ordinary shares at March 1991 and also chairman of Indequip (WA) Ltd.

Examples of former civil servants who retired at a relatively young age and entered the private sector were noted in chapter 2. They include the former federal permanent secretaries, Allison Ayida and Philip Asiodu (see Table 2.3). A further more recent case of public-sector experience follows.

Alhaji Ibrahim Aliyu, former secretary to the Niger State Government (1979–83) and former chief executive of the Nigerian Industrial Development Bank, made profitable deals in the property market in Abuja and Victoria Island.[87] In 1991, he launched a property firm, Urban Shelters with N15m. equity which has developed residential and office properties in Abuja. A mortgage-finance institution, Shelters Savings and Loans with equity of N10m., was launched in the same year.

Professionals

Among those with professional backgrounds, lawyers, with expertise in company and commercial law, have been especially prominent as shareholders and board members. Examples of lawyers who became significant investors include Chief Chris Ogunbanjo, Chief Rotimi Williams, Chief G. K. J. Amachree, Mr Fred Egbe, Mr Oludayo Sonuga and Chief Olatunde Abudu. In chapter 2, the cases of Chief Akin-George (insurance) and Mr J. O. Emanuel (accountancy) were noted. Perhaps, the individual with the largest number of company directorships in the 1970s and 1980s, was Chief O. I. Akinkugbe (b. 1928) from Ondo, who trained as a pharmacist and was secretary of the Pharmaceutical Society of Nigeria (1952–6) and chairman of Ibadan Chamber of Commerce (1962–71).[88] He pioneered Palm Chemists, Spectrum Publishing and Vitalink Pharmaceutical Industries in Ibadan and was chairman of the Nigerian Industrial Development Bank (1976–80).[89]

Chief Chris Ogunbanjo, a corporate lawyer, was legal adviser to the Western Region Development Corporation and his law firm handled some of the earliest public issues on the Nigerian Stock Exchange. He established a holding company (Union Securities) and became a shareholder and board member of many companies, including Associated Electronic Products (formerly Phillips), Brown and Root, Kloeckner Ina, Peugeot, Nigerian Sewing Machine Manufacturing, Powerlines Ltd, Nigerian Diversified Investments, Minnesota, Nigeria-French Insurance, Roche, Smurfit, Allied Biscuits, Metal Box Toyo Glass, West African Batteries, Pan African Airlines and Bougyues Nig. Ltd.

Those with professional experience of banking who have later promoted private banks, include Otunba M. O. Balogun (First City Merchant Bank, 1983), Chief S. O. Asabia (First Interstate Merchant Bank, 1987), Mr G. O. Onosode (Commerce Bank PLC, 1989) and Mr O. Olashore (Lead Merchant Bank, 1989). Mr Gamaliel Onosode, was formerly chairman and chief executive of NAL Merchant Bank (1973–9). He was a member of the Udoji Salary Commission, the Okigbo Committee on the financial system and headed a panel that reported on state corporations and parastatals.

CONCLUSION

Early in this chapter we noted the attractions of property and trade for Lagosian families and immigrant Yoruba. Later we advanced reasons for the existence of a large group of investors and intermediaries in Lagos. There is no doubt about the weight of these rentier elements in Lagos and the importance of commerce. However, over time a more complicated pattern of accumulation emerges.

The great majority of Lagos-based enterprises originated in trade and many have continued to depend on commercial activity. Petty trade, retailing, internal distribution and the produce trade often provided the starting point, but it was direct importation and, to a lesser extent, commodity exports which played a part in the subsequent growth of most enterprises. Exports of cocoa, palm kernel and rubber were significant in a few cases where individuals held a federal licence to export for the Nigerian Produce Marketing Company. The often overlooked, unscheduled, northern commodities (benniseed, coffee, ginger, gum arabic, adua kernels, shea nut) also played a minor role. As petroleum oil gradually replaced commodity exports as the major export, so importing increased in importance.

Large scale importation and commodity exporting created the incentive to move into service industries like clearing and forwarding, transportation, port services and, in a few cases, shipping. Importation of goods shifted into higher technical, more specialised areas and spread to lower-cost sources of supply in the Far East, eastern and southern Europe. The establishment of overseas offices to oversee procurement and in a few cases to manage investment portfolios was encouraged by the oil boom and the appreciation of the naira. In some cases, manufacturers' representation and agencies led to the assembly, processing or manufacture of goods formerly imported. Other concerns developed property and investment holding companies and an interest in banking. However, many trading firms did not move downstream or go into industry or services. Some trading companies that grew rapidly with the oil boom, or were associated with political patronage, proved to be vehicles for capital flight and conspicuous consumption and disappeared.

At the time of independence, substantial personal wealth led to approaches by foreign companies who sought 'names' to take shareholdings and board membership but no management functions. In the 1970s the indigenisation decrees brought new opportunities for the acquisition of shares. Relations between individuals and foreign companies did not necessarily take a completely passive, rentier form, as we saw in the case of Mobalaji Bank-Anthony who actively sought and 'introduced' foreign enterprises to Nigeria in the 1950s and Chief Abiola who bargained vigorously, secured government contracts, took substantial equity and a position on the international board of ITT.

Many larger enterprises have property portfolios which may be managed as distinct holding companies. Though some have actively traded in property, or set up residential or industrial estates, speculative property development in Lagos has not given rise to major property-development companies.[90] One reason is that families, as landowners on Lagos Island, still retain a strong interest in their properties thereby restricting the supply of land for development. The Land Use Decree made the private development of large property estates more difficult. This has not however prevented individuals from amassing property. After gaining a toe-hold in the property ladder, individuals have upgraded and expanded their portfolios eventually arriving in the expensive residential areas of Ikoyi and Victoria Island. In some cases property has absorbed a significant proportion of earnings.

With the exception of the two enterprises considered in the next chapter, the performance of older groups has been modest in terms of growth. They remain essentially trading concerns. Among the groups studied, over two-thirds had developed some industrial interests (often food processing and beverages), but the overall weight was small and in no group was it dominant.

A number of groups appear to have entered unrelated activities and lack a focus, which may impede their growth. Apart from the rationale provided by the need to spread and reduce the overall level of risk, diversification can also be seen as a rational response to other factors. Uncertainty over government policy and changes in political regime have encouraged a spread of activities to take advantage of shifts in policy and state patronage. Two other factors have contributed. Most enterprises have some activities located near the home community. Sometimes these are unprofitable and best seen as a form of welfare for the community. The difficulties of sub-contracting in Nigeria may encourage self-sufficiency and the development of in-house services like security, insurance, transport, property, packaging which leads to the spinning-off of separate companies.

The younger groups which have appeared since the civil war still have their origins in trade. All have entered industry to some extent, often agro-industry, and have taken advantage of recent opportunities to go into banking. Unlike the earlier generation of literate businessmen that were active in the late colonial period and the 1960s, they do not exhibit a pattern of shareholding and board membership in foreign companies. There has been some decline in the importance of prior employment in government service. Since 1970, the entry of graduates and those with professional qualifications marks a new departure.

Our studies of enterprises in Lagos and the western states in this chapter and in chapter 3, suggest a mixed, uneven pattern of advance in industry. The overall pattern is one of investment over a wide variety of sectors with some large-scale enterprises but no dominant position established in any one sector (food processing,[91] soft drinks and beer, distilling, soap and detergents, shoes, garments, carpets, printing and packaging, colour-photo processing,[92] paper conversion and recycling, furniture, paints, cosmetics and pharmaceuticals, plastics, electric appliances, cookers, refrigerators, motor spare parts, batteries, light engineering, flour milling, vegetable-oil milling, and fishing). Large scale investment in the textile industry is largely absent, which is not the case in Kano.[93] The poor experience of early textile ventures and the strength of Indian competition may have acted as a deterrent.

Local engineering capacities are limited to copying and are thinly spread. There is design and fabrication of process equipment (Addis Engineering), computer assembly and satellite communications assembly. Most enterprises have acquired foreign technology without adaptation and have hired expatriates directly rather than enter into management or technical agreements. Where higher technology is involved, as in unplasticised PVC fittings and manufacture of gas cylinders, the indigenous promoters have taken joint-venture partners. In another case, there was an evolution from sole distributor of electrical accessories in 1981, in which the American supplier held 40 per cent of the equity, through assembly, to local manufacture of copper cable fittings and electrical porcelain insulators in 1988, with eventual divestment by the foreign multinational in 1991.

The advance in the service sector has been stronger than in manufacture. It has been particlarly strong in banking, insurance, finance companies, mortgage institutions and other financial services. Other service activities where local capital is strongly represented include professional practices (law, accountancy, architecture, real estate), advertising, consultancy, hotels, medical services and port services.

With regard to the prospects of enterprises across the generations, evidence is still lacking not of the survival, but the capacity of successors to build on and expand the enterprise after the death of the founder/owner. As we noted in the previous chapter, a number of family enterprises have not grown appreciably despite the opportunities for growth since the 1960s. Mary Rowe reported a similar phenomenon for those second generation enterprises extant in the 1960s.[94] She also reported that, 'all but one of the Nigerian entrepreneurs seemed purposely to keep their sons in a weak position, discouraging traits which might later facilitate effective entrepreneurship of the heirs'.[95] The strategy of trying to ensure succession by educating children and bringing them into the enterprise is now more common. But family interests can prove divisive, or inimical to leadership and direction, once the founder dies. Moreover, where the founder/owner was closely identified with the enterprise and its growth was dependent on personal connections there is bound to be at the very least a hiatus and probably stagnation or contraction after death. Partial solutions to these problems can be found in the introduction of more bureaucratic, impersonal forms of management during the owner's lifetime, by partnership and by going public on the stock market. The latter option is a very new one which only a few specialist enterprises have exercised. No Lagos-based groups, or companies within groups, have gone public.

5

THE RISE OF TWO CONGLOMERATES

The Ibru Organisation and the Modandola Group are among the largest enterprises in Nigeria. The original enterprises were both set up in the same year, 1956. Their subsequent growth offers some interesting contrasts and parallels.

THE IBRU ORGANISATION

In 1990, the Ibru Organisation employed between 9,000 and 11,000 persons, depending on seasonal fluctuations and the profile of large construction projects.[1] Turnover was estimated at around N250m. in 1981.[2] I am mainly concerned here with the core of the enterprise controlled by Chief Michael Ibru which is distinct from more recent enterprises in which four junior brothers have significant interests of their own.

The Ibrus are Urhobo and hail from Agbarha-Otor, some 6 km from Ughelli in the Delta Area of Bendel State. Michael Ibru's father, Chief Peter Epete Ibru spent much of his life in missionary work in Yorubaland.[3] He worked at Igbobi Orthopaedic Hospital, close to the family house in Shomolu. His mother is an active trader who has taken a close interest in the enterprise. Michael Ibru entered Igbobi College in 1948 and left with a Cambridge School Certificate in 1951 to join the United Africa Company. He was among the first set of Nigerian managers in training.

I now trace the development of the Ibru Organisation in three phases before turning to other aspects of the business.

1956–1970

Michael Ibru left the United Africa Company as a manager in 1956 at the age of 24. He formed a general trading company, Laibru, with an Englishman, Jimmy Large, who had also worked for UAC. He also bought into an existing construction company, Ace Jimona. Among the projects executed by this company were Queen's College, Yaba; St Gregory's, Obalende; and the Police College at Ikeja.

Chief Ibru's major innovation was to pioneer the distribution of frozen fish in Nigeria from 1957. He eventually created a network of cold stores covering the whole country. The name Ibru became synonymous with frozen fish. Entry into the distribution of frozen fish and the fishing industry was not easy and the precedents were not encouraging. In the early 1950s, the Commonwealth Development Corporation had attempted to establish a fishing venture in Nigerian waters with cold-storage facilities and a distribution operation.[4] West African Fisheries and Cold Store failed. Fish stocks were insufficient off Port Harcourt, the boats were inappropriate and there were marketing and distribution difficulties.

Ibru had noticed that fish held little attraction for the European trading houses or Nigerian merchants. He examined the canning and drying of fish before he settled for frozen fish.[5] He had to overcome considerable consumer resistance. Cold stores and clouds of steam were associated in the public mind with mortuaries. Meat sellers mounted a campaign against frozen fish. To counter this propaganda, he successfully mobilised market women with processions and songs and encouraged them to smoke fish.

Two fishing ventures with Swiss and Liberian partners were unsuccessful. He then formed Ibru Sea Foods, as the sole owner, and imported frozen fish. He rented cold-storage facilities at the Ijora wharf from the UAC, using the facilities at night, and traded from the back of a Land Rover. Later, he built his own cold-storage facilities at Creek Road, Apapa. In 1963, he chartered his first fishing vessel from Taiwo of Japan. In 1965, he founded the Osadjere Fishing Company as a joint venture with Taiwo, one of the largest fishing companies in the world. The company began with three long-distance freezer trawlers. Taiwo held 30 per cent of the equity and provided the management for deep-sea trawlers and shrimpers. The company pioneered the catching of shrimps in Nigerian territorial waters. Earlier, Ibru had distributed prawns for Taiwo in Nigeria. The company experienced considerable difficulties and at times had to cease operations. In 1974, it was reorganised and the fleet then fluctuated between 8 and 25 trawlers.

A transport fleet of 200 vehicles was built up by 1967. In 1969 a vehicle-distribution agency, Rutam Motors, was acquired (Mazda, Saviem, Tata, Jeep) and agencies later set up in Bendel state (Warri Motors and Bendel Motors). Heavy construction plant was also imported and distributed. (Rutam was later appointed a Peugeot distributor by the federal government.) In Bendel State, Chief Ibru began a small palm-oil plantation (1965) and also developed a citrus and pineapple farm on a 800-hectare site which, for a time, supplied the Lafia cannery in Ibadan.

Thus, the Ibru group at the end of the 1960s included general trading, fishing and frozen-fish distribution, construction, vehicle distribution and agriculture.

1970–1982

The distribution of frozen fish was to remain at the core of the enterprise throughout the 1970s and was a stable and reliable source of profit. Ibru accounted for about 60 per cent (150,000–200,000 tons) of the Nigerian frozen-fish market and turnover reached around N90m. during the 1970s. Import policy and the appreciation of the naira were generally favourable to the expansion of fish imports during the 1970s. Local fishing ventures, on the other hand, were generally discouraged by a duty on fish caught and landed by Nigerian-owned fishing vessels (50 per cent *ad valorem*) imposed in 1969. This held up the development of a Nigerian fishing fleet. Other adverse factors were the absence of fishing terminals with facilities, over-dependence on ineffective and expensive fishing crew, the absence of training together with high duties on fishing vessels and gear. Foreign exchange earnings from the re-export of shrimps were substantial in this period. Over a slightly later period (1977–85), 6,173 tons of shrimps were caught and $33m. earned through exports.[6] Fish was also re-exported within the West African sub-region and marketed through outlets in Benin, Cameroon, Mauritania and Togo. In addition, three chartered trawler and freezer fleets were operated off Walvis Bay, Angola and Las Palmas. Plans to develop harbour facilities at the Angolan port of Cabinda were shelved.[7]

Importation through the oil-boom period was one source of growth. Another was through the whole or partial acquisition of enterprises under the indigenisation decrees of 1972 and 1977 which enforced foreign divestment. The Ibru Organisation purchased shares in, or acquired, at least fifteen companies (see the chart, Acquisition by the Ibru Organisation, p. 134). In the case of Mitchell Farms, W. F. Clarke and Zabadne, already existing shareholdings were extended. The capacity to take advantage of the indigenisation decrees distinguished the Group and it was more active than other Nigerian companies in acquiring enterprises as going concerns. In Nigeria as a whole, it was the build-up of large equity portfolios that predominated.

A third contribution to expansion was made through the setting up of joint ventures with major international companies (see the chart, Ibru joint ventures, p. 135). Finally, a few activities were spun off from in-house projects (security, shipping, agency, insurance broking and consultancy).

A major investment (N100m.) in this period was the construction of a private port complex with jetty and cold-storage facilities at Ibafon on swamp land to the west of Tin Can Island alongside the new Apapa–Isolo expressway. These facilities were financed in part by Embourg of Denmark. The decline of imports in the 1980s and the closure of private jetties by the Shagari government soon after the completion of the Ibafon complex, proved a severe blow to the company.

It is difficult to assess the rationale and subsequent performance of these

Acquisition by the Ibru Organisation.

Mitchell Farms (1973). The largest producer of day-old chicks and processed poultry in West Africa. The company was acquired from Americans who had started the enterprise in 1963. After initial problems with losses carried, a Dutch team managed the company successfully. The company has a hatchery and breeder farm for grandparent stock and uses a contract system for raising poultry. It includes a pig-breeding farm.

Nigerian Hardwoods (1974). A logging, saw-milling and wood-processing company purchased at a low price from the Lathem Group, UK. The firm was originally established in 1919 and exported hardwood logs. Located in a remote part of Bendel State, Ibru was encouraged to take over the company by the governor of the state. The offer included forestry concessions of 116 sq. miles. Because of an export ban on hardwood logs, the company was in a run-down condition. This has proved a costly long-term investment with retrenchment of workers (1,500 workers were inherited), a poor transport fleet, and obsolete equipment for replacement. The company has slowly been reactivated with the installation of a fully automated mill and wood-processing equipment. It also manufactures pallets, cranes and furniture.

George Cohen Nig. Ltd. A steel stockist and distributor with heavy crane-hire cooperation was partially acquired from the 600 Group of UK. Nigerian shareholding is 60%. The general manager, an English engineer, has lived in Nigeria since 1968 and has worked for various companies within the Ibru Group for 15 years.

W. F. Clarke. An import agency with 9 depots across the country (100%). Established 1949.

A. J. Karoumi. A Lebanese transport company based in Kano with a depot in Maiduguri, a service to Chad, and dual-purpose tankers (fuel and groundnut oil). Fleet reduced from over 100 vehicles to 30. Fuel and bitumen hauled from Kaduna refinery.

Disscol. A French company servicing the water industry (drilling and irrigation supplies). Not in operation.

Aero Contractors Company of Nigeria Ltd. 60% stake in air charter company operating from Lagos, Warri and Port Harcourt. Established 1957.

Mapel Nig. Ltd. Oil pipeline service company working for Shell.

Minet Nigeria. 40% stake in insurance company.

Lileshall (Nig.) Ltd. Importer of GKN fasteners, nuts and bolts, building materials.

Acquired interest in Western Bottlers (Pepsi Cola) but did not establish control. Established Rainbow Soft Drinks, located in Sapele and Aba. Held the Pepsi Cola franchise for the eastern states. With the intensification of competition in the soft-drinks market under recession, this company has been sold to the Nigerian Bottling Company.

F. Steiner. A Swiss company involved in watches, survey equipment, air conditioning and refrigeration. The air-conditioning division has been developed separately (Thermostein). Mr Steiner introduced the first motor car spray painting in West Africa in Accra in 1929. He began evening classes for mechanics in Kumasi (1927) and Lagos (1937). He introduced the first qualified watch-repair service in West Africa (1947).[8]

Nigerian Marine and Trading. French company providing marine services to the oil industry and holding French agencies.

NITREC. A vehicle distributor with a valuable site on the fringe of Apapa, the main dock area.

Zabadne Co. Ltd. Sale of electronics and TV assembly. Factory and shop on Broad Street, Lagos Island.

Jewellers Co. Ltd.

Source: Interviews and company directories.

Ibru joint ventures

Osadjere Fishing Co.	Venture with Taiwo of Japan (30%).
Superbru	Skol International lager brewery in Bendel State started up in 1979. Venture with Unibra of Belgium (15%) and Allied Breweries of UK (15%). In 1982 Ibru took 100% and entered into a technical agreement with Cereken of Denmark in 1984. The company has a rice farm.
Bos Kalis Nig. Ltd	Major Dutch construction company.
Spie Batgnolles	Major French construction company.
Specol Sanqui	Spanish pre-fabricated housing company.
Sheraton Hotels	Project cost was $53.1m. overall. Ibru invested $7.2m. and holds 35% of equity, a controlling interest through Ikeja Hotels Ltd NIDB holds 22% and the International Finance Corporation 6% of the equity.
Elf Marketing Nig. Ltd	Petroleum distribution with major French oil company.
Ibafon Chemicals	Venture with major US chemical company, Dow Chemicals. Dow was attracted by bulk storage facilities at Ibafon, a private port complex with a fishing jetty developed by Ibru on swamp land to the west of Tin Can Island alongside the new Apapa–Isolo expressway. Port congestion in the wake of the oil boom was a major incentive to the development of private port facilities in Nigeria. Ibru also invested in private port development and cold storage at Okereke, Bendel State.

acquisitions without further information. Some, like Mitchell Farms, George Cohen, Zabadne and Aerocontractors have proved successful. After takeover, some companies have experienced a loss of motivation and morale. The large number of acquisitions overextended management with the constant need for intervention from above. In the case of Zabadne, the original owner, a naturalised Nigerian, continued to run the company as an Ibru employee and this was successful. Some of the companies were acquired for their properties. Others involved entry into services in which the Group had little prior experience.

1982 to the Present

With a high dependence on imports, the Ibru Organisation was vulnerable to the rapid import compression in the Nigerian economy that followed the fall in oil revenues. The import of fish came under licence with the 1983 Stabilisation Order and was maintained despite a vigorous defence of frozen-fish imports by Ibru. Numerous cold-storage facilities operated by factors were closed down and concentrated on the major depots at Ijora, Ibafon, Oghareki and Port Harcourt. Fishing was expanded as the import of frozen fish declined, though the expansion has been hampered by the lack of suitable fishing grounds. Nigerian territorial waters are not rich in fish stocks. As a result, Ibru negotiated fishing rights in Mauritania and Angola for distant-water fishing.

The second major response has been the expansion of land acquisition and agricultural activities. In Bendel State, in addition to the 769-hectare oil-palm estate developed over 1965–82, a further 4,500 hectares has been acquired and a new mill opened (N2.5m.). Other land acquisitions include 7,000 hectares in Kwara where a pilot project has begun. These farms grow maize and sorghum to supply the brewery and poultry industry. In 1980, CAFAD took a shareholding in Tropic Foods, a food processing company at Agbede whose largest shareholder was Professor T. M. Yesefu.[9] In 1990, a commercial bank, Oceanic Bank International was established.

At the end of the 1980s, the recession had prompted a restructuring of the group, coordinated by a British consultant.[10] Oscar, Chief Michael Ibru's eldest son, and one of five children groomed to take over running of the companies, had joined company boards and ran a seafood firm, Waskar.

Chief Ibru helped to educate his brothers to graduate level (architecture, management, engineering, law). They participated in the core enterprises. Later, they were encouraged to set up enterprises of their own while retaining board membership in core companies. The brothers have interests in plastics, electronics, laboratory equipment, computers, advertising, architecture, hotels and newspapers. Guardian Newspapers Ltd and Ikeja Hotels Ltd have both developed into substantial enterprises.

The Guardian newspaper is probably the most authoritative newspaper in Nigeria contributing significantly to the conduct of economic and political debate. Its editorial board has generally been detached from Ibru interests. With contributions by academics and intellectuals, it was the heir to earlier campus publications like *Nigerian Opinion* and the *New Nationalist*.

The origins of the Guardian Newspapers Ltd lay in a meeting between Ibru wealth and the technocratic ideas and ambitions of Dr Stanley Macebuh and Dr Dele Cole.[11] Dr Macebuh was the editorial adviser and chairman of the editorial board of the Daily Times of Nigeria and Dr Cole, a former managing director of the Daily Times who had lost his job when the National Party of Nigeria (NPN) came to power in 1979. They wanted to launch a serious newspaper that would become the flagship of the Nigerian press. Alex Ibru, the Ibru brother with the highest public profile and chairman of Rutam Motors, also had ideas for a more down-market newspaper that would protect Ibru interests if necessary. Segun Osoba, the former managing director of the *Nigerian Herald* was instrumental in bringing the two sides together and convincing Alex Ibru of the credentials of Macebuh and Cole.

The Ibrus took 55 per cent of the equity in the new venture and Macebuh and Cole 5 per cent each. Others who bought shares in the infant company included Segun Osoba, Shehu Musa, Shehu Yar'adua, Caleb Osesami and Chris Okolie (proprietor of *Newbreed* magazine). The Ibrus spent about N7m. on equipment for the company. The chairmanship of the company went to Alex Ibru after Michael Ibru had resigned when his involvement was felt to be incompatible with his efforts to secure the NPN nomination in Bendel State. Macebuh was the effective editor and the editorial board was generally free of Ibru interests. An illustration of this was a critique of the Lagos Metroline project which was carried without the knowledge that a major French contractor in the project, Spie Batignolles, was an Ibru joint-venture partner.

Sunday and evening newspapers were added to the daily, together with a weekly magazine, the *African Guardian*. Macebuh was to stay with *The Guardian* until 1989 when differences with Alex Ibru over his involvement in a private trading company led to his departure. With Guardian Newspapers firmly established, Alex Ibru devoted time to establishing the Intra-Faith Centre, a retreat for religious study and contemplation at Agbarha-Otor, which opened in 1992.[12]

Goodie Ibru, a commercial lawyer, is chairman of Ikeja Hotels Ltd, owners of the Lagos Sheraton Hotel which opened in 1985 (see chart, p. 135). He is also vice-chairman of Triumph Merchant Bank. Ikeja Hotels had a turnover of N132m. in 1990.[13] In 1992, Ikeja Hotels acquired Federal Palace Hotels from the federal government for $50m. outbidding the Daewoo Corporation of South Korea.[14] Under the terms of the sale, Ikeja Hotels is to divest 40 per cent of the equity by public offer within 5 years. The Federal Palace, originally built by the Leventis Group to house guests for Nigerian independence celebrations in 1960, had made losses since the early 1980s largely because government officials never paid their bills.

Felix Ibru after training in Israel as an architect, lectured at the Yaba College of Technology.[15] In 1964 he set up an architectural firm with foreign partners, Ibru Vaughan-Richards. The firm was involved in the development of the Universities of Benin and Lagos. Felix unsuccessfully contested the Bendel South Senatorial District in 1983 for the Unity Party of Nigeria, losing to the Lagos-based accountant, David Dafinone. In 1992 he became governor of Delta State, his home state, whose creation he had actively lobbied for.

The Ibru Organisation combines personal control and ownership by the founder with family participation by four brothers and bureaucratic forms of corporate management that allow considerable delegation of authority. There is a strong family ideology with covers the activities of the brothers and expatriate employees who regard themselves as part of the family. The brothers meet every month.

In 1973, an 'Executive Committee' was created with Alex and Goodie Ibru, two expatriates and a Nigerian, Mr A. M. Egoh. It had responsibility for interpreting and implementing group policy.[16] Two expatriates achieved the level of executive director before leaving the company. Expatriates were recruited on terms comparable to the United Africa Company with pension schemes and gratuities. The peak of expatriate employment was in 1975 with about 110 employed. Recruitment of senior Nigerians speeded up after

1975 and a cadre of senior Nigerian management was established, several Nigerians becoming directors. Recruitment was assisted by the purge of the public sector by the Murtalla Mohammed regime which heightened the attractions of careers in the private sector. Among those recruited were academics (Dr I. A. Anaza, Dr Essien, Dr R. W. Imishue and Dr Okurume), two former federal commissioners and the former registrar of the University of Ibadan. Expatriates were retained at the plant level. A central holding company was created (Oteri) with nine divisions. Some of these divisions, like the agro-industrial wing CAFAD Ltd, which was incorporated in 1979, have begun to acquire their own identity. Others, like Oteri Properties and Oteri Services function to make the Group more independent.

Until recently, Chief Ibru has concentrated almost entirely on business interests. He was member of the Economic Council of the former Midwest State and a member of council of the University of Benin. In 1983, he stood unsuccessfully for the National Party of Nigeria gubernatorial nomination in Bendel State against the former military governor of the state, Samuel Ogbemudia. His candidacy was pressed on him at short notice four or five weeks before the primary by his home community. People from the old Delta province felt that they were not adequately represented by any of the parties and Ibru was a consensus candidate. More recently Chief Ibru was a member of the Constituent Assembly and was a leading member of the Liberal Convention, one of six parties that were disbanded by the federal government in 1990. The Liberal Convention, whose origins lay in the Constituent Assembly, was notable for the support it received from a number of wealthy businessmen, including Chief Igbinedion and Chief Onwuka Kalu. Chief Ibru was widely held to have presidential ambitions.

Like other businessmen, Michael Ibru has engaged in philanthropy. In the 1970s, he funded a college in his home town and handed it over to the government when it opened. He donated N250,000 to the University of Benin. He was awarded an honorary doctorate in 1978. He also funded scholarships for the employees of his companies to go overseas. He figured prominently in the state appeal funds of the mid-1980s. For example, as chairman of the launch of the Plateau State Industrial Development Appeal Fund in 1985, he donated N200,000.

THE MODANDOLA GROUP

This conglomerate employs about 9,000 persons of whom 5,000 work for a large construction company.[17] The Group has a low public profile and its growth has gone largely unnoticed. Individual companies are better known.

Chief Bode Akindele was born in 1932. His mother was a wealthy Ibadan trader who was also politically influential. She tried to mediate in the Action Group crisis of 1962. His father was a senior government official. Chief Akindele was educated at Olubi Memorial School, Ibadan and Lisabi Commercial College, Abeokuta. After secondary schooling, he took some commercial courses, intending to proceed later to the United Kingdom to become a chartered secretary. On several occasions, he nearly left for the United Kingdom but the growth of his own business activities eventually took precedence.

In 1952 he secured his first employment as secretary to an assistant district officer, Mr Dina. He then became a cadet manager with the United Africa Company. He was assistant to the expatriate manager at Oyo where he dealt in kerosene, spirits and bicycles. Responding to an advertisement, he then moved to Ibadan to become assistant to Mr E. A. Sanda, managing director of the Ibadan Traders Association. Mr Sanda, whose father was one of the earliest cocoa farmers near Ibadan, was active in the produce trade.[18] He was chairman of the Ibadan Chamber of Commerce and on the board of the Produce Marketing Company. This appointment brought him close to the heart of the Ibadan business elite. He stayed three and a half years during which time he gained experience of produce marketing and set up his own trading company, Okebadan Bros Ltd in 1956. Along with six others, he was also involved in the Nigerian Farmers and Commercial Bank. He also held an appointment with the Western Nigerian Union of Importers and Exporters.

His next appointment was with the Ibadan Bus Service Ltd which employed 800 workers. He was sent to sort out the accounts and spent one and a half years there. While with the bus company he imported a sample Japanese copy of a Singer sewing machine for £15. He also imported electric fans which gave him good margins. He saved £250 in a six-month period. He concentrated on the import of electrical goods and obtained an agency from Thorn Electrical of the United Kingdom which was worth some £10,000 per annum in terms of turnover. The importation of jute bags in competition with UAC, GBO (G. B. Ollivant), and later, Leventis, proved extremely profitable. He obtained a regional licenced buying agent (LBA) and used profits from the import trade to finance produce trading in cocoa and palm kernel, advancing credit for 30 to 40 days. Shops were established in Ilesha, Ife and Owo and in 1959, an office was opened in Lagos. He also obtained a sole agency for Japanese sewing machines.

He eventually gave up his regional LBA licence and took up a federal one with the Nigerian Produce Marketing Board. This gave him a licence to buy, grade and ship produce. Drawing on his experience of the produce trade in the Western Region, he was able to time his monthly purchases of cocoa and palm kernel to coincide with a period at the end and beginning of each month when other buyers who relied on bank overdrafts to advance money were not active in the market. He thought he was one of two federal agents out of about a dozen in Lagos for whom the produce trade was profitable. He bought land in Agege (a Lagos suburb) and constructed a 80 ft by 350 ft warehouse where he stockpiled and graded cocoa.

The importation of goods and the high volume of cocoa exports led to an interest in clearing and forwarding and road haulage. A company was set up (Coastal Services Ltd) and the patronage of Umarco and Panalpina terminated. Later he became a shipping agent chartering vessels in London and using old school connections with the National Bank of Nigeria which had opened a London office in 1956, to finance his transactions.

In 1965 he gave up his federal LBA licence because heavy taxation through the marketing-board system had made the controlled produce trade less profitable. He then concentrated on non-controlled produce (coffee, gum arabic, shea nuts) selling to the Japanese trading conglomerate Marubeni. In the non-scheduled produce markets there was no marketing commission to pay the board and no export duty. At this time there was no foreign exchange control. He opened his first store in Abuja in 1963, establishing sixteen branches in the North. The Chief of Suleja acted as his buying agent for high quality Kabba coffee. He directly employed some eight persons as managers and store keepers. He had eight lorries in the north and used the railways to transport produce to Lagos. In those days security was good and he would leave Ibadan every Friday night to arrive in the North early in the morning with large sums of cash to purchase produce. At one point, finding he was carrying large sums of cash, the police escorted him safely to his destination.

The setting up of Coastal Services Ltd was the beginning of the growth of a constellation of shipping and port activities that expanded in the 1970s at a time when Nigerian imports underwent extremely rapid expansion fuelled by the oil boom. Other private Nigerian enterprises also established port services and facilities (jetties, port management, warehousing, clearing and forwarding, lighterage and stevedoring, container terminals, shipping agencies and lines, ship repair and dry dock) but the Modandola Group was probably the most prominent indigenous company in this area.

With the indigenisation decree of 1972, which enforced the sale of foreign equity, Modandola secured a 40 per cent (later 60 per cent) stake in Umarco, the largest shipping agency in Nigeria owned by Saga Transport of Paris, part of the Rothschilds empire. This shareholding was secured in the face of strong competition from Chief Henry Fajemirokun, the founder and owner of the Henry Stephens Group, a company that had also been active in the produce and clearing and forwarding trade. The clearing and forwarding side of Umarco was bought and merged with Coastal Services and a ten-year management contract drawn up by Chief Akindele was signed with Umarco. Coastal Services handled a number of large public and private projects in Nigeria including the Ughelli Power Station, the Peugeot assembly plant, the Oshogbo steel-rolling mill and the Sokoto Dam for Impresit. It also operated the Ijora container terminal.

During the 1970s, the Group opened a large roll-on roll-off (ro-ro) terminal

Modandola Group industries

Standard Breweries, Ibadan	1981	1.2 hectolitres. Technical partners, El Aguila of Spain.
Diamond Foods Ltd, Ibadan	1981	7,500 tons a year. Experimenting with composite flour.
Standard Packaging, Ibadan	1983	Plastic crates, bags and household wares. Technical partners, AMS Hamburg and Acrifa of Denmark.
United Beverages Ltd, Ibadan	1986	The largest single unit in Nigeria (470,000 hectolitres) with a small share of the national market. Holds franchises from Dr Pepper of the US and Africola of Germany. Invested N6m. in distribution in 1989.
Associated Match Industry, Ibadan, Ilorin, Port Harcourt, Lagos		Four enterprises in Ibadan, Ilorin, Port Harcourt and Lagos merged to form a company with a large share of the Nigerian market. These units were acquired from Lebanese owners through the gradual build up of a controlling interest.
Standard Flour Mills Ltd, Lagos		A large flour mill with its own 380-metre jetty. $80m. investment with a milling capacity of 2,000 tons a day. Technical agreement with Somidiaa, a subsidiary of Grand Moulin de Paris.

and warehousing operation at Tin Can Island port. The Roro Terminal Company was the managing agent of the Nigerian Ports Authority for ro-ro terminals in all Nigerian ports. The Group also started a fishing venture after securing four trawlers from Ghana in 1971. Obelawo Farcha Fishing Industries Ltd currently has a fleet of 28 trawlers and 5 shrimpers are under construction. In the early 1980s, the Group expanded into boat building, and ship-repair and dry-dock facilities in a joint venture with Damen Shipyards of Holland (20 per cent).

A new phase in the development of the Group began with the start-up of manufacturing and process industries at Alomaja, a village very close to Ibadan, and in Lagos. These included a large brewery, biscuit, plastics and soft-drinks (the largest single unit in Nigeria) factories, four match factories acquired from Lebanese owners and a large flour mill with $80m. invested (see chart, Modandola Group industries, above). There are no joint ventures, the Group relying on well-known technical partners and expatriate employment. The Group has also been active in construction, real estate and equity investment, and farming. First experience in construction was a joint venture with DC Savage, an American Company that built the US embassy in Lagos and the Lagos Durbar Hotel. Savage left Nigeria and the Modandola Group sustained some losses before it closed down operations. Recently, a 50 per cent stake has been acquired in HFP Engineering, an innovative building and civil-engineering company that has grown rapidly since its arrival in

1979 to become one of the largest construction companies in Nigeria. Turn-over was N263m. in 1990.[19] It is affiliated with a German civil-engineering company. It has a pre-fabricated building factory on a 10-hectare site on the Lekki peninsula near Lagos and has set up a mortgage-finance company.

There is a large property and investment company with assets in excess of N100m. including a significant stake in the Bank of Credit and Commerce International (Nig.) Ltd. A 15,000-hectare farm was acquired in Oyo State. It has begun to provide sorghum and maize for the brewery and biscuit industry. A management agreement with the Anhui Corporation of China in 1988 proved unsuccessful and the Chinese left after a short period. A large medical diagnostic centre is currently under construction near Ibadan.

The Group opened a full service-advertising company, Oricom (Nig.) Ltd in 1983.[20] Initially, the agency did well and made publicity through the 'Oricom Lectures', sponsorship of beauty competitions and sporting events. In 1986 and 1987 the agency foundered despite bringing in a new chief executive from one of Nigeria's top agencies. At this point, a retired marketing director for Lever brothers joined the Modandola Group and advised on its reorganisation. A new chief executive was then appointed.

The Group is notable for its reliance on expatriate management both at the centre and at plant level. The number of expatriates employed has fallen from a peak of 211 to 46 (1989), and includes 17 different nationalities. The number of expatriates has declined as a result of recession, the high cost of expatriate employment and the recruitment of some Nigerians to managerial positions. The group technical director, a Spanish engineer, was originally employed by El Aguila, the technical partners in the brewery.

On the advice of foreign associates, the company has recently reorganised its corporate structure (see Figure 5.1). The appointment of a group managing director (GMD) in the hierarchy has reduced the need for downward intervention by the chairman. In addition, the creation of a group management team (GMT) of six members, five of whom each have responsibilities for four companies in the Group, has improved horizontal communication and co-ordination. Two members of the team are responsible for technical and financial matters. There is a tight system of financial control with monthly/quarterly reporting. Two members of the group management team are Nigerians who joined the Group after long careers with a bank and a major multinational company. In 1989 one of them was appointed group managing director.

CONCLUSION

The two conglomerates, which both originated in 1956, offer some interesting contrasts and parallels. Both Chief Bode Akindele and Chief Michael Ibru had early experience of working for UAC, though under different circumstances. The Ibru family through its early association with frozen fish, the

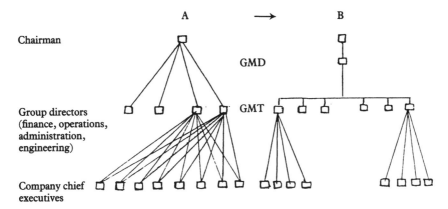

Note: For clarity, not all linkages between group and company levels are included.

FIGURE 5.1: Change in the organisation of the Modandola Group in the 1980s.

ownership of *The Guardian* newspaper and the political activities of some family members is relatively well known. The Modandola Group, on the other hand, is little known. No comparison of the enterprises in terms of performance and size is possible, since aggregate accounts are not available. The existence of strategic hard-currency earnings offshore is likely to be another complicating factor.

The Ibru Organisation was heavily dependent on the import of frozen fish to generate profit through the 1970s. It was able to finance a major programme of acquisition following the indigenisation decrees. Though some enterprises were acquired simply for property, management became overextended. Towards the end of the decade, it embarked on a number of joint ventures in the service sector (hotels, petroleum distribution and construction) and these ventures have been the main area of diversification. The pattern has generally been one of joint ventures with Ibru not being involved in the management of operations. In one case, where this was not the case, a soft-drinks venture failed because it was starved of working capital. At the centre, the management of the holding company was entirely in Nigerian hands by the end of the 1970s. During the 1980s, the Group attempted to shift from its dependence on imported commodities by promoting fishing and agricultural ventures. With the acquisition of the Federal Palace under the privatisation programme, the Group has extended its investment in hotels.

The Modandola Group has diversified more strongly away from its commercial origins and has invested more heavily in industry. Overall, the Group was probably better placed to adjust to the severe import compression in the economy. Like Ibru, it gained from the indigenisation exercise, but through a single strategic investment in a clearing, forwarding and shipping agency just prior to the enormous increase in the volume of imports that followed the oil boom. Unlike Ibru, the Group has not generally entered into joint ventures or long-term management or technical agreements, preferring the direct recruitment of expatriate staff. Reliance on expatriates at both plant level and at the centre has been strong. The central management of the Group has only recently begun to recruit Nigerian managers.

6

ENTERPRISES IN ANAMBRA STATE

In this chapter we examine the growth of enterprises in Anambra State, concentrating on the two main centres of Onitsha and Nnewi. Onitsha, as the largest commercial centre in the eastern states owes its rise to its location on the River Niger at the limit of all season navigation, 232 miles inland from the open sea. In the nineteenth and twentieth centuries, it acted as an entrepôt between the Delta ports and other trading stations on the Niger and Upper Benue rivers and was the focal point of canoe traffic. As a collecting and distribution centre in the twentieth century, its vast hinterland included the Igbo trading diaspora in the north and the dense populations of the former Eastern Region and the Cameroons. It became a great mission and education centre. It had a population of 160,000 in 1963. The large covered market completed in 1955 at the cost of £530,000,[1] which was destroyed during the civil war and subsequently rebuilt, had over 3,200 stalls in the early 1960s. The number of persons actively engaged in the market was estimated at 25,000.[2] The market was reputed to have the lowest prices for imported goods in Nigeria due to intense competition, smuggling and sale of imitation European goods that were copied and manufactured in the Far East to the order of Igbo traders.[3]

At the outset of the colonial period, supervision of Onitsha market, ownership of stalls and trade were controlled by women. After the market was moved in 1916, supervision of the market passed from the Omu's (queen's) Council to Onitsha Town Council which was dominated by men.[4] Trade in the main market still remained entirely in the hands of Onitsha women and women from the hinterland until the mid-1920s. Wealthy Onitsha women traders acted as intermediaries between the European trading companies and retailers, dealing in palm produce and imported commodities.[5] A few Onitsha men who converted to Christianity took up trading, participating as middlemen in the palm oil and kernel trade or were employed by the foreign companies.[6] Onitsha was an important centre for the palm trade up to World War II, when road transport to Port Harcourt became more competitive than the river route. In general, Onitsha men did not pursue careers in business, but turned to higher education and the professions and rented their properties to traders.

The dominant position of women traders began to be challenged by men from outside the Onitsha area in the 1920s. These immigrants built trading networks with their home towns and began to bypass indigenous women traders.[7] They also took advantage of new road and rail facilities to shift trading channels and exploit new markets for existing products. Thus men started to travel out and buy fish for Onitsha market direct from Igala fishermen, thereby undermining women's control of the trade. They also pioneered the long-distance, north–south, trade in fish and other foodstuffs. In Onitsha, they became retailers, then sub-agents and factors to the trading companies and eventually direct importers. After much controversy, Onitsha market by the late 1950s had passed under the control of non-indigenes who were attracted from all over Anambra State. They organised the powerful Onitsha Market Amalgamated Traders Association (OMATA) which extended its political influence from market regulation and policing, into local government.[8]

The career of a prominent non-indigneous trader in the 1950s, Mr B. C. Atuchukwu of Amichi, 20 miles southeast of Onitsha, shows multiple sources of income and the management of a business linking three different locations – a trading diaspora outside Igboland, a base in Onitsha market and the home community of Amichi.[9] It also demonstrates the importance of master-apprentice relations in the expansion of a trading network.

Born in 1920, Mr Atuchukwu finished elementary education in 1933 and was then apprenticed to a Nnewi trader at Uromi in the former Western Region. He went free in 1937 with £4 and traded in petty articles to build up a capital of £80 by 1939. Atuchukwu was one of the first Amichi men to trade in Yorubaland, opening up new stations and settling boys to trade for him in centres like Ibiro, Ado Ekiti and Ikare, Ekpoma and Auchi. This process of migration to new locations by former apprentices, who would in turn train and settle their own apprentices, was at the heart of the Igbo trade diaspora. By the early 1960s, 40 Amichi apprentices had served under him and 29 school leavers had been given employment including two in Sokoto and Jos on monthly salaries with trading capital of £350 each.

After one premature attempt, he felt financially secure enough to establish himself in Onitsha market with a capital of £700 in 1947. He became an agent of Holt and UAC, built houses at Onitsha and Amichi costing £2,000 and married three wives. Trading stock worth £400 was lost in the Onitsha fire of 1953. A transport business, set up just before the fire, yielded profit of £200 a year. In the 1950s, much time and energy was taken up with Amichi affairs, mediating between supporters of a former unpopular warrant chief and youths who had challenged for power. He was elected district councillor. Wealth was distributed at home through contributions to family, community and clan unions, to the church and festivals.

In 1957 he entered the furniture trade and began direct import of mattresses from Vono. He held three other agencies and built more houses for rent in Onitsha. He also invested in two Amichi trading companies yielding £1,080 a year and was a prominent money lender.

Prior to the civil war, Onitsha was primarily a commercial and transport centre. For many Igbo traders, Onitsha functioned, and continues to act, as a strategic wholesale centre within a much broader trading diaspora. There was little medium- or large-scale industry. Lorry bodies were first built in Onitsha in 1948. A small-scale industry survey of 1961 noted four bus-body building firms employing 115 persons.[10] Ottibros manufactured jewellery in the early 1960s, employing over 50 persons.[11] The only foreign manufacturer was a textile company, Textile Printers of Nigeria, established by UAC and its technical partners in 1965.

The indigenous pioneers of medium and large industry in what is now Anambra state include Mr C. T. Onyekwelu who after a long struggle with foreign competitors eventually established a record-manufacturing factory in Onitsha in 1963 (see chapter 3). Chief M. N. Ugochukwu set up a tyre retreading plant at Onitsha and a saw mill at Port Harcourt in 1958 (see chapter 3). After the civil war, he established a foam factory at Umunze, his home town. In 1963, a piggery and meat-processing plant, Niger Pork Products, was established at Ukpor by Chief Mbazulike Amechi, a federal minister.[12] It employed 300 persons and was one of the early examples of an industry being sited at home in the village. The main competitor was the UAC. Supply contracts were secured with the government of Equatorial Guinea and a number of airlines. The industry which was an important source of meat in Biafra, closed in 1973 when the cost of feedstuffs became too onerous. In 1966, Mr Edokwe of Nnewi was ready to start up a light aluminium die-casting plant in Onitsha with the assistance of the Industrial Development Centre at Owerri, but the civil war intervened and the equipment was commandeered by the army. During the war, he operated a pit furnace with bellows at his father's compound in Nnewi. He then moved to a new factory site in Nnewi and burnishing was done in Onitsha where electricity was available.

In the vicinity of Onitsha, the greatest concentrations of individual wealth in the late colonial period were associated with the palm-produce trade and LBAs. Some of these traders and transporters set up or acquired their own oil mills and small plantations. For example, Chief L. N. Obioha, established a palm-kernel mill, NIPROC, at Arondizuogu encouraged by the Okpara government.[13] Chief A. N. Okoye of Ezinifite acquired three palm-oil mills. It is possible, in these cases, to trace links between this wealth and present-day industrial activity. Thus the Obioha family own a brewery at Arondizuogu and the Okoye family have industrial interests in Aba.

It was not until 1978, eight years after the civil war ended, that medium-
and large-scale industrial development in Onitsha really started (see Table
6.1). Industrialists were drawn from many of the Igbo communities in
present day Anambra State, especially Nnewi and Awka Etiti, though not
from a wider field. The industrialisation of Nnewi, for reasons that will be
advanced, came slightly later. The post civil-war industrialisation of Igboland
is not restricted to major urban centres like Onitsha, Nnewi and Aba. Thus,
new industries have been located at Abagana, Arondizuogu, Awka, Egbema,
Ihiala, Ofeme, Ogidi, Oji River, Oko, Owerrinta, Urualla and Ozubulu
(starch, paper conversion and recycling, carpets, beer, soft drinks, biscuits,
machetes, foundry and workshops, maize milling, household utensils, oil
filters, vegetable-oil milling). The rural industrialisation of Anambra and
Imo states owes little to government policies in any direct sense. It is the
product of strong community ties, the loss of properties outside Igboland
especially in Port Harcourt and the need for security in the aftermath of the
northern massacres and the civil war. These factors made the relocation of
at least some part of business activities strategic and compelling.

The growth of Aba, the other large commercial centre of Igboland will be
treated in the next chapter. Industrialisation has been more extensive than
at Onitsha and came slightly earlier. Traders and industrialists are drawn
from a broader range of Igbo communities including many from Anambra
State and Abiriba.

ONITSHA ENTERPRISES

Our profiles of Onitsha enterprises cover seven companies. The first three
all come from a background of apprenticeship and petty trade. The Nwankwo
Group originated in petty trade in Onitsha market, moved into construction
and later diversified with five industrial concerns. The next two profiles
cover companies that started in the bicycle trade and later set up industries
in Onitsha using ties with the Far East. We then examine a motor parts
trader who was one of the pioneers in the importation of parts from Japan
in the 1950s. He ventured into industry in the 1980s. Our next case is a
cosmetics enterprise run by a second generation professional. Then we
cover a company based in Enugu which is owned by an Anambra indigene
with tertiary education. This case throws some light on construction companies and service activities. Finally, we include a section on the growth of
large-scale transport companies, many of which are based in Onitsha. The
profile here is of the Ekene Dili Chukwu Group which has at its core one of
the largest transport firms in Nigeria.

J. Nwankwo Group of Companies

Joseph Ozoemana Nwankwo was born in 1928. He completed his primary
education in 1942 and, after a brief spell as a teacher, started business as a

Table 6.1: Medium- and large-scale industry at Onitsha since 1970.

Company	Start-up	Product	Owner	Employment*	Comment
Nwa George Industries	1975	Roofing sheets	G. N. Okeke	50	Japan Tech.
Ekene Dili Chukwu Steel Structures	1976	Vehicle-body fabrication	Chief A. E. Ilodibe	?	Austrian partner 20%
Ezenwa Plastics	1978	Plastic household wares	Chief R. O. Ezenwa	200	Former distributor for Metalloplastica, the Lebanese plastics pioneer
GMO Group	1978	Roofing sheets, paper, bicycle tyres & tubes, sports shoes, nails, electrodes, pharmaceuticals	Chief J. Igwe, Late Chief G. E. Chikeluba, Chief M. O. Arinze	1,500 (1989)	Taiwan Tech.
Olympic Packers	1979	Packaging & corrugating	Sir Joe Nwankwo	180 (1989)	Belgian Tech.
Allied Steel Industries	1979	Steel rods	Chief J. E. Muoghalu	210–84	Taiwan Tech.
Allied International	1981	Galvanized sheets		280	Japan Tech.
	1985	Plastics		20	Japan Tech.
	1987	Fibreglass		18	Taiwan Tech.
	1989	Shoe soles		35	Italian Tech.
Roadmaster Industries	1979	Bicycle tyres and tubes	Chief J. S. O. Nnoruka		Taiwan Tech.
	1981	Galvanized sheets	Chief C. O. Ezenwa	250–100	Japan Tech.
	1984	Motorcycle tyres and tubes			Taiwan Tech.
	1986	Rubber solution			Japan Tech.
	1986	Wheelbarrows			Japan Tech.
	1989	Malleable pipe fittings			Korean Tech.
Geolis Cables	1981	Electric cables	Chief G. C. O. Ezebube	c. 120	Taiwan partners
Estco Industries	1979	Paper products and candles	Chief E. E. Nwosu	235	
Niger Paper Industry	1980	Toilet tissue and polythene products	Chief C. A. Ekwenibe	68	
Pesaco Chemical Industries	1981	Foam	Chief C. O. Ilodi	31 (1987)	
Pokobros Foods & Chemical Industries	1982	Rice milling, maize grits, etc.	Chief P. A. Okonkwo	240 (1987)	
Kates Associated Ind.	1982	Cosmetics	Ikem Osanakpo	110	
City Biscuits	1982	Biscuits	Chief C. A. Onyechi	200	
Memms (WA)	1982	Paper, paints	Chief F. Maduka	?	
Life Breweries	1983	Beer	Late Chief D. A. Nwandu & others	278	French partners 30%
Edeleosaka Investment Co.	1983	Nails, wire, headpans, cutlery	Chief E. A. Onwumelu	42	
Niger Auto Industries	1984	Brake linings	Bernard Maduko	100	Brazilian Tech.
Marshal Industries	1985	Garments	Chief E. E. Onunkwo	80	
Vincent Standard Steel	1986	Steel pipes	Chief V. C. Nwankwo	100	Japanese Tech. partner
Iju Industries	1987	Rubber auto parts & pvc pipes	Chief G. A. Onwugbenu	200	Indian Tech.
Anino International PLC	1987	Pins, paper clips, staples	C. L. Anapusim	29	
Brollo (Nig.)	1987	Steel pipes	Chief Dr A. I. Ekueme & others	90	Cold steel rolling. Italian partner c. 20%
A. B. Expellers	1989	Palm-kernel oil	A. B. Ezenwanne	118	Malaysian Tech.
Fenok Industries	1992	Brake pads and linings	Chief E. E. N. Ojukwu	c. 80	Argentinian Tech.

* Employment figures refer to 1992 unless otherwise stated. Where a range is indicated, the higher figure refers to peak employment.

TABLE 6.2: Industries of the J. Nwankwo Group.

Company	Start-up	Investment	Comment
Olympic Packers, Onitsha	1979	N10.0m.	Packaging and corrugating. Plastic injection moulding (1981). 180 employed, N30m. turnover (1989). Largest corrugating plant in West African sub-region. Provision of free housing for 70% of workforce. Medical and personal accident scheme
Olympic Drinks Co., Abagana			
(a) Beer	1982	N13.5m.	200,000 hectolitres capacity. Belgian technical partners terminated after 2 years. Malting plant
(b) Soft drinks	1987	N4.5m.	Own transport fleet. Marketing extends to Benue State
Olympic Maize Milling, Awka	1987	N16.0m.	75 tons a day capacity. Grits, flour, semolina, feeds, macaroni
Olympic Technical Works, Abagana	1988	N10.0m.	Foundry, machine shop and metal fabrication. Technical assistance from Taiwan
Olympic Farms, Uzo-Uwani	1985	—	260 hectares. Maize, rice, vegetables

Source: Interviews.

petty trader in Onitsha Main Market in 1943. He registered with the Compagnie Française de L'Afrique Occidentale (CFAO) in 1946 and by 1950 had become a big customer of G. B. Ollivant and sold wholesale. He purchased his first Rudge bicycle and HMV gramophone in 1945 and his first car in 1948. A strong Catholic, he was awarded a papal knighthood in 1974.

He developed links with Costain and in 1952 entered the construction industry. He was to remain in construction and general merchandising until 1979 when he launched his first industry. In 1960, under the sponsorship of GBO he attended a business management course in Manchester, England. After the civil war in Nigeria, construction activities spread beyond the former Eastern Region to include the construction of army barracks in Ogoja, Warri and Efurun and a seminary in Jos.

Both before and after the civil war, Joseph Nwankwo pursued a political career. At various times he was elected to the Njikoka County Council (1956), to the Onitsha Provincial Assembly (1960) and the House of Parliament in Enugu where he represented Onitsha Urban in 1965. He was chairman of the Onitsha Urban County Council between 1973 and 1978. He was active in politics in the Second Republic (1979–83) becoming chairman of the National Party of Nigeria in Anambra State.

After an unsuccessful foray into the bakery industry and serious consideration of a shoe factory, he launched his first industrial concern in 1979, a packaging and corrugating plant in Onitsha. Table 6.2 indicates the industrial ventures of the Group. In addition to these companies, Nwankwo has other interests and directorships – Anammco (chairman, 1980–3), Petrogas, Diamond and Life Breweries, and Orient Bank.

The Group remains a family business whose expansion has stretched the capacities of the self-made founder to the limit. A sole proprietorship with five factories, there is little delegation of authority and foreign participation is very limited. According to Nwankwo, if he went to the stock market or employed non-Nigerians to manage, the Group would collapse. The strategy has been to bring in the four sons and a daughter and the family reports every week. The sons, who have trained in law, business, political science and brewing technology are shareholders and three are executive directors.

This Group raises a more general question about how the financial surpluses that were accumulated through the oil-induced construction and import booms have been used. There has clearly been substantial industrial investment in this case. But my inquiries suggest that this is not typical of other construction companies based in Anambra State. Our last case in this section, shows a construction company that diversified into courier services and shipping. In other cases, there has been waste, a failure to build up long-term management and vulnerability to swings in construction activity.

G. M. O. & Co. Ltd

This company was formed in 1957 by three partners – Godwin, Michael and Okoye – who come from Awka Etiti, a community that has specialised in the bicycle parts and tyre trade. Total employment fluctuated between 1,000 and 1,500 persons in the 1980s. Two of the partners, who had in the early 1940s hawked garri in Sabon Gari, Zaria, had previously been involved in the reconditioning of old bicycles and the bicycle-parts trade in Aba. Here they toured Ngwa villages, purchasing old bicycles. They extended their operations to Onitsha (1949) and Lagos where they purchased bicycles and parts from Yoruba agents. Here they met the third partner and began to pool resources for bulk purchase. Eventually they diversified their sources of supply to foreign companies and became manufacturer's representatives. During the civil war, the company had a lucrative food-supply contract with the Biafran Armed Forces, but only very limited amounts of Biafran currency were convertible at the end of the war.

After the war, with assistance from friends and credit from Hero Cycles of India, the bicycle trade was revived. In addition, the company was associated, through one of the partners, with a leading drug-marketing company – United African Drugs Co. Ltd – which expanded rapidly after the war with federal and state government patronage.

In 1976, the brother of one of the partners returned from engineering studies in the United States and Taiwan and, with technical assistance from Taiwan and Japan, the company began to invest in manufacturing. Factories for bicycle and motorcycle tyres and tubes (N4.8m. invested), sports shoes

(N4.6m. invested in 1981) and roofing sheets (N3.9m. invested in 1982) were opened. Other industrial enterprises followed – floor tiles (1983); polythene bags (1984); paper milling (1986); and welding electrodes (1988). The company also participated via the United African Drugs Company, in a drug-manufacturing company in Onitsha with the Anambra State government. Two of the partners' sons have joined the business after returning from business-studies courses overseas.

Roadmaster Industries Ltd

This company employed 250 persons at peak, falling to 100 by 1992. Like GMO Ltd, the entrepreneurs come from Awka Etiti and have specialised in the bicycle trade. Awka Etiti, though a relatively small Igbo community, has a vigorous entrepreneurial tradition and is well represented among the industrialists in Onitsha. Those elders who started the bicycle business took on apprentices and gave them a one third share of the profit.[14] This enabled apprentices to achieve their independence quickly, encouraging the rapid growth of the bicycle business and community specialisation.

Mr J. S. O. Nnoruka was born in Onitsha in 1930. He attended primary school and a teacher-training college at Obosi. In 1947 he moved to Aba where he served an uncle as an apprentice for five years in the bicycle and parts trade. Here he met his future partner Chief C. O. Ezenwa with whom he worked for a year. Later he started a small trading firm in Lagos, Nnoruka Brothers Enterprises, while Ezenwa traded in Onitsha.

During the civil war, the two companies lost virtually all their assets. He was reabsorbed as a distributor of Dunlop tyres after the war and was eventually one of three Dunlop distributors in the eastern states. As manufacturers' representatives, Josiah and Cornelius bought tyres, bicycles and spare parts from India, Taiwan and Japan. During the oil boom, 2,500 bicycles were imported from India every month. Factories were visited in India and were a big influence on the decision to set up an industry. A close relationship developed with a Taiwanese partner and in 1979 an industry was established for the manufacture of bicycle tyres and tubes. Other industrial ventures followed using technology from Japan, Taiwan and South Korea. They include a rubber-solution plant, iron sheet corrugating and manufacture (1981), motor-cycle tyres and tubes, manufacture of wheelbarrows and solid-wheel production, car tubes (1986), malleable pipe fittings (1989) and car tyres (1990). Nigerian engineers were sent to South Korea for training.

Garbs Organisation

Gabriel Onwugbenu was born in 1920s at Uruagu, Nnewi. He attended primary school in Nnewi then entered apprenticeship in 1948 and traded in Calabar. His father had traded between Nnewi and Uzuakoli and had the financial resources to send all his sons to school. The first son stopped trading on his father's death and became a large-scale farmer. Gabriel, the second son, moved to Onitsha before shifting to Lagos, after the Onitsha market fire of 1951, to enter the motor-parts trade. At this time, the motor-parts trade was shared between Igbo and Yoruba traders and a few Lebanese. In 1956 his apprenticeship ended and he was settled with £150. He first traded in British parts, then German, and in late 1950s pioneered the importation of Japanese-made parts. Samples of British parts were sent to Japan by air for copying. Later no samples were needed for engine and chassis parts. Property was acquired in Lagos and Enugu.

In the mid-1970s, he began to mix Taiwanese parts with Japanese ones. In 1982 he opened a motor agency and garage for Volkswagen in Onitsha. After a long delay waiting for an import licence during which time naira costs trebled, an industry was set up in 1986 with Indian technology to manufacture rubber auto parts, pvc pipes, and latex products. 200 persons were employed together with 3 Indian expatriates. He decided to locate in Onitsha rather than Nnewi because of better infrastructure and the constant demands made by family and kin at home. A son returned from the United States with an MBA to manage the enterprise.

Kates Associated Industries

The grandfather of the present managing director was a carpenter from Ndoni who settled in Onitsha. His son trained as an accountant in the United Kingdom (1949–52) and became deputy commissioner for Internal Revenue in Eastern Nigeria. While in the United Kingdom on a course in 1958, his wife attended hairdressing school. On return, she opened a salon and school in Enugu and began to import cosmetics. A small cottage industry was developed at the family house in Onitsha where imported materials were broken down and packaged.

The father left government service before the civil war intending to start a nail factory in Port Harcourt with a partner from Nnewi. During the war, he was in charge of food processing for the Food Directorate in Biafra.

Toiletries and candles were produced in Aba after the war with the assistance of a former Pfizer employee. The father, who died in 1984, took a long-term view of the business and deliberately trained two sons and a daughter for business. They eventually took up posts as managing director, production manager and quality controller. On incorporation in 1975, all members of the family took shares. The equitable involvement of family members and monogamy helped to ensure a successful succesion. The threat of competition from former employees hastened the return of one son from business studies in the United States. A factory was opened in Onitsha in 1982 and Aba became a depot managed by the mother. Products were gradually upgraded to the level of imports and 110 persons employed. Plastic packaging was integrated into the business for fear that sub-contractors would use the packaging for competing products. An experimental farm was acquired in Cross River State with a view to sourcing raw materials for the company.

F. G. N. Okoye and Sons

F. G. N. Okoye was born in 1914 at Enugu Ukwu. He worked as a painter with the railways in the North and became a foreman. He then entered the food trade, transporting commodities between Igboland and the Northern Region. He set up a transport company, the Perseverance Line, which also carried goods for the United Africa Company. Periodic violence in the tin areas of the Jos Plateau prompted him to return to the East permanently. He secured home-maintenance work with the PWD and met expatriates who encouraged him to go into construction. The leading indigenous construction company of the 1950s was Eastern and General Contractors, which was also owned by indigenes of Enugu Ukwu. F. G. N. Okoye and Sons is the only surviving indigenous construction company from that period and has shown stability and efficiency through the cycles typical of the construction industry. It has never allied itself closely to particular regimes or political parties for the purpose of getting contracts. Manpower was trained and remuneration was sufficiently high to retain good workers and develop and maintain the company administration.

Unlike many self-made businessmen, who tend to exercise close personal control of their business in older age and hide information for reasons of suspicion and fear of the unknown, there was a gradual handover of management from 1976 and sharing of responsibility with sons who were trained abroad. This laid the foundation for continuity and succession to the next generation.

A son who trained as a lawyer in England returned home in the early 1970s and bought a 40 per cent stake in the Lagos subsidiary of International Aviation Services Ltd, a UK courier company. The stake was increased to 100 per cent in 1980 when the UK company sold out. When the son died in 1983, the company was brought into the Group and revived by another son who had returned to Nigeria in 1976 from graduate work in economics in Canada. The company secured contracts from the African Continental Bank and other banks and has grown into the largest domestic courier service in Nigeria employing over 500 persons. Lacking the capital to provide international services, the company has recently linked up with Federal Express of the United States.

Further diversification has been pursued through Globe Shipping Lines which charters vessels, including crude-oil tankers. Investment has also been made in two banks and in real-estate development.

Large-scale Transport Companies

The first generation of motor transporters in Igboland appeared in the 1920s and 1930s. In many cases transport followed trade; transport companies could be found at nodal points throughout the trading diaspora. By the late 1920s indigenous transport operators had begun to compete with expatriate transport companies like Summers Company at Aba and Weeks Transport Service. Indigenous companies had a number of advantages over expatriate ones.[15] There were practically no economies of scale where the main export crops were collected over a wide area and where the distribution of imported goods was so dispersed. There was also a strong seasonality to the business which favoured the flexibility of the dual-purpose local vehicles which could combine passenger and freight haulage. Locally constructed bodies were placed on imported chasses. The locals were also low-cost operators with low overheads and no official hours.

Nnewians were especially prominent among the transporters. Among the well known transport magnates of the 1930s and 1940s were J. C. Ulasi and D. D. Onyemelukwe at Aba, Sir Odumegwu Ojukwu at Lagos, Egwuatu at Nsukka, F. E. Okonkwo at Kano and Benson Okoli at Onitsha. These transport companies tended to run down in the lifetime of their owners and none survived the death of the founder.

In the 1950s a new wave of transport companies appeared. Two of the most well known, Ekene Dili Chukwu and Izu Chukwu Transport, originated in motor spare-parts trade (see Table 6.3). Other founders worked for vehicle owners, rising through the ranks from motor boy to transport manager, before establishing their own companies. The civil war devastated transport fleets and most transporters had to begin again. Here the assistance of the Leventis company in advancing credit and access to motor distributorships helped in recovery.

In the early 1970s, a number of state governments flush with additional oil revenues, promoted transport companies, but these proved inefficient and expensive.[16] State companies still operate, but the balance has swung back towards private operators. The scale of operation has grown and many are equipped with large service and maintenance workshops. Drivers in Nigerian transport companies receive relatively low salaries and the expectation is that income will be made up from other sources. To avoid conflict, they employ their own conductors directly. An important source of income comes from the provision of 'attachment seats', improvised seats in the bus gangway, that are occupied by roadside passengers who pay a lower fare. Preachers and medicine sellers are also allowed access to buses for a fee. Transport firms have became more specialised over time. Igbo transporters, based in Onitsha, are dominant in the luxury, long-distance passenger traffic. This presence is directly related to the depth and wide spread of

TABLE 6.3: Large-scale transport companies.

Name	Start-up	Prior employment	Approximate size	Transport related activity	Other business
C. Moore Obioha, Aba	1954	Transport manager	Group employs 450; 150 trucks in petroleum haulage	Motor distribution	Trading, manufacture of nails & water tanks
Ekene Dili Chukwu, Onitsha	1955	Motor-parts trade	c. 1,000 vehicles; 4,000 employed	Motor distribution, body building, insurance	See Table 6.4
Izu Chukwu Transport, Onitsha	1955	Motor-parts trade	142 luxury buses, 68 trailers, 10 lorries	—	Investments, detergent factory
Chi Di Ebere Transport, Umuahia	—	Conductor with Borno Motor Co.	c. 200 vehicles	Motor-parts trade	Petroleum Marketing, quarry-ing
New Tarzan Motors, Onitsha	1973	Mechanic, textile trade	100 luxury buses	—	Flour milling, paper mill acquired from state government in mid-1980s
P. N. Emerah, Onitsha	—	Motor-parts trade	100 luxury buses & mini buses	—	Agriculture (rice and cassava), civil engineering
Ekeson Brothers, Onitsha	1980	Conductor with C. Moore Obioha	65 luxury buses, 10 trucks	Motor distribution	Manufacture of brake pads & linings

Sources: *Business*, June 1991; interviews; private communications.

the trade diaspora. From their land-locked position, Hausa transporters based in Kano have tended to concentrate on haulage, while Yoruba transporters limit themselves mainly to city and intraregional services. As Table 6.4 and the following profile indicate, there has been some diversification by transporters.

The Ekene Dili Chukwu Group

Chief Augustine Ilodibe was born in 1932. His father was a produce buyer and died in 1942. His uncle Mr J. C. Ulasi, a large transporter based in Aba, paid his school fees. When his uncle died, his mother took him to work for Father Louis Kettels, the Catholic priest of Nnewi parish. In 1950 he began trading with £35 given to him by Father Kettels.

The Ekene Dili Chukwu Group has developed into a very large transport enterprise, probably the largest in Nigeria. The Group has diversified into a number of transport-related activities and also into non-transport ventures. The history of the company is set out in Table 6.4 and is largely self-explanatory.

Transport remains at the core of the enterprise and operations have continued to expand through the 1980s despite the recession. One ingredient of success has been innovation in organisation and conditions of service. The company maintains telephone and radio communications to reach its network of 59 stations for effective coordination of its 1,000-vehicle fleet. The company was the first to set up passenger terminals outside the main public motor parks. Conditions of service for drivers stipulate that they must be married and over 30 years of age, and failure to own a house after three years of active service could lead to the termination of appointment.[17] The logic here is that increased responsibilities will reduce risk taking.

Transporting has led to close ties with the Leventis group of companies and Daimler Benz of West Germany. The links with Leventis originated when Leventis held the Benz distributorship before the civil war. After the war, Leventis helped to restore the company's fortunes by advancing credit. The Group is a major supplier of transport services to the Leventis Group and Chief Ilodibe has invested in Leventis Motors and alongside Leventis in the Continental Brewery at Awomama.

In the case of Mercedes Benz, the Group is a major customer and distributor. It is a shareholder in the Mercedes Benz assembly plant at Enugu, the Anambra Motor Manufacturing Company, which is the most successful of the four lorry and bus assembly plants promoted by the federal government in the 1970s. A fabrication plant in which Emil Doll of West Germany holds 25 per cent of the equity supplies vehicle bodies to the Benz assembly plant.

Apart from transport-related activities, the Group has diversified with a rubber factory and a major long-term investment in agriculture. The Group

TABLE 6.4: The growth and diversification of a transport company: the Ekene Dili Chukwu Group.

1932	Birth of Chief Ilodibe, founder and owner
1946–50	Domestic service
1950–4	Trading in motor parts, Lagos and Gold Coast
1955	Purchased first Austin lorry from SCOA Motors
1957	Setback suffered. Forced to sell 5 vehicles
1958	Switched to Mercedes Benz vehicles supplied by Armels Transport until 1963, when Leventis became supplier. Runs locally made mammy wagons (goods and passengers) between Lagos and Onitsha. First class in cabin, second class on benches
1965	Inter-regional taxi service with Peugeot 404
1967–70	54 Mercedes trucks at the onset of civil war. Lost many vehicles during the war and properties in Port Harcourt and Onitsha

Post 1970

Transport-related activity	Transport	Non-transport ventures
Motor dealer for Leventis (Mercedes Benz, Honda motorcycle)	Re-establishes transport business assisted by Leventis. Long-distance haulage nationwide	General trading and importing
Vehicle body fabrication, 1975 (trailers and tankers). Joint venture with Emil Doll of Germany (25%). Supplier to Anambra Motors Manufacturing Company (Mercedes Benz truck assembly)	Petroleum haulage for Agip, 24 tankers (1972–6). Luxury intercity buses. Uses own bus compounds and not motor parks	Cinemas purchased from Lebanese in 1974
Mercedes distributor (1977)	Hinterland bus service	Printing and packaging, Lagos
Insurance brokerage (1978)	City bus service, Owerri, 1982	Latex rubber factory with technical assistance from Taiwan
Austin Properties (1978). Warehousing, commercial and residential properties. Ties with companies like Beechams and Leventis	728 vehicles by 1988	Austin Farms, N20m. investment (poultry, piggery, fish farms, palm-oil plantation), Philippine technical assistance

has invested some N20m. in farming and at one time employed three managers from the Philippines.

THE SILENT INDUSTRIALISATION OF NNEWI

Over the last decade, the town of Nnewi has been the location for the start-up of about twenty medium- to large-scale industries, established across a variety of sectors (see Table 6.5). Since the end of the civil war in 1970, Nnewi indigenes have controlled about 80–90 per cent of the motor-parts trade in Nigeria. Nkwo Nnewi market is the major import and wholesale point for motor spare parts in Nigeria. This extraordinary market place, which extends over a wide area, is thus located not in a major city but in an Igbo community. The trade has proved a formidable generator of wealth and a spur to industrialisation. Industrial plants are scattered over the four quarters of Nnewi, sometimes on family land and hidden from view behind compound walls. The manufacture of motor parts employed over 1,000 persons in 1989. Like other Nnewi industries it is entirely the product of private initiative and does not involve foreign or government investment. Here the common syndrome, where local communities struggle to attract government projects and indigenes complain that local sons are not investing at home, has been broken.

Nnewi town, with a population of some 100,000 persons is located 15 miles to the southeast of Onitsha. Nnewi in this century has been a relatively wealthy trading and transporting community. Farming was of little import-ance. Like some other Igbo communities with dense non-farm populations, out-migration for employment, and strong community identity and social investment at home, Nnewi was, until recently, recalcitrant to classification as urban or rural.

During and after the colonial period, Nnewi people migrated all over Nigeria, creating a trading and transport diaspora. An important early destina-tion was Aba. In the 1940s and 1950s the northern cities became more important. Two community unions were formed by those who had travelled 'abroad', the Nnewi Patriotic Association (1931) and the Nnewi Youth League (1948).

Nnewians took employment as drivers with foreign firms and the army. Other transport specialisms included mechanics, trading in motor spare parts, electricians, body building and lorry painting. At the summit of the transport specialisms were the vehicle owners. The trade in motor parts was given a boost during World War II when few motor parts were imported. Second-hand motors and army vehicles were acquired and vehicles cannibal-ised. After the war, a number of parts traders went to Ghana where supplies were less restricted. The main post-war centres of the trade were Lagos, Onitsha, Aba and Kano. In the late 1950s, Nnewians began to send European motor parts to Japan for copying and importing back to Nigeria. Nnewians

TABLE 6.5: Medium- and large-scale industry at Nnewi.

Company	Start-up	Product	Employment (1989)	Technology source
(a) Motor parts				
Cento International	1983	Motor accessories	200	Taiwan/South Korea
John White	1987	Fan belts	60	Taiwan
Uru Industries	1987	Brake cables	38	Taiwan
Edison Danzas	1987	Brake pads, shoes, linings	100	Taiwan/South Korea
Ibeto	1988	Batteries, accessories, brake pads, linings	465 (1990)	Taiwan
	1990	Shoes & clutch fibres		Taiwan
Godwin-Kris	1988	Rubber auto parts	100	Taiwan/China
OCE Filters	1988	Oil filters	120	Singapore
Dewaco	1989	Industrial moulds	60 (1992)	Taiwan
(b) Agro-industry				
Armak Industrial Mill	1987	Rice and maize processing (20 and 60 tons a day)	150	Britain/Germany (rice); Italy (maize)
Life Vegetable Oil	1988	Palm-kernel processing (50 tons)	215	Belgium (plant); Singapore (processing)
Inter-Continental Feedmills	1988	Animal feeds	?	
C. C. Ngozi Ifebi Farms	1991	Poultry, pork, fish, starch, garri	60 (1992)	
(c) Miscellaneous				
Jimex	1970	Aluminium die casting	200	
Ibeto Photo	1982	Colour photo processing	251	Britain
Cutix	1984	Domestic electric cables	60	
Adswitch	1984	Switch gear	40	
Ebunso Nig. Ltd	1985	Design and manufacture of process equipment	28	
S and M	1986	Soap, toiletries, disinfectant	16	
Ekwulumili Industrial Co.	1987	Aluminium household utensils	75	Germany
Ibeto Marble	1987	Synthetic marble	18	Germany

Sources: interviews.

controlled about 60 per cent of the parts trade in the 1960s prior to the civil war, with Yoruba from Ijebu-Ode and Abeokuta controlling much of the remainder.[18]

The civil war marked something of a watershed in the economic development of Nnewi. It was not simply that the war disrupted the growth of companies and led to the loss of substantial property especially in Port Harcourt, or that the Biafran currency was made virtually worthless at the end of the war. In fact, Nnewi was fortunate in some respects. Nnewi was already relatively developed in the early 1960s.[19] Immediately before the war, its population was swollen by returnees from the North. They were joined by others during the war, as towns fell to Federal troops. The result was that Nnewi became an important market centre and Nkwo Nnewi market was one of the largest markets in Biafra. As the home of the Biafran leader Odumegwu Ojukwu, Nnewi and its hinterland was more committed to the war effort so that security was effective. It was fortunate, too, in that local military commanders were capable of blocking federal attempts to break out of Onitsha throughout the period of hostilities.

This meant that compared with some other Igbo communities, whose inhabitants were forced to move several times during the civil war, the Nnewi population was comparatively stable. Moreover, the level of physical destruction was low. In addition, Nnewi people had some access to hard currencies both through international trading connections that were maintained through the war via the nearby Uli airstrip and through the activities of Nnewi traders resident in Lomé and Cotonou. These circumstances combined to give Nnewi people a head start in the period of reconstruction after the war.

The experience of the events leading up to the war and the war itself gave rise to a collective decision that Nnewi businessmen and traders should locate at least some of their activities at home. Nnewi was not alone in this respect and it may be argued that the pattern of rural industrialisation that has developed in Imo and Anambra states since the civil war owes much to this concern with security. Thus there are at least five medium-scale industries within the immediate vicinity of Nnewi at Amichi, Ezinifite, Ekwulumili and Ukpor (mosquito coils, biscuits, aluminium utensils, kaolin, distilling). Other factors tending to bring industry closer to home include the creation of new states (actual and prospective), and the shift from trade to manufacture which involves greater investment in fixed physical assets. In the case of Nnewi, businessmen have also experienced some difficulties getting access to land in the major commercial centres of Aba and Onitsha. Onitsha and Aba markets also have a long history of disastrous fires. Not all Nnewi industrialists have located their industries at home. For example, Memms (West Africa) Ltd has paper (1979) and paint (1982) factories at Onitsha, Iju Industries and Niger Auto Industries manufacture motor parts in Onitsha and Coscharis Group manufactures timing and roller chains (1988) for the auto industry in Lagos.

When thousands of people returned home following the massacres of Igbo people in the North, a decision was made by the Royal Nnewi Court to enlarge and relocate the Nkwo Nnewi market. During the war, an important parts market was located in Nnewi and spare parts were given priority as part of the war effort. Thus when the war ended, there was a substantial stock of parts at Nnewi and many people came to buy. The Nkwo market, which was formerly restricted to the site of the famous Nkwo triangle was moved to *Agbo-Edo* land ('sacred forest') and the site was ritually cleared by the Igwe and Obis of Nnewi. At first, old motor parts dominated the new parts section since there was very limited access to international currencies. In 1970 there were 673 members of the Nnewi Old Parts Union.[20] By 1978, membership of the New Parts Union (257) outweighed the Old Parts Union (89).

The arrival of new industries in Nnewi began in 1983 with the establishment of Cento International to manufacture plastic auto accessories and batteries. Since then, seven other motor spare-part companies have been established, together with four agro-industrial concerns and eight miscellaneous industries. All the owners of these industries, with three exceptions, had traded in motor spare parts. The timing of the industrial surge was directly related to the import restrictions and difficulties in obtaining foreign exchange that followed the decline of oil revenues. The start-up of the industry is not directly related to the presence of motor assembly plants in Nigeria which were established earlier. A number of features of the industry are of interest.

1. A common pattern of entry to motor-parts manufacture can be observed. After elementary education and a period of apprenticeship, usually lasting four or five years with an established motor-parts trader, the dealer creates his own company buying and selling locally. Later, there is a shift to direct importation and the establishment of overseas contacts usually in the Far East (Japan, Korea, Taiwan, Singapore, Hong Kong). A manufacturing venture is then started after visits to the Far East. Existing marketing channels can be used to promote the new product. This pattern can be highly compressed. In one case, there was only six years between the start of training in the motor-parts trade and the start-up of manufacture at the age of 27. Seldom can 'traditional' patterns of commercial apprenticeship be found so closely followed in time by medium- or large-scale manufacture.

2. Trade ties with Taiwan are strongly developed, especially for motorcycle parts. In addition, the most common source of technology and training for industry is Taiwan. Trading ties began to develop in the early 1970s when Nnewi traders visited Taiwan. Isaiah Nwafor was

the pioneer. It was noted earlier in this chapter that direct importation of motor parts from Japan began in the late 1950s. After 1970, Taiwan products started to replace Japanese ones as they entered a mature phase in the international product cycle. They were also favoured by exchange-rate movements in the 1980s which put a premium on low-cost sources of supply.

A number of reasons can be advanced for the Taiwan linkage in trade and industry. Taiwan trading practices have been very flexible. When trade and credit conditions deteriorated after 1983, Indian and Hong Kong companies which were then supplying Taiwan parts, withdrew from the Nigerian trade and Taiwan trading companies filled the vacuum. Taiwanese exporters are prepared to follow their goods to Nigeria in order to monitor market conditions, check margins and press for cash payment outside the banking system, so that they can pay their suppliers. The motor-parts market in Nigeria is subject to cycles and severe price fluctuations, so that timing is important. There is, moreover, very little credit in the system and import, wholesale and, sometimes, retail functions, are often combined in a single enterprise.

Taiwan has also gained from a flexible and rapid response in terms of product specification and quality for the Nigerian and West African markets. Other countries like India and mainland China may be able to produce cheaper products, but their labour intensity precludes large orders and flexibility with respect to timing, quality and packaging. Different grades of product are produced. There is a distinction between 'Taiwan' and 'Original' parts, the former being widely considered to be inferior. Intellectual property laws including copyright are not always strictly adhered to in Taiwan. Some entrepreneurs are happy to produce 'Taiwan' parts. Others are concerned to create their own 'Nnewi' brands and establish a reputation for quality.

Adaptability extends to the design of equipment and machinery for factories. The sub-contracting prevalent in Taiwan is not appropriate to Nnewi, where entrepreneurs want total control and the basis for trust and contractual efficiency between industrial concerns has not been established. Thus whole factories have to be provided. After factories are in operation, advice has been given on cost pricing and stock control, areas where traders are sometimes deficient.

Engineers are sent to Taiwan for training. Taiwanese return to Nnewi for six months or one year, to supervise the installation and start-up of machinery. Technology has been successfully acquired. A capacity to fabricate and repair parts is beginning to develop with the emergence of local workshops and a few private foundries. In a sense, the Nnewi industrialists have begun a new apprenticeship, this time with Taiwan. Like the Taiwanese, Igbo business people aspire to be independent with their own relatively small companies. Alice Amsden in her study of Korea, makes a distinction between the absorption of foreign technology through copying and self-teaching which she terms 'imitation' and technology acquisition through investing in foreign licences and technical assistance, which she terms 'apprenticeship'.[21] The distinction is a useful one and in the case of Nnewi, it is the former mode of acquisition that is completely dominant. No evidence of licensing or royalty payments was found. However, given the general importance of apprenticeship in Igbo business affairs, the term cannot be appropriated and confined to Amsden's usage, without a severe loss of meaning.

3. Infrastructure is developed privately (land, tarred roads, boreholes). A number of entrepreneurs had to purchase their own transformers in order to get attachment to the electricity grid. The private provision of infrastructure does not extend to the main roads in Nnewi town which are in a constant state of disrepair. The increase in private wealth in Nnewi has not been linked to a concomitant rise in effective taxation and the collective provision of roads by the local council. There is no industrial estate and land is acquired in a variety of ways. Land may be provided by the family, purchased on the market, or rented out by communities at cheap rates to local sons.

4. Starting wages were constant in nominal terms at N150 a month from 1982 until 1989. Early in 1992 they had risen to N275. During this period, there was a large devaluation of the naira. At rates of exchange prevailing in 1990, a mechanist in Taiwan earned the equivalent of around N7,350 a month. This may be compared with N300 a month for a Nigerian mechanist with similar skills. There is therefore a very large salary differential between Nnewi and Taiwan. More than half the industrial workforce in Nnewi has been attracted from outside the Nnewi area, sometimes from as far away as Rivers and Cross River states. Some companies have provided staff housing. Nnewi indigenes are said to prefer self-employment, but there are indications that this attitude is changing.

5. In 1990 exports were indirect and unofficial. Goods were paid for in naira in Nigeria, prior to export. With the large differential between the official and parallel rates overseas buyers had every incentive to purchase goods in this manner. The exchange rate would have to decline appreciably for exports to become official. Two manufacturers, however, were planning to make official exports.

Two Case Studies from Nnewi
Ibeto Group

The Ibeto Group is the largest enterprise based in Nnewi and early in 1989 employed 766 persons countrywide. After a period of apprenticeship to the motor-parts trade, Mr Ibeto set up his own business with assistance and funds provided by his father and elder brother. He opened a shop in Nnewi and travelled to Lagos to buy motor spare parts. In 1976 he began direct importation of auto parts. By the end of 1988, he had ended direct importation and decided to concentrate solely on manufacture.

His first non-trading venture was in colour-photograph processing. He noticed that from 1980 there was a sharp increase in demand for colour photographs. People were sending their films overseas for processing, which took two months. The industry was established in 1982 and is the second-largest business of its kind in the country, after Fototek of Lagos. Overall investment was N4m. Four fully equipped laboratories and offices were opened outside Nnewi at Aba, Enugu, Onitsha and Nsukka in addition to several other collection centres. The business has grown rapidly providing capital for expansion into other fields. The main problem in the photo-processing industry is that technological change is very fast and a competitive enterprise must keep up to date. It is also a luxury item and vulnerable to changes in market conditions. The photo-processing industry gave Ibeto experience in acquiring foreign technology and in the supply and stocking of raw materials. Given the problems of setting up a manufacturing industry, Mr Ibeto stated that had he gone into manufacture in 1982 without this prior experience he would have failed.

In 1985, Mr Ibeto entered the hotel business. The business arose from the need to accommodate his business partners in Nnewi rather than having to travel to Onitsha. He also wanted to create an environment conducive to other foreign visitors who come to Nnewi to do business.

The third venture was in marble. The overall investment in the synthetic marble plant is N3m. There is 68 per cent local content with chemicals imported. A technology agreement binds the company to the foreign supplier for three years, after which the technology will be transferred. Thereafter, cheaper sources of supply may be available. Two American expatriates are employed.

The decision to go into the manufacture of batteries and plastic auto parts was taken after conducting feasibility studies that included the manufacture of oil filters, roller chains, spark plugs and flour milling. Total investment is over N100m. ($13.3m.). The plant was commissioned in June 1988. Currently, the plant has the capacity to produce 3,000 small and 800 large batteries a day. There is A-to-Z manufacture with no assembly. Forty-one items of plastic motor accessory are also produced. Export of these products to Kenya and other African countries is planned.

Six mechanical and electrical engineers were sent to Taiwan for six months' training. Mr Ibeto also went to Taiwan for three months to familiarise himself thoroughly with the technology employed. The Taiwanese then returned with the engineers and stayed for one year. There was provision in the contract for a new contract if progress was not satisfactory after one year. The transfer was successful and Taiwanese return periodically to maintain machinery.

A lead-smelting plant is under construction which will allow old batteries to be recycled. Imported ingots will then be replaced and local content raised to 90 per cent. This will ensure regular supply of raw material. The supply of polypropylene from the local petro-chemical industry will, in future, reduce cost. A plant for brake pads and linings, clutch facings and fibres and brake-shoe kits opened in 1990. These parts are fully manufactured, unlike those produced by Ferodo, a major multinational competitor located in Ibadan. To get distribution for the new products, Ibeto was able to attract large deposits of N250,000 each from a dozen distributors. This shows that very considerable finance could be raised for working capital from the marketing network. The role which the existing marketing and trading system played in relation to industry was not therefore simply confined to providing a ready outlet for new industrial products.

The company has detailed conditions of service. There are seven salary gradings and annual and merit increments. There are bonus payments at Easter and Christmas, plus housing and transport allowances. There is a clinic and subsidised lunch is provided at a canteen. These benefits were introduced gradually as a result of experience and not worker demands. Work motivation is a problem and there is a very high rate of labour turnover among those recruited directly from school. Males leave for trading and females for sewing and hair salons. Mr Ibeto said that he saw nothing in Taiwan management practices that would be useful for Nigerian conditions which require much closer supervision and monitoring. On the other hand, employment of senior management personnel has shown much greater stability. A General Outpatients Department was donated to the local hospital.

Explaining his decision to go into industry, Mr Ibeto noted that Nnewi motor-parts traders are not wealthy in their old age. They invest in properties that deteriorate and require maintenance. The collection of rents becomes onerous in old age, and yet properties are not usually sold unless the owner is in great financial difficulty. Also, trading companies usually wind up once the proprietor is dead or incapacitated. This is not so in manufacturing where machinery and plant are involved. There is then the prospect that his family will continue to benefit from the business which he creates in his own lifetime.

Cutix and Adswitch

This is an unusual case of a second-generation graduate, Gilbert Uzodike, one of whose companies has gone public on the Lagos Stock Exchange. Two factories manufacture domestic electric cables and switchgear (feeder pillars, switch boards, busbar systems). One hundred persons are employed. The owner's father was in charge of the Public Works Department of the former Eastern Region and was executive director of a foreign construction company. The industrialist trained in engineering at the University of Lagos and later studied at Harvard Business School. He joined a multinational company producing electric cables and switchgear. He set up a Nigerian operation that achieved a sales turnover of $3m.–4m. by 1981. The multinational company then wanted more involvement and an end to the distribution agreement, but they did not want to go into manufacturing. He then left to set up his own company using savings and the proceeds from the sale of his shares. He held less than 30 per cent of the equity in the new company which had seventeen other shareholders.

The company took off in 1984 under difficult circumstances when import licensing was having an adverse effect. The industrialist estimated that of the thirteen cable companies operating in Nigeria, only the integrated ones would survive. He used an import licence for machinery and raised money for raw materials by going public on the Stock Exchange in the second-tier market (N1.4m. raised after fees). He preferred to go public rather than use private placement because he wanted the shares to be marketable and because it would be easier to raise funds in the future. In addition, he did not want large shareholders who might interfere and thought that a public company would survive him.

The companies have sufficient depth of management (the general managers are both engineering graduates) to be independent of any one individual. The employment of expatriates is deliberately avoided in order to build up local experience. The factory design, equipment selection and installation up to commissioning were handled by Nigerians. Old machines are refurbished and commissioned by the company. This saves foreign exchange and avoids sophisticated electronic controls. Also, where possible, machinery is scaled down and manufactured by the company. For example, a condensing unit, a tin-plating trough and a heat exchanger have all been manufactured by the company. Such capabilities are rare at the moment, although another enterprise in Nnewi is involved in the design and engineering of process equipment.

CONCLUSION

The most common background of those who established industries in Onitsha and Nnewi was primary schooling, apprenticeship and trade. Only one person who followed this pattern had spent a long period abroad (Cameroon). The bicycle trade in which the Awka Etiti area specialised, accounts for three cases. In the case of Onitsha, only three persons had professional or tertiary education before their entry into industry. They include the former vice-president of Nigeria (1979–83), Dr Alex Ekwueme who, after studying architecture and urban planning in the United States, returned to Nigeria in 1957 to join Esso West Africa.[22] From 1958 he built up a nationwide architectural practice, Ekwueme Associates, before entering politics in 1979. His father, Lazarus Ibeabuchi Ekwueme, was a pioneer missionary and teacher. Dr Ekwueme established a plant for roofing materials in Enugu, a chain of hotels at Enugu, Owerri, Calabar and Oko, a brewery at Oko and a steel-rolling mill at Onitsha.

In the Nnewi case, the path of apprenticeship and trade is also dominant with only two cases of tertiary education (MBA from Harvard and PhD in engineering). Limited formal education was supplemented by learning on the job and by hiring managerial and technical skills, including short-term hiring of technicians from abroad. None of the entrepreneurs considered in Onitsha or Nnewi had a long experience with foreign companies and only one had experience of government.

Foreign investment in the form of equity was completely absent in the Nnewi case and limited to three minor positions in joint ventures in Onitsha. There was no long-term expatriate employment at Nnewi. Three industrialists saw the acquisition of sophisticated foreign technology and the employment of expatriates as obstacles to the build-up of local skills and indigenous learning processes. They had adopted self-reliant strategies which included an element of trial and error.

We have advanced reasons for the strong trade links developed with Taiwan by Nnewi businessmen and the attractions of acquiring Taiwanese technology and expertise in industry. Though the sources of foreign technology are more diverse in Onitsha, four industries have acquired technology from Taiwan.

When succession to the next generation is considered, there are two cases of effective transfer to highly educated children, and another four cases where sons and daughters, who have received tertiary or professional training, have joined companies founded by their fathers. Training abroad was undertaken in Japan, Canada, Taiwan, and the United States.

Contrary to much writing about accumulation in Africa, paths of accumulation in Onitsha and Nnewi have relied on political access and state patronage to only a minor degree. Only two individuals have pursued political careers and they both were independently wealthy before their entry into politics. The existence of this economic and political space within which private accumulation is pursued may be partly explained by the distance of the Igbo elite from political power at the centre over the last two decades and hence the lack of opportunities for state patronage. But, more importantly, it also has its roots in the pre-colonial autonomy of Igbo communities and in the experience of private endeavour through a trading and transport diaspora which developed during the colonial period. There is a recognition among Nnewians that the development of the community owes little to government and in this respect the area is contrasted with the northeastern area of Igboland where government assistance has been much greater. As we noted, the common syndrome where the local community struggle to attract government projects and indigenes complain that local sons are not investing at home has been decisively broken at Nnewi. The contrast with Ilesha as depicted in the final chapter of J. D. Y. Peel's study of that Yoruba community is striking. According to Peel, Ijeshas constantly regretted the fact that despite education and migration, there was little development at home.[23] The bulk of the active population was not resident in Ilesha and the lack of local employment was a root problem. By far the most common solution proposed was for the government to establish a factory. By contrast, economic growth at Nnewi has attracted many outsiders and one ward in the town is entirely occupied by non-Nnewians. As one informant told me, 'historically we migrated and saw that it was good to have foreigners'. The lessons appear to have been taken up by the governor of Anambra State who has espoused a private enterprise philosophy and urged indigenes of the state to 'think home'.

Nnewi invites comparison with Abiriba, another wealthy Igbo trading community to the east of Umuahia. But, as we shall see in the next chapter, the Abiribans have located their industries in Aba and not at home.

7

ABA AND IMO STATE ENTERPRISES

In this century, Aba developed as a government centre and garrison town, as a major entrepôt in the palm-produce trade, and as a market centre for the southern Ngwa region. Sited along the railway line from Port Harcourt, Aba was a major produce centre, attracting seven European firms by 1919.[1] It became the hub of a transport network where expatriate and Nigerian transporters were based in the interwar period. The population of Aba reached 13,000 in 1931, climbing to 58,000 by 1953 and 130,000 by 1963.[2] Immigrants were drawn to Aba from all over Igboland. Prominent among business groups were traders and transporters from Nnewi, tobacco traders from Nkwerre,[3] shoemakers from Okigwi Division and tailors and textile traders from Item, Abiriba and Ohafia.

Ngwa indigenes of the Aba area were generally less wealthy than immigrant groups and did not establish larger-scale enterprises. Farming has remained an important activity in the vicinity of Aba. As Martin shows, past capital accumulation in farming was limited by technical and commercial constraints and there was a tendency for dispersal of wealth on death.[4] Surplus funds tended to go into education. After the civil war, new wealth tended to be associated with access to the state as employees or through political networks. There was little long-term involvement in long-distance trade and the collective strength deriving from close trading networks of other Igbo communities was absent.

Some thirty-five miles to the south of Aba lay Port Harcourt, a slightly larger city with a population of 180,000 in 1963 that experienced rapid growth just before the civil war.[5] Port Harcourt was a city dominated by Igbo immigrants and its port location and the presence of the oil industry nearby, attracted more large-scale industry than at Aba. However, Aba was second to Onitsha as a commercial centre in the East and was also important as a centre of artisan activity.[6] While Onitsha was more important than Aba for hardware and general consumer goods, Aba was strong in textiles and clothing. As at Onitsha, the intensity of economic competition kept Lebanese traders at bay and they never established a foothold.

Aba was the location of the first industrial investment by Paterson Zochonis, the Anglo-Greek merchant company, which went into partnership with a Greek soap maker in 1949 and subsequently took over the company.[7] Two other prominent soap manufacturers, Lever Brothers and the International Equitable Association also set up factories in Aba in the 1950s. Other large-scale industry established before the war included: Nigerian Breweries (1957); Pfizer (1961);[8] Aba Textiles (1964); and Major & Co.(1964).

A small-industry survey conducted in Aba in 1961 recorded a total of 2,268 firms employing 6,243 persons.[9] This figure is roughly comparable to the numbers recorded for Port Harcourt and Onitsha. Aba was distinguished as a centre of shoe and singlet manufacture. In addition, blacksmithing, welding, wrought-iron working, and plastic-bag manufacture were also prominent and undergoing rapid expansion. It was this metal-working artisan base that was to engage successfully in copying foreign technology after the civil war. Later, the local design and fabrication of items like kernel crushers, garri processors, baking machines, paper converters and shoe moulds was taken up. The 1961 report is silent about soap manufacture, but other sources suggest that there were a number of small firms selling soap to northern markets.[10] They were not in competition with the large foreign producers who sold higher-quality soap to the more sophisticated southern markets. One larger-scale indigenous soap producer was established before the war.[11]

With the creation of Rivers State in 1967 and the defeat of Biafra, Port Harcourt was virtually closed to Igbo enterprise because of hostility from ethnic minority groups. Many of the wealthiest Igbo businessmen and women had acquired extensive properties in Port Harcourt before the war and the loss of these properties proved a major setback. After the war, Aba, as the Igbo city closest to the sea, underwent rapid expansion, although growth was hampered by poor infrastructure for many years. People from Abiriba played a leading role in the economic recovery of Aba. When the new Port Harcourt–Aba–Enugu expressway was opened at the end of the 1970s, Aba became more accessible.

In the late 1970s and early 1980s, Aba experienced a wave of investment in a range of light industries (see Table 7.1). The timing of this surge was linked to the build-up of financial surpluses by traders through the oil boom. In some cases, import bans on beer, soft drinks and biscuits provided an added incentive. Overall, the incentive to industrialise was not so much a response to closure and protection as the relative inexpense of imported machinery and growth of the domestic market.

Other industries included paper conversion and recycling, garments,

TABLE 7.1: Medium- and large-scale industry at Aba since 1970.

Company	Start-up	Product	Owner	Employment	Comment
Presidential Tailors	1970	Men's suits	S. O. Ojiaku	85 (1992)	
Niger Garment	1970	Knitted fabrics & garments	Chief D. N. Orji	227 (1992)	
E. & O. Chukwu	1970	Knitted fabrics & garments	O. Chukwu	c.250 (1992)	
Rosies Garment	1971	Garments	Chief Iro Orji	300	
Rosies Textile Mill	1979	Textiles			
Iros Luggage Manufacturing		Luggage			
Udeofson Garment Factory PLC	1971	Garments	U. E. Ofuru	152 (1992)	
Baco Engineering Co. Ltd	1972	Metal fabrication	Chief B. A. Isiguzo	70	
Fabina Nig. Ltd		Brake shoes			
Starline (Nig.) Ltd	1973	Cosmetics	C. I. Onwunna	285 (1992)	
	1978	Plastics			
	1988	Pharmaceuticals			
Micco Electronics	1974	Radio/Cassette assembly	Sir Mike C. Nkwoji	400*	Electronics closed
Micco Plastic Industry	1979	Plastics			
Micco Nails Ltd	1980	Nails			
Micco Crown Cork	1982	Crown Corks			
Micco Shoe Sole	1989	Shoe Soles			
Anzzy Industrial Co.	1976	Shoes, stiffeners	A. O. Olekaibe	150 (1992)	
Toonak Group	1977	Aluminium products	Chief T. O. O. Omejua-Njoku	1,200*	Joint venture with USA
	1985	Soft drinks			
	1987	Soap			
Continental Plastics	1978	Plastics	Mazi A. C. Eneogwe	218 (1991)	
Continental Industries	1990	Flour & feed mill			
Onwuka Hi-Tek PLC	1978	Nails, spare parts	Chief Onwuka Kalu	234 (1990)	Italian technology
Star Paper Mill	1978	Paper conversion	Chief Nnana Kalu	300 (1991)	
	1983	Recycling plant			
Nibeltex	1979	Upholstery, garments	Chief K. K. Onumah	90–50	Belgian equity, 5%
Nwachukwu Shoe	1979	Shoes	Chief P. C. Nwachukwu	125 (1992)	
Okam Steel Industries	1979	Nails, roofing sheets	Chief John Okam	500–200	Royal Crown Cola franchise
	1980	Soft drinks			

TABLE 7.1 – *Comtd.*

Company	Start-up	Product	Owner	Employment	Comment
Kan Biscuits	1980	Biscuits	Chief N. O. Nwojo Chief Kalu Ndukwe	350–150 (1992)	Chiltonian Biscuits (UK) 10% of equity
Dubic Industries Ltd	1980	Jumbo paper rolls	Chief Dike Ifeagwu	c. 1,000*	Taiwan equity. Supplies 41 paper convertors
Dubic Breweries Ltd	1982	Beer			
Unijoy Paper Products	1985	Tissues			
United Steel Converters	1980	Aluminium products	Chief N. U. Okafor	110*	
UOO Agricultural Industry	1981	Animal feeds	Chief O. Eze		
Major Electrodes	1987	Electrodes	Chief U. Ozoemena Chief O. Nzedinma		
Interland Industries	1981	Soft drinks	Chief O. U. Onwruka	250–150	
Fashion Shoe Co.	1982	Shoes	Chief J. Anyaehie Lt.-Gen. T. Y. Danjuma (rtd) & others		Closed since 1985. Joint venture with Italians
Integrated Bedding	1982	Foam mattress	Late Chief I. A. Ota	106–20	
Home Charm Paints	1985	Paints	Chief O. Mang	90 (1986)	
Lee-Nobec Group	1986	Light bulbs	Chief L. I. Okoye	300* (1992)	Taiwan technology
	1989	Toilet tissue			Taiwan technology
	1990	Plastic shoes			Taiwan technology
Chieme Automobile Ind.	1987	Auto parts	Chief F. Chukwuonye	100	Taiwan technology
Nwanegbontraco Industries	1987	Shoe soles	Chief B. N. Ezissi	26	
Citraco Industry Ltd	1988	Shoe soles, shoes	Chief C. I. Oguguo	126 (1990)	N9.2m. turnover (1989)
Hic Oil Company	1988	Palm-kernel oil & cake	Nze C. O. Maduako	125	
Ndu Integrated Composite Flour Mill	1991	Flour mill	Chief N. O. Nwojo	45 (1992)	N12m. investment, UK tech.

Note: Employment figures refer to 1989 unless otherwise stated. Where a range is indicated, the higher figure refers to peak employment.
* Group employment.

Source: Interviews and communications.

upholstery, plastics, paints, nails and aluminium building products, foam, motor accessories, and shoes. There was a veritable rush to establish new industries and it became fashionable to be an 'industrialist'. Credit was easy to come by. Machinery was sometimes delivered without adequate preparation and planning and there was considerable waste as traders attempted to become industrialists overnight. Subsequently, traders entered into a much tighter commercial environment. Letters of credit were difficult to establish and import licences became hard to obtain. Many industrial projects were shelved. Some markets became so saturated with products, nails for example, that plant closures ensued.

After 1982, the pace of industrial expansion slowed down, though there was investment in the shoe industry, agro-processing, pharmaceuticals, paints and automobile parts. The single investment in vegetable-oil crushing (to be followed by refining) is of interest. The vegetable-oil industry is an area where incentives have altered since the mid-1980s to favour the domestic industry. How far have indigenous investors entered the field? The impression is sometimes given that only Indian investors have responded. While Indians possess the larger companies and have a market share of well over 60 per cent, there is a significant Nigerian presence. In the Eastern states, local investors include, Hic Oil (Aba), Ferdinand Oil Mills Group (Urualla), Unit One (Owerri), Ogbuneke at Umuahia, Life Vegetable Oil at Nnewi (see Table 6.5), and A. B. Expellers and Savoil at Onitsha.

Shoes and Garments

In 1941 there were about 15 shoemakers in Aba.[12] By 1961, shoemaking – leather shoes and rubber sandals made from automobile tyres – provided employment for 301 persons in 92 enterprises, 3 of which employed more than 10 people.[13] Shoe repairing provided employment for a further 108 persons. The shoe industry in Aba was pioneered by immigrants from Okigwi Division and Afikpo in the 1950s and 1960s. The largest indigenous companies before the war were Aba Central Shoes, Goodwill Shoes, Okigwi Shoe Company, and Eastern Shoe Industry. The latter company employed 58 persons (4 management, 38 wage workers and 16 apprentices) in 1966.[14] None of these companies survived the war, although the shoe industry, as a whole, made a vigorous comeback, led by the artisan sector.

After the war, the quality of Aba-made shoes was gradually upgraded using new adhesives. Sandals made from old motor tyres were discontinued and the latest international fashions were copied. The status of craftsmen and apprentices in the industry rose as shoe manufacture became widely recognised as a profitable activity. Aba became the shoe centre of West Africa. It is estimated that 30 per cent of its output is exported unofficially. The core of the industry is the artisan sector, which is estimated to employ 5,000 master artisans and 10,000 apprentices. The difference with the modern shoe industry in Lagos is encapsulated in the statement, 'In Aba you sit down to make shoes, while in Lagos you stand up.' The artisan output is of the order of 15 million pairs a year.[15] Although Aba produces men's dress shoes, it is particularly strong in ladies shoes, which require manual decoration.

Artisan organisation exhibits a flexible division of labour with a high degree of subcontracting within the sector. A firm that receives an order may subcontract many of the operations including manufacture of lasts, cutting of uppers, sole cutting, stitching and stamping. Low overheads and low-cost labour have led to production costs that are a quarter of those in capital-intensive units in Lagos. The competitive advantage of artisan production has become stronger since the devaluation of the naira and cut back in imports. One effect of the Structural Adjustment Programme was to dislocate the middle-class income group with a consequent migration down the market to cheaper shoes. The market has responded with cheaper 'lookalike' shoes. At the same time, lower cost, artisanal production was favoured relative to larger capital-intensive firms. The result was that large firms like Bata Nigeria began to feel competitive pressures both at the retail and wholesale levels. Demand for cheaper plastic shoes was also boosted by the decline in real incomes.

One response of Bata to this competition has been to subcontract shoe production to firms in Aba. Bata, which began subcontracting to Aba producers in 1989, subcontracted about 10 per cent of its shoe production in 1992 and expects this share to rise to 20 per cent.[16] Some other Lagos firms also subcontract to Aba. Overall the share of Aba output taken through subcontracting by large firms is small and the wholesale market for Aba-made shoes is competitive.[17]

A number of larger firms, employing up to 150 persons have emerged from within the artisan sector (Ajibu Industries, Anzzy Industrial, Johnny Christy Afro Shoe, Jonwas, O. U. Bros, Virgi Shoes). Some of these firms have secured contracts from Bata and Lennards, which have guaranteed bank loans, given technical assistance and in a few cases encouraged the adoption of machinery. Though some of these firms make whole shoes, they have little machinery. Highly mechanised enterprises have not survived in Aba due to competition from the artisanal sector and management problems. One highly capitalised, Nigerian/Italian joint venture employing expatriates, was forced to close. Another firm abandoned its machinery for more labour-intensive production. An indicator of Aba's strength is the fact that it now supplies its own shoe components, whereas before the war, components were bought in from Onitsha market. However, Onitsha traders still provide the main market and wholesale point for Aba-made shoes.

Another important area of artisan activity is the garment industry, in which people from Item, Abiriba and Bende have specialised. Sedentary and itinerant tailors (*onye obioma*) from these areas were well established in the interwar period. One firm began to sew singlets in the 1940s; the main expansion came after 1955.[18] Two firms exported to the Cameroons before protective tariffs were introduced. The small-scale industry survey of 1961 shows 733 tailoring firms employing 1,744 persons. Eleven enterprises made singlets with 5 of the firms employing more than 10 persons. The largest company at this time was Okorie and Sons, employing 45 persons to make singlets, shirts and suits. Okorie, who died in 1962, trained a number of garment manufacturers. He was member of the First Century Gospel Church and eschewed material possessions. He rented his accomodation and opened a school for his workers. Some tailors went on overseas courses in England and a few remained there to make their careers.

Several garment manufacturers re-established themselves after the war, starting with manual machines. Spinning and knitting machinery was then introduced and a few larger-scale enterprises emerged from the artisan sector (see Table 7.1). The period of the oil boom saw much greater exposure to western garments and fashions as imports increased and opportunities for international travel expanded. This forced quality improvements, though it also made local mass production more vulnerable to international trade and smuggling. Since the introduction of SAP, the devaluation of the naira and import compression have favoured the garment industry and new investment has been undertaken. Exports are significant. Overseas buyers submit designs and these are made with their generic labels. Sometimes these Aba-made goods are imported back to Nigeria as foreign goods. The custom tailoring of women's clothing also expanded as confidence increased in locally made dresses. Design work became more adventurous moving beyond simple wrapper blouses and straight lines. Since the mid-1980s, female graduates began to enter the business of fashion design for the first time. These enterprises do not generally employ more than 30 persons.

The overall size of the garment industry in Aba cannot be estimated with any accuracy. It is possible that the city is the largest centre in Nigeria. The Aba Garment Manufacturers Cooperative Society with over 400 members accounts for perhaps a quarter of the producing units.

ABA AND ABIRIBA

A striking feature of trade and industry at Aba is the prominent role played by Abiriba people. Abiriba is a specialist trading community and one of the wealthiest towns in Igboland. It is located some thirty miles to the east of Umuahia off the Arochuckwu road. In the past, Abiriban traders earned a reputation for undertaking dangerous trading missions by canoe and indulging in contraband. Abiriba is known as 'Little London' on account of the fine residences that wealthy Abiriba businessmen have built at home. The population was estimated at 40,000 in 1970.[19] Unlike Nnewi, where businessmen

have located the bulk of their industries at home (see chapter 6), Abiriba
has practically no industry and poor communications (two telephone lines in
1990). Instead, Abiriba traders and industrialists have, since the end of the
civil war, tended to concentrate their activities in Aba where they have good
relations with Ngwa people and little difficulty gaining access to land. Eleven
of the twenty-nine companies listed in Table 7.1, including the two largest
employers, are owned by Abiriba indigenes.

The Aba textile market is dominated by Abiribans who also trade in
remnants and second-hand clothing. The structure of the market in Aba
differs from that in Onitsha and Nnewi. Whereas Aba traders emphasise
volume and turnover and are essentially importers and wholesalers, Onitsha
traders control the whole marketing chain down to the retail level with
warehouses for storage. There is greater scope for market regulation and
stock can be taken off the market to protect prices and margins.

The economic history of Abiriba shows a shifting pattern of migration
and commercial specialisation in response to changing economic opportunities. Historically, Abiribans established a reputation as itinerant blacksmiths
dealing in farming implements, fishing and hunting materials like traps for
wild animals, leather pouches, and locks and keys. In the nineteenth century
and early colonial period, trade in palm produce, developed to the south
down the Igu tributary of the Inyang river, which joined the Cross river in
the Itu area, where Abiriba traders were well established.[20] In this direction,
there also developed a strong trade in smuggled gin from Fernando Po. A
separate line of trade associated with the smithing items was to Bende and
later to Uzuakoli where there was a large Abiriba quarters and along the rail
line from Umuahia to Port Harcourt.

These two lines of activity and their respective trading communities belong
to two trade associations, the riverain (Umon) and the upland (Bende),
which divide the Abiriba community and to which all Abiriban masters and
apprentices belong. Each organisation has a council composed of members
of the most senior age grade which regulates economic conduct and settles
disputes. It is age rather than wealth which rules Abiriba. Most disputes are
settled before reaching the courts. When an individual retires, relations,
business associates and friends come together to make contributions to a
retirement benefit. There is competition between the two trading 'families'
of Abiriba to bring back elements of foreign culture and fashion to the
community and attract new recruits for apprenticeship at festival time. The
apprenticeship system brings an ethic of denial, hardship and discipline in
the build-up of trading experience, to which later success in business is
attributed.

Belonging to Abiriba brings a strong sense of community and identity,
which finds expression in helping each other, in the notion of private endeavour that is 'outside government', and in the desire to build and 'retire' back

in the home community. Abiriba has a strongly competitive culture that has promoted considerable wealth and encouraged material progress. This competition goes beyond struggles for wealth and status in the community and has been institutionalised in a number of ways. There is, for example, competition between age grades to complete public projects in the community. Age grades have been responsible for the establishment of a post office, hospital, girls' secondary school, and many other projects. In an example of community endeavour in 1912, three Abiriban age groups dredged the Igu River from its mouth to Okopedi-Itu to make it navigable to canoes in all seasons.[21]

The Abiriba Communal Improvement Union was founded in 1944 by traders living away from Abiriba and branches were formed in all the major commercial centres. The Union provided many scholarships and financed the town's first secondary school, Enuda College, which opened in 1954.

The main concentration of Abiriba traders before the Second War was in Calabar. Umuahia was also an important centre. In the first decade of this century, Calabar, located on the Cross river, rivalled Lagos. Abiriban traders, acting as factors with the European trading companies, dealt in biscuits, tobacco, kippers, herrings, and by the 1930s in stockfish. With the decline of Calabar, Abiriban traders moved to Port Harcourt and Aba. In Port Harcourt, there developed a trade in second-hand clothing, originally obtained from ships and sold to Okrika people (hence the popular name for second-hand clothing in Lagos and elsewhere, 'Okrika', abbreviated from 'Okrika Wake Up'). This trade was pioneered by I. Onwuka who trained many others. The main source of this clothing was army surplus stock which appeared during and after World War II. In the 1950s, imports from the United States became available. Jewish merchants in New York were a major source of supply. Between 1946 and 1963, the proportion of stall frontage devoted to second-hand clothing in Aba main market rose from 1 per cent to 27 per cent.[22] Dealing networks in second-hand clothing were extended into Northern Nigeria by Abiribans. The largest trader in the North was Chief O. Mang.

In 1963, some Abiriban textile traders left Aba for the Cameroons.[23] The size of the potential market in the Cameroons had been signalled by Cameroonian buyers in Aba. With the civil war there was a naval blockade of the southern ports and the Cameroon government became hostile to resident Biafrans. Some Abiriba traders then moved from Cameroon to Cotonou (Benin Republic) and Lomé (Togo). Here the market for second-hand clothing was pioneered and extended to other parts of West Africa.

Access to the Nigerian market was maintained from the new import bases at Cotonou and Lomé. When the civil war ended, the textile trade continued to expand and more Abiriban traders arrived from the Cameroons. The wealth created during and after the civil war by these overseas Igbo trading communities played an important part in reviving the economic fortunes of Aba, Onitsha and Enugu in the aftermath of war when the Biafran currency was made worthless. Thus most of the Abiribans who bought property and established trading concerns in Aba following the war, had a Cotonou connection. When the oil boom expanded the Nigerian market, Abiriban traders started to return to Aba and import via Lagos and Port Harcourt. But many maintained overseas branch companies whose activities fluctuated with the strength of the Nigerian market and the degree of formal restriction on trade.

The more general role of Cotonou and Lomé as entrepôts for the Nigerian market that specialised in goods formally banned in Nigeria, should be noted.[24] Another important line of trade to Nigeria from the ports of Lomé and Cotonou, which sprang to life after 1972, involved the transit centre of Maradi in Niger.[25] Here Hausa traders, building on much older trading ties with Kano and Katsina, diversified from cattle, groundnuts and kola into cigarettes, textiles and later, rice. This official transit traffic for goods destined to be smuggled into Nigeria, peaked in 1982–3.

ABIRIBAN ENTERPRISES IN ABA

We begin with three studies of Abiriban enterprises in Aba. Nnana Kalu was a major trader in stockfish who subsequently entered the paper industry. The Chika group is a younger trading concern whose emergence throws some light on the importance of apprenticeship, the second-hand clothing trade and overseas trading. There follows the case of an apprentice to the Chika Group, who rapidly became one of the leading industrialists in Aba.

Our shorter profiles cover six other Abiriban firms. From their origins in trade, they have all made investments in light industry or services.

Chief Nnana Kalu

Chief Nnana Kalu (1924–92) attended elementary school in Abiriba. In 1934, he started work as an apprentice to a stockfish merchant in Calabar. He was a domestic servant for several years, later going to the market and working in his master's store. His master was a major dealer in stockfish, trading with the United Africa Company and G. B. Ollivant who were the major importers.

In 1943, he left the stockfish trade to assist a produce factor up river from Calabar. He then went to Umuahia where he trained as a tailor. Finally, he moved to Aba on 31 December 1949 and began to import army surplus and civilian second-hand clothing. When the import of second-hand stock was temporarily stopped he switched to importing stockfish. The UAC and GBO no longer had a monopoly in the trade. When the UAC caused a slump in stockfish prices through massive importation in 1952, he was able to survive because he had air-conditioned storage facilities. Without them, he would have been forced to sell in a week. He also imported sewing machines, gramophones, and enamelware using a confirming house in London.

In 1958, N. Kalu and Brothers Ltd was incorporated. He employed many apprentices and six non-apprentice staff. At this time, he also participated with others in the Abiriba Merchants Company, a leading firm of produce agents that had Licensed Buying Agent (LBA) status. The turnover of this company reached £500,000 per annum. Eventually, in the 1960s, his stockfish business was amalgamated with the Stockfish Marketing Company owned by UAC and he became a director and shareholder.

As a result of the war, he lost six properties he was renting out to the Shell Oil company in Port Harcourt. He retained his property in Aba, having taken his documents to Standard Chartered before the war for safe keeping. He also lost money that was held by banks during the war.

After the war he re-entered the stockfish trade and also went into transport. The UAC was forced to wind up its stockfish business because of the indigenisation decree. In 1976, the Obasanjo government banned the import of stockfish and the government took over importation through the Nigerian National Supply Company. As the stockfish trade was largely in Igbo hands, this was seen as a move against a particular section of the country. In transport, he secured Leyland vehicles from BEWAC and Mercedes from Leventis, transporting goods and passengers between Port Harcourt and Lagos. He had 120 lorries at the peak. He stopped haulage in 1975.

In 1978, he opened a paper-conversion plant in Aba (Star Paper Mill) making exercise books, envelopes and toilet tissues. In 1983, a paper-recycling plant started production at Owerrinta on five hectares of land. This plant uses waste paper and cut offs sourced from all over the country. Italian technology is used and one Italian engineer is employed. In 1988, the combined turnover of the two plants was N15m. and some 200 persons were employed. One son, who trained in Germany, later assumed executive control of the paper plants and was overseeing expansion of the recycling plant in 1992.

Chief Nnana Kalu never went into construction and argued that his business was generally outside government. At times during his business career, Chief Nnana Kalu was involved in politics. In his view, politics and business were but distant friends and he claimed that politics had some adverse effect on his business.[26] In 1961, he was elected to represent Aba in the Eastern House of Assembly (1961–5). He was also a director of the Eastern Nigerian Marketing Board and President of the Abiriba Communal Improvement Union (1965). Later he became Treasurer of the National Party of Nigeria (NPN) in Imo State (1979–83) and Chairman of the Aba Textile mill (1981–3). Chief Nnana Kalu built a hospital in Abiriba and also handed over a Presbyterian church to the community. He was conferred with a chieftaincy title by the Eze of Abiriba in 1983.

The Chika Group

Chief Chika Agu was born in Abiriba on 17 October 1939. His parents were farmers. He obtained the First School Certificate with distinction from Enuda Elementary School in 1954. He began work as an apprentice in Port Harcourt before moving to Aba in 1957. Here he attended evening classes at Progress Commercial Institute for two years, studying business practice, typing and accounts. He took the proficiency certificate in 1959.

In 1960, he started the Chika Import Company at Aba. The company specialised in the import and distribution of used clothing. Government surplus clothing (pullover, haversack, blue denim) was obtained from London companies and imported via Port Harcourt. The company also began to import used clothing from the United States. Formerly the United States had not traded freely with Nigeria.

Seven branches were established in the North (Jos, Kano, Kaduna, Zaria, Katsina, Sokoto, Maiduguri). Overall, some 300 persons were employed, with 100 at Aba. The market for used clothing was strongest among the nomadic, less privileged populations of the Sahel including northern Cameroon and Niger. The company was the second-largest used clothing and remnant dealer in the North after Chief O. Mang. During this period, Chika Agu invested in property in Aba and Umuahia.

Late in 1964, a branch of the Import Company was opened in Victoria, Cameroon. When the civil war broke out in 1967 Chika Agu was visiting the Victoria branch and he was forced to stay there and attempt to develop the business. Federal troops had cut off the waterways between Calabar and Cameroon. The normal route for Abiribans going to Cameroon was to go by canoe from Rivers State to Santa Isabel and then to Douala and Victoria. President Ahidjo supported the federal government and tried to regulate and suppress Igbo traders in the Cameroons. So in 1968, Chika migrated to Cotonou where he obtained a UN refugee passport and established temporary headquarters for the company. The company still traded in Biafra via its Libreville Office and the Uli airstrip in Biafra. Chika's older brother was in charge of these operations and the main items traded were milk, tobacco and salt.

Abiriban traders introduced second-hand clothing to Cotonou and Lomé. At first there was some resistance to these goods because they 'belonged to the dead'. But after three months, a market was established. From 1969 until the present day, this trade has been strong. The Cotonou and Lomé markets were found to be too restricted and distribution was extended northwards by opening new offices. A Hausa-speaking Dahomean was employed to enter Nigeria. Contacts were established along the border towns. The Lomé market and Togolese border locations supplied Ghanaians who traded with the Ivory Coast and Upper Volta.

The Chika Group was one of the leading Igbo merchant companies. There were about six comparable companies in Cotonou during the war period. They included Abiriban people, who had migrated from Santa Isabel and Victoria when the waterway channels with Nigeria were closed, and some Nnewi people. In general, Igbo traders specialised in second-hand clothing, remnants, and spirits. Hausa people specialised in cigarettes and damask.

The market-research division of the Chika Group operated what amounted to a grand apprenticeship scheme. While apprentices gained proficiency in typing, business-letter writing, and Pitmans shorthand, they would prospect for business overseas using trade catalogues. Each apprentice who received offers would maintain that company agency, with Chika acting as the parent company and buying the goods. The agency commission would be reserved for the apprentice and banked with his master. In this manner, considerable sums of capital could be built up for later use by the apprentice. When the apprentice had sufficient knowledge of business practices and contacts, the Chika Group would release him to go independent. The subsequent locations of the thirty or more business tycoons who began their business in this way included Aba, Uyo, Cotonou, Lomé and Douala.

With the end of the civil war, Igbo people were materially deprived. The Chika compound in Cotonou was described as a vast refugee camp. The Biafran currency was made virtually worthless and a ban was imposed on the import of stockfish and second-hand clothing. The overseas Igbo trading communities played a large part in the rehabilitation of individual businesses and the revival of the economic fortunes of Aba, Onitsha and Enugu. Many of the businesses that were launched between 1970 and 1973 were assisted by loans and advances in kind from overseas traders.

In 1982, the headquarters of the Group was transferred back to Aba. Considerable difficulty was experienced in getting back advances that had been made. Plans for a wheelbarrow, shovel and enamelware industry had to be shelved, although a warehouse was constructed. Attempts to secure an import licence failed. The introduction of the Structural Adjustment Programme then made the import of machinery too costly. Currently there are plans for a poultry industry. Meanwhile the Group has diversified to include shoe goods, luggage materials, plastics for furniture, and car upholstery.

Onwuka Interbiz Group of Companies

Chief Onwuka Kalu was born in 1954 at Abiriba, Arochukwu/Ohafia LGA, Imo State. His father died when he was about two years old. He left school early because his mother had difficulty paying the school fees. He attended Jiks Commercial Institute, Abiriba, obtaining a certificate in shorthand, typing, economics and English.

He left Nigeria in 1972 to become an apprentice to Kalu Eze, an uncle living in Lomé, Togo. Kalu Eze was in charge of the Togo operations of the

Chika Group, which had its headquarters in Cotonou (Benin). Onwuka Kalu's ability for business made an early impression and he was moved to the Group headquarters in Cotonou. He made swift progress through a series of positions – houseboy, kitchen boy, clerk, assistant company secretary, company secretary, and eventually became the managing director of an import/export company. He proved himself adept at learning business practices and he made rapid progress in French and the local dialects. He gradually became indispensable to Chika, running the business when Chief Agu travelled abroad. Foreign bankers and businessmen would insist on doing business with him in person.

While he was working for Chika, he registered a business of his own in Lomé, which was staffed by friends. Chika gave him support in making contacts with foreign companies and they assisted him in the purchase and marketing of goods. As an apprentice, his agency commissions on orders for the Togo and Cotonou sub-region were kept by his master until such time as he went independent. He secured good commissions from Japanese textile trading companies. In this manner a very considerable stock of capital was built up. Chika was very reluctant to see him leave, but he eventually went on his own in 1976. As we have seen, the experience of Chief Onwuka Kalu with the Chika Group was not unique. Many businessmen launched their careers through the market-research division of the Group with the support and assistance of Chika.

The decision to return to Nigeria in 1977 was made in the knowledge that this was the largest market in the region. Most of the goods traded by Cotonou-based companies were either destined for Nigeria or had originated there. After discussions with friends, he decided that the time was ripe to go into the manufacture of nails. He could see that traders were about to encounter problems after the initial flush of the oil boom. Moreover, the federal government had already committed itself to a local steel industry, from which raw materials could be obtained.

In 1978, Onwuka Kalu established the first indigenous large-scale nail manufacturing enterprise in Aba (NAGSMI). Land was acquired cheaply on the outskirts of Aba where infrastructure and facilities were not developed. Manufacture of nails started with two German nail presses. Expansion to twenty-eight presses later enlarged capacity to 20,000 tons of nails a year and the company became one of the largest nail manufacturers in Nigeria and a market leader. Galvanising and electro-plating facilities were added. In addition to nails, the company produces nuts and bolts, screws, staples and barbed wire. Nails currently account for about 25 per cent of turnover.

When the original nail machines broke down, machinery was purchased to manufacture spare parts. This was the start of an expansion into machine tools and a capacity to design and manufacture parts, press tools, moulds and dies. Steel and scrap from local steel-rolling mills is used. There is 10 per cent import content (chemicals, alloys and some flat steels). Initially two Indian engineers were employed for a few years. The company has experienced no difficulty in recruiting Nigerian engineers and currently twelve are employed. Management by objectives is used to set minimum targets with extra profit incentives above that level.

At no point has the company relied on state or federal contracts. Customers include multinationals (Ferodo, United Africa Company, Peugeot, Lever Brothers), public enterprises (Nigerian Airways), and larger indigenous companies (Star Paper, Ferdinand Industries, Ekwulumili Industries, etc.).

In 1986, the company raised a multiple bank credit of N21m. from eight banks together with N44m. of its own funds to finance expansion. Total investment was about $100m. and 234 persons were employed in 1990. In 1991, the company (Onwuka Hi-Tek Industries Ltd) was quoted on the first tier of the Nigerian Stock Exchange, following a public subscription. Turnover was N44m. in 1992 with net profit of N2.2m.[27]

The company forms part of the Onwuka Interbiz Group, which is still involved in general trading. In the mid-1980s, an R and D company, Basic Trust Ltd, was established. The major project envisaged was a chlorine alkali plant. This $100 investment was overtaken by the devaluation of the naira, which raised the cost of importing capital equipment prohibitively. The Group acquired a UK engineering company that made conveyor systems. This company was sold in 1989.

In 1988, Fidelity Union Merchant Bank was established. It achieved after-tax profits of N5.8m. in its first year of operation and N46m. for 1992. A boardroom struggle for control of the bank broke out in 1991, pitting Chief Kalu against Chief Victor Odili.[28] There was no run on the bank and no loans were called in, but the Central Bank dissolved the board and appointed an interim board pending a reconciliation of the conflict.[29] Victor Odili and Nebolisa Arah were eventually confirmed as chairman and managing director respectively.[30]

Chief Kalu was the founder of the Eastern Zone Area of the Manufacturer's Association of Nigeria. In 1982, he promoted the first 'Exclusively Made in Nigeria Trade Fair' to be held in Nigeria. It was held at Aba. He was nominated to serve on the Constituent Assembly in Abuja and was Chairman of the Committee for Federal Executive Bodies. He was pro-tem leader of the defunct political party, the Liberal Movement. In 1989, he took the Abiriba chieftaincy title, Okpu-Uzu ('blacksmith'), a title usually reserved for persons in their sixties.

Short Profiles

Rosies Garment

Chief Iro Orji was born in 1934. He was apprenticed to a tailor in Port Harcourt. In 1954, he started his own business. He built up a small business, which specialised in ladies dresses, with four to five apprentices using pedal machines. In 1962, he started a small sewing factory employing thirty-two men and using industrial sewing machines.

During the war, he returned to Abiriba and started farming. With the advice of a friend in the agricultural department, he cultivated swamp land near Bende to produce rice, maize, peppers and onions. He employed refugees from the rice-growing area of Abakaliki.

After the war, he managed to retrieve four sewing machines (with great difficulty) from Port Harcourt where they had been kept at the Assemblies of God Mission during the war. He started a garment business in Aba using synthetic fabric from Lagos. Later, he moved into knitting but not into weaving, which was considered too competitive. A luggage section was developed later. An Indian and a Dutch expatriate were employed, but no general manager was appointed, the owner fearing that his authority would be compromised. The company employs 300 persons.

Aku International/Nibeltex

This company employed about 300 people in 1990 and was involved in general trading, textile production and construction. Chief K. K. Onumah started general trading and a second-hand clothing business in Aba with his brothers in the mid-1950s. In 1964 he left for the Cameroons where he remained during the civil war. He returned to Aba in 1972. Aku International specialised in textiles, building materials and stockfish. The trading company has offices in Aba, Lagos, Togo, Cotonou, Cameroon and Equatorial Guinea. In 1975 a construction company was founded. In 1980 a joint venture with a Belgian company was established to knit, weave and produce upholstery. The Belgian company took 40 per cent of the equity and two Belgian expatriates were employed. In 1988, a garment division was created. The level of employment has fluctuated between 40 and 90 persons.

John Okam

John Okam traded in second-hand clothing in northern Nigeria before the civil war. After the war, he moved to Lomé where the volume of second-hand clothing imports had risen. Subsequently, he returned to Nigeria and went into industry when credit was easy to obtain. His first venture in 1979 was in the manufacture of nails, nuts and roofing sheets. The second business was a soft-drinks venture with a franchise from Royal Crown Cola who sold concentrates and advised on the running of the plant. His third activity was in food processing and cold storage with the establishment of Jojo Cold Storage Ltd.

He employed expatriates up to 1985 when costs became too great. The peak of employment was in 1982. In 1983 the group began to move into shipping. In 1990, four ships were on charter and one vessel, owned by the company, carried limestone for the Delta Steel plant.

Interland Industries Ltd

Chief Onwukah was educated up to class 3 at the secondary level and then left school for financial reasons. After a period of trade apprenticeship, he went independent in 1962. During the war, his company supplied foodstuffs to the Biafran army.

After the war, a new company was established, specialising in beverages – especially imported malt drinks and beer. In 1976 the import of beer was banned. This prompted the decision to go into the production of soft drinks as an independent concern (rather than a franchise). Funds were obtained from personal savings, bank loans, and friends who lent money and the size of the investment was N7.8m. Three Germans were employed initially. They trained Nigerian counterparts and left in 1983. Staff were also trained overseas in Canada and the owner's brother, an engineer, became the general manager. A single line plant was obtained second-hand in the international market. No technical problems have arisen that could not be solved locally. Plans for expansion were abandoned with the introduction of the Structural Adjustment Programme in 1986. The company has a carbon-dioxide plant and makes sales to other beverage companies. A fleet of trucks is operated with a depot system.

Michael Nwoke Okocha

Michael Okocha is one of the largest textile and remnant dealers who is active in the Aba market.

He left Abiriba at the age of 7 without schooling for Umuahia where he enrolled in elementary school. He left school in 1964 and travelled to the Cameroons. His first port of call was Bamenda and Mankom where he traded in used clothing. He left for Victoria in 1969 and was appointed manager for the Utah Associated Trading Company. Subsequently he left to join the Abiriba Merchants Company in the Ivory Coast. He resigned the appointment after disagreement and formed his own company, Nokoprise Intermark Company in 1971.

He moved to Togo where living expenses were lower and sold other people's used clothing and textiles on commission. He raised sufficient capital to begin direct importation of remnants from the United States. He knew a wide network of buyers because many people had come to Lomé from the Cameroons. With 1m.F CFA profit achieved over a six-month period, he made his first import of 50 bales of used clothing from the United States and began to import by container. In 1983 he had credit outstanding of $900,000 and 20 containers from the United States. At that time, Nigerians were coming to buy at Lomé because textile imports were banned in Nigeria. Lomé was also a major staging point for imports to Ghana, Burkina Faso and Niger. He later moved to Aba market, keeping offices in the United States, Togo and Lagos. The company has diversified into petrol filling stations and hotels.

Ezera International

After elementary education, Chief N. O. Nwojo was apprenticed to a textile dealer in Calabar. When he left his master, he moved to Aba where he traded in patent medicines. In 1957, he made his first importation of used clothing from the United States. The ban on the importation of used clothing into Nigeria prompted his departure for the Cameroons in 1963. He traded in textiles and used clothing at Victoria and stayed in Cameroon throughout the war. When the war ended, he moved to Cotonou and food and textiles were sent to Aba to assist those who had lost their livelihoods. The trade in general goods, textiles and used clothing at Cotonou proved profitable and some funds were used to finance a biscuit factory in Aba. Following a ban on the import of biscuits in 1977, the factory was opened in 1980 in partnership with Chief Kalu Ndukwe who had trained in catering and had acted as agent for Chiltonian Biscuits of the United Kingdom since 1971. The Nigerian Industrial Development Bank gave loans. Chiltonian Biscuits took 10 per cent of the equity and two expatriates were employed. Output and employment peaked during the early 1980s. The ban on the importation of wheat and the Structural Adjustment Programme affected the business adversely. A flour mill opened in 1991 to process local grains. The company has diversified into colour photo-processing.

OTHER ENTERPRISES IN ABA

We present six enterprise profiles – Niger Garments, one of four larger garment firms in Aba; Starline, a cosmetics and pharmaceutical enterprise with steady growth that is investing in chemical manufacture to supply the oil industry; Toonak, a mini-conglomerate with a strong property base; the Maduako Group, which grew from its origins in transport to enter the cement trade and vegetable-oil milling and processing; Baco Engineering, a metal fabrication and civil engineering firm; and UOO Nig. Ltd, a partnership that originated in the textile trade before the civil war and subsequently switched to building materials and moved into light manufacture.

Niger Garments

Chief David Nwokocha Orji was born in 1933 at Ikoko Item in Bende Local Government Area. He was apprenticed at the age of 7 to a master tailor in Aba. At this time, tailoring in Aba was dominated by Item people. As an itinerant tailor in Aba, he mended clothes and collected orders for his master. He set up on his own in 1948 using a hired manual sewing machine and concentrated on singlets.[31] In 1963 he incorporated Niger Garments Manufacturing Company which employed 60 people (including 10 apprentices), mainly Item people, making singlets, underwear, school uniforms and sportswear. The first batch of knitting machines worth £26,000, was ordered before the civil war but was stranded in Lagos when the blockade began.

The company lost all its assets during the war. Start-up after the war was assisted by Union Bank and later the Nigerian Industrial Development Bank which made loans for knitting machinery. The concern was forced to close during the Second Republic (1979–83) as imports flooded the Nigerian market. A subsequent ban on the import of garments and the introduction of the Structural Adjustment Programme boosted demand. Over 220 people are employed, many of them local Ngwa who live in outlying villages and cycle to work in Aba, thereby lowering labour and welfare costs to the company. There is considerable delegation of authority within the company and four university graduates are employed. The only diversification outside garments is a small investment in a hotel.

Starline (Nig.) Ltd

The company started in the mid-1950s marketing pharmaceuticals as a sole proprietorship, Owunna & Sons, under Chief P. S. Owunna. Starline Chemists was established in 1962. Manufacture of candles started in 1964 and was revived again in 1973 after the war. A pilot cosmetics factory opened in 1975 with an investment of £30,000. Plastic containers followed in 1978 and pharmaceuticals in 1985. The company still imports pharmaceuticals and general goods and has retail pharmacy outlets. Manufacturing accounts for about 60 per cent of turnover and 285 persons are employed. Overall more than 500 persons are employed in the group.

In addition to trading and manufacturing interests, two palm-oil mills and refining capacity were acquired in 1989 from the Agricultural Development Corporation, Cross River State. A palm plantation was added in 1990. Fish farming was started near Okigwe in 1990. A major investment in chemical manufacturing to supply oil companies is currently being undertaken in Aba in partnership with the Nigerian Industrial Development Bank.

The family also has a property portfolio in the United States and investments in the United Kingdom. These interests are held by a discretionary family trust.

The company has adopted a strong marketing-led strategy for cosmetics, undertaking consumer surveys in local government areas in the northern states. Its small size allows it to be more adaptable to local consumer preferences than larger multinational companies. It has a cautious strategy with respect to expansion, maintaining a low debt/equity ratio.

The Group is notable for a successful intergenerational transition. The senior son trained in the United States as a pharmacist and in business administration. He also gained work experience with US companies. He returned to Nigeria in 1983 and worked in a government hospital for one year. He then joined the family company, supervising the trading shop, and then the trading division. He then moved in sequence to manufacture, banking and importation. With full exposure to all aspects of the business, he took over all operations in 1988, two years before his father's death. This kept potentially disruptive family pressures at bay and ensured continuity.

Toonak International (Nig.) Ltd

Toonak International is a small conglomerate, employing some 1,200 persons. Chief Titus O. Njoku was born in 1932 at Ozuitem, Bende Division. He started trading in general commodities in Aba in the 1950s. Prior to the civil war, he built up widespread international trading contacts especially with the United States. A strong property base was established in Aba, Umuahia, Onitsha and Lagos. After the war, he traded in second-hand clothing at Cotonou. Some properties were converted to cash after the war to provide liquidity. The group has benefited from property appreciation in Aba and owns part of the central textile trading area.

In the mid-1970s, the company began to diversify. An aluminium building products venture was started with a US company. The company operates nationally with contracts in Abuja. An oil-marketing company with fifty filling stations in prime locations was established. In 1985, a soft-drinks plant was opened under franchise from Canada Dry. And in 1987 a soap-manufacturing plant was opened with German participation. A construction company was also established with offices nationwide. A major hotel is planned in Aba and the group hopes to attract a joint-venture partner after establishing the core business.

The Group has diversified as the need arises and still maintains its trading base. Diversification has been given impetus by unpredictable government policies. The senior son returned from business studies in the United States in 1984 and is deputy chairman and managing director. An expatriate general manager is employed.

Maduako Group

Nze C. O. Maduako left secondary school in 1950 and joined CFAO as a clerk in the transport section. He began his own transport service with a single Morris truck operating out of Port Harcourt. He registered as a transporter with CFAO. He became a major transporter for the Nkalagu cement factory at Emene near Enugu, which opened in 1957 (The Nigerian Cement Co. Ltd). He carried imported gypsum from Port Harcourt. Before the war, he had a fleet of 120 lorries and was a clearing and forwarding agent for the Nigerian Cement Co., the Nigerian Coal Corporation, and Nigersteel.

During the civil war, he was involved in distributing food aid for Caritas and the Red Cross and he visited Portugal. After the war, he founded a cement importing and bagging enterprise with Norwegian partners (40 per cent) in 1981. The company, Eastern Bulkcem Co. Ltd, located in Port Harcourt, had a turnover of N35m. and employed 198 persons in 1986.[32] This business was established in partnership with a chemical engineer who was the first indigenous manager at the Nkalagu Cement Factory. Bags were produced in 1983. Subsequently, a palm-kernel processing plant was established in Aba in 1989 at the cost of N13m. and a vegetable-oil refinery, costing about N5m., is in the pipeline.

Baco Engineering

Before the war, the owner of Baco Engineering, Chief B. A. Isiguzo, was the chief engineer with Lever Brothers in Aba. During the war, Lever Brothers (Biafra) was transferred to Ukpor where 150 persons were employed. The factory used caustic soda that had been bought and stored before hostilities began. Soap-cutting tables were fabricated and the soap was stamped by hand. The unit was given army protection.

After the war, Lever Brothers reinstated their workers. In 1972, Chief Isiguzo left Lever Brothers and set up a metal fabrication unit in Aba. The company made steel and iron windows and doors; there was steady custom from churches because the main competitor, Crittal Hope, only made items in standard sizes. The firm subsequently moved site, bought a roller and guillotine machine, and began making underground tanks. It also made bonded-brake linings and machinery for vegetable-oil processing. A civil engineering section was also started.

UOO Nig. Ltd

This company was established in 1956 by four partners from Unubi, Nnewi Local Government Area. It began trading in fancy goods, worsted woollen terylene, and other merchandise at Aba. At Lagos a branch was established in 1958, followed in 1960 by a branch in Ibadan on Lebanon Street, where goodwill was paid to the Lebanese owners. By 1966, eight branches were established in the Western Region and four branches in the East. There was also a ready-made ladies-wear shop near the Marina in Lagos. Whereas the Lebanese, who were dominant in the textiles trade, mixed different materials in the same shop, UOO concentrated on wool. UOO All Wool Stores were the largest importers of terylene worsted material from the United Kingdom, taking over 60 per cent of imports. Plans to move into the textile industry were thwarted by the civil war. Many properties were lost in Port Harcourt as a result of the war.

After the war, the company concentrated its trade on building materials, especially roofing sheets. Entry into the motor trade ended in 1986. A corrugated-roofing plant was established at Aba in 1980 and this was followed by a galvanising plant in 1985. In 1987, the Group established the first electrode plant east of the Niger. It has experienced strong competition from cheap Chinese imports. In neither of these industries are the basic raw materials, wire rods and rolled sheets being produced locally.

Earlier, the company had diversified into poultry, animal feeds, and farming on a small scale (cassava and pineapples). The latest venture is a filling station integrated with a cooking gas bottling plant. The Group which employs over 500 persons combines its industrial activities with importation and distribution of pharmaceuticals, cosmetics and automobile and refrigeration parts. Turnover in the trading division in 1990 was N24m.[33]

IMO STATE ENTERPRISES

Our last two case studies cover the Ferdinand Group of Companies with operations at Urualla, Imo State and Enugu; and Rokana Industries PLC, located near Owerri, Imo State.

Ferdinand Group of Companies

This group, which employs over 3,000 permanent staff, is one of the largest enterprises in Igboland. From a background in trade, the Group has diversified into manufacturing and agro-processing.

Chief Ferdinand Anaghara was born in 1937 in Urualla, Ideato Local Government Area in Imo State.[34] He attended primary school in Urualla and had two double promotions. He was sent to a Roman Catholic priest in Onitsha as a house boy and mass server. The priest soon left Nigeria because of ill health and Anaghara became an apprentice to a food trader in Onitsha. As an apprentice, he travelled widely in eastern and northern Nigeria. In 1953, he graduated as a master trader and established his own retail business.

For four years he remained in the food trade. In 1958, however, he diversified into transport and placed a bus on the Urualla–Onitsha route. He then went into the motor-tyre trade and registered a company, Messrs F. Anaghara and Brothers Ltd. The transport fleet was expanded into northern Nigeria and depots were established in the Mid-West Region.

After the civil war, he was again appointed a dealer in motor tyres by Dunlop industries. Ferdinand Enterprises Nig. Ltd was registered with headquarters in Enugu. The company consolidated old lines of business in motor tyres and parts with increasing patronage from the Leventis Group. A dealership in Honda motorcycles and electric generators was obtained. Later, the company became a distributor for Daihatsu vehicles (1977) and Mercedes trucks from Anambra Motor Manufacturing Co. (ANAMMCO) (1980). Volkswagen-approved sales and service garages were established in Lagos, Aba, Enugu, Onitsha and Abakaliki. Other activities included general merchandising and sale of scientific and medical equipment. A London buying office was also established. In addition, the Group established a property division (which is currently constructing a shopping complex in Enugu) following the decline of the retail outlets of the older foreign trading companies.

An industry for aluminium kitchen and domestic ware was established in Urualla in 1978. This was followed, in 1981, by fabrication of steel structures (motor trailers and tankers, underground storage tanks, motor chassis, doors, and windows). In the same year, a garment industry was started in Onitsha with the assistance of a British firm owned by a Greek couple. £130,000 was invested and 66 sewing machines installed. Because of the ban on imported fabrics, the enterprise concentrated on the production of school uniforms using local fabrics.

In 1982, a filter manufacturing company was established in Urualla under licence from Soparis SA of France, whose products were previously imported. In addition to motor filters, the company makes filters for industrial applications. Production has not reached half the rated capacity since inception.[35] Clients include the Nigerian Railway Corporation, Delta Steel, the Nigerian National Petroleum Corporation and several breweries.

The Group has made large agro-industrial investments including a palm kernal crushing mill, a rubber-processing plant (1988) and a cocoa bean processing plant. A vegetable-oil refinery is being added and will process 150m. tons of oil a day (N300m. investment). Palm-kernel cake and crumb rubber exports were worth N197m. in 1991.[36] A Belgian company is sole management agent for the rubber plantation and sales of rubber. Ferdinand Oil Mills went public in 1991 and had a turnover of N77m. in 1989–90. The Group has leased palm plantations and rubber estates and is finalising arrangements to acquire 10,000 hectares in Rivers State for a palm and rubber plantation. The Group has also acquired a 3,000-hectare site in Uzo-Uwani, Anambra State (1988). Rice, maize and cowpeas are cultivated and livestock reared.

The flow of social recognition and philanthropic activity that often surrounds a successful business career in Nigeria can be gauged from the following information about the Group. Chief Anaghara has extended financial and material support to the following: 15 church organisations; 37 state and federal government ventures, student and women's organisations and professional associations; 10 sporting clubs and associations; 6 educational institutions, including the University of Nigeria, Nsukka.

The Group has over 25 awards and certificates to its credit, while Chief Anaghara is patron of over 26 social and sporting organisations, and member of over 17 social and business organisations. He is also the recipient of six chieftaincy titles from various communities in the country and an honorary doctorate in business administration (1992) from the University of Nigeria, Nsukka.

Rokana Industries PLC

Located near Owerri (Imo State), this company had a turnover of N10.3m. in 1990 and employed 108 persons (200 at its peak). The owner, Engineer

Ugwuh, studied mechanical engineering in the United Kingdom at Borough Polytechnic and went on to take an M.Sc. at Birmingham University. On return to Nigeria in 1972, he joined ICI. He marketed chemicals and became marketing manager and executive director in 1978. He performed a number of feasibility studies for the company, but none was taken up, leaving him frustrated.

In 1978, he registered a company with his senior brother that resold chemicals. He imported toothbrushes from Norway. He attempted to manufacture toothpaste on a small scale in a warehouse, buying flavours and components from Boots, but failed to produce a marketable product.

He wanted to make toothbrushes and the Norwegian firm was willing to give him a licence and to train personnel. Lever Brothers collaborated in a joint pack promotion (toothbrush and toothpaste). In addition to toothbrushes, an oil and skin lotion was produced. In 1982-3, an insecticide aerosol plant was opened using equipment from Italy. Igbo workers, who had formerly worked in the plastics industry in Lagos, were recruited, attracted by the higher quality of life at Owerri. The major problem was investment in LPG storage facilities with a high fire risk. In addition, the company also manufactures complementary products, like insecticides and toothpaste, on a contract basis for multinational companies such as Cadbury and G. B. Ollivant.

CONCLUSION

We have traced in some detail the movement from trade to industry in Aba since the end of the civil war. The onset of new industries was particularly marked after 1977 when trading profits from the oil boom had been built up. A wide range of light industries have been established. The background of those who have founded larger enterprises in Aba is predominantly that of elementary education, apprenticeship and trading, often with an international component. All Abiriba enterprises fall into this category. Trading still remains an important part of the activity of most enterprises. Two other routes to medium-scale industry can be distinguished. In the shoe and garment industries, enterprises have emerged from apprenticeship and small-scale artisanal activity. On the other hand, there were only two cases of industrialists with tertiary education and experience of employment with a foreign company (both engineers).

It must be emphasised that the artisan base in Aba has itself grown and in the case of shoe making, a major industry has developed. A major reservoir of skills has been built up over many years and the quality of products upgraded. This growth of small-scale enterprise (the so-called informal sector) is not in any direct sense functionally subordinate to larger capitalist enterprises, nor can it be linked to economic decline and strategies of survival. Like the shift to industry from trade, it is not the direct result of government policies. Any attempt to read into the recent economic history of Aba a development strategy would be a serious distortion. Debate about whether an 'informal sector' or a larger-scale strategy for enterprise growth and entrepreneurial development should be adopted, seems irrelevant and presumptuous, when the broad contours of economic change (involving, in this instance, growth through new enterprises at both scales) and its dynamic are so little understood.[37]

In the same way, arguments about the limitations of apprenticeship, that focus simply on its capacity to promote technical training, risk missing its broader significance for economic advancement and social well-being. Our work underlines the enduring importance of apprenticeship in trade and artisanal production throughout this century. In the Abiriban case, apprenticeship is linked to a strong ethic of hardship and sacrifice which is associated with business discipline and the capacity to undertake a successful career. Instances have been noted where apprenticeship was significant for allowing the initial accumulation of capital, but generally apprenticeship is more important for the business connections which are established. In trading organisations, where recruitment through apprenticeship has been the norm, business networks tend to be restricted to kin and community. These networks endure through individual careers. Where a movement to manufacture or significant increase in scale has occurred, the opportunity for individual control is weakened and the need for delegation arises. Then the basis of recruitment may shift from kin and community to more meritocratic procedures especially when relatives, whose performance has been found wanting, cannot be effectively disciplined.

As we have seen elsewhere, a trading background tends to give rise to greater diversification. In some instances, diversification has been unfocused leading to dispersion of effort. A succession of perceived profit opportunities has been followed and as competitors have rushed into similar lines, excess capacity has resulted. Examples include nails, toilet tissues and shoe soles.

In four enterprises, there has been full or partial succession to the next generation. In three cases, this has brought young, US-trained business graduates to top executive positions. The key condition for a successful transition and continuity in company growth appears to be the transfer of authority during the founder's lifetime, so that no vacuum exists for family pressures to exploit at death.

Most trajectories of accumulation in Aba did not rely on access to the state. In one case, political connections to the ruling party were instrumental in securing import licences which in turn created a trading profit that was used for investment in manufacture. But this was exceptional. Abiriban entrepreneurs in particular, have a long tradition of private initiative, operating outside, or across, formal state structures. Nor has the growth of enterprises been closely linked to foreign investment or management. Equity participation by foreign interests was very limited. Only one group consciously pursued a joint-venture strategy. The employment of expatriates in technical positions, often Indians or Taiwanese, was more common.

In the case of Abiriba, a pre-colonial trading community has maintained its relative wealth and a distinct pattern of private entrepreneurial activity involving migration and international trade throughout this century. Abiribans pioneered the importation and distribution of second-hand clothing, used offshore bases in Cameroon, Cotonou and Lomé to great effect, played a strategic role in the recovery of Aba after the civil war and were at the forefront of movement into industry in the late 1970s.

Although our work was not expressly concerned to examine the impact of the civil war on enterprises and the nature of the subsequent recovery, we will draw together some preliminary observations on the subject based on our findings in the Aba and Onitsha/Nnewi areas. Overall, there is little doubt that enterprises suffered a severe set-back from the war. Very often a virtually new start had to be made after the war, because assets had been destroyed, transport fleets run down, properties lost and the Biafran currency made worthless. Though no accurate assessment can be made, there are indications that the war blocked some important paths of local accumulation, especially in Port Harcourt area, where entry to the oil-service sector had begun before the war, and other industries were set up, or had reached an advanced stage of preparation.

Yet there were continuities. Some concerns like Niger Pork Products at Ukpor simply continued to run throughout the war uninterrupted. Others, like Lever Bros (Biafra) shifted from Aba and produced soap in a new location. Some enterprises changed their activities to work for the Food Directorate or provide transport for relief agencies. One entrepreneur, who was forced to drop garment manufacture, turned to rice production near Bende, employing refugees from the rice-growing area of Abakaliki, and then returned to garments. Several garment manufacturers who were in business in Aba before the conflict, quickly set up again, albeit on a small scale.

Most of the larger enterprises that emerged after the war were also present before the war. Two of the wealthiest businessmen in Port Harcourt before the war, F. U. Anyanwu and John Anyaehie were able to re-establish themselves. F. U. Anyanwu set up an aluminium roofing factory in Owerri and John Anyaehie established factories in Aba and Owerri. Other business people who re-emerged included Nnana Kalu, Augustine Ilodibe, Clement Maduako, Ferdinand Anaghara, Josiah Nnoruka, Joe Nwankwo, Mathias Ugochukwu, and the partnerships, GMO and UOO Group. In a number of cases, distributorships and agencies were resurrected and links with overseas suppliers repaired. For transport companies, like Ekene Dili Chukwu and C. Moore Obioha, the Greek Cypriot firm of Leventis played an important role in extending credit and restoring dealerships after the war ended.

With respect to communities, the impact of the war varied a great deal. As we saw in the case of Nnewi, it became an important market centre during the war, and was poised to resume the trade in motor parts when peace came. In the case of Abiriba, the overseas trading component was clearly very significant in explaining its revival. Other communities, that suffered from physical destruction and displacement of population, were altogether less fortunate.

After the war, trade networks were recreated and migrant populations settled all over the country. The pivotal role of Onitsha market as an entrepôt within a trading diaspora was re-established with the difference that more goods were locally produced. Perhaps the most remarkable outcome was the shift from reinvestment in the diaspora before the civil war, to the repatriation of capital and the build-up of enterprises and properties closer to home. This has brought a measure of economic recovery and a new pattern of industrial location.

8

THE ADVANCE OF INDIGENOUS CAPITAL IN KANO AND KADUNA

KANO

The city of Kano was, for centuries, a terminus in the trans-Saharan and West African trades. It was also in the nineteenth century at the centre of a vigorous regional trade in textiles, kolanut, livestock, grain and craft production.[1] It formed part of a textile belt which included northern Zaria, southern Katsina and Zamfara and was itself integrated into a wider region of cotton and grain production. At the core of the textile area were the dye works of southern Kano and northern Zaria. In the last quarter of the nineteenth century, Kano emirate, a territory of some 13,000 square miles, supported between three and four million people.[2]

Many of the leading businessmen of today descend from the long-distance traders of the pre-colonial period. The Agalawa were the largest single group of traders in the Sokoto Caliphate and Kano gradually became the focus of their activities. Like other immigrant groups, they traced their origin to the desert side of the Tuareg economy.[3] And like Tuaregs, Arabs, Kanuri, Fulbe, Nupe and Jukun, they were assimilated into Hausa society. One of the most important routes was to North Africa. Cloth, leather goods, slaves and kolanut were exported. Weapons, gowns, salt and manufactured goods were imported. Another route was to Adamawa, which took cloth and leather goods in return for slaves and ivory; another was the kolanut trade from Gonja and the Akan forest. These wealthy merchants stood at the apex of diversified commercial organisations that were based on complex patterns of kinship, clientage, slave labour and religious affiliation.[4] They sometimes combined caravan trading with local trading, the production of crafts, food production and credit services. Large-scale urban merchants produced large quantities of grain, using slave labour on estates and during the nineteenth century, they started to invest in the cottage production of textiles. The slave estates expanded and by the end of the century, merchants and wealthy craftsmen probably owned more plantations than the aristocracy.[5] Many of these merchants, who lived in Kano city and formed part of an absentee class of merchant planters, were kola importers, salt dealers, slave traders and textile brokers.

During the colonial period, Kano emerged as the premier city of the North and became a vital commercial centre, principally for the bulking and shipping of groundnuts, for the cattle trade, and for a flourishing petty commodity economy. The wealthy merchants had to respond to a number of new factors among which were the reorientation of trade away from the Sahara, the undermining of slavery, the arrival of foreign merchant companies, the coming of the railway in 1911, and the rise of new commodities. One response was to become agents for European and Lebanese companies engaged in the import of merchandise and the export of groundnuts, cotton, and hides and skins. Many local merchants, especially former kolanut dealers, converted their old commercial networks, that had been developed during the era of long-distance trading, to the demands of produce buying and merchandise distribution.[6] They also traded, in their own right, in other commodities, like grain. A related adjustment was a shift from residence in centres like Ringim and Bebeji to settlement inside Kano city. Most of them came originally from outside Kano city and in some cases, it was not until wealth had been accumulated in the wider Hausa trading diaspora, which stretched from Senegal to the Congo and the Sudan, that movement to Kano occurred. Traders did not generally allow their children to enrol in western education. Madugu Iliasu Dangomba (d. 1952) was an exception.[7]

With the expansion of groundnut and cotton production, the number of middlemen expanded.[8] At the beginning of each buying season, they were advanced large sums of money by the foreign companies to support a myriad of hamlet and village wholesalers. Through this system of advances and through control over the banking system, the foreign merchants were able to restrict the sphere of operation of local merchants, keeping them out of direct importation and export. The expansion of the groundnut trade attracted an influx of Lebanese, and Yemeni and Tripolitanian Arabs, especially after World War I.

The Lebanese occupied an intermediary position between European companies and the indigenous traders at times competing with one or both groups.[9] Initially they bought and sold European goods as agents. They did not begin direct importation until 1926. They were also involved in gold prospecting and the cattle and kola trades.[10] Some Lebanese arrived from Sierra Leone from where they imported kolanuts. The cattle trade was a risky activity with a complicated system of credit and the Lebanese never really made headway against competition from Hausa traders. Prices fell sharply in the depression and the Lebanese withdrew from both the cattle and kola trades. In groundnut purchasing and transporting, they fared better, especially after 1925, when produce market regulations in Kano and new trading practices by foreign buyers, disadvantaged Hausa merchants.[11]

By 1928, many Hausa merchants had been supplanted. Among the important Lebanese merchants were George Ferris, the Akle brothers, the Minaise brothers, the Shour family and Mohammed Chiranci. The most well known foreign merchant was a Tripolitanian Jew, Saul Raccah (1895–1970) who arrived in Kano in 1915, began exporting groundnuts in 1921 and succeeded in building up an important share in the export trade.

During the 1950s, Nigerian traders made advances in produce buying, direct importation of merchandise, real estate, transport and large-scale cattle dealing. This enlargement in the scale and scope of business was associated with the expansion of the domestic market, a larger volume of international trade, and the beginnings of a withdrawal of foreign merchants from the retail and produce trades. There were also shifts of power as some merchants began to make alliances with aristocrats, politicians, and the new class of state officials in the regional government.[12] These links were important in securing access to state patronage, finance and contracts, which became progressively more important as power shifted away from the colonial rulers, and surplus funds generated through the marketing board system were used to finance individual loans, infrastructure and industrial projects through institutions like the Northern Nigerian Development Board (later Northern Region Development Corporation) and the Bank of the North which opened in 1960.

The *sarauta* group, or aristocracy, began to look for alternative sources of income to maintain their large households and patronage networks as traditional sources of revenue were eroded under colonial rule. The involvement of the *sarauta* in business was generally low key and largely behind the scenes as backers and financiers. In the 1950s and 1960s collaboration and cooperation with the Lebanese increased as the latter came under pressure from local traders and began to invest in industry.[13] Formal links with foreign companies also increased as title holders became board members. Shehu Ahmad (d. 1986), Madakin Kano, was chairman of Nigerian Spinners and Dyers and Mandrides, and director of Royal Exchange Assurance, Nigerian Sweets and Confectionery, Nigerian Leather Works, Nigerian Fibre Products, Coledense, and Baertle and Company.

The first Nigerian licensed buying agents (LBA), Alhassan Dantata and Ibrahim Gashash, were appointed in 1953–4. By 1959–60 there were 29 Nigerian LBAs in Kano alone.[14] By the mid-1950s, some 12 businessmen were importing directly.[15] The opportunities for advances in commerce increased. The United Africa Company and John Holt encouraged local middlemen and customers to establish their own concerns as they withdrew from certain trading activities. New overseas companies wanting to expand their activities in Nigeria appointed Nigerian businessmen as their dealers and provided them with 90-day credit facilities.

The produce trade was closely linked to transporting. Among the early indigenous transporters and haulage groups were Dantata Transport, Muhammadu Nagoda, Haruna Kassim, Sani Marshal Transport, Garba Bichi and Sons, as well as Bello Bichi Transport.[16] Garba Bichi (b.1926) traded in grain and bicycle spare parts, purchased unserviceable vehicles in Kaduna and entered lorry transporting in 1953, becoming an LBA in 1960 with thirty lorries at the peak of his activity, a large-scale farmer and civil engineering contractor.[17] Sani Marshal (b.1927) began business in bicycle hire and repair.[18] His father was a financier and organiser of the dyed-cloth industry at Kura. Marshal worked as a motor boy on the Chad route and was employed as a driver in Maiduguri. He acquired his first lorry in 1955 operating in the North. In the early 1960s, he shifted to Lagos and operated on the Accra route. In 1966 he had thirty lorries and was a transporter for the Northern Region Marketing Board operating from Lagos. He established biscuit and macaroni factories and a hotel in Kano in the 1970s and was a financier of the People's Redemption Party. A member of the Tijaniyya brotherhood, he built a mosque and Islamia school at Kura and other mosques in Kano.

There also emerged a group of indigenous businessmen who started dealing in motor vehicles. Alhaji Uba Dan Maiwaina traded in second-hand motors, while new vehicles were imported by Yakudima and Sons, a company owned by the Abdullah Brothers, descendants of pre-colonial merchants.[19] Another avenue for the use of trading surpluses was real estate and there was a property boom in Kano in the early 1950s.

The expansion of small- and medium-scale light industry in Kano gathered momentum in the second half of the 1950s overshadowing earlier industrial development in Jos.[20] Until the early 1960s, there was practically no involvement by merchants in medium-scale industry. The industrial expansion did however, provide some opportunities for members of the administrative class and title holders to secure lucrative advisory positions in the new management structures. State officials tried to channel the interests of local merchants away from large-scale schemes on the grounds that it was the foreign companies who were interested in these areas.[21] Thus, the Northern Region Development Loans Board directed applicants into such spheres as rice milling, river transport, and bakeries. An early exception to the absence of investment in large-scale industry was the Kano Citizens Trading Company (KCTC), one of the first modern textile mills to be set up in Nigeria (1952). The mill was part of the Textile Development Scheme launched in 1946 as a project of the Department of Commerce and Industry.[22] A loan of £35,000 was granted to a group of local merchants by the Northern Region Development Loans Board in 1949. The KCTC had subscriptions from 300 local businessmen who held 59 per cent of the equity alongside the Northern Nigeria Development Corporation (NNDC). The Department undertook the management of the company and ordered used equipment from Lancashire. After a second loan for working capital, production started and the mill operated at a modest level. In the 1960s, it secured contracts for army amd police uniforms and by 1965 had 300 looms.[23]

It was Lebanese businessmen who played a central role in promoting industry in the 1950s.[24] They used capital from the groundnut trade to go into oil milling and, later, other industrial activities. George Calil set up the first mill on an experimental basis in 1942 followed by a larger mill in 1947. In 1953, P. S. Mandrides, K. Maroun Ltd, and Kano Oil Millers Ltd were established. Other areas of Lebanese investment included furniture making, soap production, shoes, bees wax, wheat mills and leather tanning. This movement to light industry was partly a response to growing pressures from Nigerian merchants who resented their activities in the retail and produce trades, road haulage and the wholesale trade in imported textiles. This opposition to foreign and, especially Lebanese interests, led eventually to the appointment of the Zanna Laisu Commission in 1960, which recommended that the retail trade, distribution from local industries, the produce trade, and transport should all be reserved for Nigerians.[25] Opposition to foreign control over tobacco distribution was especially strong and the first local distributors were appointed about this time.

These nationalist pressures, together with uncertainities created by changes in the marketing-board system led the Lebanese to align themselves with the ruling party, the NPC. In 1958, the Northern Region Development Corporation bought a Lebanese transport company from the Arab Brothers, who were based in Jos.[26] The Arab brothers then became the largest shareholders in the Bank of the North (1960) until the northern government took a controlling share. Lebanese interests were later involved with the Kano State Investment Company when it was founded in 1971 at the onset of the indigenisation exercise.[27] The Kano State government under Audu Bako was persuaded to take up shareholdings in a number of Lebanese companies of doubtful viability.

In the 1960s, Nigerian businessmen made further inroads in transport, construction, and the importation of general merchandise. A number of industrial projects were undertaken and minority shares acquired in foreign enterprises, though it was in the next decade that the shift to manufacture really gained strong momentum. In 1963, Sanusi Dantata set up Nigerian Leather Works with the assistance of the Northern Nigerian Development Corporation.[28] The shoe factory later diversified into football and military boots, and tennis and basketball shoes. Sanusi also invested in a small-scale oil mill. So, too, did the Rabiu brothers and Uba Ringim, whose oil mill employed 500 persons in a labour-intensive operation.[29] Uba Ringim also set up a small unit to produce leather goods. The Gashash brothers invested as minority partners in the Kaduna textile industry (1963), in a tannery (1963), in Nigerian Carbon Dioxide (1958), Kano Nails and Wires (1962) and Northern Steel Works (1964).

Advances in transportation were assisted by the Igbo exodus from the northern states and the switch to road traffic that followed the disruption of the railways and produce evacuation.[30] Local transporters secured an increased share on the crucial Kano–Lagos route. In 1966, the Northern Transporters and Merchant Syndicate emerged, promoted by the government. Six Kano businessmen led by Aminu Dantata, Musa Iliasu, Mahmoud Gashash and Haruna Kassim had 100 lorries by the end of 1966, rising to 700 by 1970. The company secured cement and fertiliser contracts from the new state governments. Other major transporters included Sanusi Dantata, Garba Bichi and Inuwa Wada. By 1976 there were 30 large-scale indigenous road haulage and transport companies in Kano, rising to 61 in 1980.[31] Road haulage enterprises became involved in the distribution of petroleum products, the most prominent being Garba Bello.[32]

The construction industry boomed with strong government expenditures in the 1970s. Chains of housing estates and office blocks were established to take advantage of the housing shortage and the enlargement of the state bureaucracy. Among the investors were Isiaku Rabiu, Miko Abdallah, Kabiru Bayero, Sani Marshal, Aminu Dantata and Sani Buhari Daura. Some like Haruna Kassim started hotels and guest houses. Others, like Sani Buhari Daura, established building and construction companies (Standard Construction). By 1976, there were 26 indigenous building-construction companies operating in Kano.[33]

During the 1970s, new manufacturing companies were promoted, some Lebanese companies acquired, and extensive industrial equity portfolios built up, following the indigenisation decrees of 1973 and 1977. Among the major industrial investors in this period were Isiaku Rabiu, Nababa Badamasi, Aminu Dantata, the Gashash brothers, Garba Inuwa, Baba Nabegu, Sani Marshal and Inuwa Wada.

Lebanese enterprises were hardest hit by phase one of the indigenisation exercise. In 1972, just prior to the decree, the Fagge-Ta-Kudu market in Kano, the nerve centre of the textile trade for the northern states, had 204 foreign-owned textile enterprises and 74 Nigerian-owned ones.[34] Many of the former were closed down or sold with the advent of the decree. In a survey of Fagge-Ta-Kudu and adjacent areas, Albasu found that over 100 buildings were sold by Lebanese to Hausa businessmen for more than N10m.[35] However, evidence at the end of the 1980s suggests that the Lebanese managed to retain an important share of the textile trade at wholesale and retail levels.

The two indigenisation decrees promoted the growth of large equity portfolios. Hoogvelt, in a study of 54 enterprises affected by the decree, found that N15.2m. of the N21m. divested went to some 219 individuals.[36] The degree of concentration was high with some 6 persons securing 50 per cent of the shares by value. A few businessmen took over enterprises as going concerns, but this was the exception. Thus, the Gashash brothers, who had already bought a cosmetics company before the decree, acquired companies involved in the wholesale and retail distribution of medicines and suitcase manufacture.

The NNDC and state investment companies were active during the 1970s, moving beyond a support role for foreign capital to active support for indigenous capital by encouraging the aggregation of small local capitals. There was also a clear tendency for the largest merchants in various centres to come together to invest in new ventures and extend the geographical range of their investments. For example, Mai Deribe, the Maiduguri merchant, joined Aminu Dantata of Kano as a major shareholder in Preussag Drilling Engineering established in 1976. Sani Buhari Daura and Nababa Badamasi made investments in Zaria, Kaduna and Funtua. Some of the largest companies expanded their interests to Lagos with the development of private jetties (Aminu Dantata), banks (Isiyaku Rabiu) and corporate headquarters (Dangote Group).

In the early 1980s, Nigerian capital was strongly represented in food and beverages, vegetable-oils, metal and wooden furniture, soap, perfumes and cosmetics.[37] In the vegetable-oil milling sector, a number of Lebanese enterprises (A. J. Karoumi, K. Maroun, and Fahdoul) were sold to Nigerian interests. Nigerian capital was also well represented in textiles, metal fabricating, pharmaceuticals, candles, paint, enamelware, paper and packaging, confectionery, foam and rubber, plastics and leather tanning. Nigerian businessmen collaborated and competed with foreign companies, whose presence also expanded in the 1970s and early 1980s. Apart from joint ventures and equity investments, there were also numerous licence and trademark agreements. Areas where there was significant competition between local businessmen and foreign companies included tanneries, soft drinks, textiles, paper milling, and cosmetics.[38]

In the mid-1980s, the largest single industrial investment (N12m.) was by Nababa Badamasi in Gaskiya Textiles. The company entered full production in 1986.[39] Badamasi, a large textile trader, had earlier opened the first indigenous sweet factory in 1972, Moon Confectionery. He also became a large shareholder in Raleigh Industries and made small investments in Funtua Cottonseeds Crushing Company and Eslon Nig. Ltd. Gaskiya Textiles, with fixed assets of N60m., was the product of great perseverance and determination to complete a project that had been conceived in the early 1970s. The participation of the Nigerian Industrial Development Bank, which took 12 per cent of the equity, was crucial to financing the project. When the founder died in 1986, a friend and former managing director of the Bank of the North became an executive director and appointed board members, thereby filling a vacuum that threatened to disrupt the early progress of the company. A technical and training agreement with Arvind Mills of India

was terminated after two years because of divided loyalties. Indians were
then employed directly (7 in 1990).

The Lebanese were strongest in plastic products, sweets, confectionery
and sugar products, mineral water, aluminium, iron and wood processing,
textile products, rubber products, candles and flush doors. Leading industrial
investors included the Raccah brothers, the Moukarim brothers, H. A.
Shour, Ali K. Fawaz, Suhail Akar, F. Akle and M. S. Fadlallah.[40] The
indigenisation decrees had the effect of encouraging the take-up of Nigerian
citizenship and forcing greater collaboration with Nigerian partners. For
example, Alhaji Mustapha Danlami took a shareholding in H. W. Romain
and Alhaji Bukar Balori became a major shareholder in Yassin Confectionery.[41] Many of the Lebanese companies that started business after 1978 took
on local partners.[42]

Before turning to examine the experience of indigenous enterprises in
more detail, we will look briefly at the evolution of two Lebanese enterprises.
Lebanese investors remain a major presence in Kano commerce and industry.

Mr George Calil came to Kano in 1928 and became a large groundnut
trader.[43] By 1942 he began processing groundnuts on an experimental basis
and in 1951, he founded Nigerian Oil Mills, which is still the largest and
most consistent vegetable-oil unit in Kano. In 1959, a separate company
was incorporated to select better quality nuts for the overseas confectionery
trade. An aluminium holloware plant and foundry was also established to
manufacture tea kettles, brass calabashes, and silver plate ware. From its
small foundry and machine shop came casting for the Nigerian Railway
Corporation, bushings for local industry and spare parts. The company was
consistently profitable. Surplus profits from these enterprises were invested
in property with over 90 units in Kano, Lagos and Apapa.

In 1967, the year of Nigeria's largest ever commercial groundnut crop,
George Calil died and the company was taken over by his son, Ely Calil,
who was 22 years old. George Calil, who was fluent in fourteen languages,
had provided his children with university education and business training.
In the mid-1970s, the oil mill was closed down as supplies of groundnuts,
cotton seed, soyabeans and benniseed dwindled. In 1976, the company was
the first to import groundnut oil on a large-scale. By late 1981, 10,000 tons
of refined oil a month was being imported and the company was manufacturing
its own tins.

When Nigeria's petroleum exports declined, a ban was imposed on vegetable-oil imports in 1984. The milling industry then began a slow recovery.
The mill was redesigned and refurbished. Two defunct palm kernel oil mills
and palm plantations in the eastern states were purchased and a fractionation
refinery plant with two soap lines installed in Kano. Other investments
made inside and outside the Group, include a company selling water-drilling
equipment (1979), the manufacture of graphite pencils (1979), a stake in a

Kaduna brewery (1980) and a major shareholding in a tin-smelting company in Jos (1986). The latter is seen as a platform for entry into mining. Overall turnover for the foregoing activities was about N200m. in 1990.

Our second example, a group owned by the Moukarim family, also originated from a base in the groundnut trade in 1930. In 1959, Moukarim Metalwood Factory was established at Bompai, Kano to manufacture metal and wood furniture.[44] To meet the growth of the market, subsidiaries were established in Ikeja in 1971 (foam blocks, furniture sheetings and mattresses), Katsina in 1973, Jos in 1977 and Kaduna in 1979 (steel structures, wrought-iron works, containers and furniture). In 1979, turnover of the enlarged Kano factory on the Sharada Industrial Area was N15m. with 800 persons employed. The Moukarim brothers also diversified into shoe manufacture holding about 40 per cent of the equity in Shoe Manufacturers Ltd at Sharada. Since furniture production was heavily dependent on the custom of state governments, the market collapsed after 1983. The Jos and Kano branches were closed as competition from roadside artisans, who paid no tax and could absorb small margins, became intense. Staff were transferred to Lagos, where steel working, pipe making, foam and mattress ventures were less exposed. Other Lebanese furniture makers that had expanded through the oil boom were also forced to close down (Raccaform and Nigerian Iron Wood) and the shift to Lagos was paralleled by some other Lebanese ventures in Kano.

Enterprises in Kano

The growth of indigenous enterprises is now considered in more detail. The Dantata Organisation is probably the most well-known company in Kano with a long commercial pedigree. The Isiyaku Rabiu Group diversified into industry in the 1970s from its base in the textile trade. The Gashash Holding and Investment Company is probably the largest indigenous industrial investor in Kano. Hamza Holdings, a multifarious trading conglomerate is now based in Lagos, but is included here because it throws light on trading activity in the North. Nabegu Holdings controls the most extensive tanning interests in Kano. The Dangote Group, which is based in Lagos, is one of the largest commodity traders in Nigeria. The last case is an insurance brokerage, Koguna, Babura and Co., the first and largest brokerage to originate in the northern states. There follow brief profiles of the Garba Industrial Group and Yakamata Group of Companies, Ceramics Manufacturers Nig. PLC, Falacol Pharmaceutical Industries Ltd and Star Modern Paper.

The Dantata Organisation

This company forms part of what is popularly known as the 'Dantata Group'. The latter is often perceived by outsiders as a single family group, but the

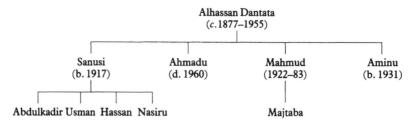

FIGURE 8.1: The Dantata family.

interests of family members are often independent of each other, and sometimes in competition. The Dantata Organisation is owned by Aminu Dantata
who succeeded to the company on the death of his brother, Ahmadu, in
1960. It is entirely independent of the enterprises run by Sanusi Dantata. In
1987, the company was employing over 2,500 persons. Although the Dantata
enterprises are perhaps the most well known indigenous group in Nigeria,
there are other enterprises in Kano of comparable size.

The Dantata family has a long pedigree in business that extends back to
the *Attajirai* ('rich merchants') of the pre-colonial period (see Figure 8.1).
The Dantatas were important kola traders in the nineteenth century and
owned large client- and slave-based grain estates, south of Kano city and in
five other emirates.[45] Alhassan Dantata, whose father was a wealthy trader
and caravan leader, was born in Bebeji. He later travelled to Accra to join
his mother, who was a wealthy trader in her own right. He traded in the Gold
Coast, on behalf of his mother, first in kolanut, and then in livestock, and
beads and European cloth. He returned to Kano in 1910 after his mother
had died.

With the expansion of groundnut production, he established a large network
of agents and sub-agents to purchase the crop. Approached by the Niger
Company in 1918, he had by 1922 become one of the wealthiest men in
Kano. From 1926, he took advantage of the railway to promote the cattle
trade with Lagos and revitalised the kolanut trade with western Nigeria.[46]
The following year he sponsored 16 persons for pilgrimage including his
teacher from Accra.[47]

The complex nature of his trading networks is best described by Watts
who cites Tahir:[48]

> The supply system consisted of at least five different levels of operation-
> subsuming factors, clients, agents, and business associates; each level
> occupied a quite different social and political space and each was granted
> distinctive levels of autonomy from the patron (*uban gida*), namely
> Dantata himself.
>
> Firstly, there was a system of direct delivery from rural speculators
> (*madugai*) who approached and bought directly, using advances, from

the farmers, usually within a restricted domain. Secondly, there were the so-called 'balance men' (*yan balas*); the Dantata system included six, who were clients or effectively quasi-kin. They received cash and goods advances, purchased and stored commodities for the patron, and received interest-free loans for their own operations. Thirdly, there were Dantata's close business associates (*abokin ciniki*), independent and significant trade magnates in their own right, with their own networks and clientage systems but who were, nonetheless, tied to Dantata through loans and, not infrequently, marriage. Fourthly, there were independent agents who were of much lesser significance in terms of size and scale of operation, but were financed through short-term credits. And finally, there were Dantata's 'boys' (*yara*), consisting of kin and houseboys who, by virtue of trust and kinship, worked closely with the patron but often ran a small-scale, independent, trade line financed by Dantata himself. These ramifying networks of clientage and religious affiliation allowed Dantata to operate over long distances and to seek out and support locally influential scholars and clerics who reinforced his trading dominance in local communities. The centre piece of the system was the diversified urban-based merchant who made use of clients and business associates, rural connections, and local storage to acquire staples that could yield considerable speculative profits in view of the seasonally volatile grain markets. Conversely, the middle and lower echelon traders who resided and operated in rural communities, gained access to urban credit and interest-free loans during the buying seasons, which were the basis for their own revenues of accumulation.

Alhassan Dantata used his trading networks in grain, kola and groundnuts to distribute imported consumer goods for the foreign trading companies. With the assistance of the UAC he became a direct importer of consumer goods from Europe in the early 1950s.[49] He was the leading agent for the United Africa Company and was advanced credit of up to £500,000 for crop purchase.[50] In 1953, he became the first Nigerian licensed buying agent for the Northern Nigeria Marketing Board. Apart from the produce, grain and livestock, and merchandise trades, he was also active in transporting, direct importing, real estate and the construction industry, handling projects for the Native Administration. His three eldest sons were put in charge of land, building, and contracting and transport sections of the business, each of them backed by a separate organisation.[51]

When Alhassan Dantata died in 1955, the estate was divided. Sanusi started his own enterprise in 1959 and Ahmadu, the eldest son, died in 1960. Aminu Dantata then carried on in business in his father's name. Mahmud Dantata had gone independent much earlier, successfully importing and operating corn mills in the 1940s.[52] He was also one of the first to go into the import/export business. He imported concentrates for the manufacture of local soap, hitherto the exclusive preserve of southerners. In 1948 he was a promoter of the successful West African Pilgrims Association (WAPA) along with Ibrahim Gashash and Haruna Kassim. He was convicted of possessing forged currency notes in 1957 and after his release from prison in 1964, he entered business again with interests in hotels, catering and the pools. He converted the WAPA headquarters into a night club, the largest in Kano. His interests in the hotel and entertainment business were later carried on by his son, Majtaba Dantata.

The pattern of activity in the 1950s was again apparent in the 1970s in an expanded and more advanced form in the enterprise owned by Aminu Dantata. The company was appointed supplier to many state governments trading in fertilisers, cement, rice, and jute bags. As manufacturer's representatives, the company handled the import of building materials, construction machinery, generating sets, air conditioners and household appliances. It became a distributor for Mercedes Benz. In 1978, the Building and Engineering Division employed 1,500 persons. The company was also active in transport. After the Igbo exodus from Kano in 1966, Aminu Dantata headed the Northern Transporters and Merchants Syndicate, which had a fleet of 700 vehicles by 1970. A container shipping service from Warri port was established as a joint venture with Walford Lines of the United Kingdom, and operated for five years. In manufacturing, the pattern was one of sole ownership with foreign technical assistance. At the end of the 1970s, there were four industries – candles, a small tannery, soft drinks, and sugar processing. At the end of the 1980s, however, only the sugar plant was still active.

The group also built up an extensive investment portfolio. In 1972, Aminu Dantata resigned as Commissioner for Commerce and Industry in Kano Sate and became very active in acquiring shares sold in the indigenisation exercise. Among the companies in which Aminu Dantata took large shareholdings were Raleigh Industries, Mentholatum, Funtua Cotton Seed Crushing Co., Nigerian Cable Manufacturing and Engineering, SCOA, Northern Nigerian Flour Mills, Northern Asbestos Cement Ltd, Universal Textiles, Mandrides, Nigerian Pipes Ltd, Preussag Drilling Engineering and Metoxide. In the 1980s, a 60 per cent interest was acquired in Kano State Oil Mills from Uthman Sanusi Dantata. The mill, with the largest capacity in Kano, used a chemical-extraction process, and had been set up by the state government in the mid-1970s, just as the supply of oil seeds collapsed. A shareholding was also acquired in Kano Textile Printers through privatisation and a major investment (N280m.) made in a fertiliser-blending plant at Madobi. In general, the company followed a passive, rentier role with no active part in management or board representation in these companies. Dantata Investment and Securities Ltd, the investment and financial wing of the enterprise, recorded a turnover of N153m. in 1989–90.[53]

The rapid expansion of the 1970s, fuelled by the oil boom, led initially to management difficulties, poor accounting, and problems with recruitment. Like other Kano enterprises, expatriates were preferred as senior managers rather than the recruitment of senior Nigerians from other parts of the country. The company set up a training school and recruited Nigerian graduates, employing thirty in 1990. As a supporter of the National Party of Nigeria in a state held by the People's Redemption Party (PRP), the company experienced difficulties getting licences and land allocation from 1979 to 1984.

The companies owned by Sanusi Dantata showed a similar pattern of diversification. In 1963, Nigerian Leather Works (making shoes and boots) was established with paid-up capital of N£140,000 and support from the Northern Nigerian Development Corporation. Oil milling and furniture enterprises were also started. Sanusi was the largest groundnut LBA in the 1960s and a very large transporter. At the time of the indigenisation exercise, he teamed up with Panalpina, one of the world's largest clearing, forwarding, and shipping agents.[54] He was chairman of the National Party of Nigeria, Kano State branch. After the defeat of the NPN in 1979, he became increasingly involved in religious activities. He sold all his business holdings to his sons who developed their own businesses.[55] The eldest son, Abdulkadir Sanusi Dantata started Asada Farms and Motors and a civil engineering firm, Dantata and Sawoe Construction, a German joint venture with headquarters at Abuja, the new Federal capital. Turnover of the latter enterprise was N100m. in 1990.[56] Another son, Usman, developed Anadariya Farms which went into liquidation.

Isiyaku Rabiu Group of Companies

This Group employed about 1,000 persons in 1990. Isiyaku Rabiu, the son of a Koranic Mallam, is descended from a powerful family of Koranic teachers and merchants.[57] He became an independent trader in 1949, after completing Arabic and Islamic education. In 1952, he became an importer and exporter and factor with UAC. In 1957, he registered as a distributor with the new textile industry in Kaduna. He became a major textile dealer, creating the Kano Merchants Trading Company with other business associates in 1963. He also set up a small oil mill with his brother. In 1970, he took a 40 per cent share in Kano Suit and Packing Cases Ltd when a Lebanese, who had dominated the industry, pulled out. The company later diversified into briefcases and handbags. In the same year, he established the Victory Insurance Company with Mustapha Danlami and Garba Bichi. In 1972, he established Bagauda Textile mill with Bala Rabiu, Nababa Badamasi, and Umaru Na'Abba to manufacture woollen and terylene materials at a cost of £1.5m. Other industries established in the 1970s included a frozen chicken and fish enterprise, vehicle distribution (Daihatsu), sugar and soft drinks

TABLE 8.1: Gashash Holding and Investment Company Ltd.

Company	Start-up/acquisition	Comment
Nortex	1963	14% share in Kaduna textile mill
Darum Enterprises (later Gashash Tanneries)	1963	Tannery. Acquired full ownership in 1985. Turnover N8m. in 1990
Nigerian Perfumery	1964	Venture with Mr Seroussi. Acquired 100%
Fedco Foam	1970	First foam mattress plant in North
NIMADCO	1971	Vegetable-oil mill
United Consolidated Industries	1971	Metal containers
Wehbe Industries	1974	Suitcases. 60% acquired via indigenisation
Bauchi Oil Mills	1974	Closed 1981
Berkeley Pharmaceutical	1974	Distribution. Acquired via indigenisation
First Lady	1974	Cosmetics. Sold to partner Alwan Naif in 1989
Elephant Plastics	1977	Sold to partner Gambo Mohammed in 1989
Magasons	1980	Trading
Marbrex	1985	Artificial marble and ceramics. $2.5m. investment

Sources: Interview and personal communication.

(management agreement with a German company), and a Brass Lisbon Pan factory. The group also developed large housing estates and office blocks and started a construction company.

The group suffered from overcentralised family management, with the parent company controlling individual units through a single managing director. Expatriate management staff at the centre were largely redundant. When industrial activities came under pressure from falling demand, import compression, and foreign exchange shortages in the 1980s, they were closed down. Bagauda Textiles, which closed in 1987, was reopened in 1990 under Indian contract management. It supplies uniforms to the armed forces. The Group's fortunes were not enhanced by the imprisonment of the owner for twenty months under the Buhari regime in 1984–5. In 1984, a merchant bank was launched. Overall, the Group has tended to revert back to its trading role. It is one of the largest indigenous trading companies with a turnover of N742m. reported in 1990–1.[58]

Gashash Holding and Investment Company

The Gashash Holding and Investment Company is one of the largest indigenous industrial investors in Kano.[59] In 1990, wholly owned enterprises included a tannery, vegetable-oil mill, metal containers, foam mattress, artificial marble, and ceramics (see Table 8.1). The Group employed six expatriates.

Ibrahim Musa Gashash, father of the Gashash brothers (Ibrahim, Abdallah and Mahmoud) came to Kano from Tripoli in 1904 and was a prominent exporter of hides and skins.[60] He made the trip to Europe seven times.[61] He imported incense, Arabic cloth, house blankets, and jewellery from Morocco.

Ibrahim Gashash entered the groundnut trade in Kano and Katsina in 1938 and was a transporter.[62] He was the leading business figure and a major political strategist in the Northern People's Congress (NPC).[63] He became a minister in 1959 and deputy premier of the Northern Region. He assisted the regional premier, the Sardauna of Sokoto, who wanted to attract new industries to the region. Contacts were made with the Seroussi family in Sudan, which had interests in cotton and tanning. Ibrahim invested with E. A. Seroussi in the Kaduna textile industry.

Of the three brothers, it was Mahmoud who committed himself most strongly to business and provided the leadership. He was born in 1931 and attended Arabic School in Kano city, Dala Primary School, and Kano Middle School where the future Emir, Ado Bayero, was his classmate. He left school in 1948 and was given £280 and textile goods worth £320 to start trading in the old city. In 1950, he opened a shop in the city market where he specialised in enamelware, getting supplies from Holts, GBO, and the UAC. In 1951, he started to import directly from Hong Kong, Czechoslovakia, and Liverpool, England. He extended his sales to Zaria and Jos, then to Chad and Cameroon. In Cameroon, he traded textiles and enamelware for hides and skins, travelling as far as Ngaoundéré. In Kano, he established corn-grinding machines all over the city. He was appointed to the board of the Nigerian Coal Corporation and the Nigerian Bank for Commerce and Industry.

The Gashash brothers invested in the 1960s in Nigerian Carbon Dioxide as minority partners with Baba Danbappa, in the Kano Nails and Wires and in Northern Steel Works in partnership with NNDC and some Lebanese businessmen. Mahmoud also invested with Seroussi in a tannery and perfume factory in Kano. Other significant shareholdings acquired later included Kano Confectionery, and Atlas Construction and Engineering.

In 1970, two years before indigenisation, they took over a Lebanese cosmetics company (N1.4m. turnover in 1981 with 60 persons employed). Another cosmetics company was acquired in 1974 together with a wholesale and retail distributor of pharmaceuticals. Using contacts established at the 1967 Expo in Montreal, the Gashash brothers established the first foam factory in the North in 1970. Initially this was a franchise from Fedco Foam International of the United States. The company proved successful, with a turnover of N17m. in 1981 and 380 persons employed in 1980. In 1971 an oil mill and metal container factory were set up and in 1977 a plastics plant was established. In the following decade, the perfumery and plastics concerns were sold to partners and a factory for artificial marble and ceramics established in 1985.

The group acquired substantial shareholdings in a number of foreign companies, among them Union Carbide (12 per cent), Bayer (25 per cent), Saviem Berliet (25 per cent), and Eltec, a large telecommunications company in partnership with Siemens AG of West Germany. It also has interests in property, banking and a brewery.

Hamza Holdings Ltd (Formerly, G. N. A. Hamza & Co. (Nig.) Ltd)

This trading conglomerate, which has a long history of commercial activity, is based in Apapa and employs about 500 persons directly.[64] Over time, it demonstrates a veritable kaleidoscope of short-term trading and contract activity that sometimes required access at high levels of the state.

Alhaji Garba Nautan Hamza was born in 1934 at Utai, Wudil Local Government Area in Kano State. He attended evening classes at local Koranic schools in Nguru, Borno State. Three times he was enrolled in primary school but each time his parents quickly withdrew him. He entered business in 1947 assisting his father in textile and general goods trade at Nguru. In 1948, he traded between Nguru and Kano dealing in sugar, soap, perfumes, cosmetics, umbrellas and educational books. He also entered the dried meat business which was a major item of trade to southern Nigeria. In 1949, he extended his business into bicycle hiring. The following year, he controlled 80 per cent of the market in Nguru, Gashua and Geidam in Borno State and about 40 per cent of the market in Mallam-Madori and Hadejia in Kano State. In 1951 assisted by a Yoruba trader, he took English lessons and was introduced to an International Trade Directory. He then went into the direct importation of textile materials, white tarpaulin, umbrellas, perfumes and corn-grinding machines (1952) from Manchester and Birmingham companies, using a mail-order business, before he started to clear goods through the ports. By 1955 he had a virtual monopoly of grinding machines and bicycles in the locations mentioned above. In 1953 he started to export gum arabic, and cow bones and hooves to France and the United States. He was the first indigenous exporter of gum arabic and became a major supplier to the French market joining the Gum Arabic Association. In 1957 and 1958 he entered car hire and lorry transport. He owned twenty-three trucks and competed with Lebanese and Igbo transporters. In 1958 he was appointed a licensed buying agent for groundnuts and cotton, purchasing for UAC (1958–63). A Lagos office was opened the following year.

He pressed the government for an end to the UAC monopoly on cigarette distribution and as a result was appointed one of the first indigenous distributors for the Nigerian Tobacco Company in the Northern Region. This lasted for six years (1960–6) and was a very lucrative business. Other areas of activity included the export of adua kernels after the UAC had found a market for them with Rowntree, the British confectionary company and the import of second-hand clothing which was very profitable. He was also an agent for the Nigerian Produce Marketing Company selling cocoa in London. During this period, he came to know Ahmadu Bello, the regional premier, and provided many items, including party badges, for the ruling party, the Northern People's Congress.

By means of money lending to one Alhaji Inua Usman, who bought army lorries at the annual Kaduna auction, he developed contacts with the Nigerian army in Kaduna. According to his biographer, he eventually became the leading supplier of general goods and software to the army during the civil war, buying from England, Europe, Brazil and the United States. When the army decided to centralise orders in Lagos, he moved his headquaters to Lagos. In 1970 he became National President of the Organisation of Nigerian Indigenous Businesses.[65] During the 1970s, Alhaji Hamza traded to Niger where there was a strong demand for soap, textiles, beverages and generators. He also tried and failed to get a contract to lift crude oil.

Though the Group acquired some industrial, banking and insurance interests in the 1970s and 1980s including stakes in a Lagos textile mill, a furniture factory, a building-materials plant in Ikorudu, and started a perfumery and cosmetics factory in Kano, it has not really diversified away from its trading origins. As executive chairman, the owner retains personal direction and management of the enterprise. In 1983, the company acquired a licence for an airline but did not operate.

In the 1958 general elections, Alhaji Hamza contested unsuccessfully for a seat in the House of Representatives on the platform of the Northern Elements Progressive Union (NEPU). During the Second Republic, he identified with the NPN. A strong involvement in sporting philanthropy began in 1956 when he was appointed executive secretary of the Nguru Race Club. Horse racing was the only recognised sport of those days. He is life patron of the Youth Sports Federation of Nigeria and he founded the Traditional Sports Promotion Council of Nigeria to promote and protect games that are neglected or hidden. He was chairman of the Sub-Finance Committee of the All-African Games in 1973.

Nabegu Holdings

Nabegu Holdings owns the largest indigenous tanning company in Kano and through its control of another company has the most extensive tanning interests in Kano.[66] It has diversified through downstream investment in shoes and through acquisition. It employs approximately 800 persons. Other indigenous tanneries in Kano include Arewa Tanneries, owned by Alhaji Baballe Illa[67] and Gashash Tanneries, owned by Mahmoud Gashash.

The Nabegu family from Bunkure Local Government Area have been involved in the business of hides and skins for over six generations. Addulkarim Nabegu, the present managing director's grandfather, was the largest supplier of hides and skins to European companies and imported and distributed salt and cloth. He became an agent for the Italian company Ambrosini, as did his son, Baba Nabegu, in his turn.

In 1961, Ambrosini established a tannery in Kano, the Great Northern Tanning Company. This was the second tannery in Kano, following the establishment of First Tannery (Nig.) Ltd by John Holt in 1949. As a supplier, Baba Nabegu initially purchased a 10 per cent shareholding in the company, obtaining a controlling interest in the 1970s. He also acquired a small interest in International Tanneries and began to export raw skins on his own. In partnership with Alhaji Baballe Illa, he also acquired, at the time of indigenisation, the large network of stores and warehouses belonging to Ambrosini.

In 1978, his son, Aminu Nabegu, who had been assisting his father since 1975, when he was a university student, visited Spain, the main export market. On return, he urged his father to establish a tannery. His father's trading friends and peers had argued against the idea because it was seen to erode the personal control that a trader has over his business. In 1981, Baba Nabegu visited Spain and was persuaded to establish a tannery. Aminu Nabegu became managing director of Nabegu Holdings. Three other sons also joined the group after graduation, one of them undergoing training in leather technology in Spain.

The tannery began production in 1983, with technical assistance from Spain. It broke even in six months, expanded rapidly, and became one of the largest tanneries in Kano with a turnover of N10.2m. in 1986. In 1990, 200 persons were employed and 70 per cent of the output was exported to Spain. One Spanish manager was employed.

In 1989, forward integration was achieved with the start-up of a shoe factory, the Superior Shoe Co. Ltd. Investment was N15m. with output of 2,000 pairs a day and employment of 250 persons. A technical and management agreement was signed with an Italian firm and one Italian was employed in 1990.

In 1982, the Nabegu Company established a technical division to supply equipment to water projects. This followed the expansion of irrigated agriculture in the northern states and, World Bank assisted, urban water contracts. In 1985, the company purchased a 52-bed hospital from an expatriate who was leaving the country. In the same year, Gazal Industries, a Lebanese enterprise founded in 1959 by Chale Gazal, was purchased when the owner left the country at the age of 75. The industry manufactures precast concrete, flush doors, tiles, candles, polish, school chalk, and cosmetics. In 1986, Gazal Industries had a turnover of N13m. and employed over 300 persons. Other investments include large holdings in three banks as well as in pharmaceutical companies.

Dangote Group

The Dangote Group, with headquarters in Lagos, is one of the largest trading organisations in Nigeria and has diversified into textiles, banking, property, shipping, fishing and oil services. Alhaji Aliko Dangote, President of the Group, was born in 1957.[68] His father, Muhammed Dangote, who came from Kura, was a business associate of Alhassan Dantata. His mother, Hajiya Mariya Sanusi Dantata is the eldest daughter of Sanusi Dantata.

After Islamic education his uncle gave him work as a store manager in Kano. He started his own business in Kano in 1976 under the name Alco Aviations trading in commodities and cement. In 1977 he moved to Lagos and continued trading in cement and other goods. Between 1981 and 1986 he imported baby food, frozen fish, rice, vegetable-oil, flour, granulated sugar, aluminium sheets, batteries, tyres, and motor spare parts. Since the advent of the Structural Adjustment Programme, the Group has concentrated on the importation of salt, cotton and sugar.

Since the early 1980s, the Group has been the largest sugar importer in Nigeria with a current volume of about 1.2m. tons and turnover of about N1bn. Frozen fish was imported until 1986. Three factory freezer vessels were then chartered for operation in European waters with a view to supplying the Nigerian market. The Group owns a general cargo vessel and is acquiring fishing trawlers.[69]

Exports of cocoa, cashew nuts, and gum arabic are worth about $15m. annually. Cotton buying of about 18,000 tons a year led to investment in ginning and textile production. Dangote General Textile Products was acquired in 1989. It had started in 1981 as a joint venture between Alhaji Dandawaki and some development banks and had run into financial difficulties. The plant is being renovated and reactivated with a large investment in additional looms and a new spinning mill costing N100m. A controlling interest was taken in Nigerian Textile Mills, Lagos, in 1993.[70] Turnover of this company was N90m. in 1989–90. A ginnery at Kankara went into operation in 1992. Thus the Dangote Group has begun to move towards an integrated textile operation.

The Group also has interests in construction, property, banking, and oil-services. With a strong property base in Kano, the Group has extended its portfolio to Abuja. Liberty Merchant Bank was floated in 1990 with a paid up capital of N30m. and made an after-tax profit of N18m. in its first year of operation.

Family control is exercised through the President, Aliko Dangote, two brothers in the banking and textile divisions and a cousin in shipping operations and distribution. Recruitment of specialist first line management includes several US-trained MBAs.

Koguna, Babura and Company

Mohammed Hassan Koguna was born in 1936 in Kano.[71] His father was a village head in Dambatta Local Government Area. He attended Dambatta Primary School (1945–9) before proceeding to Kano Middle School (1949–57). With no opportunities to pursue higher studies, he was recruited by UAC who were desperately looking for northerners at that time. Initially he trained in the general goods division, but agreed to move to Marina Agencies, the insurance division, on the understanding that he would be sent abroad for professional training. In 1965 he was sent for one-year attachment with Commercial Union Insurance Co. in London. On return to Nigeria, he became manager of the United Nigeria Insurance Company (as the insurance division of UAC was then known) in Ibadan before moving to Kano. Eventually, he rose to be assistant general manager in charge of the northern states (1973–9).

He retired in 1979 to form a partnership with his cousin and school friend, Alhaji Sani Babura, a distributor for the Nigerian Tobacco Company. Equity was shared in a trading and import company (Koguna and Babura Ltd) and in the NTC distributorship (A. S. Babura and Sons). In addition, insurance clients of UNIC convinced him to register as an agent and he eventually re-registered a broking company, Koguna Babura and Co., in which equity was again shared with his partner. A Lagos office was opened and an expatriate manager employed for six years before a Nigerian managing director was recruited who had spent sixteen years with Hogg Robinson. In 1992, 65 persons were employed. The company acquired a 17 per cent stake in another insurance company, Kapital Insurance, when Commercial Union, which Mohammed Koguna had represented on the board, divested in 1991.

By January 1993, ownership was restructured with 30 per cent owned by staff. The idea was to delegate authority and give incentives and a feeling of security to staff and enhance the prospects of company longevity. Senior staff were also given high salaries and fringe benefits. The example of the Nigeria International Bank in which Alhaji Koguna was a foundation shareholder was influential here. With the death of his partner, 35 per cent of the shareholding was divided among Babura's family according to Islamic principles.

In 1987 Alhaji Koguna promoted a reinsurance company, Continental Reinsurance, as chairman and major shareholder along with other wealthy individuals. The initiative came from two experienced insurance professionals who approached him. This was the second private reinsurance company following the establishment of Universe Reinsurance in 1985. In 1992 he became chairman of Red Star Express, an indigenous courier company, with a small equity holding after two Nigerians with experience in DHL and IMNL had approached him.

Brief Profiles

Garba Industrial Group and Yakamata Group of Companies

In 1990 this group employed some 370 persons directly. Alhaji Garba Inuwa was born in Kano in 1940 and after Koranic education entered business selling textiles and jewellery. He left for Ghana in 1959 to import kolanuts. He then settled at Mubi, Gongola State (1960) importing animal skins, ivory and general trade goods from Japan. He returned to Kano in 1969. He invested in a lace factory with British and Austrian partners in 1975, holding 55 per cent of the equity. This was followed by investment in aluminium building products with Lebanese partners in 1977 and a soft-drink venture with French technical partners in 1982. A construction company, vehicle distribution and air charter operations were also started, but only motor distribution proved viable. The lace factory closed in 1983 and the trading wing of the Group has generally become more prominent, dealing in sugar, rice, salt and grains.

Ceramics Manufacturers Nigeria PLC

Alhaji M. S. Umoru, the executive chairman of Ceramics Manufacturers was born in Agbede, Bendel State in 1934.[72] He schooled in Kano and studied banking at the Zaria College of Science and Technology. He then studied accountancy in the United Kingdom. After a spell with the United Bank of Africa, he joined Mobil Oil becoming financial coordinator. He then joined the Central Bank (1968–72) and subsequently became general manager of Bagauda Textiles (1972–6). He started to import office and laboratory equipment and formed a company to undertake electricity and water supply projects obtaining a large contract from the Benue-Plateau State government.

Ceramics Manufacturers opened in Kano in 1985 with a total investment of N81.5m. investment. In 1990, 65 per cent of the equity was held in the family, with French technical partners 12 per cent, New Nigeria Development Company 10 per cent, Kano State 9 per cent, and Nigerian Bank for Commerce and Industry 4 per cent. In 1992 shares were offered for public subscription and publicly quoted on the Stock Exchange. The family holding was reduced to 51 per cent with new private Nigerian investors holding the bulk of the remaining equity.

The company is the leading producer of ceramic wares in the country and unlike two competing companies at Umuahia and Abeokuta, sources all its raw materials locally. Technical problems and a high reject level initially reduced output and profitability to low levels. Turnover for 1992 was N27.3m. with profits after tax of N2.8m.[73] The introduction of semi-automated equipment to reduce drying time is expected to raise production.

The managing director, a son of the chairman, received his business education at Boston University (1983) followed by an MBA from New Hampshire College in 1985. He then qualified in ceramic technology at North Staffordshire Polytechnic, England.

Falacol Pharmaceutical Industries Ltd

Alhaji Farouk Labaran was born in Kano city in 1944.[74] He attended Government Secondary School, Kano (1960–5) and took a diploma in commercial accounting at Ahmadu Bello University. He joined the Bank of the North where he served from 1970 to 1979.

He then started a company engaged in general merchandising, construction, import and export. A private hospital led to trade in medical equipment and interest in pharmaceuticals. Falacol Pharmaceuticals started operations in 1990 with liquid preparations and employs 50 workers. It is the second pharmaceutical company in Kano following the establishment of an earlier Lebanese enterprise. The managing director was highly trained in pharmacology in the United Kingdom for 10 years. Foreign technical assistance was limited to the supply and installation of equipment. Critical to the future is effective inspection and control by drug agencies to improve credibility in the market and reduce competition from fake preparations. Containers and caps have to be sourced in Lagos and this raises costs.

Star Modern Paper

The father of the present proprietor, who migrated to Kano from present-day Delta State, worked with the Native Authority in Kano for many years and owned a printing press, Mid-West Printing Press. His son trained as a teacher, and became manager of the press. He gradually left the family business, starting a printing press before envelope making and paper conversion. A new plant was opened at Challawa in 1984, with 100 persons employed. Two children were trained in Germany to operate the German machinery.

KADUNA

Unlike Kano with its long commercial history, the city of Kaduna is a recent colonial creation. It was the administrative centre of the former Northern Region. It attracted immigrants from all over the North and grew from a population of about 45,000 in 1952 to 150,000 in 1965.[75] It became a military and industrial centre notable for its textile industry. It was also the seat of the Northern Nigerian Development Corporation (later, New Nigerian Development Company), a regional investment institution which played a major role in attracting foreign investors and acted as a training ground for local managers, investors and business people. Kaduna became a second home for former civil servants and retired military officers from all over the northern states.

Large-scale indigenous enterprise in Kaduna is more restricted than in Kano and has, in the main, been undertaken by individuals with a background in government or the parastatal sector. Lebanese investment is also more limited though it includes a flour mill and a large plastics company. Before looking at four case studies, it is worth considering the nature of the opportunities that were open to individuals in the three decades since independence since this affects the manner in which energies were absorbed, attitudes to business and trajectories of accumulation.

There was in fact a range of possible private strategies that individuals with education, professional qualifications, or experience and connections gained in the civil service, parastatals, or the military, could pursue, short of launching, owning and managing his or her own enterprise which, of course, entailed greater initiative and risk. As we saw in chapter 4, such opportunities first became available on a limited scale in the South. They became more widespread after independence with the arrival of more foreign companies and the growth of state investment institutions and banks and probably reached their zenith during the heady days of oil boom, state creation and indigenisation in the 1970s. Foreign companies and parastatals would actively search for prominent individuals to take up board membership. Such opportunities were spread all over the country, though they are possibly observed in sharpest relief in the northern states. State institutions and regulation were generally seen as a means to securing adequate indigenous participation and experience, and a way of obtaining a share of federal resources that would allow the northern states to catch up with more developed areas in the South.

Individual responses ranged from contentment with board membership, perks and shares in an essentially rentier position to a more active consultancy or 'arrangee' role in which the individual promoted projects (sometimes at his home location) by attracting foreign interests and facilitating contact with state personnel and institutions, through to cases where the build-up of a private investment portfolio was pursued more systematically and sometimes combined with the launching of companies, wholly or partially owned by the individual. A distinctive feature here was that the individual did not actively manage the enterprises though he might chair the boardroom and commit his own funds. Usually, there was a diversity of interests without concentration on any line.

Movement to the private sector first occurred when Ahmadu Coomassie joined the Nigerian Tobacco Company in 1965.[76] Others followed with the creation of states in 1967. Rather than take positions in the new states, some very senior civil servants opted to retire, stay in Kaduna, and join company boards. Thus Yahaya Gusau was associated with NTC, Shell and Kueppers, and Isa Kaita with Chellarams, Kaycee, UAC, and the Songhai Group. Further impetus to involvement in the private sector came with the indigenisation exercise which prompted foreign companies to look for local investors and made the acquisition of shares very attractive. A third factor was the wave of retirements from the civil service, parastatals and universities in 1976, at a time when the economy was booming.

The NNDC played an important role in providing formative business experience for a number of individuals. Among those who worked for the NNDC for a period in their careers, or were board members, were Aliko Mohammed (b. 1934), former chairman of NICON, Daily Times and Bank of the North; Hamza Zayyad (b. 1937), chairman of NNDC and Phoenix Investment Services; Mamman Daura (b. 1939), former managing director, New Nigerian Newspapers, chairman African International Bank (formerly BCCI) and Kaduna Furniture and Carpets Company; U. A. Mutallab (b. 1939), former chief executive of United Bank for Africa, chairman of New Africa Merchant Bank and Barade Holdings; and Alhaji Hassan Adamu (b. 1941), former chairman of NICON, NAFCON, and chairman of Bulkship (Nig.) Ltd and Abuja City Press. All these individuals had overseas professional training, the majority in accountancy. Some established holding companies like Balm Holdings, Barade Holdings, Bells Holdings and HH Holdings.

Others with a background in the civil service include the former federal permanent secretary, Alhaji M. T. Usman, chairman of Julius Berger, who invested in Spring Waters Nig. Ltd, Hamada Carpets, and the late Alhaji Abdu Abubakar, former secretary to the Interim Common Services Association and chairman of Peugeot, who promoted Imani Aviation, Imani and Sons (property development) and Imani Mortgage Finance. Those with a background in the armed forces include Rtd Lt.-Gen. T. Y. Danjuma, Rtd Lt.-Gen. Shehu Yar'adua, Rtd Lt.-Gen. M. I. Wushishi (chairman, Chartered Bank) and Rtd Air Commodore Dan Suleiman (chairman, North-South Bank).

While certainly not typical by virtue of his privileged birth and the extent of the opportunities open to him, the business career of Alhaji Shehu Malami does illustrate some characteristic features of this period. Shehu Malami, nephew to the Sultan of Sokoto, Sir Abubakar III, was born in 1936.[77] He schooled in Sokoto, Kano, Katsina and Bida and made many lasting acquaintances among his classmates. He studied law in Britain and was secretary-general of the NPC in London. On return to Nigeria in 1963, he was close to the Sultan of Sokoto and had political ambitions which were thwarted by the military coup of 1966. Through connections that were first made in London, he joined the board of Costain in 1964 and then Paterson Zochonis. In 1966 he joined the board of the Nigerian Industrial Development Bank and remained there for nine years. This awakened his interest in industrial promotion. He also served on a number of government commissions and institutions like the Northern States Marketing Board and was a member of the CDC and the Constituent Assembly where he argued in favour of a mixed economy. In 1974 he was appointed Sarkin Sudan of Wurno (district head of Wurno).

He served on the board of Kaduna Textiles Ltd (1970–5) and became a director of Barclays Bank in 1973 and chairman in 1980. Other directorships included Alraine, Guinea Insurance, Brown Boveri and BASF. He was also chairman of Paterson Zochonis, Major & Co., Indo-Nigerian Merchant Bank and Pan African Consultancy. The latter firm, was founded, entirely managed, and 30 per cent owned by Birla Brothers, the Indian multinational.[78] Shehu Malami held 40 per cent of the equity, the remaining 30 per cent being held by Alhaji Mai Sango, a wealthy Lagos-based merchant from Bauchi.[79] Pan African was the project coordinator for the Ajaokuta Steel project with a fee income estimated at over $70m. and it had the management contract for a number of other large projects. It also designed, set up and managed a number of projects promoted by Malami including Zaki Bottling in Wurno and Nigeria Pipes in Kano.

Shehu Malami was involved in a number of attempts to promote projects in the former Northwestern and Sokoto states where there was practically no medium- or large-scale industry. These efforts, by his own account, ended in disaster.[80] Some of the difficulties were reminiscent of the troubles experienced with the turnkey projects of the First Republic. The projects included the Sokoto Tannery in which he lost his investment as director and shareholder; Gusau Oil Mill where he favoured the participation of the Raccah family over John Holt Ltd, and later had his shares confiscated by government; Wurno Construction Materials Company, a brick plant in which he had a 8 per cent share alongside the state government and Italian investors, and where the state government declined to pay for all its shares; Consolidated Industries, a match project with inflated costs, which was abandoned by the overseas shareholder and technical partners; Tradev, a trading company with a monopoly over supplies of essential commodities for Sokoto State, which was riddled with corruption and never paid dividends; and finally, Zaki Bottling Company, where electricity and water supplies were not forthcoming and equipment proved defective. Elsewhere, Shehu Malami was the main promoter and chairman of Nigeria Pipes in Kano in which Aminu Dantata, Phillip Asiodu and M. S. Umoru were also shareholders. And he participated in Summit Furniture, a venture promoted by the former federal permanent secrtary, Phillip Asiodu at Asaba, Delta State.

Kaduna Enterprises

We now turn to examine four Kaduna enterprises and one enterprise in Ilorin in more detail. EOA Holdings is a mini-conglomerate which has grown rapidly over the past two decades. The Lemaco Group with origins in agro-industry was also a child of the oil boom. The ABG Group is a smaller enterprise that shifted its product lines from office equipment and stationery to electronics assembly and satellite and cable communications with changes in market conditions. The fourth case is Dagazau Carpets Ltd which is part of a broader group owned by Alhaji Tijani Dagazau that also emerged during the boom. The last profile is Bio-Medical Services Ltd owned by a medical practitioner in Ilorin.

TABLE 8.2: Companies of EOA Holdings.

Company	Start-up	Initial investment ($m.)	Comments
Vulcan Gases, Kaduna	1978	0.6m.	
Okin Biscuit, Offa	1979	0.3m.	N60m. assets (1990). Coaster and short-cake. Cash and carry distribution. 500 employed
Okin Foam, Offa	1980	0.5m.	Mattresses
Okin Bottling, Kaduna	1982	3.0m.	Brazilian concentrate. Tetrapak of Sweden. Fruit juice
Omicron International	1983	—	International trading company. Frozen fish
First Nigerian Insurance Company, Kaduna	1984	3.0m.	Life insurance. First GM was Jack Farnsworth, an expatriate with years of experience in Nigeria
Laxamy, Kaduna	1986	1.0m.	Electrical and mechanical engineering
Supasteel, Kaduna	1987	5.0m.	Steel structures, motor, and water tankers
Kwara Breweries	1989	—	Acquired 70% of the equity of Kwara State Breweries under privatisation. N7.5m. loan syndication

Sources: Interviews.

EOA Holdings

This group of ten constituent companies had a turnover of about N150m. in 1990 and employed over 2,000 persons.[81] The group, which is based in Kaduna, is owned by Chief E. O. Adesoye of Offa, Kwara State.

Chief Adesoye's father worked with Nigerian Railways at the locomotive workshop at Ebutte Metta in Lagos. He was a technician in charge of overhead crane operations. His late mother traded in textiles and commodities. After secondary schooling, Chief Adesoye joined the Northern Civil Service in Kaduna. He obtained an in-service scholarship and after studying at the Nigerian College of Arts and Technology, Enugu Campus, continued his studies at the South East London College of Technology, where he qualified as a quantity surveyor. His scholarship still had two years to run, so he gained experience with two UK companies before returning to Nigeria. He rose to the position of chief quantity surveyor in the northern states, the summit of his profession, at the age of 28. In 1967, he planned to establish a brick factory, but the project did not materialise for lack of support.

In 1968, he left government service to establish a consultancy in Kaduna, E. O. Adesoye and Partners. The timing was fortunate because the oil inspired construction boom was soon to come. At the peak of activity, the company employed nine British quantity surveyors. Operations extended to all the states of the Federation. The first industrial investment, a gas plant in Kaduna, was undertaken in 1978 (see Table 8.2); six other industrial ventures were to follow. In addition, an international trading company and an insurance firm were established.

In terms of turnover, the leading companies are Omicron International, Okin Biscuit, and Kwara Breweries. Investment was also undertaken in another gas plant, two banks, and a weekly newspaper in Kwara Sate. In-house printing and clearing and forwarding facilities were developed.

10,000 hectares were acquired for farming. The group was close to investing $40m. in capital equipment when devaluation made hard currency costs prohibitive. Attempts were made to grow irrigated wheat at Hadejia in Kano State, but 30 per cent of the crop was lost due to the late arrival of harvesting machinery. Farming currently employs about 50 persons in the small-scale cultivation of wheat, sorghum, maize, cassava and yam. A small cattle and goat herd has been established, as have experimental fish ponds.

The Group has no joint ventures or management and technical agreements with foreign partners. Direct employment of expatriates is preferred. Chief Adesoye argued that such arrangements would only be justified in higher areas of technology. Expatriate staff have no loyalty where the partner's objective is to maximise returns, offshore. This loyalty is better secured by direct recruitment. At its peak, expatriate employment was about 20. The Group does its own feasibility studies on the grounds that no outside agency will provide a negative assessment of a proposal.

The owner knows each business thoroughly and generally aims to secure the best technology available. General managers are given freedom to operate. Managers meet every two months to discuss strategy and cash flows. While a holding company has been formed, group management has not developed. Apart from the consultancy unit, which provides finance for private consumption, the Group has pursued a strategy of reinvestment with total equity financing and zero debt.

Chief Adesoye, who has avoided participation in partisan politics, is perhaps best known as the proprietor of Adesoye College, an elite school that opened at Offa in 1986. The college cost about N45m. and consists of fifty-two brick buildings. The college, which employs six expatriates, has highly competitive entrance examinations and small classes. Leadership and sacrifice are stressed and the college has a strong Christian ethic.

Lemaco Group of Companies

The Lemaco Group employs about 1,000 persons and has turnover of approximately N40m. (1991).[82] Both employment and turnover (in naira terms) were about double these figures in the early 1980s. Expatriate employment has fallen from 46 at its peak to 5. The Group was vulnerable to the high cost of imports after devaluation and the high cost of debt servicing.

Alhaji Lema Jibrilu, who comes from Katsina, spent seventeen years in

TABLE 8.3: Lemaco Group of companies.

Company	Start-up	Initial investment	Comment
Lemaco Farms	1977	?	4,500-hectare farm
Lemaco Enterprises	1980	$7.0m.	Meat distribution, cold storage
Leman Industries	1980	?	Nails, nuts and bolts. Brazilian partner
Projex West Africa	1980	$5.0m.	Land clearance. Brazilian partner
Northern Dairies, Funtua	1982	$6.0m.	Danish technical partner
Funtua Bottling Company	1982	$6.0m.	German technical partner
Modular Aluminium Fabrication	1984	$5.0m.	Austrian technology
Delema Ltd (Kaduna, Funtua, Katsina)	1985	?	Bakery
Lemaco Retreads	1987	$0.5m.	Tyre retreading
Fine Dairy Products, Katsina	1988	$2.0m.	Ice cream
Lema Agricultural Technical, Lagos	?	?	Generator sales and service

Source: Interview.

government service between 1958 and 1976, before leaving for the private sector. Throughout this period, he was involved with livestock. He trained in the United Kingdom and specialised in poultry. He was appointed livestock officer, Kaduna, in 1962. He was involved in attempts to upgrade poultry through the importation of exotic stock. After the creation of states, he moved to the new Nigerian Livestock and Meat Authority (NLMA), which took over many of the livestock establishments including the Kaduna abbatoir and an intensive feed lot operation at Mokwa with 10,000 head of cattle.

In 1972, he was seconded to the Nigerian Agricultural Bank and it was here that he began to see the opportunity for private enterprise. Later, he returned to the NLMA as chief development officer. He began to acquire land for farming. His first farm was not successful, suffering from erosion caused by mechanised ground clearance. A second farm of 4,500 hectares acquired in 1977 was to prove more successful with about 80 per cent of the area cropped at the end of the 1980s.

The origins of his first venture arose from a federal government mission to Argentina and Brazil to explore the possibility of a meat programme in the aftermath of the 1973–4 drought. This sowed the seeds of a company involved in cold storage and refrigerated transportation that would move meat from the northern abbatoirs to the southern states. Lemaco Enterprises (1980) was a joint venture with a Brazilian company – Cotia Comercio – involved in the distribution of frozen meat and poultry (see Table 8.3). The same Brazilian company was involved in another venture, Leman Industries, which was set up simultaneously. This company manufactured nails and nuts and bolts with a British company as a technical partner. In both cases, the Brazilian partner was subsequently bought out.

A third venture with Cotia was a land-development company. He was attracted to the venture because of his own experience of difficulties with land clearance, the very high cost of land preparation, and the fact that his partner had many ranches in Brazil. Among the companies for whom large-scale land clearance were undertaken were Bhojsons (10,000 acres in Gongola), UAC Agro Industries (6,250 acres in Kaduna), Northern Nigerian Flour Mills (5,000 acres in Niger), Guinness (7,500 acres in Niger), Norbru (5,000 acres in Plateau), Lemaco Farms (4,500 acres in Kaduna State), Nigerian Breweries (3,500 acres in Niger), Maize Products Ltd and Greenland Farms (2,500 acres in Kwara). The demand for land clearance, which had risen with the banning of some food imports and incentives for local sourcing, fell once deregulation set in and devaluation made the importation of agricultural machinery very costly.

Two industries were established in Funtua. The Funtua Bottling Company proved uneconomical and demonstrated the high costs of an unintegrated enterprise in which crown corks, bottles, crates and transport had to be bought in. Northern Dairies was established in the expectation that local milk supplies could be tapped from the old grazing reserve at Dutsinma, which had 200,000 head of cattle in the early 1960s. But the Fulani cattle herders had left with land encroachment and the drought which had adversely affected many small dams. Use was made of imported butter oil and powdered milk. The venture had to be restructured with the onset of the Structural Adjustment Programme. It is planned to revitalise the project and produce fruit juice.

In Kaduna, an aluminium building-material plant was established with Austrian technical assistance in 1984 and this was followed by a bakery in 1985 and a tyre-retreading unit. In Lagos, the original intention was to establish an engine-reboring plant but the project was uneconomical after devaluation and the enterprise concentrates on generator sales and service. In Alhaji Jibrilu's home of Katsina, a series of cottage industries have been developed on a small estate (candles, milk and ice cream plant, bakery and confectionery). Finally, the Group is involved in sales of agricultural equipment, insurance brokerage, and computer servicing.

ABG Group

Alhaji Bawa Garba was born in 1942 and comes from Garkida Gombi LGA in Adamawa State.[83] He worked for a Kaduna textile company as a production clerk (1963) and then with the Arewa Construction Company as an accounts clerk (1965). He set up Arewa Commercial Institute in 1966 with 50 students. Enrolment grew to 2,000 students by 1972. He was also the northern representative of Novesty Press Agency (USSR) and circulation manager for *New World* magazine (1968–71). His first major enterprise was Arewa Advancement Enterprises incorporated in 1969, which dealt in office stationery and equipment. It secured sole agencies for Thomas Wyatt, the stationers, and Olympic typewriters. Strong ties were developed with the Union Trading Company (UTC) for the distribution of photocopier machines.

By the mid-1970s, there was strong competition in the field of office equipment and Alhaji Garba began to shift into the marketing of electronic products. He established ABG Electronic Manufacturers Ltd and entered a technical partnership with Bosch Group of West Germany, representing the Blaupunkt company of West Germany for several years. Components for the assembly of television, car radio and video systems were imported. Staff underwent training in Germany. At first, there was protection and low duties on CKD components. The local production of components was expected but never materialised. With the Structural Adjustment Programme of 1986 it became more expensive to assemble locally and the luxury market collapsed. Assembly was discontinued and the source of supply later switched away from Germany to South Korea using the ABG brand. ABG Magnetic Tapes Industries established in 1982, succumbed to trade liberalisation by 1985. In 1986 ABG Communications began to assemble satellite systems with locally manufactured satellite dishes and imported receivers. In 1993 ABG Communications Systems was granted a licence for satellite and cable redistribution and transmission. Cable satellite systems have been gradually extended to the main urban centres of the northern states and now account for 75 per cent of turnover. Satellite dishes are now only purchased by rich people in rural areas where cable facilities are not available.

Dagazau Carpets Ltd

Alhaji Tijani Dagazau was born in 1932. He attended Barewa College (1946–9) and worked for the Bornu Native Authority (1950–6). He was then employed at the Federal level in the Ministry of Mines and Ministry of Works, Lagos. He resigned from government service in 1970 to enter private business.

During the 1970s, he set up companies engaged in importation, in the sale of crude oil and in civil engineering. Dagazau International was one of the first indigenous companies to commence sale of Nigerian crude oil. It was also involved in the construction of the Warri and Kaduna refineries. Alhaji Dagazau was a pioneer shareholder and director in Nigeria International Bank (1984).

The attempt to translate some of the profits of the oil boom into manufacture was not successful. Dagazau Carpets, the largest modern carpet factory in West Africa with a capacity of 6m. square metres of top quality dyed and printed carpets, opened in Kaduna in 1985 on a 54-acre site. Equity was held in the Dagazau family. The carpet industry in Nigeria is led by Kings Carpets International, an Indian enterprise with high quality management and external foreign support, which aims at medium-quality products and exports.

The company made losses for three years and suspended production in

1987 with the retrenchment of most of the workforce. Four qualified expatriates, who were recruited for production, left the company. There was over-investment in fixed assets and the decision to use bank overdrafts to fund permanent assets meant that there was no working capital for raw materials. The management structure was oriented towards production. Administrative and financial management were weak. The company hopes to reopen if a technical partner or foreign investor can be found.

Bio-Medical Services Co. Ltd

Dr Farouk Abdulazeez was born in 1938.[84] He was educated at Government College, Keffi (1952–57) and Ibadan University (1960–5). After experience in several hospitals and a brief spell as a university lecturer, he became medical adviser to Ciba-Geigy (1973–8) and since 1978, medical director of Okene Clinic Hospital. He later attended Harvard Business School.

He pioneered the local manufacture of intravenous fluids when he set up Bio-Medical Services in 1978. The NIDB and NNDC together provided 37 per cent of the equity of N1m. and loans of N1.7m. A Swiss technical partner took 10 per cent of the equity and supplied a technical manager for one year after commissioning. The company started production in 1981 and by 1991 had about 20 fluids on the market with a turnover of N23.6m. and 177 employees. Current net worth of the company was N55m. It controls about 30 per cent of the market and is the only local producer of the full range of intravenous and irrigation fluids. Local competitors include Unique Pharmaceuticals in Lagos and Ashimina in Ibadan. In 1986 it successfully formulated its own brand of haemodialysis concentrate for treatment of renal diseases. The company has recently begun production of medical grade plastic containers which will increase capacity utilisation.

Dr Abdulazeez was elected a member of the Constituent Assembly in 1988 and was national chairman of the People's Front of Nigeria before the party was disbanded by the government.

CONCLUSION

Under colonial rule, Kano grew as a centre of trade. Merchants, who had conducted long-distance trade from smaller settlements, tended to relocate their activities to the city, pulled by the new north–south orientation of trade in imported commodities from the coast and the export of new crops like groundnuts and cotton. The wealthiest merchants established themselves as agents of foreign commercial companies. Yet older activities and career patterns persisted. Involvement in the produce trade was often combined with trade in cattle, grain and kolanut. The movement of kola continued and was now transported by rail from the south. And merchants would still make their fortunes beyond the confines of Nigeria in the wider trading diaspora, before settling in Kano.

The careers of those merchants who were born before 1917 commonly followed a pattern of koranic education at a young age, followed by hawking, petty trade and an apprenticeship served in long-distance trade. Trade was then organised within *gandu* ('joint family unit') until a son was given trade goods to start his own enterprise or the household unit broke up following the death of the household head. With very few exceptions, trading organisations and estates did not survive after the death of the founder. Traders generally aspired to leave a name and their wealth but not a business organisation. The personal control of their networks, trading friendships and credit relations could not be transmitted. There was too, the practice of subdividing estates according to Islamic principles which tended to reduce the incentive for heirs to commit themselves to their father's enterprises.[85] A gap in communication and lifestyle with the younger generation could develop when children got early access to wealth, leading to the rapid liquidation of assets on death.

These factors are still relevant today. The expectation that all male children will share equally in the estate has encouraged first sons, if they are active and ambitious, to establish their own enterprises in their fathers' lifetime. A senior or favourite son may receive support from his father and may take some of the father's business goodwill with him, leaving other children disadvantaged. Cases where a father had established a limited company and brought in children as shareholders in his lifetime, which might in principle increase the chances of company survival at death, were not encountered. Very few cases of enterprise survival and growth were found. In the case of Gaskiya Textiles, a heavily indebted company was protected from family interests at the death of the founder by creditors and a strong administrator who managed to turn the company round. In the case of the Nabegu Group, a transition has been made to management by a younger, highly educated generation in the lifetime of the father.

In the 1950s, advances were made in road transport, in the direct importation of new items like bicycle parts and corn-grinding machines and in the produce trade, where government intervention assisted those who were formerly agents of foreign companies to become LBAs and command large cash advances from the banks. The effect of government pressure was also felt at the end of the decade in the opening of access to the distribution of commodities like textiles and tobacco, and in the arrival of industries, which gave opportunities for distributors, some private shareholding and advisory positions for the few merchants and members of the *sarauta* group who had access to western education. Later, the influence of government patronage was vastly increased through the expenditure of new state governments and the expansion of the armed forces.

Indigenous investment in a wide range of light industries in Kano which began in the 1960s, gathered momentum in the 1970s and was maintained up to 1983. Generally, investment was undertaken as part of the diversification of trading groups and not by specialist newcomers. Some of this investment proved vulnerable to the decline of the oil economy and to the political impact of the collapse of the Shagari regime in December 1983. Much of the investment during the oil boom was undertaken at overvalued exchange rates and was capital and import intensive. Companies which lacked a lifeline to sources of hard currency after 1983, or failed to get an import licence once the National Party of Nigeria fell from power, had difficulty sustaining production. Thus some larger groups have tended to revert back to their trading functions. The large trading companies of Aminu Dantata, Isiyaku Rabiu, Garba Inuwa and the Lagos-based Dangote Group still on occasion constitute a powerful commercial lobby with access to the federal government.

But it was not just the change in economic and political environment which caused a retreat. There were management problems of a kind that were identified in the literature on entrepreneurship in Nigeria in the 1960s. Personal control associated with a lack of trust and an inability to delegate authority as an enterprise expanded was evident. In two early cases of industrial partnerships, the Kano Citizens Trading Company and Bagauda Textiles Ltd, a single individual came to dominate the companies and other investors lost interest and were not prepared to put in more funds. This experience was widely known and remarked on in Kano and may have acted as a deterrent to older traders venturing into industry.

Within the last decade, a few larger enterprises have emerged from non-trading backgrounds. Apart from Koguna, Babura and Company, Falacol Pharmaceuticals, Ceramics Manufacturers and Star Modern Paper, which we profiled, there is Kabo Air owned by a former employee of Nigerian Airways and Tofa General Enterprises. Kabo Holdings has diversified into real estate, hospitals and hotels. In 1993, it acquired Durbar Hotel, Kaduna for N90m. under the privatisation programme.[86] Tofa General Enterprises, a trading and paper conversion enterprise, with a turnover of N32m. in 1990–1[87] is owned by Isiyaku Umar Tofa.[88]

At a number of points in this chapter, the continued strength of Lebanese business interests in Kano has been underlined. In retrospect, the indigenisation exercise does not appear to have been much of a set-back to Lebanese firms. In the distribution of textiles, where the Lebanese have financial strength and strong ties to the textile companies, it has long been a dead letter and its provisions were not followed through. The only change is the arrival of more small Hausa textile dealers whose market share is low.

The case of the Lebanese demonstrates the frailty of economic nationalism and the artificiality of international boundaries. Since the end of the Second Republic, Nigerians have not perceived the economic benefits of being identified as Nigerians as being very great. Moreover, Nigerians themselves straddle international borders and have property and business interests abroad. As we have seen, the Lebanese adopted a number of strategies to secure their position, including taking Nigerian citizenship and making joint investments with Nigerian businessmen. They also made a number of strategic alliances with powerful individuals. Unlike the Libyans, Egyptians, Yemeni and Sudanese who have settled in Kano and become entrenched, the Lebanese have not, with very few exceptions, integrated themselves into the host society through marriage and religious practice. They have maintained a tightly organised community with its own schools and social clubs.

In Kaduna, by contrast with Kano, the major indigenous investment has been undertaken by individuals whose first experience of business was in the public sector as civil servants, parastatal employees, and professionals. Some highly capitalised or import-dependent enterprises have not been successful or have contracted. The promotion of enterprises has generally been more restricted. One explanation would seem to lie in the opportunities which the expansion of the public sector (including state creation) and foreign investment have provided for the relatively risk free acquisition of wealth. In Kaduna, the timing of industrial investment at the end of the 1970s adhered to a broader pattern evident in Ibadan, Onitsha, Aba and, to some extent, Lagos, in which investment was undertaken after financial surpluses had been accumulated through the oil boom.

9

CONCLUSION

ENTREPRENEURIAL ORIGINS AND PATTERNS

The origins of entrepreneurs who have developed larger-scale enterprises in Nigeria are diverse. The field ranges from petty traders and artisans with limited formal education who have built up large enterprises, to professionals, graduates and MBAs, who have entered business relatively recently. These very different trajectories may intersect, as I witnessed, when bankers from an indigenous merchant bank in Lagos came to an Igbo village to discuss loan terms for a maize-milling complex, owned by a former trader in Onitsha main market.

Persons with trading backgrounds and limited education are still important among those who own large-scale business in Nigeria, but their position has been steadily eroded by persons from other backgrounds. Throughout the colonial period, government service and employment with foreign companies remained consistent strands in the careers of business people. Persons tended to retire from junior positions in government departments like the railways and public works, sometimes late in their careers, to start their own businesses. The structure of incentives and hierarchy of status usually ruled out a business career for the few who gained access to secondary education. The exceptions tend to have had their education interrupted and so prove the rule. In the 1950s and 1960s, the advent of parastatal bodies gave a few professional people (lawyers and accountants) the connections and business experience to launch themselves privately. In the 1970s and 1980s, a new wave of senior public officials and executive officers with parastatal agencies, retired at a relatively young age to enter business.

The other strand of experience with foreign companies, sometimes of brief duration, evolved through the colonial period from employment as clerks, store keepers and produce agents to more senior management positions and a few technical posts. The numbers passing through the management training programmes of the UAC in the late 1940s and early 1950s to eventually establish their own companies bear witness to this movement. The arrival of graduates and younger professionals without experience of the public sector or corporate enterprise, is a more recent phenomena, starting in the 1970s and gathering momentum in the 1980s. Today, those who enter commerce and the produce trade may well be graduates.

It is, in general, erroneous to suppose that modern industry is necessarily associated with a new type of business owner with higher education and experience of modern fields of enterprise. John Iliffe has drawn the contrast too sharply, claiming that experience in older economic spheres becomes irrelevant with modern enterprise.[1] There is no break or jump in the overall pattern of entrepreneurship that the literature of the 1960s on the weakness of Nigerian enterprises might lead one to expect. Many entrepreneurs, especially in Igboland, emerge from a background of apprenticeship and trade. As their enterprises have grown, so they have raised their level of managerial, organisational and technical expertise through experience on the job and employment of expertise from outside.

The importance of trading backgrounds in Nigeria confirms the broad contrast between Nigeria and eastern and southern Africa where western education and official employment play a larger role in the careers of those who invest in industry. Entrepreneurs with government and professional backgrounds are not lacking in Nigeria, especially in Lagos and the western states. As we have seen, prior to independence many had experience in government departments. A number of federal ministers in the First Republic set up businesses while holding office. In the 1970s, many civil servants and army officers retired to go into business. But the process of straddling, which is so emphasised and officially sanctioned in the Kenyan case, has been much less important. Writing in the late 1970s, Swainson saw the use of official position within the state to advance private business interests as the hallmark of the present stage of indigenous accumulation in Kenya.[2] Médard has tried to generalise the Kenyan case to Nigeria and other African countries.[3] Bayart, too, gives straddling a central place in his paradigm of trajectories of power and accumulation across Africa.[4] He views accumulation in the private and public spheres as complementary and sharing the same ethos. Contrary to Bayart, Iliffe is correct, at least for Nigeria, to draw a contrast between West Africa with its strong private trading traditions, and East and Central Africa where straddling is more systematic and visible.[5] Straddling mechanisms are not central to large scale accumulation in Nigeria.

Nigerians do use connections made in the state sector to accumulate wealth, obtain bank loans and influence government policy. Some may run businesses or use proxies while holding state appointments. But straddling, in the classic Kenyan sense of the term, is of much less importance. Unless straddling is limited to a process of initial accumulation, it is hard to see how holding political or bureaucratic office in the state sector could be compatible with the time and energy required to build up large corporate forms of enterprise. There is little evidence that those who straddle in Kenya have built up significant enterprises, as distinct from property and investment portfolios. As I will argue later, the reasons for its prominence and persistence in Kenya lie in the absence of alternative political structures and the need for security.

ENTERPRISE GROWTH, GROUPS AND DIVERSIFICATION

Have small enterprises grown into large ones? A number of authors who have addressed this question in Africa have advanced cogent reasons why small producers tend to stay small. In Berry's work, the emphasis is on the difficulty of managing larger-scale enterprises and supervising labour where customers and suppliers require the personal attention of the owner.[6] Hart also stresses the difficulties of delegating responsibility.[7] McCormick argues that risk-management strategies in Kenya lead to the maintenance of small-scale enterprises that are more flexible and more profitable than larger-scale enterprises.[8] All authors note a tendency for business owners to start other concerns or make other investments, once enterprises reach a certain size.

It is necessary to distinguish clearly cases where a small enterprise expands into a large-scale enterprise and the much more common situation where a small enterprise, usually a trading firm, is the progenitor of other companies which may eventually form a diversified group. In the latter case, the original enterprise may cease to exist or only play a minor role. Studies of company mortality that do not follow these trajectories through will completely miss the dynamic of accumulation. Many medium- and large-scale enterprises, especially in Onitsha, Nnewi and Aba, have a background of small-scale trading and formal apprenticeship. Examples across the country include the Nwankwo Group of Onitsha, the Toonak Group of Aba and the Eleganza Group of Lagos. All these groups have entered manufacture.

The emergence of medium- or large-scale enterprises from petty production is much rarer. In the 1960s, examples were found in the printing and saw-milling industries. The only examples I found were in Aba in the shoe and garment industries. Here the owners had served formal apprenticeship, gone independent, relocated, purchased machinery and were employing up to 250 persons.

During our investigation, we have found a number of large groups employing from 1,000 to 10,000 persons, and the emergence of effective group-management structures. These groups are family owned and tend to be strongly diversified across trade, manufacture, finance, property and services. No group has concentrated its activities in a particular sector and with the possible exception of one sugar trader, none has established monopoly powers. Younger groups give little indication of a more focused approach.

The strong impulse to diversify into unrelated fields among larger enterprises can be partly explained by strategies designed to spread and reduce risk and minimise unavoidable losses. Nigeria is a high-risk environment emanating from economic instability, political uncertainty and from inconsistent and unpredictable changes in government policies. General responses to risk include overseas investment, property holdings well in excess of business requirements, a tendency to widen the territorial spread of activities to encompass the home area, and a reluctance to commit funds to long-term investment in fixed assets. The latter certainly acts as a deterrent to manufacture though it by no means excludes it. Another indicator is the reluctance to give up trading opportunities. Further impetus is given to diversification by the adoption of strategies that allow flexible responses. Two informants spoke of the need for rounded, well balanced enterprises that are positioned to take advantage of new profit opportunities should they arise as a result of unexpected shifts in government policy or changes in regime. Not all cases of diversification result from strategic thinking of any kind. In the case of Aba, some groups resulted from a succession of perceived profit opportunities in industry that turned out to be short term as competing enterprises rushed to enter similar lines of business.

MANAGEMENT AND BUSINESS CULTURE

Our investigations highlighted a number of issues relating to the internal culture of owner-managed enterprises that adversely affected performance and the potential for growth. In the broadest terms, these matters were all linked to the willingness and capacity of a founder/owner to share the benefits and responsibilities of the enterprise with others. Among the interrelated issues were the capacity to delegate authority and share information with others, including partners; a recognition of the need for adequate rewards and remuneration for employees, the ability to recruit and maintain non-family management, and the management of relations with kin and home community. Where terms of service are negotiable, employee expectations may be at variance with owners own. Deficiencies in managing these relations could lead to tension, conflicts of interest and the failure of enterprises. Conversely, the more successful enterprises had addressed these issues and begun to shift the identity of the company away from the person of the owner to the wider family or corporate organisation. Three interelated problems were most commonly found.

While our findings did not generally give support to the common stereotype of business owners hampered by the demands of the extended family, whose members, especially brothers, are said to insist on sharing the wealth of the owner; they did underline the tensions that arise from the use of business resources and the owners' wealth to support conspicuous expenditures (housing, marriage, title taking, etc.) for self and close kin. When this was combined with low pay and benefits for employees, it created a particularly debilitating environment within the firm, undermining morale, work discipline, and recruitment.

Second, the inability of the founder to share information with others could create a culture of secrecy, that effectively blocked delegation, ruled out partnership and ruined any chance of succession. The underlying question of trust was not necessarily solved by employment of close kin, even sons and daughters. Some owners deliberately avoided the employment of relations because they could not be effectively disciplined.

Finally, in a number of cases, the failure to create a company identity distinct from the personal identity of the founder/owner had the effect of increasing the demands of employees, raising the pressure on a 'Big Man' to launch and donate at public functions, and meant that all matters relating to the bureaucracy had to be attended to personally.

In retrospect the difficulties of delegating authority that were emphasised by studies in the 1960s do not appear so formidable. There are instances where the failure of the 'self-made' businessman (Wolsey Hall and the bush lamp) to delegate authority has hampered growth and taken its toll on the health of the owner. The common strategy of educating children and bringing them into the business does not necessarily lighten the burden since paternal authority is still exercised. But there are many cases where changes in organisation, more bureaucratic forms of management and recruitment from outside the family, have allowed large increases in the scale of enterprise. The rise of the large conglomerates testifies to this. So too, does the growth of private professional firms in accountancy, architecture, banking, engineering and medical services.

The employment of professional managers and accountants by Nigerian enterprises since 1970 marks a significant change. Lall has suggested that in sub-Saharan Africa the development of managerial capabilities outstripped entrepreneurial ones.[9] However in the case of Nigeria, the growth of African enterprise has itself been dependent on the recruitment of outside management. As we saw in chapter 2, there is evidence that difficulties of recruitment in the 1960s, when the public sector had higher status and offered higher relative rewards, retarded the growth of some indigenous enterprises.

Pius Okigbo in his 1986 Ahiajoku lecture has lamented that Igbo businesses are smaller and more closed than those of their counterparts elsewhere.[10] In his argument, Igbo individualism, which generally acts as a positive spur to enterprise, becomes a fetter on the growth of enterprises. He argues that partnerships, which would create larger enterprises, fail because of conflicts of interest generated by the tendency of the Igbo businessman to use resources from the business to meet social-security payments and expenses for the extended family. While there is no doubt that these forces do operate and are detrimental to growth, our evidence does not fully bear out Okigbo's argument. First, Igbo enterprises are not appreciably smaller when account is taken of the impact of the war years. Even in those cases where firms made a rapid recovery after war, there is little doubt that the civil war and the currency change constituted a severe set-back to the growth of companies. Second, the incidence of formal partnership appears to be as great, if not greater, in Igboland, than it is elsewhere. In general, I would put less emphasis on classical partnership as a requisite for growth and more on the ability to share the responsibilities and especially the rewards of enterprise with others – in other words, the ability to create a corporate identity and business practice that is distinct from the personal interests of the individual.

TECHNOLOGY ACQUISITION AND CAPACITIES

During the colonial period, levels of technology and skills employed by Nigerian enterprises outside agriculture and some crafts, were low. Very limited access to western education at home and abroad, reduced the opportunity to acquire skills or technological know-how. Moreover, the hierarchy of status and rewards under colonial rule was biased towards general education and administrative skills. The obstacles to importing technology, or gaining experience on the job, were also formidable. Foreign companies tended to exclude Nigerians from positions of technical and organisational responsibility. Strong bilateral ties with Britain and the element of monopoly in colonial business acted to restrict foreign business contacts and the avenues for technology acquisition. It was in the 1950s that technology sources began to diversify in a more competitive environment.

Under conditions of autarchy in wartime Biafra, scientists and engineers demonstrated a capacity to innovate and adapt existing technology. The colonial pattern of high status accorded to generalist administrators with a far lower ranking for engineers and technical personnel was dramatically reversed. Although the value of this experience was recognised, attempts to carry over the achievements to peacetime were largely unsuccessful. The scientific personnel and engineers involved, quickly scattered. Far more damaging was the oil boom, which encouraged easy access to a flood of imported technology that was extremely wasteful and disruptive of local learning processes. In the public sector, administrators superintended the import of advanced technology for state projects and generally adopted a fully packaged, low-risk, high-cost approach. There was no cumulative build-up of experience through public-sector projects. Many technocrats left public companies out of frustration and highly trained personnel found employment in areas far from their field of expertise. Nor was there any indication that the purchasing policy of federal and state governments was geared to the capacities and needs of local firms in any systematic way.

There are a variety of strategies relating to the acquisition to foreign technology and management by private indigenous firms. Joint ventures, where the local partner originally promoted the enterprise and is actively involved in management, appear comparatively rare. Whether joint ventures give local enterprises better prospects for growth and greater technical capacities cannot be decided *a priori*. It will depend on many factors including the initial strategy and strength of the local partner. Joint ventures and long-term technical and management agreements with foreign companies run the risk of the enterprises being run in the interests of an overseas partner by expatriates loyal to overseas employers with the local partner being relegated to a rentier or agency role. Unless a high level of technology and management demands close collaboration with foreign firms, a better option may be the purchase of technology overseas, the training of Nigerians at home and abroad and the direct employment of expatriates where necessary. Both the Nnewi industrialists and the owners of oil-service companies, from their very different backgrounds, have adopted this strategy.

The degree of reliance on expatriate employment varies from heavy recruitment at managerial and technical levels, through temporary hiring for technical, service and training functions, to deliberate strategies of avoidance designed to build up local skills and capacities. In recent years, the heavy foreign-exchange costs of expatriate employment have substantially reduced the numbers employed.

The importance of technology and skills imported from Taiwan is striking. In an earlier article, which examined Brazil's relations with Nigeria, I briefly contrasted the Brazilian economic presence in Nigeria with that of India and related it to differences in domestic development strategies and geopolitical interests.[11] India had more direct investment and larger technology exports than Brazil. It may be that Taiwan's technology exports are as important in aggregate as those of India despite greater direct investment by Indian companies. In our study of Nnewi enterprises, reasons were advanced for the competitive nature and attraction of Taiwanese technology and its successful introduction to Nigeria. The adaptability of trading practices among small firms, the wide range of product specification and production technology and cost advantages were noted.

SUCCESSION AND SURVIVAL

In the past, owner-managed, family firms in Nigeria have very often died with their founders. Our studies suggest that this situation is changing, but only very slowly. A few examples of successful succession were cited. In many cases, where children had been brought into the enterprise, it was too early to judge the prospects for succession and subsequent growth.

The prospects for business longevity and sustained growth across generations depend on a multiplicity of factors which cannot be reduced to a neat instrumental formula. Among them are the type of activity (trading and transport ventures tend to run down during the owner's lifetime), the degree of bureaucratic organisation and delegation achieved during the owner's lifetime, the strength of family business traditions, the existence of polygamy which tends to accentuate pressures to divide responsibilities and share assets on the death of the founder, and patterns of inheritance. Perhaps the most important factor accounting for successful transitions that could be identified was a capacity to bring in children and give them gradual responsibility and authority during the lifetime of the founder, though this, in itself, was no guarantee of success. Children, who had assumed executive positions in this manner, were likely to have sufficient authority at the death of the founder to deter or resist family pressures to subdivide assets. The chances of coming to a judicious settlement of property which safeguarded the business firm were improved. Among the factors undermining the strategy of trying to ensure succession by bringing children into the family business were a tendency to delay the hand over until it was too late, a failure on the part of the older generation to trust their heirs and pass on the detailed understandings and confidences of business life, the entry of children at high executive levels without adequate on-the-job experience, and easy access to wealth at a young age, which undermined motivation and discipline among children.

Studies in Lagos suggest that wealth (especially landed property) is transmitted across the generations through strong family organisation and leadership, but that business enterprises have rarely survived the death of the founder. The highly educated children of the present generation often set up in fields different from their fathers. Of the African companies listed in *The Red Book of West Africa* in the early 1920s, only one appears to have survived in a modest form.[12] We noted in the conclusion to chapter 3 that even where firms have survived, they tended to remain small. In Kano, there is greater continuity in family-business traditions, though here, sons expecting that the estate will be divided among the family according to Islamic principles, have generally tried to establish their own enterprises in their fathers' lifetime, rather than commit themselves to a career within the existing organisation. The fact that most enterprises have been trading concerns is also very relevant, since the personal credit relations characteristic of these enterprises cannot be easily transferred to the next generation.

In principle, going public on the stock exchange could provide a solution to business longevity, where family pressures might otherwise lead to the break-up or atrophy of a business. In the case of one older enterprise, preparations were being made to float the industrial concerns (with a family shareholding), while the main family interests were taken care of by property and investment trusts. By early 1993, about thirty, relatively young, privately owned companies had gone public. None of the larger groups, or companies associated with them, were involved. A few private companies, notably in the insurance and banking industry, had opened share ownership and board membership to senior management. Here there was a clear recognition that the survival of the firm depended on a core of committed professionals who had a stake in the future of the business.

WEALTH, HOME COMMUNITY, TITLES AND PHILANTHROPY

At various points in our work, reference has been made to the links between entrepreneurs, home communities and philanthropy. The accumulation of wealth is often justified by the ultimate social, philanthropic or religious purpose to which the money is put. Ideally, studies of enterprises and individual paths of accumulation need to be set within an understanding of the legitimation of wealth, and status and power in the community and wider society. Because our studies have ranged very widely over different communities and cultures and been focused on enterprises, this was not possible. This section takes up a few issues in what is clearly a large field of study. What contribution do wealthy business people make towards the development of their home communities? What form does philanthropy and the search for social recognition and approval take? How significant is the redistribution of wealth to community and others through voluntary contributions, levies and title taking? What impact do these transfers have on the material welfare of the community? In Nigeria, such contributions take on added significance because wealthy individuals are rarely taxed and local government taxation is at a low level.

The picture that emerges on these questions in Yorubaland is uniformly rather negative. Berry sees local elites as engaged in a process of unproductive accumulation and wasteful competition engendered by a struggle for access to state resources outside the community.[13] Surplus funds are absorbed by political monuments and duplication of existing facilities. Guyer sees only limited benefits for communities from the activities of wealthy office holders (chiefs and government officials) and professionals who have access to private and public resources outside the community.[14] She also suggests that the effectiveness of collective endeavours as a means of overcoming the absence of taxation are limited especially for projects that cover a wider area.[15] Peel found that Ilesha residents were critical of the contributions to home development made by wealthy Ijesha who had gone abroad, and despondent at the lack of local employment opportunities.[16] Their solution was to secure better access to the state.

In the case of Lawrence Omole, the Ilesha entrepreneur we treated in chapter 3, his views evolved from the unattainable goal of attracting a government project to Ilesha through the patronage of a political party, to the successful strategy of bringing together a small group of private investors, some of whom were not from Ilesha. His desire to contribute to the industrialisation of Ilesha clearly involved an investment in individual and group identity and a welfare component. He was conscious of the past failure of *osomaalo* traders to create lasting enterprises and contribute to development at home. Recognition for self and family took the form of an honorary doctorate from the University of Ife and the second highest Ilesha title for his senior brother.

Our remaining observations are drawn from Igboland – from Anambra State in particular – and are restricted to business owners. Though caution needs to be exercised because of variation across communities, I am inclined to take a slightly more positive view of individual contributions to the home community and the impact of collective endeavour on community welfare than that presented in the Yoruba cases.

In the case of Nnewi and a number of other communities in Anambra State, industries have been located in the home community. Complaints that local business people are not investing or providing employment are not common. Sometimes investment in industry brings spin-offs for close residents in the form of electricity, piped water and roads. Many of the goods produced are for sale outside the community and therefore likely to be viewed as an additional source of revenue to the community.

Private philanthropy by wealthy individuals beyond contributions to extended kin is directed at education, health, infrastructure, social clubs and churches. Though it is clearly related to a search for individual recognition and social approval, it is not necessarily part of a Big Man syndrome where a stream of patronage is directed at building up networks of influence and adversely affects the growth and longevity of the enterprise. Three younger businessmen resident in Nnewi have financed infrastructure projects at the local teaching hospital.

Before the civil war, contributions by wealthy individuals to public projects were generally given privately or were part of development union or church levies. Collective fund raising for projects through public launching started just after the war ended and then spread from Igboland to the rest of the country. It was seen as a means to speed urgent reconstruction which allowed for contributions that were more in line with ability to pay than the flat-rate contributions of the town union levies. These public donations, in which business people take a prominent part, are a form of competitive philanthropy which ranks contributors in public. They can be seen as a very partial substitute for the absence of effective tax assessment and payment. In some communities and local government areas, substantial sums have been raised and used for water, road, educational and health projects. The Ukpor Development Union raised over N2m. for road building from launchings in Lagos and Ukpor in 1990. The Aguata Local Government Area raised over N5m. at a launching in 1992 for a water scheme and road rehabilitation.

Community recognition of success in business, financial contributions to local development or an individual's role as a political representative, or broker, at higher levels in the national hierarchy, may lead to chieftaincy titles. Most titles are honorary ones and do not entail much redistribution of wealth or waste through lavish installation ceremonies. The building of large mansions that signal wealth and sometimes connote political influence and can accommodate a visiting governor or head of a multinational corporation, is probably a more significant drain on resources. In some communities, indigent elders have encouraged the commercialisation of chieftaincy titles. Sometimes, titles are collected as a means of buying political support or in an attempt to gain social respectability by young men whose wealth was acquired illegitimately.

At higher levels, many semi-official statewide appeal funds were launched after 1983. They were widely seen as an admission of failure to tax and as an opportunity for wealthy individuals to recycle wealth through the state. I know of no assessment of their achievements. For those who are national figures there are many calls to launch appeal funds and contribute to specific projects at a national or regional level. The sponsorship of sports is well developed.[17] Private school proprietorship is an older tradition which varies in the degree to which business or philanthropic objectives are in the ascendancy. Recent examples include Adesoye College at Offa, Igbinedion College at Benin and Olashore International School at Iloko-Ijesha.

Recognition of wealth and achievement at state or federal levels, includes the award of honorary doctoral degrees by Nigerian universities. A far from complete listing of doctorates awarded to Nigerian business people since 1965, when Chief Odutola was honoured by Ibadan University (38 cases), shows that awards proliferated after 1985 and became common to the country as a whole.[18] This proliferation was linked to the creation of new universities and the parlous financial condition of the universities which made a search for private sources of funds and endowments more compelling. A contributory factor was the permeation of academia by monetary values which received a great boost with the oil boom.[19] The award of honorary degrees became commercialised. Beyond Nigeria, degrees were purchased by wealthy individuals from as far away as the diploma mills of California and Singapore.

FORMS AND PATTERNS OF ADVANCE OF INDIGENOUS CAPITAL

Our studies show that the rentier, unproductive view of local private accumulation in Nigeria, which came into fashion during the oil boom and its aftermath, needs to be severely qualified. Modification is also required of the older picture of merchant capital. All these elements are present but none is dominant. There is clear evidence of a general advance of local capital from trade to manufacture and services. Movement from an agrarian base direct to industry, or from trade to large-scale agriculture, is much more limited. Studies in Kano, Anambra State, Aba and among Lagos-based companies confirm this. Sometimes construction and transport combined with trade provide the route to industry. Yet the shift from trade to industry should not be exaggerated. Many enterprises retain their trading functions within a diversified group. Moreover, it would be misleading to suppose that indigenous capital controls the import, wholesale and retail sectors. Many large companies operate their own distribution networks and despite the well known withdrawal of the UAC from supermarkets, foreign capital remains dominant in this sector. For example, it is Indian capital, entrenched in the importation of general consumer goods and electronics, with extensive overseas networks, that has been most active in the field of large supermarkets in the Lagos area. In Kano, the Lebanese remain active in the textile trade at all levels.

The advance into industry has been patchy and in some areas has been vulnerable to less favourable economic conditions in the 1980s. Nevertheless, compared with the position in the 1960s when African capital was typically in saw milling, furniture making, printing, garment making, baking, building materials and motor transport, there have been important advances in scale and technology. This has occurred in existing areas like food and beverages, garments, textiles, furniture, printing, vegetable-oil and rubber processing. There has also been entry to new areas like carpets, ceramics, cotton ginning, starch, detergents, distilling, industrial gases, pharmaceuticals (including injectibles), motor parts, motor body panels, steel rolling and fabrication, condensers, windscreens, electric cables, plastics, paper conversion and recycling, packaging, oil and other technical services (computers and telecommunications). Large indigenous companies exist in many industrial sectors though they do not have a dominant position in aggregate. For example, in agro-industry, Lebanese and Indian investors have an important stake. In textiles, the Nigerian advance has been weak and the Indian and Chinese presence correspondingly strong. Only in Kano does there appear to be sizeable indigenous investment in this sector. In the metallurgical and engineering sector, technical capacities remain at a low level, but there have been some small advances with the establishment of private foundries and workshops with a capacity to design and fabricate spare parts and moulds.

With respect to the promotion of industrial enterprises, I do not think the Nigerian case really bears out the picture painted by Lall in a recent survey of sub-Saharan Africa.[20] He sees a general failure of African private enterprise to enter modern industry. Lall links the weakness of African entrepreneurial capabilities (managerial, organisational and technical) to a missing range of medium- to large-scale industrial enterprises lying between small-scale enterprises and large foreign enterprises. Our work shows that African entrepreneurs have set up industrial enterprises, though their presence in some parts of the country and in some sectors like textiles and engineering is weak. Certainly the 'gap' is not as extensive, and the capabilities as weak, as suggested. When the existence of Lebanese, Indian and other smaller foreign enterprises are taken fully into account, the 'missing middle' disappears.

Outside of industry, a strong advance in banking has been evident since 1980. This development has no parallel in other sub-Saharan African countries. It has been encouraged by high profits, more relaxed conditions for entry, and the prospect of access to foreign exchange after the regime of import licensing was abolished. The speculative character of some of this activity should not hide the fact that this is a significant development for the long-term growth of indigenous capital. Within two decades, there has been a breakdown of expatriate ownership and control, greater access for indigenous borrowers to banks and a steady build-up of banking expertise in a progressively more competitive environment. The scope of financial activity extends to insurance, mortgage finance, discount houses, stockbroking, unit trusts and equipment leasing.

Other areas of service activity that have also seen strong advances include legal services, accountancy, architecture and real estate, hotels, advertising, domestic airlines, port services, various forms of technical services and private education.

THE IMPACT OF THE OIL BOOM AND THE STRUCTURAL ADJUSTMENT PROGRAMME

Our work on the growth of individual enterprises suggests that existing ideas about the impact of the oil boom need some modification. The 1970s are often seen as a time of rapid accumulation of private wealth through state contracts and privileged access to the state bureaucracy, with many opportunities for corruption and the privatisation of state resources. The oil boom is held to have shifted incentives in favour of intermediary and rentier activity (shares and property) rather than directly productive activity and to be associated with excessive consumption, waste and debt.

There is no doubt that these views are in part correct, but they do not give the whole picture. The oil boom did encourage rentier values through easy access to shares via indigenisation, through property speculation, and through commission agencies and fees. Later, high financial returns in the banking sector, attracted an influx of capital. There was also a build-up of offshore wealth in property and financial assets through capital flight and commissions paid abroad by foreign companies. This picture needs to be tempered by the recognition that some of the wealth acquired, later found its way into more productive forms of investment, including industrial investment. Also, a small part of the investment abroad, provided hard-currency earnings which were used to finance business at home.

We noted that in a number of locations the initial impact of the oil boom was to increase profitability in commerce and in service industries. This later provided the finance for investment. Among the younger groups to emerge in this period were Concord Group, Desam Group, EOA Holdings, Onwuka Interbiz, Devcom, Honeywell and Lemaco. In terms of timing, there is clear evidence of an increase in industrial investment by indigenous entrepreneurs in the late 1970s, after the initial impact of the oil boom had provided the finance for investment.

The precise timing and rhythm of the advance has varied according to location and the origin and strength of local capital. In the major commercial centres of Aba and Onitsha where the civil war had interrupted the growth of local enterprises and set back accumulation, a trading regime began to shift quite rapidly towards industrial investment towards the end of the 1970s. At the same time, Aba experienced growth in artisan production. In Nnewi, the wealth created from a strong market share in the motor-parts trade was the basis for an industrial thrust that did not get underway until after 1983 following the closure of the economy. A broader pattern of rural industrialisation was also initiated in Enugu, Anambra, Abia and Imo states, as investors located industries closer to their home communities for political and security reasons. Other locations where indigenous investment in manufacture was marked after 1977 were Lagos, Ibadan and Kaduna. In Kano, where local industrial investment kept up momentum through the decade of the 1970s, continued into the early 1980s and then slackened, there was no particular acceleration at the end of the 1970s.

In the case of the indigenisation programmes, both the conglomerates we investigated in detail, gained from the exercise. In the one case, there was a heavy programme of acquisition. Other cases of Lebanese companies being taken over as going concerns were noted. These cases, and a few others where joint ventures were created, do in particular instances modify the general picture of indigenisation as an exercise in share transfer with the build-up of passive equity portfolios by wealthy individuals and a much broader distribution of shares to those who subscribed to public offers. In Kano, the programme does not appear to have significantly reduced the importance of the Lebanese presence in industry or textile distribution.

The advent of the Structural Adjustment Programme in 1986, which originated from pressures applied by the IMF and World Bank and not from domestic sources, brought deregulation and an emphasis on market solutions and private initiatives.[21] While its impact on economic ideas and attitudes cannot be determined with any precision, it did open up a debate about the role of the government in the economy and gave a voice to those in favour of private enterprise who had been silent before.[22]

The direct impact of SAP on indigenous enterprise is difficult to assess. The increase in cost of foreign exchange following sharp devaluation of the naira and the shrinkage of the domestic market as deflationary fiscal measures were introduced, made capital-intensive and import-intensive industries less competitive. Some of the investment undertaken under oil-boom conditions had already proved vulnerable to import compression. This was true of the assembly of electrical goods, flour milling, building materials and other activities that relied heavily upon imported materials. Access to foreign exchange was probably broadened but at the same time the uncertainty and problem of sourcing foreign exchange while depreciation continued, delayed the take-off of many projects and absorbed much time and energy. Capital-intensive, large-scale farming was undermined, but at the same time invest-ment in agro-industries like vegetable-oil processing, rubber processing and cotton ginning was encouraged. Artisans and roadside producers with low overheads and wage costs gained at the expense of capital-intensive producers in lines like furniture and shoes. Traders in second-hand machinery and motors were also favoured as were those importing from cheaper sources of supply. The employment of expatriates became more expensive leading to a further reduction in their numbers and the substitution of Asians for more expensive Europeans. Devaluation encouraged the growth of manufactured exports though rarely through official channels because of the costs associated with bureaucracy and tariffs in francophone countries. Unofficial manufac-tured exports to the West African sub-region, which outweigh official ones by a wide margin, include motor parts, shoes, garments, cosmetics and pharmaceuticals.

The privatisation programme at federal and state levels, opened up some opportunities for acquisitions by indigenous capital, especially of agricultural plantations, agro-processing facilities, breweries and hotels. Here there was competition with Indian and Lebanese companies. It is too early to judge the effect of other government policies aimed at deregulation and increasing indigenous participation in the shipping, oil-services and production, TV and radio and the effect of parastatal commercialisation. There are indications, though, that indignenous capital is poised to advance in oil-services and the electronic media.

THE STATE AND PRIVATE ENTERPRISE

In the introduction a number of authors were cited who emphasised the close relation between the state and private accumulation in Nigeria. By virtue of its large size, the state was held to offer all manner of opportunity for corruption, predatory behaviour, patronage, and the exercise of discretion-ary power through subsidy, loan, licence and contract. Elsewhere in Africa, state-centric approaches to private accumulation have been common. All share the view that access to state resources and power have been the central avenue to capital accumulation, upward mobility and class formation. Some go further and see the existence of a ruling or political class that monopolises the channels of accumulation through control of state power and policy.

There has been a tendency to project assumptions about the state, class and power at the macro-level on to the economy without adequate empirical investigation. In reality, interaction between state and society in Africa has created a great deal of variation in the origin and size of the social spaces open to private accumulation. For example, private trajectories may evolve from long established trading networks and be shaped by the specific socio-cultural ethos of the home communities. They may also originate in more recently created spaces at the centre. Here firms, that are national in the scope of their operations, have emerged with corporate forms of culture and business management. They maintain legal, bureaucratic relations with the state rather than privileged or clientilistic access or straddling relations. The rise of financial institutions in Nigeria is a case in point.

Relations between the state and private accumulation show much variation, with different combinations and relative weighting, over time. They range from acute dependence on forms of political accumulation to autonomy from the state and reliance on the market. Each linkage, or combination, has differ-ent implications for forms of accumulation, the individual strategies associated with them and the development of capitalist institutions. Access to the state and corruption are commonplace and unless specified more precisely and contextualised, their significance will remain unclear. In Kenya, we have noticed forms of straddling where positions are secured in the public domain and used to simultaneously develop private business. In Nigeria, cases where an initial stage of accumulation in the public sector leads to retirement and the pursuit of essentially private trajectories are much more important. Other cases, where primary accumulation occurs outside the state and is maintained, or is followed by occasional, limited access to the state have also come to our attention. All these cases can co-exist with other forms where entrepreneurs actively seek access to state resources, adopt strategies of avoidance, or acquire existing assets through more predatory forms of behaviour.

Before we conclude with some observations about accumulation in different national contexts, we examine the views of Jean-Francois Bayart.[23] Bayart gives primacy to politics and attempts to find a common paradigm for African politics and accumulation. While all the logics that Bayart presents exist in Nigeria, they are not as pervasive, or as dominant, as he suggests. At the centre of his account is a close link between power and the acquisition of wealth. Access to positions of power, whether in the state or more local forms of authority, are seen as central to strategies of accumulation and social mobility. Here Bayart gives prominence to the practice of straddling between private and public domains which is a major mechanism linking power and wealth. The pursuit of private business interests is combined with salaried positions and public office in the public sector. Boundaries are blurred, through overlapping and constant interaction and the two domains come to share the same ethos of personal enrichment and munificence. In addition, Bayart invokes a powerful logic of extraversion which turns profit making away from the exploitation of the domestic economy towards the acquisition of external resources by power holders who control points of access to the international economy.[24]

The result of these processes is an economy of profit and political predation in which rents, licences, contracts, sinecures, privileged access to credit, private appropriation of existing assets and unproductive forms of accumulation, loom large. There is little or no autonomous private accumulation of capital, merely, the personal acquisition of wealth through multiple interactions between private and public channels and the domestic and international economies. All this does not augur well for the economic future of Africa. In a characteristic provocation, Bayart informs his readers that political predation has become systematised and the African continent is being erased from the map of world capitalism.[25]

Bayart's view of accumulation through access to power leads him to recognise private accumulation only under exceptional circumstances. An escape from the logic of political accumulation and the control exercised by an emergent, dominant class may occur as a result of sheer territorial and demographic scale, which makes control difficult. Yet the divergent cases of Nigeria and Zaire suggest that state/civil society relations are more fundamental than scale in determining the size of the social space open for private accumulation. It can also result from the existence of extremely wealthy and powerful individuals who can resist the state. This begs the question of how they grew and freed themselves in the first instance. The only other case of autonomous accumulation mentioned is that of older private commercial networks like the Bamileke and Bamenda businessmen of the Cameroon Grassfields, who are relatively independent of the political and administrative elite and have a disciplined and ascetic lifestyle. Here a local hierarchy of notability and status affects access to land, the concentration of capital through rotating credit associations, paternalistic forms of business management and control over the labour of junior persons.[26]

Bayart's blurring of the public and private domains through hybridisation and complementarity and his emphasis on extraversion and transnational mobility lead him to misinterpret the phases of indigenisation and privatisation in Nigeria and to oversimplify relations between local and foreign capital.[27] The nationalist impulse behind the indigenisation decrees in Nigeria cannot be reduced to the acquisition of assets by elements of dominant class whose relations of extraversion and collaboration with foreign capital ensure a non-conflictual, non-antagonistic relation with foreign capital. Likewise, it is erroneous to interpret privatisation simply as another opportunity for acquisitive political predators to acquire existing assets and consolidate their power and wealth from within the interstices of the state. Privatisation like indigenisation, has, in some instances, promoted the private accumulation of capital outside the state. Finally, the capacity to use external links to acquire foreign technology in order to build up domestic production has no place in Bayart's logic of extraversion.

Bayart's views may be more appropriate to francophone Africa than anglophone West Africa. One factor at work is the legacy of French colonial rule and neo-colonial tutelage with its strong political, economic (including the franc zone), technical and military linkages between France and Africa. Tight central control and policing was maintained over local societies. Over time this has encouraged state-centred patterns of accumulation and wealth that have left less space for private accumulation. It has also contributed to more coherent economic management and the longevity of civilian regimes. A broad contrast can be drawn between neighbouring pairs of states, Senegal and the Gambia, Côte d'Ivoire and Ghana, and Cameroon and Nigeria.[28]

For Kenya, it has been argued that the business class that acquired land and labour in the colonial period was able to extend control to large-scale agriculture with the assistance of legislation and administrative action.[29] From there, it started to enter other sectors including industry, the import/export trade, tourism, banking and other services. In the mid-1970s, economic nationalist pressures surfaced within the ruling party and the Kenya National Chamber of Commerce.[30] These advances took place under the political hegemony of President Kenyatta and the Kikuyu were particularly favoured. Individuals would use their position in the state to acquire existing assets, get credit, profit from state monopolies and get preferential access to licences. Observers saw the process of straddling by bureaucrats and politicians as favourable to the advance of private capital and a source of Kenya's exceptionalism.[31] The leading role of Indian capital in promoting industrial development was largely ignored by analysts at the time, perhaps because the Indian community was not seen as a stable political presence.

After President Moi came to power in 1979, the minority Kalenjin group was favoured and started to enrich themselves. More predatory forms of political accumulation were fastened on to existing tiers of patronage exercised through control of import licences and foreign exchange, grain milling and distribution, and the parastatals. More personalised, authoritarian structures narrowed the channels for private accumulation outside the state, checking advances and the opportunities for more private trajectories. Individuals who lacked political support could find their industrial projects suddenly undermined by an influx of imports. The growth of some larger indigenous companies was inhibited and their asset bases became swollen relative to turnover.

While land remained the most reliable form of accumulation for wealthy Kenyans, strategies became more short term, rentier and commercial. Trading interests were favoured over industrial interests which lacked political muscle.[32] Profits from trade sparked a property boom which led to the collapse of prices and unsold office space. There was greater capital flight abroad sometimes linked to the financing of international projects. With one or two exceptions, private banks that were launched in the mid-1980s and early 1990s used parastatal funds and proved vulnerable to political faction fighting.

Under these conditions, the persistence of straddling is better seen as a response to uncertainty and the high political risks attached to large-scale enterprise. It has been reinforced by the decline in real incomes in the public sector.

In Zaire, the predatory, acquisitive nature of the ruling class is seen as quite inimicable to its functions of providing the conditions for sustained capitalist accumulation. Here private accumulation has been undertaken by producers in the second economy outside the hegemony of the ruling class.[33] In Senegal, a dominant rentier class, that was created through state patronage and clientilist mechanisms of control, is held to have blocked productive patterns of private investment.[34]

In the Côte d'Ivoire, the group of indigenous cocoa planters who emerged after 1945, developed political links with ruling groups and did not go on to establish strong private trajectories of accumulation in other fields.[35] The 'entrepreneurial planters' are absentee landowners, who belong to the political and administrative elite of the towns. An independent Ivoirian commercial class has not arisen from the import, export and wholesale trades.[36] A strong Lebanese presence persists in cocoa and coffee buying. A select group of Ivoiriens, the 'Abidjan' elite, who have extensive holdings in real estate and shares in agro-industry, commerce and industry, have relied on political connection and access to the centralised state for the acquisition of wealth. The political class and bureaucracy have created and shaped these opportunities for private accumulation through political patronage and state policies.

A very different view of the Côte d'Ivoire is provided by John Rapley who sees a well organised indigenous bourgeoisie effectively controlling the state and creating a favourable climate for private business.[37] The dominant role of the state was transitional. The business class, which has emerged partly from agriculture, urban real estate and shareholding, and partly from the civil service and parastatals, is actively engaged in accumulation across a wide range of activities.

In Nigeria, the state is not so central to the process of private accumulation as to warrant the adoption of any of the above perspectives. All of them tend to draw the link between private accumulation and the state too tightly. While many instances of political accumulation and privileged private access to the fruits of state policies like indigenisation, privatisation and the earlier loans programme can be found, the advances we have outlined have not been critically dependent on them. The fact that state office and resources are often used for private purposes and that an issueless, patronage-based, money politics is pervasive, does not preclude substantial private productive accumulation. Our work conducted at enterprise level, suggests the need to recognise that there are political and social spaces in which long-run, private trajectories of accumulation take place to a large extent independent of the state and those who control it.

The precise role of the state has varied across different locations and communities and at the risk of oversimplification, some comparisons can be made between Igboland and Yorubaland. In Igboland, access to the state for the purpose of accumulation has generally played a smaller role. A strong private trading diaspora which was established in the colonial period provided the basis for recovery after the civil war and movement to industry, services and agriculture. The opportunity for social mobility by individuals in the community through accumulation of wealth was greater in Igbo society and the need for investment in relations of seniority less compelling. In some communities, like Nnewi and Abiriba, with a long tradition of trade and community autonomy, reliance on state patronage for business has been negligible. It is not a coincidence that these communities have been in the vanguard of recent efforts to industrialise. Exclusion from power and fewer opportunities for state patronage have also played a part. There was the loss of political office and bureaucratic and parastatal employment in the wider Federation with the outbreak of the civil war. The government of Michael Okpara in the former Eastern Region was more favourable to private enterprise than the Action Group in the West.[38] No large state investment corporation similar to the New Nigeria Development Company in Kaduna or the Odu'a Investment Company in Ibadan emerged in the East.

In the western states, the opportunities and attractions of state employment and patronage have been greater. The perception of business opportunities and orientation of economic activity was less resolutely private and more oriented towards government patronage. The Yoruba trading diaspora was less extensive and trading practices less tightly organised and competitive than in Igboland, allowing, for example, considerable penetration by Lebanese traders. The incidence of 'clerkly' occupations and straddling across government and foreign-company employment and private business was probably higher than in Igbo communities, even amongst the Ijebu, the Yoruba group most strongly involved in trade.[39] There was, too, the dominance of cocoa which tended to bring trade and the bureaucracy closer together. Yoruba people in their proximity to Lagos and with their head start in education and the professions were able to take first advantage of the opportunities to join boards of foreign companies and parastatals, and patronise the Lagos Stock Exchange. These investments built on the rentier and professional presence that already existed in Lagos. The high level of financial resources available to the former Western Region government and the Fabian developmental programme of the Action Group and stronger party structures were also instrumental in impeding private initiatives and diverting private energies towards political connection and the state.

In this study we have generally given a more positive view of the advances made by indigenous capital in Nigeria than previous writers. At the enterprise level, we have shown that the constraints thought to impede the growth of firms are less binding. At the macro-level, the often remarked negative features of Nigerian political economy – distributive struggles over centralised oil rent, uncontrolled borders, extensive corruption, the decline in public morality and security, the inconsistency of government policies, the overbearing bureaucracy, and the weight of political patronage – have not proved as adverse to private capital accumulation as commonly supposed. Yet this study should not be taken as a signal to swing the pendulum very far in the opposite direction. It is not claimed that a rapid economic transformation is underway with indigenous capital playing a leading role. At the very least, the contribution of foreign capital, including the Indian and Lebanese components, would have to be assessed. The amalgam of elements that make up the Nigerian advance defies any easy summary or blanket generalisation about the prospects for capitalism or a market society. In the past, such statements have obscured more than they have revealed. The reality is altogether more complicated and the future more open and less predictable.

NOTES

CHAPTER 1

1. The main exception to this statement is the thesis on Kano by 'Bayo Olukoshi. A. O. Olukoshi, 'The multinational corporation and industrialisation in Nigeria: a case study of Kano', unpublished Ph.D. thesis, University of Leeds, 1986. An earlier work was Peter Kilby's study of the bread industry. P. Kilby, *African Enterprise: the Nigerian Bread Industry*, Stanford, Hoover, 1965. See, also E. O. Akeredolu-Ale, *The Underdevelopment of Indigenous Entrepreneurship in Nigeria*, Ibadan, Ibadan University Press, 1975.

2. Swainson's work on indigenous enterprise in Kenya tends to focus on share ownership, directorships and company registration. She stresses, as do others, the centrality for accumulation of the process of straddling between permanent official employment and other private business interests. The importance of state support for the advance of indigenous capital is also given great emphasis. N. Swainson, *The Development of Corporate Capitalism in Kenya, 1918–1977*, London, Heinemann, 1980.

3. D. Himbara, 'Myths and realities of Kenyan capitalism', *Journal of Modern African Studies*, 31, 1, 1993, pp. 93–107.

4. Important contributions to the debate were: N. Swainson, 'The rise of a national bourgeoisie in Kenya', *Review of African Political Economy*, 8, 1977; C. Leys, 'Capital accumulation, class formation and dependency: the significance of the Kenya case', in J. Saville and B. Miliband (eds), *Socialist Register 1978*, London, 1979; C. Leys, 'Kenya: what does "dependency" explain?', *Review of African Political Economy*, 17, 1980; R. Kaplinsky, 'Capitalist accumulation in the periphery – the Kenyan case re-examined', *Review of African Political Economy*, 17, 1980, pp. 83–105; S. Langdon, 'Industry and capitalism in Kenya: contributions to a debate', in P. Lubeck (ed.), *The African Bourgeoisie: Capitalist Development in Nigeria, Kenya and the Ivory Coast*, Boulder, Lynne Rienner, 1987 (originally presented in 1980); a critique of the debate is given by Bjorn Beckman in 'Imperialism and capitalist transformation: critique of a Kenyan debate', *Review of African Political Economy*, 19, 1980, pp. 48–62. For a trenchant analysis of the whole debate, its background, and the essential reading, see the article by Gavin Kitching, 'Politics, method and evidence in the "Kenya debate"', in H. Bernstein and B. K. Campbell (eds), *Contradictions of Accumulation in Africa*, Beverly Hills, Sage, 1985; For Leys' later views, see *Learning from the Kenya debate*, Sheffield Papers in International Studies, 15, University of Sheffield, 1992.

5. S. Berry, *Fathers Work for their Sons: Accumulation, Mobility and Class Formation*

in an Extended Yoruba Community, Berkeley and Los Angeles, University of California Press, 1985, pp. 8–13, 66–7, 75–81, 188–90.

6. J. Iliffe, *The Emergence of African Capitalism*, London, Macmillan, 1983.
7. T. McCaskie, 'Accumulation, wealth and belief in Asante history, Part 2, The 20th century', *Africa*, 56, 1, 1986.
8. A. A. Mazrui. 'Privatisation versus the market:cultural contradictions in structural adjustment', in H. B. Hansen and M. Twaddle (eds), *Changing Uganda*, London, James Currey, 1991. J.-F. Bayart, *The State in Africa: The Politics of the Belly*, London, Longman, 1993.
9. C. C. Wrigley, 'Aspects of economic history', in A. Roberts (ed.), *The Colonial Moment in Africa: Essays on the Movement of Minds and Materials 1900–1940*, Cambridge, Cambridge University Press, 1990, pp. 126–7.
10. Most notably in his essay, 'Rival views of market society'. A. O. Hirschman, *Rival Views of Market Society and Other Recent Essays*, Cambridge, Harvard University Press, 1992.
11. See the references cited in A. G. Hopkins, 'Imperial business in Africa, Part I: Sources' and 'Part 2: Interpretations', *Journal of African History*, 18, 1976, 29–48, 276–90; A. G. Hopkins, 'Big business in African studies', *Journal of African History*, 28, 1987.
12. A. G. Hopkins, 'Big business in African studies'.
13. International Labour Organisation (ILO), *Employment, Incomes and Equality: A Strategy for Increasing Productive Employment in Kenya*, Geneva, ILO, 1972.
14. S. Berry, *Fathers Work for their Sons*, pp. 136–7. For a recent example of developmental populism combined with a belief in market deregulation see, W. Elkan, 'Entrepreneurs and entrepreneurship in Africa', *Research Observer*, 3, 2, 1988. Elkan argues that African entrepreneurship is best suited to small scale enterprise and has been impeded by state subsidies and protection that have favoured the growth of larger scale enterprises.
15. J. MacGaffey, *Entrepreneurs and Parasites: The Struggle for Indigenous Capitalism in Zaire*, Cambridge, Cambridge University Press, 1987; J. MacGaffey, *The Real Economy of Zaire: The Contribution of Smuggling and Other Unofficial Activities to National Wealth*, London, James Currey, 1991.
16. P. Kilby, *Industrialisation in an Open Economy: Nigeria 1945–1966*, Cambridge, Cambridge University Press, chapter 10; E. O. Akeredolu-Ale, *The Underdevelopment of Indigenous Entrepreneurship in Nigeria*; S. P. Schatz, *Nigerian Capitalism*, Berkeley, University of California Press, 1977.
17. P. C. Garlick, *African Traders and Economic Development in Ghana*, Oxford, Oxford University Press, 1971.
18. J. R. Harris, 'Nigerian entrepreneurship in industry', in C. K. Eicher and C. Liedholm (eds), *Growth and Development of the Nigerian Economy*, Michigan, 1970.
19. P. Kilby, *Industrialisation in an Open Economy: Nigeria 1945–66*, pp. 341–2.
20. S. Berry, *Fathers Work for their Sons*, chapter 6.
21. F. Cooper, 'Africa and the world economy', *African Studies Review*, 24, 2 and 3, 1981, p. 49.
22. W. M. Freund, *The Making of Contemporary Africa: The Development of African Society Since 1800*, London, Macmillan, 1984, pp. 241–3.
23. L. Diamond, J. J. Linz, and S. M. Lipset (eds), *Democracy in Developing Countries*, vol. 2, *Africa*, Boulder, Lynne Rienner, 1988, pp.84–5.
24. C. Leys, 'African economic development in theory and practice', *Daedalus*, 3, 1982, p. 113.
25. T. M. Callaghy, 'The state and the development of capitalism in Africa:

theoretical, historical, and comparative reflections', in D. Rothchild and N. Chazan (eds), *The Precarious Balance: State and Society in Africa*, Boulder, Westview, 1988.

26. S. P. Schatz, 'Pirate capitalism and the inert economy of Nigeria', *Journal of Modern African Studies*, 22, 1, 1984.
27. S. Berry, *Fathers Work for their Sons*, pp. 7–11, 82–3, 192–4.
28. R. A. Joseph, *Democracy and Prebendal Politics in Nigeria: The Rise and Fall of the Second Republic*, Cambridge, Cambridge University Press, 1987, pp. 55–7 and chapter 6.
29. J.-F. Bayart, *The State in Africa: The Politics of the Belly*, pp. 80–1, 87, 90–7, 103. According the Bayart, the space for private accumulation stems from three sources: the existence of old commercial networks; sheer demographic or geographic scale, which makes control difficult; and economic scale in terms of private finance, industry or individual wealth that is strong enough to stand up to interference by those in power.
30. J.-F. Médard, 'Le "Big Man" en Afrique: equisse d'analyse du politicien entrepreneur', *L'année sociologique*, 42, 1992.
31. P. T. Bauer, *Economic Analysis and Policy in Underdeveloped Countries*, London, Routledge, Kegan and Paul, 2nd edn, 1965, pp. 11–14.
32. A. Sen, 'Description as choice' in *Choice, Welfare and Measurement*, Oxford, Blackwell, pp. 432–48.
33. E. L. Inanga, *History of Akintola Williams & Co, 1952–1992*, Lagos, West African Book Publishers, 1992.
34. M. Young, 'The contributions of women to national development with special reference to business', in J. Akande, O. Jegede, C. Osinulu and F. D. Oyekanmi (eds), *The Contribution of Women to National Development in Nigeria*, Nigerian Association of University of Women, 1990.
35. The main difficulties I encountered were with a few younger informants who had recently accumulated wealth through corrupt means.
36. There is a paradox here. In the struggle to legitimate themselves through lavish entertainment and title taking, some young people succeed only in raising questions about the origins of their wealth.
37. W. G. Runciman, *A Treatise on Social Theory*, vol. 2, *Substantive Social Theory*, Cambridge, Cambridge University Press, 1989, p. 78.

CHAPTER 2

1. C. Gertzel, 'Relations between African and European traders in the Niger Delta 1880–1896', *Journal of African History*, 3, 2, 1962, pp. 361–6.
2. A. G. Hopkins, 'An economic history of Lagos 1880–1914', Unpublished Ph.D. thesis, University of London, 1964, pp. 41–2.
3. Among them were J. P. L. Davies, Samuel and Josiah Crowther, and J. S. Leigh. A. Olukoju, 'Elder Dempster and the shipping trade of Nigeria during the First World War', *Journal of African History*, 33, 2, 1992, pp. 257.
4. C. Newbury, 'Trade and technology in West Africa: the case of the Niger Company, 1900–1920', *Journal of African History*, 19, 4, 1978, p. 555.
5. W. I. Ofonagoro, *Trade and Imperialism in Southern Nigeria, 1881–1929*, New York, Nok Publishers International, 1979, pp. 397–8.
6. A. G. Hopkins, 'Richard Beale Blaize 1854–1904: merchant prince of West Africa', *Tarikh*, 1, 2, 1966, p. 73.
7. A. G. Hopkins, 'The Lagos Chamber of Commerce 1888–1903', *Journal of the Historical Society of Nigeria*, 3, 2, 1965, p. 243.

8. A. G. Hopkins, 'An economic history of Lagos', pp. 394–6.
9. A. G. Hopkins, 'The Lagos chamber of commerce', p. 247.
10. A. G. Hopkins, 'An economic history of Lagos', p. 433–7.
11. Another relatively early hotel owner was the Igbo gold prospector, Chief Green Mbadiwe from Arondizuogu. He opened Greens Hotel along Ahmadu Bello Way, Kaduna in 1939. The hotel closed in 1957 when the site was redeveloped. *National Concord*, 16 March 1992.
12. A. Macmillan, *The Red Book of West Africa*, London, Frank Cass, 1920, reprinted 1968, pp. 95–6.
13. C. Newbury, 'Trade and technology in West Africa', p. 560.
14. A. Olukoju, 'Elder Dempster and the shipping trade of Nigeria during the First World War', p. 261.
15. For details of Sir Alfred Jones' interests and the growth of monopoly, see W. I. Ofonagoro, *Trade and Imperialism in Southern Nigeria, 1881–1929*, New York, Nok Publishers International, 1979, ch. 8.
16. J. Mars, 'Extra-territorial enterprises', in M. Perham (ed.), *Mining, Commerce and Finance in Nigeria*, London, Faber and Faber, 1948, p. 52.
17. P. T. Bauer, *West African Trade: A Study of Competition, Oligopoly and Monopoly in a Changing Economy*, Cambridge, Cambridge University Press, 1954, p. 123.
18. J. G. Deutsch, '"Educating the middlemen", a political and economic history of statutory cocoa marketing in Nigeria, 1936–1947', Ph.D. thesis, University of London, 1990, pp. 74–5.
19. A. G. Hopkins, 'Economic aspects of political movements in Nigeria and in the Gold Coast 1918–1939', *Journal of African History*, 7, 1966, pp. 138–9.
20. J. G. Deutsch, '"Educating the middlemen"', pp. 33–4.
21. J. G. Deutsch, '"Educating the middlemen"', p. 54.
22. P. T. Bauer, *West African Trade*, p. 190.
23. A. G. Hopkins, 'Economic aspects of political movements', p. 139 and p. 145.
24. This argument has been advanced by Laurens van der Laan, who notes that lorries became more competitive at the expense of rail and river transport. H. van der Laan, 'Modern inland transport and the European trading firms in colonial West Africa', *Cahiers d'études africaines*, 84, 1981, pp. 567–70.
25. For the early history of the bread industry see, P. Kilby, *African Enterprise: The Nigerian Bread Industry*, Stanford, Hoover Institute, 1965.
26. J. D. Y. Peel, *Ileshas and Nigerians: The Incorporation of a Yoruba Kingdom, 1890s-1970s*, Cambridge, Cambridge University Press, 1983, pp. 130–45.
27. J. Hogendorn, *Nigerian Groundnut Exports*, Zaria, Ahmadu Bello University Press, 1978, pp. 82–5.
28. F. Ekejiuba, 'Omu Okwei, the merchant queen of Ossomari. A biographical sketch', *Journal of the Historical Society of Nigeria*, 3, 4, 1967, pp. 633–46.
29. This section draws on my book, *Politics and Economic Development in Nigeria*, Boulder, Westview, 1993, ch. 2.
30. Large-scale slave plantations, owned by the aristocracy and rich merchants, were a prominent feature of the Sokoto Caliphate in the nineteenth century. In some areas, title holders controlled large farms throughout the colonial period and later. P. E. Lovejoy, 'The characteristics of plantations in the nineteenth-century Sokoto Caliphate (Islamic West Africa)', *American Historical Review*, 84, 5, 1979; P. E. Lovejoy and J. S. Hogendorn, *Slow Death for Slavery*, Cambridge, Cambridge University Press, 1993, pp. 129–34.
31. P. Hill, 'The lack of an agrarian hierarchy in pre-colonial West Africa', chapter

16 in *Dry Grain Farming Families – Hausaland (Nigeria) and Kanakata (India) Compared*, Cambridge, Cambridge University Press, 1982.

32. G. Williams, 'Why is there no agrarian capitalism in Nigeria?', *Journal of Historical Sociology*, 1, 4, 1988, p. 360.

33. On colonial land policy and the plantation issue, see A. Phillips, *The Enigma Of Colonialism: British Policy in West Africa*, London, James Currey, 1989.

34. S. Berry, *Fathers Work for their Sons: Accumulation, Mobility and Class Formation in an Extended Yoruba Community*, Berkeley, University of California Press, 1985, p. 30.

35. J. D. Y. Peel, *Ijeshas and Nigerians*, p. 128.

36. S. M. Martin, *Palm Oil and Protest: An Economic History of the Ngwa Region of South-Eastern Nigeria, 1800–1980*, Cambridge, Cambridge University Press, 1988, pp. 86–9.

37. P. Drummond-Thompson, 'The rise of entrepreneurs in Nigerian motor transport: a study in indigenous enterprise', paper presented to African History Seminar, SOAS, London, 1991.

38. 'Commemoration. Benjamin Fagbemi Mabinuori Dawodu', *Guardian* (Lagos), 6 February 1992.

39. A. G. Hopkins, 'An economic history of Lagos', pp. 370–2.

40. P. Drummond-Thompson, 'The rise of entrepreneurs in Nigerian motor transport'.

41. G. O. Olusanya, 'Charlotte Olajumoke Obasa', in B. Awe (ed.), *Nigerian Women in Historical Perspective*, Lagos and Ibadan, Sankore/Bookcraft, 1992, pp. 111–13.

42. G. O. Olusanya, 'Charlotte Olajumoke Obasa', p. 119.

43. P. O. Sada and A. A. Adefolalu, 'Urbanisation and problems of urban development', in A. B. Aderibigbe (ed.), *Lagos: The Development of an African City*, Ibadan, Longman, pp. 98–100.

44. For an account of J. N. Zarpas in the 1950s see, G. Walker, *Traffic and Transport in Nigeria*, London, HMSO, 1959, pp. 267–9.

45. J. D. Y. Peel, *Ijeshas and Nigerians*, pp. 134–5.

46. P. Drummond-Thompson, 'The rise of entrepreneurs in Nigerian motor transport'.

47. S. Silverstein, 'Socio-cultural organisation and locational strategies of transport entrepreneurs: an ethno-economic history of the Nnewi Igbo of Nigeria', Ph.D. thesis, Boston University, 1983, pp. 156–7.

48. T. Falola, 'Lebanese traders in southwestern Nigeria, 1900–1960', *African Affairs*, 89, 357, 1990, pp. 525–7.

49. A. G. Hopkins, 'An Economic History of Lagos', pp. 406–7.

50. T. Falola, 'Lebanese traders', Table 2, p. 533.

51. T. Falola, 'Lebanese traders', pp. 526–8, 540–9.

52. T. Falola, 'Lebanese traders', p. 526.

53. H. V. Merani and H. L. van der Laan, 'The Indian Traders in Sierra Leone', *African Affairs*, 78, 311, 1979, p. 241.

54. P. Kilby, *African Enterprise: the Nigerian Bread Industry*, Stanford, Hoover Institution, 1965, pp. 7–8.

55. *West Africa*, 11 February 1961, p. 145. Kweku Biney also owned a nightclub and a zoo in Yaba. The largest Nigerian dock-labour contractor in the 1950s was S. B. Bakare & Son, owned by Chief S. B. Bakare (b. 1922) from Ilesha. Bakare bought some sheds at Apapa and Lagos port from W. Biney & Co.

56. P. T. Bauer, *West African Trade*, p. 69.

57. P. T. Bauer, *West African Trade*, p. 220.

58. F. Longe, *A Rare Breed: The Story of Chief Timothy Adeola Odutola*, Lagos, Academy Press, 1981, pp. 30–1.
59. F. Longe, *A Rare Breed*, pp. 25–6.
60. T. Falola, 'Lebanese traders', p. 530.
61. S. Osoba, 'The phenomenon of labour migration in the era of British colonial Rule: a neglected aspect of Nigeria's social history', *Journal of the Historical Society of Nigeria*, 4, 4, 1969, p. 537.
62. A. O. Olukoshi, 'Some remarks on the role of the Levantine bourgeoisie in the capitalist industrialisation of Kano', *Nigerian Journal of Political Science*, 4, 1 and 2, 1985, pp. 55–6.
63. T. Falola, 'Lebanese traders', pp. 550–1.
64. In the 1950s, tyre retreading firms were set up by the two Odutola brothers and by Mathias Ugochukwu.
65. Among the early Nigerian pools companies were Nigerpools, J. K. Randle Pools and P. J. Osoba.
66. G. K. Helleiner, *Peasant Agriculture, Government and Economic Growth in Nigeria*, Homewood, Illinois, Irwin, 1966, p. 248.
67. The literature on these schemes is usefully summarised by Peter Kilby in his *Industrialisation in an Open Economy: Nigeria 1945–66*, Cambridge, Cambridge University Press, 1969, chapter 10.
68. P. Kilby, *Industrialisation in an Open Economy*, p. 321.
69. C. C. Wrigley, 'The development of state capitalism in late colonial and post colonial Nigeria', mimeo, African Studies Association of the United Kingdom, Liverpool, 1974.
70. P. Kilby, unpublished report to the Federal Ministry of Commerce and Industry and the Western Nigerian Ministry of Trade and Industry, mimeo, pp. 7–8, 1962. Cited in J. R. Harris, 'Industrial entrepreneurship in Nigeria', Ph.D. thesis, Northwestern University, 1967, p. 356.
71. J. O'Connell, 'The political class and economic growth', in P. Kilby, *Industrialisation in an Open Economy: Nigeria 1945–66*, Cambridge, Cambridge University Press, 1969, p. 376; S. Osoba, 'The Nigerian power elite 1952–65', reprinted in P. C. W. Gutkind and P. Waterman (eds), *African Social Studies: A Radical Reader*, Heinemann, 1977 p. 368; C. C. Wrigley, 'Some aspects of the political economy of Nigeria', mimeo, Institute of Commonealth Studies, London, 1968.
72. John Harris cites two cases of very successful businessmen who deliberately withdrew from politics. J. R. Harris, 'Industrial entrepreneurship in Nigeria', pp. 224, 297.
73. E. O. Akeredolu-Ale, 'Nigerian entrepreneurs in the Lagos State: a study in the origins and performance of indigenous business leadership in a young economy', Ph.D. thesis, University of London, 1971, p. 190.
74. Proceedings of the 1977 Annual Seminar on Indigenisation, *Management in Nigeria*, vol. 1, 1978.
75. *Industrial Survey 1963*, Lagos Federal Office of Statistics.
76. Apart from British companies, the construction industry in Nigeria was notable for the early presence of Italian companies. Thus the Cappa family has been associated with construction in Lagos since 1931.
77. Professor A. C. Callaway, unpublished papers.
78. J. S. Coleman, *Nigeria: Background to Nationalism*, Berkeley, University of California Press, 1958, p. 90.
79. P. Kilby, *Industrialisation in an Open Economy*.
80. P. Kilby, 'Manufacturing in colonial Africa', in P. Duignan and L. H. Gann

(eds), *Colonialism in Africa 1870–1960*, vol. 4, *The Economics of Colonialism*, Cambridge, Cambridge University Press, 1975, p. 494.

81. P. Kilby, 'Manufacturing in colonial Africa', p. 494.
82. J. R. Harris, 'Industrial entrepreneurship in Nigeria', p. 131.
83. J. R. Harris, 'Industrial entrepreneurship in Nigeria', p. 123–4.
84. Alfred Rewane, a close political associate of Chief Awolowo, supplied food to the army and exported cow bones before he entered the timber trade in the 1950s. Later he promoted a series of companies at Sapele with the Seaboard Group of the United States. Although he was the largest single shareholder in these companies, he deliberately left management to foreign partners. Companies included West African Shrimps (1969), Life Flour Mills (1971) (the second flour mill in Nigeria following Flour Mills of Nigeria), Top Feeds (1977) and Deltapack. The same strategy was employed with a Swiss pharmaceutical company and with Ovaltine, the foreign beverage producer where he held 60 per cent of the equity. In addition, Rewane had interests in two casinos and a lace factory. Interview with Mr Ebison Rewane, Victoria Island, Lagos, March 1993.

    Joseph Asaboro, who married into the wealthy Thomas family, had a large saw-milling operation at Sapele which started in 1958. It employed over 1,000 workers and the investment was worth £268,000 in the early 1960s. He also owned extensive rubber plantations covering 3,884 acres and a rubber processing facility. See R. K. Udo, 'British policy in the development of export crops in Nigeria', *Nigerian Journal of Economic and Social Studies*, 9, 3, 1968, p. 311; A. Sokolski, *The Establishment of Manufacturing*, New York, Praeger, p. 342.

    M. I. Agbontaen started business in the rubber trade in the early 1940s, after returning from the Gold Coast. He then went into timber, exporting logs and experimenting with the export of sawn timber. Later, he concentrated on the local market, setting up a saw-milling operation and furniture company, Agbontaen Brothers Ltd. *Business*, July 1991, p. 111.
85. Chief Ben Sutherland, after he left school, worked with UAC Sawmills before becoming an agent for the Royal Navy. He was a major exporter of timber from Sapele and Lagos, using contractors from Benin and Ondo. He introduced Alfred Rewane to the timber trade in 1951.
86. 'A short biography of High Chief Samuel Akinbolaji Oladapo, MBE, the Lisa of Ondo.'
87. A. Sokolski, *The Establishment of Manufacturing in Nigeria*, p. 342.
88. Commonwealth Development Corporation, *Report and Accounts 1992*, London, p. 32. The CDC returned to Nigeria in 1992 after an absence of thirteen years. The CDC left Nigeria in 1979 after it had failed to gain exemption from the Nigerian Enterprises Promotion Decree.
89. Interviews with Alhaji S. O. Gbadamosi and Alhaji Garba Hamza.
90. P. Kilby, *Industrialisation in an Open Economy*, p. 83.
91. *New Nigerian* (Kaduna), 22 February 1979.
92. *Financial Post*, 14 April 1990 p. 28.
93. There were 250 wholly private firms and 19 joint ventures in which Nigerian interests were dominant, see J. R. Harris, 'Nigerian entrepreneurship in industry', in C. K. Eicher and C. Liedholm (eds), *Growth and Development of the Nigerian Economy*, Michigan, 1970, pp. 299–324. See also J. R. Harris, 'Industrial entrepreneurship in Nigeria'.
94. J. R. Harris, 'Industrial entrepreneurship in Nigeria', p. 164.
95. A. Sokolski, *The Establishment of Manufacturing*, p. 336.
96. These were small-scale manual operations employing 10 to 20 persons. By the

mid-1960s, most indigenous soft-drink bottlers had been put out of business by the arrival of large-scale, foreign-owned, automated plant.

97. United Development Trading Company, Ibadan. The company founded in 1933 by Chief Makanjuola had originally engaged in the produce trade. It also undertook kapok cleaning.

98. Nigerian Paper Converters, Apapa, started in 1962. It was a subsidiary of Nigerian Office and Stationery Supply Stores begun in 1944 and owned by the Adebajo family.

99. Denchukwu Ltd at Isieke Iheku near Enugu employed about 300 workers in various activities in 1963. In 1957, the proprietor, who had attended secondary school and developed an interest in science subjects, opened a quarry to supply limestone to a foreign construction firm. Soon after, he opened a second quarry to supply granite for a port extension project. Learning that Shell-BP was spending $3,000 daily to import drilling mud, he began to search for a local substitute. He found a satisfactory local clay and with Shell's assistance developed a satisfactory product, the bulk of which was sold to Shell from 1961. After experimentation, he also set up in 1963 a small emulsion paint factory whose product was recommended for use by government departments. He also developed a fertiliser which he supplied to the Ministry of Agriculture and a face powder. T. Geiger and W. Armstrong, *The Development of African Private Enterprise*, Washington, National Planning Foundation, 1964, pp. 139–40. A. Sokolski, *The Establishment of Manufacturing*, p. 295.

100. P. Kilby, *Industrialisation in an Open Economy*, p. 159.

101. D. E. Welsch, 'Rice marketing in eastern Nigeria', *Food Research Institute Studies*, 6, 3, 1966, pp. 331–2.

102. Mary Rowe, cited by P. Kilby, 'Manufacturing in Colonial Africa'.

103. E. O. Akeredolu-Ale, 'Nigerian enterprise in the Lagos state', pp. 262–3.

104. The UAC claimed that it had eight Nigerians in senior executive positions in 1961. A. Sokolski, *The Establishment of Manufacturing*, p. 91.

105. E. O. Akeredolu-Ale, 'Nigerian enterprise in the Lagos state', p. 274.

106. E. O. Akeredolu-Ale, 'Nigerian enterprise in the Lagos state', pp. 245, 261.

107. P. Kilby, *Industrialisation in an Open Economy*, p. 337.

108. M. P. Rowe and J. R. Harris, 'Entrepreneurial patterns in the Nigerian sawmilling industry', *Nigerian Journal of Economic and Social Studies*, 8, 1, 1966, p. 79.

109. Two other factors may be relevant to the decision to employ expatriates. First, there was some prestige attached to employing expatriates. Second, expatriate employment was sometimes preferred, when the option was employment of a Nigerian from another part of the country. In Kano and other northern business centres, indigenes often preferred to recruit expatriates rather than Nigerians from the South. This policy followed the more general practice of Northernisation, which was first applied to recruitment in the Northern Region public service.

110. O. Oni, 'Development and features of the Nigerian financial system: a Marxist approach', *Nigerian Journal of Economic and Social Studies*, 8, 3, 1966, p. 388.

111. D. Rowan, 'The native banking boom in Nigeria', *The Banker*, XCVII, 309, 1951, pp. 244–9.

112. D. Rowan, 'The native banking boom in Nigeria', p. 246.

113. G. Olusanya, *Fifty Years of National Bank of Nigeria Ltd. A Golden Jubilee Souvenir*, Lagos, 1983.

114. S. O. Banjo, 'Why National Bank must not be "scrapped"', *Sunday Times*, 17 May 1992.

115. Supplement on Chief A. G. Leventis, *New Nigerian*, 19 December 1978.
116. O. Oni, 'Development and features of the Nigerian financial system', p. 391.
117. *Sunday Concord*, 28 January 1990.
118. Chief J. Akin-George became a leading company director. Among his director-ships were Abiola & Sons Bottling Company, Cash Data Services, Ecobank Transnational Incorporated, Fountain Trust Merchant Bank, Gacol, Ikeja Hotels, JKN Construction, Kilpatrick, Liz Olofin, Marine and General Assurance, Milestone Investment Services, Poly Products and Afroil PLC.
119. *Financial Post*, 14 April 1990.
120. Personal communication.
121. For general accounts, see M. E. Zuckerman, 'Nigerian crisis: economic impact on the North', *Journal of Modern African Studies*, 8, 1, 1970, pp. 37–54; E. W. Nafziger, 'The economic impact of the Nigerian civil war', *Journal of Modern African Studies*, 10, 2, 1972, pp. 223–45.
122. *African Guardian*, 15 March 1993, p. 24.
123. A. Oraegbu, *Hamza!*, Lagos, Sovereign Publications, 1991, p. 41–5.
124. Waziri Ibrahim (1926–92) held senior management positions with the UAC of Nigeria in Jos, Lagos and Kano in the 1950s. He was a minister in the First Republic (1962–6). He was involved in fishing (Mesurado Fishing Company purchased from Stephen Tolbert), and the importation of frozen fish (Nigeria Cold Stores). He established Herwa tin mining in Jos and soap and flour mill industries in Maiduguri. In 1976 he opened the Herwa Clinic in Kano at the cost of N5m. with Dr Abubakar Imam. He was the founder and leader of the Great Nigeria People's Party and, according to his biographer, spent a total of N50m. on the 1979 and 1983 elections. His businesses went into decline after 1983. N. Anyaegbunam, *Waziri Ibrahim: Politics Without Bitterness*, Lagos, Daily Times, 1992, pp. 73–4, 81–4, 98.
125. *Commerce in Nigeria*, 11, 1969, pp. 20, 65.
126. Monetary Policy Circular 3, 1971.
127. Interview with Allison Ayida, Lagos, August 1982.
128. Further details of the decrees can be found in T. G. Forrest, *Politics and Economic Development in Nigeria*, pp. 153–7. The fullest account of the exercise is T. J. Biersteker, *Multinationals, the State and Control of the Nigerian Economy*, Princeton, Princeton University Press, 1987. I have drawn my figures on the value of share transfers from this source.
129. A. Hoogvelt, 'Indigenisation and foreign capital: industrialisation in Nigeria', *Review of African Political Economy*, 14, 1979, p. 62.
130. Adeosun Commission. As reported by Biersteker, *Multinationals*, Table 3.1b, p. 145.
131. Although not legally bound to do so, Bata Nigeria Ltd transferred 77 retail stores to Nigerians at the time of NEPD (Nigerian Enterprises Promotion Decree) 1972. Bata Nigeria Ltd, *Prospectus for Sale of Shares*, 1977, p. 3.
132. These companies were Deltapack at Sapele (1982), SIO Industries at Asaba (1988), and Bellhope Plastics at Port Harcourt (1988).
133. *Business Concord*, 7 March 1989.
134. *African Concord*, 28 September 1992.
135. *Sunday Vanguard* (Lagos), 15 March 1992.
136. *Business*, 3,2, 7 February 1990.
137. Major indigenous investments in hotels include Modotels (Dr Alex Ekueme), Ikeja Hotels (Ibru Organisation), Agura Hotel (Joseph Ayonmike), Alpha Sofitel (Jimi A. Lawal) and Rita Lori (Chief (Mrs) Rita Lori Ogbebor).

138. A leading owner is Chief Solomon Adebayo Ayoku with casinos in Lagos, Owerri and Abuja, and three restaurants in Lagos.
139. A pioneer of indigenous publishing in the late 1960s was Onibonoje Press and Book Industries of Ibadan. Others in the 1970s were Spectrum Books of Ibadan (Olu Akinkugbe and Joop Berkhout) and Fourth Dimension (Arthur Nwankwo) of Enugu. Some of the multinational publishers became effectively indigenised, for example, Heinemann Educational Books Nigeria Ltd under Aig Higo.
140. A study of 46 firms with Japanese equity that invested in Nigeria between 1964 and 1991 showed that 4 divestments occurred between 1980 and 1985 and 13 divestments between 1986 and 1992. This suggests that the devaluation of the naira, which accelerated after 1986, encouraged divestment. The scale, causes, and consequences of foreign divestment in Nigeria are in need of research. I owe this information to Kweku Ampiah.
141. The Iyayi Group, which was founded in the early 1960s by Mr Iyayi Efiananyi, employed 2,250 persons in 1992. It is one of the leading indigenous rubber exporters and has invested in new rubber plantations. Other activities include fishing, plywood manufacture and aluminium building materials. From about 1967, Mr Efiananyi began to improve the infrastructure in his home village of Igba and contribute to education and health facilities. *Corporate*, March 1992, pp. 141–3. Interview with Mr Emeka Ogbeide, Lagos, October 1993.
142. *African Concord*, 19 October 1992. Associations of indigenous companies have also been formed recently in shipping, in oil exploration and production, and in the pharmaceutical industry.
143. J. R. Harris, 'Nigerian entrepreneurship in industry', pp. 224–5.
144. A leading independent oil-marketing company was General Oil which began operations in 1981. By the end of the 1980s, it had built up a turnover of over N100m. and employed about 200 persons. It had diversified into bitumen and lubricants.
145. *Newswatch*, 17 February 1992, p. 26.
146. *Newswatch*, 17 February 1992, pp. 24–5.
147. C. Oraegbu, *Hamza!*, pp. 71–8.
148. Dubri Oil Company produces an average of 1,000 bpd. Staff strength is about 85. Personal communication from Dr U. J. Itsueli, April 1993.
149. For example, Aero Contractors, Pan African Airlines and Bristow Helicopters. *Business*, November 1991.
150. *West Africa*, 22 July 1985.
151. *African Business*, May 1979, p. 73.
152. *African Business*, May 1979, May 1980, July 1989.
153. *African Business*, August 1988, p. 21.
154. Further discussion of large-scale farming and land aquisition in Nigeria can be found in T. G. Forrest, *Politics and Economic Development in Nigeria*, pp. 196–200. Very little is known about the economic history of large-scale farms.
155. *New Nigerian*, 1 August 1985. For land and farming in the Sokoto area, see A. A. Labaran, 'Land appropriation and capitalist farming in the Sokoto region: some preliminary findings', in M. Mortimore, E. A. Olofin, R. A. Cline-Cole and A. Abdulkadir (eds), *Perspectives in Land Administration and Development in Northern Nigeria*, Kano, Bayero University Department of Geography, 1987; K. Swindell and A. B. Mamman, 'Land expropriation and accumulation in the Sokoto periphery, northwest Nigeria, 1976–86', *Africa*, 60, 2, 1990.
156. *New Nigerian*, 29 August 1985.
157. *New Nigerian*, 2 October 1985.

158. *New Nigerian*, 26 September 1985.
159. 'High profile farmers', *Newswatch*, 14 August 1989.
160. *African Concord*, 30 July 1990.
161. *Newswatch*, 14 August 1989.
162. *African Business*, May 1980, pp. 83–5.
163. C. Clarke, C. Peach and S. Vertovec (eds), *South Asians Overseas: Migration and Ethnicity*, Cambridge, Cambridge University Press, 1990, p. 2.
164. Address by Acting High Commissioner of India at Nigerian Institute of Policy Studies, *National Concord*, 26 August 1992.
165. For the development of the Chandaria Group see, R. Murray, 'The Chandarias: the development of a Kenyan multinational', in R. Kaplinsky (ed.), *Readings on the Multinational Corporation in Kenya*, Nairobi, OUP, 1978.
166. The following paragraph relies on an unpublished paper by Chief S. O. Asabia, 'The Nigerian banking system', mimeo, 1989, pp. 12–19.
167. Five new state banks owned by the Bendel, Cross River, Rivers, Kaduna and Kano State governments, opened between 1971 and 1975.
168. The Chairman of BCCI Nigeria Ltd (1979–89) was Alhaji Ibrahim Dasuki (b. 1923), former Chairman of the Northern Region Marketing Board (1966–9) and the Nigerian Railway Corporation (1969–77). In 1988, Ibrahim Dasuki became the Sultan of Sokoto. *Who's Who in Nigeria*, ed. Nyaknno Osso, Lagos, Newswatch, pp. 243–4. BCCI Nigeria Ltd changed its name to African International Bank Nigeria Ltd and became wholly owned by Nigerian private interests after the liquidation of BCCI Holdings (Luxembourg).
169. Societe Generale was an exception. Here one individual held 60 per cent of the equity.
170. *Nigeria Banking, Finance and Commerce*, 1991–2 edn, Lagos, Research and Data Services Ltd, 1992.
171. *Nigeria Banking, Finance and Commerce*, 1988–9, Lagos, Research and Data Services Ltd, 1988, pp. 145–6. The Nigerian investors, drawn from all parts of the country, included Chief C. S. Sankey, chairman and managing partner, Akintola Williams; Chief E. J. Amana, chairman of the Desam Group; Alhaji T. Dagazau, chairman of Dagazau International; Alhaji M. H. Koguna, an insurance broker from Kano; Chief A. O. Lawson, former chairman of Lagos State Development Board and West African Breweries; and Chief J. O. Udoji, former chief secretary and head of service, Eastern Region and former chairman of Nigeria Tobacco Company.
172. *Nigerian Enterprise*, 2, 4, November 1981.
173. *Business*, April 1992, p. 34.
174. Joseph Olabode Emanuel was also chairman of Eko International Bank, Ferodo, Hogg Robinson Nigeria, Macmillan Nigeria Publishers, Saipem (Nig.) Ltd, Tara Consulting Company, Trevi Foundations, West Africa Engineering Company, and director of Foremost Dairies and Incar (Nig.) Ltd.
175. *National Concord*, 9 September 1992.
176. Arthur Nzeribe was born in 1938 to a prominent Oguta family (Imo State). He attended Holy Ghost College, Owerri, and then got a Nigerian Ports Authority scholarship to study marine engineering in England in 1958. By 1960 he was selling life insurance to black immigrants in Britain. In the same year he met Kwame Nkrumah. He was then employed in public relations in London and Africa on behalf of Nkrumah. Within twelve months he purchased his first Rolls Royce. After Nkrumah fell in 1966, he worked with General Ankrah of the NLC to promote his regime through Jeafan

Ltd. When Colonel Afrifa came to power in 1969, he was asked to leave Ghana.

In 1969 he opened Travellers Bank in Guernsey and the following year the bank received $10m. from arms sales. Over the next 9 years, $95m. was to accrue. Nzeribe built up the Fanz Organisation based in London; it was involved in heavy construction, arms dealing, computers, oil brokerage, scientific and medical products, publishing and property investment. Much business was conducted with the Middle East and Gulf States. In 1979 Fanz had an annual trading turnover of £70m. and assets in excess of £120m. The UK property portfolio was worth £30m.

In Nigeria, Nzeribe built up Sentinel Assurance using expatriate managers. Many of his Nigerian companies were subsidised from abroad. In 1983 he spent N12m. to win a senatorial seat in Orlu. In 1993 Nzeribe was prominent as a supporter of the Association for a Better Nigeria which attempted to get General Ibrahim Babangida to stay on in power. (Dillibe Onyeama, *African Legend: The Incredible Story of Francis Arthur Nzeribe*, Enugu, Delta Publications, 1984, pp. 29, 50–4, 56–7, 63, 65, 92, 112; *African Business*, May 1980; *Newswave*, 11 December 1989.)

177. *The Guardian* (Lagos), 5 March 1989.
178. Eades estimated the Yoruba community in Ghana at over 200,000 persons in 1969. The great majority came from Oyo North, the Ogbomosho area, Offa and Ilorin. J. S. Eades, 'The growth of a migrant community: the Yoruba in Northern Ghana', in J. Goody (ed.), *Changing Social Structure in Ghana*, London, International African Institute, 1975, p. 39.
179. *Financial Times*, 2 August 1977.
180. *Le Soleil* (Dakar), 3 December 1980.
181. *African Guardian*, 15 March 1993, p. 25.
182. Nina E. Mba, *Ayo Rosiji: Man with Vision*, Ibadan, Spectrum Books, 1992, pp. 176–7.
183. *Business*, November 1992, p. 20.
184. For details of these problems, see *Business*, November 1992, pp. 20–5.
185. *Financial Post*, 14 April 1990.
186. *Business*, 5, 6, June 1993, pp. 53–6.
187. Interview with Mr Smart Binitie, Accra, March 1993.
188. *African Concord*, 2 November 1992, p. 33.

CHAPTER 3

1. See, F. Longe, *A Rare Breed: The Story of Chief Timothy Adeola Odutola*, Lagos, Academy Press, 1981.
2. E. A. Ayandele, 'The changing position of the Awujales of Ijebuland under colonial rule', in M. Crowder and Obaro Ikime (eds), *West African Chiefs: Their Changing Status under Colonial Rule and Independence*, University of Ife Press, 1970.
3. Much of the following narrative is drawn from F. Longe, *A Rare Breed*.
4. *West Africa*, 12 February, 1949, p. 129.
5. National Archives Washington, Record Group 84, Lagos Consulate, 1935, vol. 4, 610.1, cited in A. Harneit-Sievers, *Zwischen Depression und Dekolonisation: Afrikanische Handler und Politik in Sud-Nigeria 1935–1954*, Saarbruchen and Fort Lauderdale, Breitenbach Publications, 1991, p. 82.
6. E. A. Ayandele, *The Ijebu of Yorubaland 1850–1950: Politics, Economy and Society*, Ibadan, Heinemann, 1992, p. 210.

7. 333 tons of cocoa were exported in 1943. Palm-kernel exports were only a 0.31 per cent share of the total. M. Perham (ed.), *Mining, Commerce and Finance in Nigeria*, London, Faber, 1948, p. 56.
8. T. Falola, 'Cassava starch for export in Nigeria during the Second World War', *African Economic History*, 18, 1989.
9. J. G. Deutsch, '"Educating the middlemen", a political and economic history of statutory cocoa marketing in Nigeria, 1936–1947', Ph.D. thesis, University of London, 1990, p. 409.
10. E. A. Ayandele, *The Ijebu of Yorubaland*, p. 214.
11. E. A. Ayandele, *The Ijebu of Yorubaland*, p. 213.
12. A. Harneit-Sievers, *Zwischen Depression und Dekolonisation*, pp. 382–6.
13. Speech on the Appropriation Bill, 7 March 1950, cited in F. Longe, *A Rare Breed*, pp. 24–32.
14. A. A. B. Agbaje, *The Nigerian Press, Hegemony, and the Social Construction of Legitimacy*, Lewiston, Edwin Mellon Press, 1992, p. 150.
15. J. R. Harris, 'Industrial entrepreneurship in Nigeria', Ph.D. thesis, Northwestern University, 1967, p. 166.
16. Interview, Odutola Industries, Ijebu-Ode, March 1989.
17. J. R. Harris, 'Industrial entrepreneurship in Nigeria', p. 176.
18. Interview, Odutola Industries, Ijebu-Ode, March 1989.
19. The profile is based on interview at Ugochukwu & Sons, Apapa, November 1990, and supplemented with other sources.
20. R. L. Sklar, *Nigerian Political Parties*, New York, Nok, 1983, pp. 206, 221.
21. 'Igwe Ugochukwu: a tower of diligence', *Daily Times*, 13 July 1990.
22. *West Africa*, no. 2445, 11 April 1964.
23. Mbonu Ojike in his column in the *West African Pilot* called on his readers to 'boycott the boycottables' and do away with all forms of conspicuous consumption. He advised them to drink palm wine and not take imported spirits or beer and to boycott European dress. Mbonu Ojike, *My Africa*, London, Blandford Press, 1989. (originally published 1946, New York, John Day).
24. M. I. Okpara, 'Long live the Boycott King', in Ukwu I. Ukwu (ed.), *The Spirit of Self-Reliance, Mazi Mbonu Ojike Memorial Lectures*, Enugu, Institute for Development Studies, University of Nigeria, 1984, p. 19.
25. A. Harneit-Sievers, *Zwischen Depression und Dekolonisation*, pp. 303, 347, 349.
26. M. I. Okpara, 'Long live the Boycott King', p. 19.
27. See P. Kilby, *Industrialisation in an Open Economy: Nigeria 1945–1966*, Cambridge, Cambridge University Press, 1969. pp. 106–7.
28. *Daily Times*, 8 October 1992.
29. My account draws on the work of Peter Kilby ,'Manufacturing in colonial Africa' in P. Duignan and L. H. Gann (eds), *Colonialism in Africa 1870–1960*, vol. 4, *The Economics of Colonialism*, Cambridge, Cambridge University Press, 1975; and on the *Nigerian Eagle* (Onitsha), no. 4, July 1963.
30. D. E. Welsch, 'Rice marketing in eastern Nigeria', *Food Research Institute Studies*, 6,3, 1966.
31. My account draws on the work of Peter Kilby supplemented by a portrait in *West Africa* magazine and the writing of E. A. Ayandele. P. Kilby, 'Manufacturing in colonial Africa', pp. 514–15; *West Africa*, 17 April 1965; E. A. Ayandele, *The Ijebu of Yorubaland*, pp. 325–7.
32. 'Mr De Facto', *West Africa*, 17 April 1965, p. 421.
33. This account is based on an interview at Fawehinmi Furniture, Lagos, March 1990 and on 'Fawehinmi Furniture Factory Ltd', mimeo, no date.

34. Interview, Lisabi Mills, Lagos, November 1990.
35. H. Sodipo, *A Dynasty of 'Missioners'*, Ibadan, Spectrum Books, 1992, p. 123.
36. The following profile is based on a biography of Chief Bisoye Tejuoso by Omodele Karunwi, *A Woman Industrialist: A Biography of Chief (Mrs) Bisoye Tejuoso*, Lagos, Cowlad Ent., 1991.
37. E. E. Eribo (1916–82) was born in Benin. He attended Edo College, became a typist with UAC and a clerk in the Nigerian Railways (1941–6). He later established the Ribway Group of companies in Benin which included textiles, carpets, plastics, tyre retreading, construction, insurance brokerage, rubber products and a farm. None of these enterprises survived his death in 1982. *Africa Who's Who*, Africa Book Ltd, 2nd edn, 1991.
38. *West Africa*, no. 2078, 9 February 1957.
39. 'Sir Mobalaji Bank-Anthony: a Nigerian business icon', *Spear*, March 1986.
40. Communication from Dr Axel Harneit-Sievers.
41. *Spear*, March 1986.
42. *Spear*, March 1986.
43. I owe this information to Dr Axel Harneit-Sievers.
44. Obituary, *The Independent*, 1 June 1991.
45. Communication from Dr Axel Harneit-Sievers.
46. Other bilateral chambers of commerce did not follow until the late 1970s.
47. *West Africa*, 20 July 1963, no. 2407; *Who's Who in Nigeria*, ed. Nyaknno Osso, Lagos, Newswatch Communications Ltd, 1990.
48. *West Africa*, 18 July 1953, p. 653.
49. B. Odogwu, *No Place to Hide: Crisis and Conflicts Inside Biafra*, Enugu, Fourth Dimension, 1985, p. 249.
50. O. Orizu, *Inside Nnewi*, Onitsha, Ana-edo Trading Company Ltd, 1960.
52. Interview with Chief Jerome Udoji, Ozubulu, March 1992.
53. *The Guardian* (Lagos), 19 April 1987 and 3 May 1987.
53. *The Guardian* (Lagos), 19 April 1987 and 3 May 1987.
54. My account of Chief Edo-Osagie's career relies almost entirely on the writing of H. K. Offonry. H. K. Offonry, *Investment in Goodwill: The Story of a Nigerian Philanthropist*, Owerri, New Africa Publishing Company, 1987.
55. The *Comet* (1933–45), Nigeria's first news weekly, was Duse Mohammed Ali's most successful and enduring business venture. In the 1940s, it had a circulation of 8,000 and the Comet Press employed 70 persons. See J. Duffield, 'The business activities of Duse Mohammed Ali: an example of the economic dimension of Pan-Africanism, 1912–1945', *Journal of the Historical Society of Nigeria*, 4, 4, 1969, pp. 593–6.
56. In 1955 John Edokpolo set up a rubber-processing plant in Benin, investing £81,000. In the early 1960s, over 200 persons were employed. A. Sokolski, *The Establishment of Manufacturing in Nigeria*, New York, Praeger, 1965, p. 336.
57. This profile draws on A. U. Dan-Asabe, 'Comparative biographies of selected leaders of the Kano commercial establishment', MA thesis, Bayero University, 1987.
58. J. N. Paden, *Ahmadu Bello, Sardauna of Sokoto*, London, Hodder and Stoughton, 1986, p. 266.
59. Ibid., p. 147.
60. This section is based on Omole's autobiography and newspapers. L. Omole, *My Life and Times: Reflections*, Lagos, MIJ Professional Publishers for Cardinal Investments Ltd, 1991; *The Guardian* (Lagos), 26 April 1986 and 7 December 1988.

61. Osomaalo trade is discussed at length by John Peel. See J. D. Y. Peel, *Ijeshas and Nigerians: The Incorporation of a Yoruba Kingdom, 1890s–1970s*, Cambridge Cambridge University Press, 1983, pp. 147–59.

62. J. D. Y. Peel, *Ijeshas and Nigerians*, pp. 202–3.

63. The directors of the WRDLB were Chief T. A. Odutola of Ijebu-Ode, Chief W. E. Mowarin of Warri, Chief S. A. Oladapo of Ondo and Mr. E. A. Sanda of Ibadan.

64. T. A. Oni (1913–75) after his primary education, joined the Public Works Department (PWD) in 1930. He resigned in 1945 with £2,000 capital to set up as a civil engineering and construction company in Ibadan. In the mid-1950s, his firm had contracts worth £0.5m. In the early 1960s, the company along with two partnerships, Adebayo and Olatubosun, and Abdulai and Awomolo, were the only indigenous construction companies classified in category G, allowing them to bid for contracts of over £100,000. Four of his children were trained abroad with a view to joining the company. A metal-furniture factory was opened in 1965 and investments made in Lagos property, insurance and brewing. In 1973 the company merged with Royal Netherlands Harbourworks to form Harboni. The merger was never successful. Oni died in 1975 after illness and there were problems over sharing assets among the family. Apart from a family estate, the main public legacy of this very well known Ibadan firm is the T. A. Oni Memorial Hospital which was converted from Chief T. A. Oni's residence at his bequest. *West Africa*, 21 July 1962, p. 789; Interview with Mr Kunle Oni, Ibadan, April 1992; G. A. Ogunpola, 'The pattern of organisation in the building industry – a Western Nigeria case study', *Nigerian Journal of Economic and Social Studies*, 10, 3, 1968.

65. Interview with Alhaji S. O. Gbadamosi, Lagos, November 1990.

66. 'A patriot goes home', *Nigerian Economist*, 15 March 1993, p. 33.

67. I have drawn extensively on the account given by Peter Kilby in 'Manufacturing in colonial Africa', pp. 515–16.

68. *Business* (Lagos), July 1991, p. 31.

69. *Business* (Lagos), July 1991, p. 31.

70. See, P. Kilby, 'Manufacturing in colonial Africa', pp. 508–9; and A. A. Ayida, 'Contractor finance and supplier credit in economic growth', *Nigerian Journal of Economic and Social Studies*, 7, 2, 1965.

71. *West Africa*, 21 July 1962, p. 789.

72. R. L. Sklar, *Nigerian Political Parties*, p. 183.

CHAPTER 4

1. M. Peil, *Lagos: The City is the People*, London, Bellhaven Press, 1991, p. 19.

2. M. Peil, *Lagos*, p. 30.

3. M. Peil, *Lagos*, p. 30.

4. *Industrial Survey 1964*, Lagos Federal Office of Statistics. 'Large scale' refers to industry with ten employees or more.

5. Investments included Gacol in 1977 (Chief Akinrele) at Sango Otta; Marston Barrow Foods at Sango Otta in 1980; Isoglass Industries at Ibadan in 1979 (Chief I. O. Akinmokun); Bodefoam and Atlantic Carpets at Ibadan in 1979 (Chief J. O. Amao); Standard Breweries and Diamond Foods at Ibadan in 1981 (Chief Bode Akindele); Shokas Industries at Ijebu-Igbo in 1978 (Alhaji S. O. Kassim); International Breweries at Ilesha in 1978 (Lawrence Omole); Bisrod Furniture at Ijebu-Ode in 1978 (Chief Bisi Rodipe).

6. W. I. Ofonagoro, *Trade and Imperialism in Southern Nigeria, 1881–1929*, New York, Nok Publishers International, 1979, pp. 70–5.

7. The following paragraph relies entirely on Kristin Mann's excellent work. Kristin Mann, 'The rise of Taiwo Olowo: law, accumulation, and mobility in early colonial Lagos', in K. Mann and R. Roberts (eds), *Law in Colonial Africa*, London, James Currey, 1991.

8. My understanding here owes much to discussion with Kristin Mann.

9. A. G. Hopkins, 'Innovation in a colonial context: African origins of the Nigerian cocoa-farming industry, 1880–1920', in C. Dewey and A. G. Hopkins (eds), *The Imperial Imprint: Studies in the Economic History of Africa and India*, University of London, published for the Institute of Commonwealth Studies; London, Athlone Press, 1978, p. 88.

10. P. Cole, *Modern and Traditional Elites in the Politics of Lagos*, Cambridge, Cambridge University Press, 1975, pp. 89–97.

11. J. R. Harris, 'Industrial entrepreneurship in Nigeria', Ph.D thesis, Northwestern University, pp. 154–5.

12. A. Sokolski, *The Establishment of Manufacturing in Nigeria*, New York, Praeger, p. 91.

13. S. Barnes, *Patrons and Power: Creating a Political Community in Metropolitan Lagos*, London, Manchester University Press for the International African Institute, 1986, pp. 67–9.

14. P. H. Baker, *Urbanisation and Political Change: The Politics of Lagos 1917–1967*, Berkeley, University of California Press, 1974, pp. 85–7.

15. E. O. Akeredolu-Ale, 'A socio-historical study of the development of entrepreneurship among the Ijebu of western Nigeria', *African Studies Review*, 16, 3, 1973, pp. 347–65.

16. E. O. Akeredolu-Ale, 'A socio-historical study of the development of entrepreneurship', pp. 362–3.

17. E. A. Ayandele, *The Ijebu of Yorubaland 1850–1950: Politics, Economy, and Society*, Ibadan, Heinemann, 1992, p. 325.

18. Enterprises include The Ibru Organisation, Maiden Electronics, Odogwu Group, Okada Group, and South Atlantic Seafood Company.

19. J. R. Harris, 'Nigerian entrepreneurship in industry', in K. Eicher and C. Liedholm (eds), *Growth and Development of the Nigerian Economy*, Michigan, 1970, p. 308.

20. *Who's Who in Nigeria*, ed. Nyaknno Osso, Lagos, Newswatch Communications Ltd, p. 437.

21. Henry Stephens Group of Companies, Group Public Relations Department of Henry Stephens, Lagos, n.d.

22. Nigeria-British Chamber of Commerce, *1991 Directory*, Lagos, p. 5.

23. I. B. Jose, *Walking a Tightrope: Power Play in the Daily Times*, Ibadan, Ibadan University Press, 1987.

24. 'First anniversary of Late Chief (Dr) Henry Fajemirokun', *Daily Times Supplement*, 15 February 1979.

25. *Who's Who in Nigeria*, p. 333.

26. Yinka Folawiyo Group of Companies (profile).

27. *Financial Times*, 2 August 1977.

28. *National Concord*, 22 November 1990. p. 19.

29. Details of Chief Igbinedion's career are drawn from *This Week*, 21 December, 1987, pp. 8–18.

30. *Nigeria Banking, Finance and Commerce, 1988/89*, Research and Data Services Ltd, Lagos, 1988, p. 211.

31. Interview with Prince Samuel Adedoyin, Lagos, November 1990.

32. Abimbola Awofeso, *M. K. O. Abiola: To Make Whole Again*, Lagos, Update Communications Ltd, 1990, p. 288.
33. A. Awofeso, *M. K. O. Abiola*, pp. 409–10.
34. A. Awofeso, *M. K. O. Abiola*, p. 206.
35. The following details of Chief Abiola's career are drawn from his own account in 'A Principal, not an Agent' in A. Awofeso, *M. K. O. Abiola*, pp. 127–54.
36. *Who's Who in Nigeria*, ed. Nyaknno Osso, Lagos, Newswatch Communications Ltd, 1990, p. 19.
37. *African Concord*, 23 November 1992, p. 43.
38. G. Andrae and B. Beckman, *The Wheat Trap: Bread and Underdevelopment in Nigeria*, London, Zed Press, 1985.
39. *African Concord*, 17 July 1989.
40. *Nigerian Economist*, 13–26 September 1988.
41. *Nigeria Banking, Finance and Commerce, 1988/89*, Research and Data Services Ltd., Lagos, p. 105.
42. *Weekend Concord*, 14 March 1992.
43. *African Concord*, 23 November 1992, p. 43.
44. *Nigeria Now*, 2, July/August 1993.
45. *West Africa*, 12–18 April 1993, p. 590.
46. Interview with Mr Oba Otudeko, London, August 1991.
47. *African Concord*, 12 August 1991, p. 39.
48. *Nigerian Industrial Directory*, Manufacturer's Association of Nigeria, Lagos, 1988, p. 38.
49. *Nigeria Industrial Directory*, p. 227.
50. *Sunday Concord*, 24 February 1991, p. 15.
51. *Guardian* (Lagos), 8 February 1992.
52. Interview with Paul Kehinde Fashanu, Lagos, May 1992.
53. *Sunday Concord*, 28 January 1990, p. 13, 24 February 1991, p. 29.
54. *African Concord*, 30 July 1990.
55. Interview with Michael Murray-Bruce, Lagos, March 1993.
56. The National Economic Reconstruction Fund began in 1989 with the aim of providing long term loans to small- and medium-scale enterprises. Over 141 projects had been approved by the end of 1991, over half of them, agro-allied projects. Disbursements of $19m. and N110m. had been made to 73 projects. NERFUND, *Annual Report and Accounts*, Lagos, NERFUND, 1991.
57. This profile is based on an interview with Chief Ayo Rosiji, Lagos, March 1992 and on his biography by Nina Mba.
58. Nina E. Mba, *Ayo Rosiji: Man with Vision*, Ibadan, Spectrum Books, 1992, p. 166.
59. The following paragraph draws on the biography of Ayo Rosiji by Nina Mba, p. 167–9.
60. Chief A. S. Guobadia established his own electronics company, Maiden Electronics in the mid-1960s. Assembly of TV and radio started in 1968 and later the manufacture of some components was begun. The company was a supplier of telephones and telecommunications equipment to Post and Telegraph, the armed forces and the police. Chief Guobadia was a nominated member of the Constituent Assembly in 1978.
61. The following account is largely taken from E. L. Inanga, *History of Akintola Williams & Co, 1952–1992*, Lagos, West African Book Publishers, 1992.
62. A further instance of a Nigerian professional who trained abroad and was instrumental in the establishment of local training facilities is the case of Chief C. O.

Otubushin. His father, Otunba M. S. Otubushin set up Pacific Printing Works in Yaba in 1935. After his father's death in 1952, he trained as a printer in Germany. He returned to establish Pacific Printers in 1957. In 1973 he established the Nigerian Institute of Printing and Graphic Arts which was approved for London City and Guild examinations. *National Concord*, 7 September 1992.

63. Interview with Mr T. A. Braithwaite, Lagos, October 1990.
64. *Nigeria Industrial Directory*, p. 379.
65. *Nigeria Industry Directory*, p. 391.
66. Interview at Onward Stationery, Lagos, April 1992.
67. Profile of Alhaji Chief Abdul Rasaak Olajide Sanusi, Sanusi Group of Companies, mimeo.
68. Interview with Dr M. O. Akinrele, Lagos, February 1992.
69. Interview with Mrs Olu Ponnle, Lagos, April 1992.
70. *Tell*, 15 March 1993, pp. 33–4.
71. The following profile draws on O. A. Oyenuga, 'Women entrepreneurs: a case study of Chief (Mrs) Olutoyin Olusola Olakunri', BA dissertation, Department of History, University of Lagos, 1990.
72. Interview with Mr B. A. Onafowokan, Lagos, April 1992.
73. Interview at Majekodunmi Ventures, Lagos, February 1992.
74. Interview with Chief Edet Amana, Lagos, March 1993.
75. *Corporate*, March 1992, p. 169.
76. Interview with Mr Abidoye Ayoola, Lagos, May 1992.
77. Interview at Continental Pharmaceuticals, Lagos, March 1989.
78. This profile draws on a Corporate Profile of Liz-Olofin & Co. and on the Annual Report for 1991.
79. *Sunday Concord*, 28 January 1990.
80. Eko Hospitals PLC, Prospectus for issue of 36m. shares at 85 kobo, 1992.
81. Interview with Chief J. O. Amao, Lagos, March 1993.
82. Interview with Chief Bisi Rodipe, Ijebu-Ode, October 1993.
83. Interview with Otunba Ojora, Lagos, May 1992.
84. Interview with Chief N. O. Idowu, Lagos, May 1992.
85. The following paragraphs draw on a profile of Prince Ado Ibrahim in *Business*, July 1991, p. 33.
86. *Business*, April 1992, p. 33.
87. *Business*, April 1992, p. 34.
88. *Africa Who's Who*, London, Africa Books Ltd, 2nd edn, 1991, p. 128.
89. Among the chairmanships and directorships held by Akinkugbe (not necessarily at the same time) were Academy Press, African Prudential Insurance, Barclays (later Union) Bank, Beecham, Blue Straps, Brightstar, R. T. Briscoe, Caxton Press, Cogemat, Fan Milk, Leyland Nigeria, Nigerian Textile Mills, Nigerian Tobacco Company, Nitro Atlasco, PZ Industries, Prudent Finance, SCOA, Triplex Glass, West African Batteries, West African Milk Company, West African Portland Cement, Thomas Furniture, Sanitas.
90. C. S. O. Okoye, 'Commercial property development in Lagos', paper presented to Estate Management Students' Association, University of Lagos, April 1987.
91. Food-processing companies include Quality Foods (1968) established by food technologist Peter Jegede at Ibadan; Marston Barrow Foods (1980) at Otta, the leader in jams and marmalades; and Jobitex Foods (1985) at Otta. Otunba Mohammed Jobi, the founder of the last company, was born in 1940 at Ikare-Akoko, Ondo State. He trained in textile technology in Manchester, United Kingdom, became a distributor for Lever Bros, Cadbury and Food Specialities,

before starting to import food items in 1977. In the 1980s, a sardine-canning plant was set up with Portuguese technical assistance. Local foodstuffs are also canned. In 1990 the semi-automated plant employed 200 persons.

92. The leading company in photo processing is Fototek Industries with branch offices in Benin, Port Harcourt, Sokoto, Kano and Jos. The company began as a one-room photographic studio known as 'Bola Oguns' in Ebute Metta in 1963. It is owned by Alhaji Adebola Adegunwa of Ososa. In 1988–9 it had a turnover of N51m. and employed over 500 persons. *Guardian Financial Weekly*, 13 March 1989.

93. An exception is Shokas Industries, Ijebu-Igbo, which started to manufacture lace in 1978 with Swiss technical assistance. Alhaji S. O. Kassim was born in 1936. He was a timekeeper with Costain and a driver in Ibadan. He started trading around 1962, importing guinea brocade and lace materials. *Nigeria Who's Who in Business*, Lagos, Mednet, 1992, p. 152.

94. M. P. Rowe, 'Indigenous industrial entrepreneurship in Lagos, Nigeria', Ph.D. thesis, University of Columbia, 1971, pp. 180–1.

95. Ibid.

CHAPTER 5

1. In addition to the sources cited, this section is based on interviews with Mr G. Robertson, London, May 1983 and Chief B. O. W. Mafeni, Lagos, June 1987; and a personal communication from Chief J. E. Uduehi, March 1989.

2. *Financial Times*, 29 November 1982.

3. *Business* (Lagos), November, 1988.

4. Colonial Development Corporation, *Report and Accounts*, 1949–55.

5. 'Private enterprise beyond the orthodox', paper presented by Olorogun Michael Ibru to seminar organised by City Securities Ltd and First City Merchant Bank at the Nigerian Institute for International Affairs, Lagos, 1988.

6. Ibru Internal Report: (a) Industrial Marine Fishing/Shrimping in Nigeria: The Ibru Contribution; (b) Ibru, over 25 years; (c) Osadjere.

7. 'Fishes and riches', *Business*, November 1988, p. 44.

8. *Who's Who in Nigeria 1956*, Lagos, Daily Times Publications, p. 257.

9. *Nigeria Business Guide*, 1989–90, Lagos, ICON Ltd, p. 216.

10. 'Fishes and riches', *Business*, November 1988, p. 36.

11. *This Week* (Lagos), 13 February 1989.

12. *Guardian on Sunday*, 6 September 1992.

13. *The Top 1000 Companies, Corporate* (Lagos), March 1992–February 1993, p. 44.

14. *The Guardian* (Lagos), 30 January 1992.

15. 'Ibru destined to rule Delta State', special report, *National Concord*, 21 February 1992.

16. 'Fishes and riches', *Business*, p. 41.

17. Interview with Chief Bode Akindele, Lagos, August 1988.

18. For details of Mr Sanda's career, see *West Africa*, 8 July 1950.

19. *The Top 1000 Companies, Corporate* (Lagos), March 1992–February 1993, p. 42.

20. *The Guardian* (Lagos), 28 January 1990.

CHAPTER 6

1. R. K. Udo, *Geographical Regions of Nigeria*, London, Heinemann, 1970, p. 53.

2. B. W. Hodder and U. I. Ukwu, *Markets in West Africa: Studies of Markets and Trade among the Yoruba and Ibo*, Ibadan, Ibadan University Press, 1969, p. 238.

3. R. K. Udo, *Geographical Regions of Nigeria*, p. 54.
4. N. E. Mba, *Nigerian Women Mobilized: Women's Political Activity in Southern Nigeria, 1900–1965*, Berkeley, University of California, 1982, p. 51.
5. I. A. Mbanefo, *A Friend of the Gods*, Onitsha, Etukokwu Publishers, 1990, p. 41. For the case of Omu Okwei, see chapter 2. For the case of Madam Ruth of Oguta, see N. E. Mba, *Nigerian Women Mobilized*, p. 48.
6. N. E. Mba, *Nigerian Women Mobilized*, p. 49.
7. N. E. Mba, *Nigerian Women Mobilized*, p. 49.
8. For an Onitsha indigene's hostile view of OMATA, see I. A. Mbanefo, *A Friend of the Gods*, pp. 112–13.
9. Unpublished papers of the late Professor A. C. Callaway.
10. P. Kilby, *The Development of Small Scale Industry in Eastern Nigeria*, Lagos, United States Agency for International Development, 1962, p. 36.
11. A. Sokolski, *The Establishment of Manufacturing in Nigeria*, New York, Praeger, 1965, p. 302.
12. Interview with Chief Mbazulike Amechi, Ukpor, February 1992.
13. P. N. C. Okigbo, *Okparanomics: The Economic and Social Philosophy of Michael Okpara*, Enugu [no publisher stated], 1987, p. 13.
14. Interview with Chief J. S. Nnoruka, Lagos, May 1992.
15. O. N. Njoku, 'Development of roads and road transport in southeastern Nigeria, 1903–1939', *Journal of African Studies*, 5, 4, pp. 471–97.
16. Armels Transport based in Benin, one of the largest Lebanese transport companies, was taken over by the Mid-West State government.
17. *Business*, June 1991.
18. The membership of the spare parts union in Lagos in 1964 was split equally between Igbo and Yoruba from Ijebu-Ode. S. B. Silverstein, 'Sociocultural organisation and locational strategies of transportation entrepreneurs: an ethnoeconomic history of the Nnewi Igbo of Nigeria', Ph.D. thesis, Boston University, 1983, pp. 311–12.
19. In the early 1960s, apart from a post office, piped water and 4 secondary schools it was estimated that Nnewi had 20 saloon cars, 6 electric generators, 2,000 bicycles, 400 sewing machines, over 100 storied buildings, and 4 gas-filling stations. Unpublished papers of Professor A. C. Callaway.
20. S. B. Silverstein, 'Sociocultural organisation and locational strategies of transportation entrepreneurs', pp. 309–10.
21. A. H. Amsden, *Asia's Next Giant: South Korea and Late Industrialisation*, Oxford, Oxford University Press, 1989, p. 20.
22. *Who's Who in Nigeria*, ed. Nyaknno Osso, Lagos, Newswatch Communications Ltd, 1990, p. 280.
23. J. D. Y. Peel, *Ijeshas and Nigerians: The Incorporation of a Yoruba Kingdom, 1890s–1970s*, Cambridge, Cambridge University Press, 1983, pp. 258–60.

CHAPTER 7

1. S. Martin, *Palm Oil and Protest: An Economic History of the Ngwa Region, South-Eastern Nigeria, 1800–1980*, Cambridge, Cambridge University Press, 1988, p. 93.
2. S. Martin, *Palm Oil and Protest*, p. 123.
3. R. K. Udo, *Geographical Regions of Nigeria*, London, Heinemann, 1970, p. 71.
4. S. Martin, *Palm Oil and Protest*, pp. 86–9.
5. B. N. Floyd, *Eastern Nigeria: A Geographical Review*, London, Macmillan, 1969, p. 280.

6. The competitive strength of Aba in textiles, garments and shoes is vividly demonstrated today at the weekly Oil Mill market held by Aba traders in Port Harcourt along the Port Harcourt–Aba expressway.

7. P. Kilby, *Industrialisation in an Open Economy: Nigeria 1945–1966*, Cambridge, Cambridge University Press, 1969, pp. 72–3.

8. The Pfizer plant was the first pharmaceutical manufacturing plant in Nigeria. It was damaged beyond repair, and after the war, production was shifted to Ikeja, Lagos (1976).

9. P. Kilby, *The Development of Small Scale Industry in Eastern Nigeria*, Ministry of Commerce, USAID, March 1962, p. 34.

10. J. H. Jennings and S. O. Oduah, *A Geography of the Eastern Provinces of Nigeria*, Cambridge, Cambridge University Press, 1966, p. 124. And interviews in Aba.

11. R. K. Udo, *Geographical Regions of Nigeria*, p. 71.

12. E. Nafziger, *African Capitalism: A Case Study in Nigerian Entrepreneurship*, Stanford, 1977, p. 142.

13. P. Kilby, *Development of Small Scale Industry in Eastern Nigeria*, p. 34.

14. Interview with Mr Robert Obialor, Aba, September 1990.

15. Assuming a production capacity of 60 pairs a week, this gives an annual output of 14.4 million pairs from the artisanal sector. This estimate owes much to discussions with Mr Chris Enenya, general manager (marketing) at Bata Nigeria Ltd, who insisted that I increase my original estimate.

16. Interview with Chris Enenya, Bata Nigeria, Lagos, March 1993.

17. A contrast may be drawn with small-scale production of sandals in Calcutta, India, where four large wholesalers/retailers, including Bata, control the market, fix the price, and take almost the entire output from 2,000 production units. The supply of raw materials is also highly monopolistic. T. Basu, 'Calcutta's sandal makers', *Economic and Political Weekly*, 12, 32, 1977, p. 1262. I owe this reference to Barbara Harriss.

18. J. H. Harris, 'Industrial entrepreneurship in Nigeria', Ph.D. thesis, Northwestern University, 1967, p. 209.

19. A. C. Smock, *Ibo Politics: The Role of Ethnic Unions in Eastern Nigeria*, Cambridge, Harvard University Press, 1971, pp. 27, 245.

20. *Annual Reports of Bende Division, South Eastern Nigeria, 1905–1912*, with a commentary by G. I. Jones, Cambridge Occasional Paper 2, African Studies Centre, University of Cambridge, 1986, pp. 37, 83.

21. A. C. Smock, *Ibo Politics*, p. 29.

22. B. W. Hodder and U. I. Ukwu, *Markets in West Africa: Studies of Markets and Trade among the Yoruba and Ibo*, Ibadan, Ibadan University Press, 1969, p. 246.

23. The movement of Igbo to Cameroon was of long standing. In the interwar period, many migrated to anglophone southern Cameroons to work as labourers. Later, they came to dominate trade in local foodstuffs and imported goods as well as transport, the retail and wholesale distribution of palm oil, and buying of cocoa in the Kumba area. Following unification into an independent federal republic in 1961, restrictions were placed on many of these activities. G. W. Kleis, 'Confrontation and incorporation: Igbo ethnicity in Cameroon', *African Studies Review*, 23, 3, 1980.

24. J. O. Igue and B. G. Soule, *L'État-entrepôt au Bénin: commerce informel ou solution à la crise?*, Paris, Karthala, 1992.

25. E. Grégoire, 'Les chemins de la contrabande: étude des réseaux commerciaux en pays hausa', *Cahiers d'études africaines*, 124, 1991.

26. Interview, Owerrinta, July 1989.
27. *The Guardian* (Lagos), 19 October 1993.
28. See *The Guardian*, 12 February 1992, pp. 17–19 and 'Fidelity Union Merchant Bank crisis', *Daily Champion*, 13 March 1992.
29. *Banking Survey, Business*, 1992, p. 99.
30. *The Guardian* (Lagos), 28 October 1993.
31. 'Perservering to succeed', *Sunday Statesman*, 27 November 1988.
32. *Nigeria Industrial Directory*, Manufacturers' Association of Nigeria, 1988, p. 481.
33. *Corporate*, March 1992, p. 56.
34. This profile is based on 'Ferdinand Group of companies: corporate profile', mimeo; and 'A profile of Chief Ferdinand Anyaoha Anaghara', mimeo.
35. *Business* (Lagos), 3 February 1990.
36. *Business*, August 1992–July 1993, p. 52.
37. For a summary of these issues and a negative view of traditional apprenticeship, see K. Marsden, *African Entrepreneurs*, Discussion Paper No. 9, International Finance Corporation, 1990. This paper draws on two publications: *World Bank, Sub-Saharan Africa: From Crisis to Sustainable Growth*, Washington DC, World Bank, 1989; and ILO, *African Employment Report 1988*, Addis Ababa, JASPA, 1989.

CHAPTER 8

1. P. Shea, 'The development of an export-oriented dyed cloth industry in Kano emirate in the nineteenth century', Ph.D. thesis, University of Wisconsin, 1975; P. E. Lovejoy, 'Plantations in the economy of the Sokoto Caliphate', *Journal of African History*, 19, 3, 1978, pp. 341–68; P. E. Lovejoy, *Caravans of Kola: A History of the Hausa Kola Trade, 1700–1900*, Ahmadu Bello University, Zaria, 1980; M. Watts, 'Brittle trade: a political economy of food supply in Kano', in J. I. Guyer (ed.), *Feeding African Cities*, Manchester, Manchester University Press for the International African Institute, 1987, p. 61.
2. M. Watts, 'Brittle trade', p. 61 (citing Polly Hill).
3. P. E. Lovejoy, 'Plantations in the economy of the Sokoto Caliphate', p. 358.
4. M. Watts, 'Brittle trade', p. 66.
5. P. E. Lovejoy, 'Plantations in the economy of the Sokoto Caliphate', p. 358.
6. J. Hogendorn, *Nigerian Groundnut Exports*, Zaria, Ahmadu Bello University Press, 1978, pp. 84–5.
7. A. U. Dan-Asabe, 'Comparative biographies of selected leaders of the Kano commercial establishment', MA thesis, Bayero University, Kano, 1987, pp. 92–8. Of the sons, Baba Iliasu became a produce buyer. Musa Iliasu (d. 1972) attended Kano Middle School, was employed by UAC and was a produce buyer, transporter and pharmaceutical distributor. Salihu Iliasu took a degree in water-resources management and became an employee of the Northern Region government. He was chairman of the Kano State People's Redemption Party (PRP) and loyal to Malam Aminu Kano.
8. On the expansion of Nigerian groundnut exports and the role of local merchants, see J. Hogendorn, *Nigerian Groundnut Exports*.
9. Albasu provides a full account of early Lebanese activity in Kano. S. A. Albasu, 'The Lebanese in Kano: an immigrant community in a Hausa-Muslim society in the colonial and post-colonial periods', Ph.D thesis, Bayero University, 1989.
10. S. A. Albasu, 'The Lebanese in Kano', pp. 177–94.
11. S. A. Albasu, 'The Lebanese in Kano', pp. 197–214.

12. M. Watts, 'Brittle trade', p. 94.
13. S. A. Albasu, 'The Lebanese in Kano', pp. 315, 382.
14. A. O. Olukoshi, 'The multinational corporation and industrialisation in Kano', Ph.D. thesis, University of Leeds, 1986, p. 221.
15. A. O. Olukoshi, 'The multinational corporation', p. 222.
16. A. O. Olukoshi, 'The multinational corporation', p. 222.
17. A. U. Dan-Asabe, 'Comparative biographies', pp. 161–4.
18. A. U. Dan-Asabe, 'Comparative biographies', pp. 165–8.
19. A. U. Dan-Asabe, 'Comparative biographies', p. 223.
20. J. N. Paden, *Religion and Political Culture in Kano*, Berkeley, University of California, 1973, p. 319.
21. J. N. Paden, *Religion and Political Culture in Kano*, p. 224.
22. P. Kilby, *Industrialisation in an Open Economy: Nigeria 1945–66*, Cambridge, Cambridge University Press, 1969, p. 311–16.
23. J. R. Harris, 'Industrial entrepreneurship in Nigeria', Ph.D. thesis, Northwestern University, 1967, p. 223.
24. A. O. Olukoshi, 'Some remarks on the role of the Levantine bourgeoisie in the capitalist industrialisation of Kano', *Nigerian Journal of Political Science*, 4, 1 and 2, 1985, pp. 55–6.
25. A. O. Olukoshi, 'The multinational corporation', p. 231.
26. S. A. Albasu, 'The Lebanese in Kano', pp. 318–22.
28. A. O. Olukoshi, 'The multinational corporation', p. 234.
29. A. O. Olukoshi, 'The multinational corporation', p. 234.
30. A. O. Olukoshi, 'The multinational corporation', pp. 232–3.
31. A. O. Olukoshi, 'The multinational corporation', p. 233.
32. A. O. Olukoshi, 'The multinational corporation', p. 234.
33. A. O. Olukoshi, 'The multinational corporation', p. 233.
34. *Kano State Commercial and Industrial Handbook*, Kano, Ministry of trade and Industry, 1974.
35. S. A. Albasu, 'The Lebanese in Kano', pp. 388.
36. A. Hoogvelt, 'Indigenisation and foreign capital: industrialisation in Nigeria', *Review of African Political Economy*, 14, 1979.
37. A. O. Olukoshi, 'The multinational corporation', pp. 244–5.
38. A. O. Olukoshi, 'The multinational corporation', p. 246.
39. This account is based on interview.
40. A. O. Olukoshi, 'Some remarks on the role of the Levantine bourgeoisie', p. 59.
41. S. A. Albasu, 'The Lebanese in Kano', pp. 378–9.
42. A. O. Olukoshi, 'Some remarks on the role of the Levantine bourgeoisie', pp. 61–2.
43. 'A brief history of the Nigerian Oil Mills Ltd and the Cedar Group', mimeo, June 1989.
44. A. O. Olukoshi, 'Some remarks on the role of the Levantine bourgeoisie', pp. 69–70.
45. M. Watts, 'Brittle trade', p. 88.
46. M. Watts, 'Brittle trade', p. 216 (citing Tahir).
47. *Alhassan Dantata Memorial Almanac*, 1990.
48. M. Watts 'Brittle trade', pp. 88–9.
49. A. O. Olukoshi, 'The multinational corporation', p. 229.
50. A. O. Olukoshi, 'The multinational corporation', p. 213.
51. A. O. Olukoshi, 'The multinational corporation', p. 229.
52. A. U. Dan-Asabe, 'Comparative biographies', pp. 136–9.

53. *The Top 1000 Companies, Corporate* (Lagos), March 1992–February 1993, p. 42.
54. A. O. Olukoshi, 'The multinational corporation', p. 233.
55. A. U. Dan-Asabe, 'Comparative biographies', p. 129.
56. *The Top 1000 Companies, Corporate* (Lagos), March 1992–February 1993, p. 44.
57. 'Focus on the Isiyaku Rabiu Group of companies', *New Nigerian* (Kaduna), 22 February, 1979.
58. *The Top 1000 Companies, Corporate* (Lagos), March 1992–February 1993, p. 40.
59. Interview with Alhaji Mahmoud Gashash, Kano, November 1990.
60. *West Africa*, 18 November 1950.
61. *Kano Advertiser*, vol. 3, January 1979.
62. *West Africa*, 18 November 1950.
63. J. N. Paden, *Ahmadu Bello*, pp. 147–9.
64. This section is based on the biography of Alhaji Hamza by Chukwuma Oraegbu and on an interview with Alhaji Hamza, Apapa, October 1990.
65. The organisation was not the first of its kind. As Akeredolu-Ale points out, a Nigerian Association of African Importers and Exporters was formed in 1942 to obtain for its members a share of the controlled import trade during the war period. E. O. Akeredolu-Ale, *The Underdevelopment of Indigenous Entrepreneurship in Nigeria*, Ibadan, Ibadan University Press, p. 49.
66. Interview with Aminu Baba Nabegu, Kano, May 1992.
67. Alhaji Baballe Illa is a major produce buyer and transporter. He is chairman of the Northern Nigeria Transporters Association. He is a major shareholder in Noma Oil and Cake Mills Ltd. He acquired Arewa Tanneries from Spanish owners in 1981. In 1993 he opened a new cotton ginnery investing $2m. His eldest son established a tannery, Globus Enterprises, in 1991.
68. This account is based on a company brochure and an interview at Dangote Group, Lagos, March 1992.
69. *The Guardian* (Lagos), 23 August 1992.
70. *Business Times*, 10 May 1993.
71. Interview with Alhaji Mohammed Koguna, London, December 1991.
72. Interview at Ceramics Manufacturers, Kano, May 1992.
73. Ceramics Manufacturers Nigeria PLC, Prospectus for offer of subscription 60m. shares of 50K each at 80k per share, Lagos, 1992.
74. Interview, Falacol Pharmaceutical Industries, Kano, February 1992.
75. J. N. Paden, *Ahmadu Bello*, p. 579.
76. J. N. Paden, *Ahmadu Bello*, p. 231.
77. 'His Highness Alhaji Shehu Malami, banking and industrial potentate', *Nigerian Enterprise*, 3, 6, June 1983, pp. 18–53.
78. 'Birla Brothers – experience and low profile wins friends in Nigeria', *Africa Economic Digest*, 24 July 1981.
79. Alhaji Mai Sango has substantial investments in Lagos, Kaduna and Bauchi. In Kaduna, he promoted with foreign partners, Kaduna Marble Industries (1978) and the Blanket Manufacturing Company (1980). In Bauchi, he owns a hotel, is a shareholder in Nigerian Asbestos Industries and is chairman of Inland Bank. He is chairman of Sunflag, one of the largest textile companies in Lagos with a turnover of over N600m. He is also a director of International Bank for West Africa, Merchant Bank of Commerce, New Africa Holdings Ltd, Roche Nigeria, Minnesota Nig. Ltd, Sonatel IG, and Tiger Batteries.
80. 'The frustrations of indigenous enterprise', *The Democrat* (Kaduna), 8–13 October 1990.
81. Interview with Chief Adesoye, Kaduna, November 1990.

82. Interview with Alhaji Lema Jibrilu, Kaduna, April 1992.
83. Interview with Alhaji Bawa Garba, Kaduna, November 1993. 'Alhaji Bawa Garba; from grass to grace', *Sunday Concord*, 24 February 1991.
84. Personal communication from Dr Farouk Abdulzazeez.
85. Estates are divided in the following way. If living, parents each take a one-sixth share of the total estate. The balance is then subdivided among wives, each receiving a one-eighth share. The remainder is then shared among all children, each male child receiving twice the share of female children.
86. *The Guardian* (Lagos), 6 March 1993.
87. *The Top 1000 Companies, Corporate* (Lagos), March 1992–February 1993, p. 54.
88. Isiyaku Umar Tofa studied public administration at Ahmadu Bello University. In the early 1970s, he was posted to the office of the Governor of Kano State, Audo Bako, and was involved in the provision of drought relief supplies. He later studied in the United States before returning to Nigeria to pursue private business.

CHAPTER 9

1. J. Iliffe, *The Emergence of Modern Capitalism*, London, Macmillan, p. 67.
2. N. Swainson, *The Development of Corporate Capitalism in Kenya 1918–1977*, London, Heineman, 1980, p. 191.
3. J.-F. Médard, 'Le "Big Man" en Afrique: equisse d'analyse du politicien entrepreneur', *L'Année sociologique*, 42, 1992.
4. J.-F. Bayart, *The State in Africa: The Politics of the Belly*, London, Longman, English edn, pp. 81–2, 96–9.
5. J.-F. Bayart, *The State in Africa*, p. 96.
6. S. Berry, *Fathers Work for their Sons: Accumulation, Mobility and Class Formation in an Extended Yoruba Community*, Berkeley and Los Angeles, University of California Press, 1985, chapter 6.
7. K. Hart, 'Swindler or public benefactor? The entrepreneur in his community,' in J. Goody (ed.), *Changing Social Structure in Ghana*, London, International African Institute, 1975, pp. 23, 27.
8. D. McCormick, 'Why small firms stay small: risk and growth among Nairobi's small-scale manufacturing', Working Paper no. 483, Institute for Development Studies, University of Nairobi, 1992.
9. S. Lall, 'Long term perspectives in sub-Saharan Africa', background paper, Industry, Washington DC, World Bank, 1987.
10. P. N. C. Okigbo, 'Towards a reconstruction of the political economy of Igbo civilization', Ahiajoku lecture, Owerri, 1986.
11. T. G. Forrest, 'Brazil and Africa: geopolitics, trade and technology in the South Atlantic', *African Affairs*, 81, 322, 1982.
12. The firm of J. H. Doherty. See A. Macmillan, *The Red Book of West Africa*, London, Frank Cass, 1920, reprinted 1968, pp. 98–9.
13. S. Berry, *Fathers Work for their Sons*, chapter 7.
14. J. Guyer, 'Representation without taxation: an essay on democracy in rural Nigeria, 1952–1990', *African Studies Review*, 35, 1, 1992, pp. 57–62.
15. J. Guyer, 'Representation without taxation', p. 62.
16. J. D. Y. Peel, *Ijeshas and Nigerians: The Incorporation of a Yoruba Kingdom, 1890s–1970s*, Cambridge, Cambridge University Press, 1983, pp. 258–62.
17. Major sponsors of sports include Alhaji G. N. Hamza, Bashorun M. K. O. Abiola and Chief Emmanual Iwuanyanwu.
18. The most prominent Lebanese businessman in Ibadan, Chief Raymond Zard (b.

1938), was awarded a doctorate by the University of Ibadan in 1991. Raymond Zard heads a conglomerate employing about 4,000 persons with 35 expatriates. The group has for many years been the leading exporter of cocoa and owns substantial property in central Ibadan.

19. P. N. C. Okigbo, 'Crisis in the temple', public lecture, University of Lagos, 5 March 1992, published in *Sunday Times*, 8 March and 15 March 1992. Okigbo found that in the period 1980 to 1990, Nigerian universities made over 600 awards and that less than 15 of them went to academics or intellectuals.

20. S. Lall, 'Long term perspectives in sub-Saharan Africa: industry', background paper, Washington DC, World Bank, 1987.

21. The political conditions surrounding the introduction of SAP are examined in my book, *Politics and Economic Development in Nigeria*, Boulder, Westview, 1993, chapter 10.

22. A small example was a seminar organised in 1988 by an indigenous merchant bank, First City Merchant Bank, on the theme 'Private entrepreneurship as a motivating force for economic development' at the Nigerian Institute for International Affairs, Lagos. Even five years earlier, the climate would not have been propitious for such an event.

23. J.-F. Bayart, *The State in Africa*.

24. J.-F. Bayart, *The State in Africa*, pp. 20–31.

25. J.-F. Bayart, *The State in Africa*, p. 208.

26. J.-P. Warnier, *L'Esprit d'enterprise au Cameroun*, Paris, Karthala, 1993; M. Rowlands, 'Accumulation and the cultural politics of identity in the Grassfields', in P. Geschiere and P. Konings (eds), *Itinéraires d'accumulation au Cameroun*, Leiden and Paris, Africa-Studiecentrum and Karthala, 1993.

27. J.-F. Bayart, *The State in Africa*, pp. 84–6. J.–F. Bayart, 'Finishing with the idea of the Third World: the concept of the political trajectory', in J. Manor (ed.), *Rethinking Third World Politics*, London, Longman, 1991, p. 63.

28. For an excellent comparative essay on Côte d'Ivoire and Ghana, see R. Crook, 'State, society and political institutions in Côte d'Ivoire and Ghana', in J. Manor (ed.), *Rethinking Third World Politics*, London, Longman, 1991. For francophone Africa, see D. B. Cruise O'Brien, 'The show of state in a neo-colonial twilight: francophone Africa', in J. Manor (ed.), *Rethinking Third World Politics*, London, Longman, 1991.

29. C. Leys, 'Capital accumulation, class formation and dependency: the significance of the Kenyan case', in J. Saville and B. Miliband (eds), *Socialist Register 1978*, London, pp. 251–61.

30. G. Dauch and D. Martin, *L'Heritage de Kenyatta*, Paris, L'Harmattan, 1985, chapter 2.

31. P. Kennedy, *African Capitalism: The Struggle for Ascendancy*, Cambridge, Cambridge University Press, 1988, pp. 95–6.

32. P. Coughlin, 'Toward the next phase', in P. Coughlin and G. K. Ikiara (eds), *Kenya's Industrialization Dilemma*, Nairobi, Heinemann, 1991, pp. 375–8.

33. J. MacGaffey, *Entrepreneurs and Parasites: The Struggle for Indigenous Capitalism in Zaire*, Cambridge, Cambridge University Press, 1987.

34. C. Boone, 'The making of a rentier class: wealth accumulation and political control in Senegal', *Journal of Development Studies*, 26, 3, 1990.

35. See Y.-A. Fauré and J.-F. Médard, 'Classe dominante ou classe dirigeante?'; and J.-M. Gastellu and S. Affou Yapi, 'Un mythe à décomposer: la "bourgeoisie de planteurs"', in Y.-A. Fauré and J.-F. Médard (eds), *Etat et bourgeoisie en Côte d'Ivoire*, Paris, Karthala, 1982.

36. C. Boone, 'Commerce in the Côte d'Ivoire: Ivoirianisation without Ivoirian traders', *Journal of Modern African Studies*, 31, 1, 1993, pp. 67–92.
37. J. Rapley, *Ivoirien Capitalism: African entrepreneurs in Côte d'Ivoire*, Boulder, Lynne Rienner, 1993.
38. The best account of the policies of the Okpara administration is an essay by Pius Okigbo. See P. N. C. Okigbo, *Okparanomics: The Economic and Social Philosophy of Michael Okpara*, Enugu, no publisher stated, 1987.
39. In a brief survey of eleven owners of sixteen medium-scale enterprises in Ijebu-Ode, I found that six came from non-trading backgrounds.

BIBLIOGRAPHY

PUBLISHED BOOKS AND ARTICLES

A. A. A. Agbaje, *The Nigerian Press, Hegemony, and the Social Construction of Legitimacy*, Lewiston, Edwin Mellon Press, 1992.

E. O. Akeredolu-Ale, 'A socio-historical study of the development of entrepreneurship among the Ijebu of western Nigeria', *African Studies Review*, 16, 3, 1973, pp. 347–61.

—— *The Underdevelopment of Indigenous Entrepreneurship in Nigeria*, Ibadan, Ibadan University Press, 1975.

—— 'Private foreign investment and the underdevelopment of indigenous entrepreneurship in Nigeria', in G. Williams (ed.), *Nigeria: Economy and Society*, London, Rex Collings, 1976.

J. O. Alutu, *Nnewi History*, Enugu, Fourth Dimension Publishing Company, 3rd edn, 1986.

S. Amin, *Le développement du capitalisme en Côte d'Ivoire*, Paris, Editions de Minuit, 1967.

—— *Le monde des affaires sénégalais*, Paris, Editions de Minuit, 1969.

A. H. Amsden, *Asia's Next Giant: South Korea and Late Industrialisation*, Oxford, Oxford University Press, 1989.

G. Andrae and B. Beckman, *The Wheat Trap: Bread and Underdevelopment in Nigeria*, London, Zed Press, 1985.

N. Anyaegbunam, *Waziri Ibrahim: Politics without Bitterness*, Lagos, Daily Times, 1992.

B. Awe (ed.), *Nigerian Women in Historical Perspective*, Lagos and Ibadan, Sankore/Bookcraft, 1992.

A. Awofeso, *M. K. O. Abiola: To Make Whole Again*, Lagos, Update Communications Ltd, 1990.

E. A. Ayandele, 'The changing position of the Awujales of Ijebuland under colonial rule', in M. Crowder and O. Ikime (eds), *West African Chiefs: Their Changing Status under Colonial Rule*, Ile-Ife, University of Ife Press, 1970.

—— *The Ijebu of Yorubaland 1850–1950: Politics, Economy and Society*, Ibadan, Heinemann, 1992.

A. A. Ayida, 'Contractor finance and supplier credit in economic growth', *Nigerian Journal of Economic and Social Studies*, 7, 2, 1965, pp. 175–86.

P. H. Baker, *Urbanisation and Political Change: The Politics of Lagos 1917–1967*, Berkeley, University of California Press, 1974.

A. Banjo, 'The principal problems of indigenisation', in *Management in Nigeria*, September 1976.

S. Barnes, *Patrons and Power: Creating a Political Community in Metropolitan Lagos*, London, Manchester University Press for the International African Institute, 1986.

T. Basu, 'Calcutta's sandal makers', *Economic and Political Weekly*, 12, 32, 1977, p. 1262.

P. T. Bauer, *West African Trade: A Study of Competition, Oligopoly and Monopoly in a changing Economy*, Cambridge, Cambridge University Press, 1954.

—— *Economic Analysis and Policy in Underdeveloped Countries*, London, Routledge and Kegan Paul, 2nd edn, 1965.

J.-F. Bayart, 'Finishing with the idea of the Third World: the concept of the political trajectory', in J. Manor (ed.), *Rethinking Third World Politics*, London, Longman, 1991.

—— *The State in Africa: The Politics of the Belly*, London, Longman, English edn, 1993.

B. Beckman, 'Imperialism and capitalist transformation: critique of a Kenyan debate', *Review of African Political Economy*, 19, 1980, pp. 48–62.

—— 'Neocolonialism, capitalism, and the state in Nigeria', in H. Bernstein and B. K. Campbell (eds), *Contradictions of Accumulation in Africa*, Beverly Hills, Sage, 1985.

P. Bennell, 'Industrial class formation in Ghana: some empirical observations', *Development and Change*, 15, 1984, pp. 593–612.

S. Berry, *Fathers Work for their Sons: Accumulation, Mobility and Class Formation in an Extended Yoruba Community*, Berkeley and Los Angeles, University of California Press, 1985.

T. J. Bierstecker, *Multinationals, the State, and Control of the Nigerian Economy*, Princeton, Princeton University Press, 1987.

C. Boone, 'The making of a rentier class: wealth accumulation and political control in Senegal', *Journal of Development Studies*, 26, 3, 1990, pp. 425–49.

—— *Merchant Capital and the Roots of State Power in Senegal 1930–1985*, Cambridge, Cambridge University Press, 1992.

—— 'Commerce in Côte d'Ivoire: Ivoirianisation without Ivoirian traders', *Journal of Modern African Studies*, 31, 1, 1993, pp. 67–92.

T. M. Callaghy, 'The state as lame leviathan: the patrimonial administrative state in Africa', in Zaki Ergas (ed.), *The African State in Transition*, New York, Macmillan, 1987.

—— 'The state and the development of capitalism in Africa: theoretical, historical and comparative reflections', in D. Rothchild and N. Chazan (eds), *The Precarious Balance: State and Society in Africa*, Boulder, Westview, 1988.

A. Callaway, 'Nigeria's indigenous education; the apprenticeship system', *Odu*, 1, 1, 1964, pp. 62–79.

—— 'From traditional crafts to modern industries', *Odu*, 2, 1, 1965, pp. 62–79.

C. Clarke, C. Peach, and S. Vertovec (eds), *South Asians Overseas: Migration and Ethnicity*, Cambridge, Cambridge University Press, 1990.

P. Cole, *Modern and Traditional Elites in the Politics of Lagos*, Cambridge, Cambridge University Press, 1975.

J. S. Coleman, *Nigeria: Background to Nationalism*, Berkeley, University of California Press, 1958.

P. Collins, 'Public policy and the development of indigenous capitalism: the Nigerian experience', *Journal of Commonwealth and Comparative Politics*, 15, 2, 1977, pp. 127–50.

F. Cooper, 'Africa and the world economy', *African Studies Review*, 24, 2 and 3, 1981, pp. 1–86.

P. Coughlin, 'Toward the next phase', in P. Coughlin and G. K. Ikiara, *Kenya's Industrialization Dilemma*, Nairobi, Heinemann, 191.

R. Crook, 'State, society and political institutions in Côte d'Ivoire and Ghana', in J. Manor (ed.), *Rethinking Third World Politics*, London, Longman, 1991.

D. B. Cruise O'Brien, 'The show of state in a neo-colonial twilight: francophone Africa', in J. Manor (ed.), *Rethinking Third World Politics*, London, Longman, 1991.

G. Dauch and D. Martin, *L'Heritage de Kenyatta*, Paris, L'Harmattan, 1985.

C. Dennis, 'The limits of women's independent careers: gender in the formal and informal sectors in Nigeria', in D. Elson (ed.), *Male Bias in the Development Process*, Manchester, Manchester University Press, 1991.

L. Diamond, 'Nigeria: pluralism, statism and the struggle for democracy', in L. Diamond, J. J. Linz and S. M. Lipset (eds), *Democracy in Developing Countries*, vol. 2, *Africa*, Boulder, Lynne Rienner, 1988.

J. Duffield, 'The business activities of Duse Mohammed Ali: an example of the economic dimension of Pan-Africanism, 1912–1945', *Journal of the Historical Society of Nigeria*, 4, 4, 1969, pp. 571–600.

J. S. Eades, 'The growth of a migrant community: the Yoruba in Northern Ghana', in J. R. Goody (ed.), *Changing Social Structure in Ghana*, London, International African Institute, 1975.

—— 'Kinship and entrepreneurship among Yoruba in Northern Ghana', in W. A. Shack and E. P. Skinner (eds), *Strangers in Africa*, Berkeley, University of California Press, 1979.

F. Ekejiuba, 'Omu Okwei, the merchant queen of Ossomari: a biographical sketch', *Journal of the Historical Society of Nigeria*, 3, 4, 1967, pp. 633–46.

—— 'Omu Okwei of Osomari', in B. Awe (ed.), *Nigerian Women in Historical Perspective*, Lagos and Ibadan, Sankore/Bookcraft, 1992.

W. Elkan, 'Entrepreneurs and entrepreneurship in Africa', *Research Observer*, 3, 2, 1988, pp. 171–88.

T. Falola, 'Cassava starch for export in Nigeria during the Second World War', *African Economic History*, 18, 1989, 73–98.

—— 'Lebanese traders in southwestern Nigeria, 1900–1960', *African Affairs*, 89, 357, 1990, 523–53.

Y.-A. Fauré and J.-F. Médard, 'Classe dominante ou classe dirigeante?', in Y.-A. Fauré and J.-F. Médard (eds), *Etat et bourgeoisie en Côte d'Ivoire*, Paris, Karthala, 1982.

—— (eds), *Etat et bourgeoisie en Côte d'Ivoire*, Paris, Karthala, 1982.

B. N. Floyd, *Eastern Nigeria: A Geographical Review*, London, Macmillan, 1969.

T. G. Forrest, 'Brazil and Africa: geopolitics, trade and technology in the South Atlantic', *African Affairs*, 81, 322, 1982, pp. 3–20.

—— 'The advance of African capital: the growth of Nigerian private enterprises', in F. Stewart, S. Lall and S. M. Wangwe (eds), *Alternative Development Strategies in Sub-Saharan Africa*, London, Macmillan, 1992.

—— *Politics and Economic Development in Nigeria*, Boulder, Westview, 1993.

W. M. Freund, *The Making of Contemporary Africa*, London, Macmillan, 1984.

P. C. Garlick, *African Traders and Economic Development in Ghana*, Oxford, Oxford University Press, 1971.

J.-M. Gastellu and S. Affou Yapi, 'Un mythe à décomposer: la "bourgeoisie de planteurs"', in Y.-A. Fauré and J.-F. Médard (eds), *Etat et bourgeoisie en Côte d'Ivoire*, Paris, Karthala, 1982.

T. Geiger and W. Armstrong, *The Development of African Private Enterprise*, Washington, National Planning Association, 1964.

C. Gertzel, 'Relations between African and European traders in the Niger Delta, 1880–1896', *Journal of African History*, 3, 2, 1962, pp. 361–6.

P. Geschiere and P. Konings (eds), *Itinéraires d'accumulation au Cameroun*, Leiden and Paris, Afrika-Studiecentrum and Karthala, 1993.

E. Grégoire, 'Les chemins de la contrabande: étude des réseaux commerciaux en pays hausa', *Cahiers d'études africaines*, 124, 1991, pp. 509–32.

J. Guyer, 'Representation without taxation: an essay on democracy in rural Nigeria, 1952–1990', *African Studies Review*, 35, 1, 1992, pp. 41–79.

W. K. Hancock, *Survey of Commonwealth Affairs, Problems of Economic Policy 1918–1939*, part 2, 1940, London, Oxford University Press.

A. Harneit-Sievers, *Zwischen Depression und Dekolonisation: Afrikanische Handler und Politik in Sud-Nigeria 1935–1954*, Saarbruchen and Fort Lauderdale, Breitenbach Publications, 1991.

J. R. Harris, 'Nigerian entrepreneurship in industry', in C. K. Eicher and C. Liedholm (eds), *Growth and Development of the Nigerian Economy*, East Lansing, Michigan State University Press, 1970.

—— 'Nigerian enterprise in the printing industry', *Nigerian Journal of Economic and Social Studies*, 10, 2, 1968, pp. 215–27.

K. Hart, 'Swindler or public benefactor? The entrepreneur in his community', in J. Goody (ed.), *Changing Social Structure in Ghana*, London, International African Institute, 1975.

E. K. Hawkins, *Road Transport in Nigeria*, London, Oxford University Press, 1958.

G. K. Helleiner, *Peasant Agriculture, Government and Economic Growth in Nigeria*, Homewood, Illinois, Irwin, 1966.

Polly Hill, *Studies in Rural Capitalism in West Africa*, Cambridge, Cambridge University Press, 1970.

—— 'The lack of an agrarian hierarchy in pre-colonial West Africa', in *Dry Grain Farming Families – Hausaland (Nigeria) and Kanakata (India) Compared*, Cambridge, Cambridge University Press, 1982, ch. 16.

D. Himbara, 'Myths and realities of Kenyan capitalism', *Journal of Modern African Studies*, 31, 1, 1993, pp. 93–107.

A. O. Hirschman, *Rival Views of Market Society and Other Recent Essays*, Cambridge, Harvard University Press, 1992.

B. W. Hodder and U. I. Ukwu, *Markets in West Africa, Studies of Markets and Trade among the Yoruba and Ibo*, Ibadan, Ibadan University Press, 1969.

J. Hogendorn, *Nigerian Groundnut Exports*, Zaria, Ahmadu Bello University Press, 1978.

A. Hoogvelt, 'Indigenisation and foreign capital: industrialisation in Nigeria', *Review of African Political Economy*, 14, 1979, pp. 56–68.

A. G. Hopkins, 'The Lagos Chamber of Commerce 1888–1903', *Journal of the Historical Society of Nigeria*, 3, 2, 1965, pp. 241–8.

—— 'Economic aspects of political movements in Nigeria and in the Gold Coast 1918–1939', *Journal of African History*, 7, 1966, pp. 133–52.

—— 'Richard Beale Blaize 1854–1904,:merchant prince of West Africa', *Tarikh*, 1, 2, 1966, pp. 70–9.

—— *An Economic History of West Africa*, London, Longman, 1973.

—— 'Imperial business in Africa, part 1: sources' and 'part 2: interpretations', *Journal of African History*, 18, 1976, pp. 29–48, 276–90.

—— 'Innovation in a colonial context: African origins of Nigerian cocoa-farming industry, 1880–1920', in C. Dewey and A. G. Hopkins (eds), *The Imperial Impact: Studies in the Economic History of Africa and India*, University of London, published for the Institute of Commonwealth Studies, London, Athlone Press, 1978.

—— 'Big business in African studies', *Journal of African History*, 28, 1987.

A. Hourani and N. Shehadi (eds), *The Lebanese in the World*, London, I. B. Tauris, 1992.

J. O. Igue, 'Le Nigeria et ses périphéries frontalières', in D. C. Bach, J. Egg and J. Philippe (eds), *Le Nigeria: un pouvoir en puissance*, Paris, Karthala, 1988.

J. O. Igue and B. G. Soule, *L'État-entrepôt au Bénin: commerce informel ou solution à la crise?*, Paris, Karthala, 1992.

J. Iliffe, *The Emergence of African Capitalism*, London, Macmillan, 1983.

E. L. Inanga, *History of Akintola Williams & Co., 1952–1992*, Lagos, West African Book Publishers, 1992.

International Labour Organisation (ILO), *Employment, Incomes and Equality: A Strategy for Increasing Productive Employment in Kenya*, Geneva, ILO, 1972.

—— *African Employment Report 1988*, Addis Ababa, JASPA, 1989.

E. Isichei, *A History of the Igbo People*, London, Macmillan, 1976.

J. H. Jennings and S. O. Oduah, *A Geography of the Eastern Provinces of Nigeria*, Cambridge, Cambridge University Press, 1966.

I. B. Jose, *Walking a Tightrope: Power Play in the Daily Times*, Ibadan, Ibadan University Press, 1987.

R. Joseph, *Democracy and Prebendal Politics in Nigeria: The Rise and Fall of the Second Republic*, Cambridge, Cambridge University Press, 1987.

R. Kaplinsky, 'Capitalist accumulation in the periphery – the Kenyan case re-examined', *Review of African Political Economy*, 17, 1980, pp. 83–105.

O. Karunwi, *A Woman Industrialist: A Biography of Chief (Mrs) Bisoye Tejuoso*, Lagos, Cowlad Ent., 1991.

P. Kennedy, *Ghanaian Businessmen: From Artisan to Capitalist Entrepreneur in a Dependent Economy*, Munich, Weltforum Verlag, 1980.

—— *African Capitalism: The Struggle for Ascendancy*, Cambridge, Cambridge University Press, 1988.

P. Kilby, *The Development of Small-scale Industry in Eastern Nigeria*, Lagos, United States Agency for International Development, 1962.

—— *African Enterprise: The Nigerian Bread Industry*, Stanford, Hoover Institute, 1965.

—— *Industrialisation in an Open Economy: Nigeria 1945–66*, Cambridge, Cambridge University Press, 1969.

—— 'Manufacturing in colonial Africa', in P. Duignan and L. H. Gann (eds), *Colonialism in Africa 1870–1960*, vol. 4, *The Economics of Colonialism*, Cambridge, Cambridge University Press, 1975.

G. Kitching, 'Politics, method and evidence in the "Kenya Debate"', in H. Bernstein and B. K. Campbell (eds), *Contradictions of Accumulation in Africa*, Beverly Hills, Sage, 1985.

G. W. Kleis, 'Confrontation and incorporation: Igbo ethnicity in Cameroon', *African Studies Review*, 23, 3, 1980, pp. 89–100.

R. R. Kuczynski, *Demographic Survey of the British Colonial Empire*, vol. 1, *West Africa*, London, Oxford University Press, 1948.

H. L. van der Laan, 'Modern inland transport and the European trading firms in colonial West Africa', *Cahiers d'études africaines*, 84, 1981.

A. A. Labaran, 'Land appropriation and capitalist farming in the Sokoto region:

some preliminary findings', in M. Mortimore, E. A. Olofin, R. A. Cline-Cole and A. Abdulkadir (eds), *Perspectives in Land Administration and Development in Northern Nigeria*, Kano, Bayero University, 1987.

S. Langdon, 'Industry and capitalism in Kenya: contributions to a debate', in P. Lubeck (ed.), *The African Bourgeoisie: Capitalist Development in Nigeria, Kenya and the Ivory Coast*, Boulder, Lynne Rienner, 1987.

D. K. Leonard, *African Successes: Four Public Managers of Kenyan Rural Development*, Berkeley, University of California Press, 1991.

C. Leys, *Underdevelopment in Kenya: The Political Economy of Neo-colonialism, 1964–1971*, London, Heinemann, 1975.

—— 'Capital accumulation, class formation and dependency: the significance of the Kenyan case', in J. Saville and R. Miliband (eds), *Socialist Register 1978*, London, 1979.

—— 'Kenya: what does "dependency" explain?', *Review of African Political Economy*, 17, 1980, pp. 108–13.

—— 'African economic development in theory and practice', *Daedalus*, 3, 1982, pp. 99–124.

—— *Learning from the Kenya Debate*, Sheffield Papers in International Studies, 15, University of Sheffield, 1992.

F. Longe, *A Rare Breed: The Story of Chief Timothy Adeola Odutola*, Lagos, Academy Press, 1981.

P. E. Lovejoy, 'Plantations in the economy of the Sokoto caliphate', *Journal of African History*, 19, 3, 1978, pp. 341–68.

—— 'The characteristics of plantations in the nineteenth-century Sokoto Caliphate (Islamic West Africa)', *American Historical Review*, 84, 5, 1979, pp. 1267–92.

—— *Caravans of Kola: A History of the Hausa Kola Trade, 1700–1900*, Zaria, Ahmadu Bello University, 1980.

P. E. Lovejoy and J. S. Hogendorn, *Slow Death for Slavery*, Cambridge, Cambridge University Press, 1993.

P. M. Lubeck (ed.), *The African Bourgeoisie: Capitalist Development in Nigeria, Kenya, and the Ivory Coast*, Boulder, Lynne Rienner, 1987.

T. McCaskie, 'Accumulation, wealth and belief in Asante history, Part 2, the 20th century', *Africa*, 56, 1, 1986, pp. 3–23.

D. McCormick, 'Why small firms stay small: risk and growth in Nairobi's small-scale manufacturing', Working Paper no. 483, Institute for Development Studies, University of Nairobi, 1992.

J. MacGaffey, *Entrepreneurs and Parasites: The Struggle for Indigenous Capitalism in Zaire*, Cambridge, Cambridge University Press, 1987.

—— *The Real Economy of Zaire: The Contribution of Smuggling and Other Unofficial Activities to National Wealth*, London, James Currey, 1991.

A. Macmillan, *The Red Book of West Africa*, London, Frank Cass, 1920, reprinted 1968.

K. Mann, 'The rise of Taiwo Olowo: law, accumulation, and mobility in early colonial Lagos', in K. Mann and R. Roberts (eds), *Law in Colonial Africa*, London, James Currey, 1991.

P. Marris and A. Somerset, *African Businessmen: A Study of Entrepreneurship and Development in Kenya*, London, Routledge and Kegan Paul, 1971.

J. Mars, 'Extra-territorial enterprises', in M. Perham (ed.), *Mining, Commerce and Finance in Nigeria*, London, Faber and Faber, 1948.

K. Marsden, *African Entrepreneurs*, Discussion Paper No. 9, International Finance Corporation, 1990.

S. M. Martin, *Palm Oil and Protest: An Economic History of the Ngwa Region of South-Eastern Nigeria, 1800–1980*, Cambridge, Cambridge University Press, 1988.

A. A. Mazrui, 'Privatisation versus the market: cultural contradictions in structural adjustment', in H. B. Hansen and M. Twaddle (eds), *Changing Uganda*, London, James Currey, 1991.

Nina E. Mba, *Nigerian Women Mobilized: Women's Political Activity in Southern Nigeria, 1900–1965*, Berkeley, University of California Press, 1982.

—— *Ayo Rosiji: Man with Vision*, Ibadan, Spectrum Books, 1992.

I. A. Mbanefo, *A Friend of the Gods*, Onitsha, Etukokwu Press, 1990.

J.-F. Médard, 'Le "Big-Man" en Afrique: equisse d'analyse du politicien entrepreneur', *L'Année sociologique*, 42, 1992, pp. 167–92.

H. V. Merani and H. L. van der Laan, 'The Indian traders in Sierra Leone', *African Affairs*, 78, 311, 1979, pp. 240–50.

R. Murray, 'The Chandarias: the development of a Kenyan multinational', in R. Kaplinsky (ed.), *Readings on the Multinational Corporation in Kenya*, Nairobi, Oxford University Press, 1978.

E. W. Nafziger, 'The economic impact of the Nigerian civil war', *Journal of Modern African Studies*, 10, 2, 1972, pp. 223–45.

—— *African Capitalism: A Case Study in Nigerian Entrepreneurship*, Stanford, Hoover Institute, 1977.

C. Newbury, 'Trade and technology in West Africa: the case of the Niger Company, 1900–1920', *Journal of African History*, 19, 4, 1978, pp. 551–75.

O. N. Njoku, 'Development of roads and road transport in southeastern Nigeria, 1903–1939', *Journal of African Studies*, pp. 471–97.

D. C. North, *Structure and Change in Economic History*, New York, Norton, 1981.

A. I. Nwabughuogu, 'From wealthy entrepreneurs to petty traders: the decline of African middlemen in eastern Nigeria, 1900–1950', *Journal of African History*, 23, 3, 1982, pp. 365–79.

I. N. C. Nwosu, *The History and Genealogy of Nnewi Town*, [no publisher stated], 1988.

J. O'Connell, 'The political class and economic growth', in P. Kilby, *Industrialisation in an Open Economy: Nigeria 1945–1966*, Cambridge, Cambridge University Press, 1969.

B. Odogwu, *No Place to Hide: Crisis and Conflicts inside Biafra*, Enugu, Fourth Dimension, 1985.

H. K. Offonry, *Investment in Goodwill: The Story of a Nigerian Philanthropist*, Owerri, New Africa Publishing Company, 1987.

W. I. Ofonagoro, *Trade and Imperialism in Southern Nigeria, 1881–1929*, New York, Nok Publishers International, 1979.

G. A. Ogunpola, 'The pattern of organisation in the building industry – a Western Nigerian case study', *Nigerian Journal of Economic and Social Studies*, 10, 3, 1968, pp. 339–60.

Mbonu Ojike, *My Africa*, London, Blandford Press, reprinted 1989 (originally published New York, John Day, 1946).

P. N. C. Okigbo, *Towards a Reconstruction of the Political Economy of Igbo Civilization*, Owerri, Ministry of Information, Culture, Youth and Sport, 1986.

—— *Okparanomics: The Economic and Social Philosophy of Michael Okpara*, Enugu [no publisher stated], 1987.

M. I. Okpara, 'Long live the Boycott King', in Ukwu I. Ukwu (ed.), *The Spirit of Self Reliance, Mazi Mbonu Ojike Memorial Lectures*, Enugu, Institute for Development Studies, University of Nigeria, 1984.

O. O. Olakunri, 'The contribution of women to commerce and industry', in J. Akande, O. Jegede, C. Osinulu and F. O. Oyekanmi (eds), *The Contribution of Women to National Development in Nigeria*, Lagos, Nigerian Association of University Women, 1990.

D. Olowu, *Lagos State: Governance, Society and Economy*, Lagos, Malthouse Press, 1990.

A. Olukoju, 'Elder Dempster and the shipping trade of Nigeria during the First World War', *Journal of African History*, 33, 2, 1992, pp. 255–71.

A. O. Olukoshi, 'Some remarks on the role of the Levantine Bourgeoisie in the capitalist industrialisation of Kano', *Nigerian Journal of Political Science*, 4, 1 and 2, 1985, pp. 53–75.

G. O. Olusanya, *Fifty Years of National Bank of Nigeria Ltd. A Golden Jubilee Souvenir*, Lagos, 1983.

—— 'Charlotte Olajumoka Obasa', in B. Awe (ed.), *Nigerian Women in Historical Perspective*, Lagos and Ibadan, Sankore/Bookcraft, 1992.

L. Omole, *My Life and Times: Reflections*, Lagos, MIJ Professional Publishers for Cardinal Investments Ltd, 1991.

O. Oni, 'Development and features of the Nigerian financial system: a Marxist approach', *Nigerian Journal of Economic and Social Studies*, 8, 3, 1966, pp. 383–402.

D. Onyeama, *African Legend: The Incredible Story of Francis Arthur Nzeribe*, Enugu, Delta Publications, 1984.

C. Oraegbu, *Hamza!*, Lagos, Sovereign Publishers, 1991.

O. Orizu, *Inside Nnewi*, Onitsha, Ana-edo Trading Company Ltd, 1960.

S. Osoba, 'The phenomenon of labour migration in the era of British colonial rule: a neglected aspect of Nigeria's social history', *Journal of the Historical Society of Nigeria*, 4, 4, 1969, pp. 515–38.

—— 'The Nigerian power elite 1952–65', reprinted in P. C. W. Gutkind and P. Waterman (eds), *African Social Studies: A Radical Reader*, New York, Heineman, 1977.

J. N. Paden, *Religion and Political Culture in Kano*, Berkeley, University of California Press, 1973.

—— *Ahmadu Bello, Sardauna of Sokoto*, London, Hodder and Stoughton, 1986.

A. Pallinder-Law, 'Aborted modernisation in West Africa? The case of Abeokuta', *Journal of African History*, 15, 1974, pp. 65–82.

J. D. Y. Peel, 'Olaju: a Yoruba concept of development', *Journal of Development Studies*, 14, 1978, pp. 135–65.

—— *Ijeshas and Nigerians: The Incorporation of a Yoruba Kingdom, 1890s-1970s*, Cambridge, Cambridge University Press, 1983.

—— 'Social and cultural change', in M. Crowder (ed.), *The Cambridge History of Africa, vol. 8, c. 1940–1975*, Cambridge, Cambridge University Press, 1984.

M. Peil, *Lagos: The City is the People*, London, Bellhaven Press, 1991.

M. Perham (ed.), *Mining, Commerce and Finance in Nigeria*, London, Faber, 1948.

A. Phillips, *The Enigma of Colonialism: British Policy in West Africa*, London, James Currey, 1989.

Proceedings of the 1977 Annual Seminar on Indigenisation, *Management in Nigeria*, vol. 1, 1978.

J. Rapley, *Ivoirien Capitalism: African Entrepreneurs in Côte d'Ivoire*, Boulder, Lynne Rienner, 1993.

D. C. Rowan, 'The native banking boom in Nigeria', *The Banker*, XCVII, 309, 1951, pp. 244–9.

M. P. Rowe and J. Harris, 'Entrepreneurial patterns in the Nigerian sawmilling industry', *Nigerian Journal of Economic and Social Studies*, 8, 1, 1966, pp. 67–95.

M. Rowlands, 'Accumulation and the cultural politics of identity in the Grassfields', in P. Geschiere and P. Konings (eds), *Itinéraires d'accumulation au Cameroun*, Leiden and Paris, Afrika-Studiecentrum and Kathala, 1993.

W. G. Runciman, *A Treatise on Social Theory*, vol. 2, *Substantive Social Theory*, Cambridge, Cambridge University Press, 1989.

P. O. Sada and A. A. Adefolalu, 'Urbanisation and problems of urban development', in A. B. Aderibigbe (ed.), *Lagos: The Development of an African City*, Ibadan, Longman, 1975.

R. Sandbrook, *The Politics of Africa's Economic Stagnation*, Cambridge, Cambridge University Press, 1985.

S. P. Schatz, *Nigerian Capitalism*, Berkeley, University of California Press, 1977.

—— 'Pirate capitalism and the inert economy of Nigeria', *Journal of Modern African Studies*, 22, 1, 1984, pp. 45–57.

A. Sen, 'Description as choice', in *Choice, Welfare and Measurement*, Oxford, Blackwell, 1982.

R. W. Shenton, *The Development of Capitalism in Northern Nigeria*, London, James Currey, 1986.

R. L. Sklar, *Nigerian Political Parties*, New York, Nok, 1983.

M. G. Smith, *The Economy of Hausa Communities of Zaria*, London, HMSO, 1955.

—— 'Exchange and marketing among the Hausa', in P. Bohannan and G. Dalton (eds), *Markets in Africa*, Evanston, Illinois, Northwestern University Press, 1962.

A. C. Smock, *Ibo Politics: The Role of Ethnic Unions in Eastern Nigeria*, Cambridge, Harvard University Press, 1971.

H. Sodipo, *A Dynasty of 'Missioners'*, Ibadan, Spectrum, 1992.

A. Sokolski, *The Establishment of Manufacturing in Nigeria*, New York, Praeger, 1965.

N. Swainson, 'The rise of a national bourgeoisie in Kenya', *Review of African Political Economy*, 8, 1977, pp. 39–55.

—— *The Development of Corporate Capitalism in Kenya 1918–1977*, London, Heinemann, 1980.

K. Swindell and A. B. Mamman, 'Land expropriation and accumulation in the Sokoto periphery, northwest Nigeria, 1976–86', *Africa*, 60, 2, 1990, pp. 173–87.

T. N. Tamuno and A. Aderinwale, *Abebe: Portrait of a Nigerian Leader*, Abeokuta, ALF Publications, 1991.

R. K. Udo, 'British policy in the development of export crops in Nigeria', *Nigerian Journal of Economic and Social Studies*, 9, 3, 1968, pp. 299–314.

—— *Geographical Regions of Nigeria*, London, Heinemann, 1970.

Ukwu I. Ukwu (ed.), *The Spirit of Self Reliance, Mazi Mbonu Ojike Memorial Lectures*, Enugu, Institute for Development Studies, University of Nigeria, 1984.

E. Vercruijsse, *The Penetration of Capitalism: A West African Case Study*, London, Zed Press, 1984.

G. J. Walker, *Traffic and Transport in Nigeria*, London, HMSO, 1959.

J.-P. Warnier, *L'Esprit d'enterprise au Cameroun*, Paris, Karthala, 1993.

M. Watts, 'Brittle trade: a political economy of food supply in Kano', in J. I. Guyer (ed.), *Feeding African Cities*, Manchester, Manchester University Press for the International African Institute, 1987.

D. E. Welsch, 'Rice marketing in eastern Nigeria', *Food Research Institute Studies*, 6, 3, 1966, pp. 329–52.

G. Williams, 'Why is there no agrarian capitalism in Nigeria?' *Journal of Historical Sociology*, 1, 4, 1988, pp. 345–98.

World Bank, *Sub-Saharan Africa: From Crisis to Sustainable Growth*, Washington DC, World Bank, 1989.

C. C. Wrigley, 'Aspects of economic history', in A. Roberts (ed.), *The Colonial Moment in Africa: Essays on the Movement of Minds and Materials, 1900–1940*, Cambridge, Cambridge University Press, 1990.

O. Yemitan, *Madam Tinubu: Merchant and King Maker*, Ibadan, Ibadan University Press, 1987.

M. Young, 'The contributions of women to national development with special reference to business', in J. Akande, O. Jegede, C. Osinulu and F. D. Oyekanmi (eds), *The Contribution of Women to National Development in Nigeria*, Nigerian Association of University Women, 1990.

A. B. Yusuf, 'Capital formation and management among the Muslim Hausa traders of Kano, Nigeria', *Africa*, 45, 2, 1975, pp. 167–82.

M. E. Zuckerman, 'Nigerian crisis: economic impact on the North', *Journal of Modern African Studies*, 8, 1, 1970, pp. 37–54.

UNPUBLISHED PAPERS

'A brief history of the Nigerian Oil Mills Ltd and the Cedar Group', mimeo, June 1989.

S. O. Asabia, 'The Nigerian banking system', mimeo, 1989.

Professor A. C. Callaway, unpublished papers.

P. Drummond-Thompson, 'The rise of African entrepreneurs in Nigerian motor transport: a study in indigenous enterprise', paper presented to African History Seminar, SOAS, London, 1991.

J. S. Henley, 'The state and foreign investor behaviour in Kenya: capitalism in a mercantilist state', Proceedings of the Oxford Joint British–Soviet Roundtable Conference, 'Nigerian and Kenya: Indigenous Paths to Capitalism', Institute for African Studies, Moscow and St Antony's College, Oxford, 1990.

M. Ibru, 'Private enterprise beyond the orthodox', paper delivered to seminar organised by City Securities Ltd and First City Merchant Bank at Nigerian Institute for International Affairs, Lagos, 1988.

'Indo-Nigerian relations in perspective', text of an address by the Acting High Commissioner of India at the Nigerian Institute for Policy Studies, *National Concord*, 26 August 1992.

S. Lall, 'Long term perspectives in sub-Saharan Africa: industry', background paper, Washington DC, World Bank, 1987.

P. N. C. Okigbo, 'Crisis in the temple', public lecture, University of Lagos, 5 March 1992, published in *Sunday Times*, 8 March, 15 March 1992.

C. S. O. Okoye, 'Commercial property development in Lagos', paper presented to Estate Management Students' Association, University of Lagos, April 1987.

C. C. Wrigley, 'The development of state capitalism in late colonial and post colonial Nigeria', mimeo, African Studies Association of the United Kingdom, Liverpool, 1974.

—— 'Some aspects of the political economy of Nigeria', mimeo, Institute of Commonwealth Studies, London, 1968.

UNPUBLISHED THESES

E. O. Akeredolu-Ale, 'Nigerian entrepreneurs in the Lagos State. A study in the origins and performance of indigenous business leadership in a young economy', Ph.D. thesis, University of London, 1971.

S. A. Albasu, 'The Lebanese in Kano: an immigrant community in a Hausa-Muslim society in the colonial and post-colonial periods', Ph.D. thesis, Bayero University, 1989.

A. U. Dan-Asabe, 'Comparative biographies of selected leaders of the Kano commercial establishment', MA thesis, Bayero University, Kano, 1987.

J. G. Deutsch, '"Educating the middlemen", a political and economic history of statutory cocoa marketing in Nigeria, 1936–1947', Ph.D. thesis, University of London, 1990.

J. R. Harris, 'Industrial entrepreneurship in Nigeria', Ph.D. thesis, Northwestern University, 1967.

A. G. Hopkins, 'An economic history of Lagos 1880–1914', Ph.D. thesis, University of London, 1964.

A. O. Olukoshi, 'The multinational corporation and industrialisation in Nigeria: a case study of Kano', Ph.D. thesis, University of Leeds, 1986.

O. A. Oyenuga, 'Women entrepreneurs: a case study of Chief (Mrs) Olutoyin Olusola Olakunri', BA dissertation, Department of History, University of Lagos, 1990.

M. P. Rowe, 'Indigenous industrial entrepreneurship in Lagos, Nigeria', Ph.D. thesis, University of Columbia, 1971.

P. Shea, 'The development of an export-oriented dyed cloth industry in Kano emirate in the nineteenth century', Ph.D. thesis, University of Wisconsin, 1975.

S. Silverstein, 'Sociocultural organisation and locational strategies of transport entrepreneurs: an ethno-economic history of the Nnewi Igbo of Nigeria', Ph.D. thesis, Boston University, 1983.

I. Tahir, 'Sufis, saints and capitalists in Kano, 1904–1974: pattern of a bourgeois revolution in an Islamic society', Ph.D. thesis, University of Cambridge.

NEWSPAPERS AND PERIODICALS

London

African Business
Africa Economic Digest
Financial Times

Nigeria Now
The Independent
West Africa

Lagos

African Guardian
African Concord
Business
Business Concord
Commerce in Nigeria
Corporate
Daily Champion
Daily Times
Financial Post
Guardian Financial Weekly
Guardian on Sunday
National Concord

Newswatch
Nigerian Economist
Nigerian Enterprise
Spear
Sunday Concord
Sunday Times
Sunday Vanguard
Tell
The Guardian
This Week
Weekend Concord

Other

Kano Advertiser (Kano)
Le Soleil (Dakar)
New Nigerian (Kaduna)

Nigerian Eagle (Onitsha)
Sunday Statesman (Enugu)
The Democrat (Kaduna)

OTHER

Africa Who's Who, London, Africa Books, 2nd edn, 1991.

Annual Reports of Bende Division, South-Eastern Nigeria, 1905–1912, with a commentary by G. I. Jones, Cambridge Occasional Paper 2, Cambridge, African Studies Centre, University of Cambridge, 1986.

Central Bank of Nigeria, Annual Reports, Lagos, Central Bank of Nigeria.

Colonial Development Corporation, *Report and Accounts*, London, Colonial Development Corporation, 1949–55.

Commonwealth Development Corporation, *Report and Accounts 1992*, London.

ICON Nigeria Company Handbook, Lagos, Jikonzult Management Services, 1982.

Industrial Survey 1963, Lagos, Federal Office of Statistics.

Industrial Survey 1964, Lagos, Federal Office of Statistics.

Kano State Commercial and Industrial Handbook, Kano, Ministry of Trade and Industry, 1974.

Members' Directory, Manufacturers Association of Nigeria, Ogun State Branch, 1st edn, 1987.

NERFUND, *Annual Report and Accounts*, Lagos, NERFUND, 1991.

Nigeria Banking, Finance and Commerce, 1988–9, Lagos, Research and Data Services, 1988.

Nigeria Banking, Finance and Commerce, 1991–2 edn, Lagos, Research and Data Services, 1992.

Nigeria-British Chamber of Commerce, *1991 Directory*, Lagos, 1991.

Nigeria Business Guide, 1989–90, Lagos, ICON Ltd.

Nigeria Business Guide, 1990–1, Lagos, ICON Ltd.

Nigeria Industrial Directory, Manufacturers' Association of Nigeria, Lagos, 1988 (information refers to 1986).

Nigeria Who's Who in Business, Lagos, Mednet, 1992.

Redasel's Companies of Nigeria, Lagos, Research and Data Services Ltd, 1988.

Stock of Private Direct Investments by DAC Countries in Developing Countries, end 1967, Paris, OECD, 1972.

Who's Who in Nigeria, ed. Nyaknno Osso, Lagos, Newswatch Communications Ltd, 1990.

Who's Who in Nigeria 1956, Lagos, Daily Times Publications.

INDEX

Italicised page numbers refer to figures and tables.